# ENJOYING
# WORLD
# HISTORY

# ENJOYING WORLD HISTORY

**Henry Abraham**
**Irwin Pfeffer**

*Dedicated to serving*

**AMSCO**

*our nation's youth*

When ordering this book, please specify:
*either* **R 188 P** *or* ENJOYING WORLD HISTORY

**AMSCO SCHOOL PUBLICATIONS, INC.**
**315 Hudson Street          New York, N.Y. 10013**

ISBN 0-87720-618-X
Copyright © 1977 by Amsco School Publications, Inc.
No part of this book may be reproduced in any form
    without written permission from the publisher.
Printed in the United States of America

Illustrations on pages 111, 129, 182, and 323
    by courtesy of The Bettmann Archive
Cartoons by Edward Malsberg
Line drawings by Charles Molina
Maps and charts by Delos D. Rowe Associates

# Preface

Over the years some of our students have complained that their history courses were dull and lifeless. "Why can't history be interesting?" they asked.

*Enjoying World History* was written to show students that the study of the past is not just memorizing names, dates, battles, and treaties. History is all of these things, of course, but it is also people. Real people made history—our past was their present.

*Enjoying World History* surveys the history of Western Europe from the days of the Roman Empire to the present. To make history come alive, we have written 91 stories about the people and events of the past. Many of the characters in our stories are or were real people; some of the incidents in the stories are fictional, but many actually did happen. Those incidents that are imaginary are based on solid historical evidence. They might very well have occurred.

We have used a variety of literary forms—short stories, plays, newspaper reporting, interior monologues, letters. The illustrative materials—maps, charts, cartoons, line drawings—are the basis for comprehension questions in the exercise sections following each story.

The stories are introduced by a short historical narrative which sets the time and place and explains in easy-to-understand terms the political, social, and economic setting. When a name or term that may cause difficulty is used for the first time, a definition or pronunciation guide is given in parentheses.

The units are introduced and concluded by conversations between a history teacher and his student. These conversations are unit previews as well as summaries of their highlights.

Short-answer questions follow each of the stories. Ten different types of questions are used throughout the book. Two different types of questions are used after each story. In addition, the Activities and Inquiries sections provide opportunities for student research and the development of social studies skills.

It is our hope that the stories in *Enjoying World History* will interest students and give them insight into how people lived and the forces that shaped their lives. We also hope that students will gain an understanding of the contemporary world.

We wish to acknowledge the valuable suggestions made by Sidney Langsam, Assistant Principal, Social Studies, Springfield Gardens High School, New York City, while we were preparing this book.

To our wives, Elsa Abraham and Gloria Pfeffer, we wish to express our gratitude for their understanding and encouragement.

*Henry Abraham*
*Irwin Pfeffer*

# Contents

## Unit IV. France—The Beginnings of Democracy    *109*

## Unit V. Nationalism    *157*

## Unit VI. The Industrial Revolution    *179*

## Unit VII. Imperialism    *203*

# The Roman Empire and the Middle Ages

Many students find their history classes interesting and exciting. Others, however, find their history classes dull. As our story opens, Mr. Miller, a history teacher, and Jack, one of his students, are meeting after school. They are discussing why Jack does not pay attention in class.

"Come on, Mr. Miller, the real reason I don't pay attention in your history class is that history doesn't have anything to do with me."

Mr. Miller sighed. He had heard this many times from students. He knew that he was in for a long afternoon.

"Jack," said Mr. Miller, "maybe, just maybe, you've got it all wrong."

"Look, Mr. Miller," interrupted Jack, "you don't have to give me any song and dance. You can tell me all about how history is going to help me to improve my reading, writing, and thinking. I'm still going to say that for me it's boring and a waste of time. I mean, who cares about dead people and dead civilizations and dead wars? In fact, how can you waste so much time talking about those things when so many more serious things are happening to us today?"

"Like what, Jack?"

"Oh, you know, inflation and depression, and corruption and crime, war and hunger, and things like that. My father says that this is the worst time to be alive, and I believe him!"

"Are you worried, Jack?"

"Are you kidding? Aren't you?"

"Sure, a little bit, I guess," admitted Mr. Miller. "But I think we'll all manage to get through these problems."

"You sound so sure," said Jack in a slightly mocking tone. "You must have a crystal ball in front of you."

"Well, maybe that's what history is," said Mr. Miller. "Maybe history is a crystal ball."

"I don't follow you."

"Just think of what we talk about in our history class."

"You mean the Romans and French and Italians and Chinese and Germans and Russians?"

"That's exactly what I mean, but I think that you're missing the point."

"Why?"

"Because," said Mr. Miller, warming to his subject, "we don't just talk about those people. We talk about people's problems and fears, and how people dealt with them."

"What does this have to do with us?" asked Jack.

"Everything," answered Mr. Miller. "Their fears are now our fears, and their problems are now ours too. Just as each person writes his or her own story, so each civilization does the same."

"What if we do know their stories? What does that do for us?"

Mr. Miller thought a long time before answering. "Their stories are over, and ours are still being written. We who are confused by so many things are searching for answers that have already been written down."

"Are you saying what I think you're saying?"

"If you're thinking that the past can help us to understand the present and to unlock the secrets of the future, then that's exactly what I am saying," said Mr. Miller in a very serious tone.

"Then you must know all the answers," exclaimed Jack.

"No," answered Mr. Miller, "but I'm still searching."

"But you're a teacher—"

Mr. Miller smiled. "History makes students of us all, and the course takes a lifetime."

Jack thought for a moment. He said, "If I were really interested in searching out the secrets of the future—and remember, I didn't say that I was—how would I get started?"

"You have just taken the first step, Jack," said Mr. Miller.

# 1. Freedom Recalled

*Our first story is set* in the days of one of the great empires of all time, the Roman Empire. In the 2nd century A.D., Rome had gained control of all the land from the Strait of Gibraltar on the Atlantic Ocean eastward to the Caspian Sea in Asia. Rome's power extended from Egypt in Africa northward to the North Sea in Europe. The 2nd century was a time of peace and prosperity. The people of the empire were well off.

But this was not to last. In the 3rd century *barbarian tribes* (outsiders not as civilized as Romans) such as the Goths were beginning to raid the empire. In Rome itself, the government was no longer secure. Rebellion followed rebellion. From the years 235 to 285 there were 19 emperors; only two died natural deaths! Roman soldiers no longer fought against invaders. Instead, they fought for power at home. Soldiers stole from the peasants and bankers. They took as much as they could from the wealthy. The great Roman Empire was crumbling.

By the 4th century, the once great Roman Empire had become a hollow shell. Rome had been weakened by barbarian invasions. Food was in short supply, and many people were starving. Business and trade were on the downturn.

The free farmers who owned small plots of land were hit hard. Taxes rose higher and higher. Many of these small farmers found themselves unable to pay their debts and were forced to give up their farms. These farms were then taken over by the rich, who in turn hired the poor to work on them as tenants. At first the tenants paid the landlord with part of their crops. They also had to work a certain number of days each year for the landlord.

As the years passed, however, the tenants came under the complete control of the landlords. By the year 332, any tenant farmer who left the land could be brought back in chains. These once-free farmers had become *serfs*. They

3

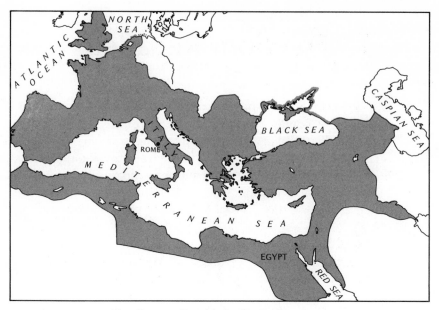

*The Roman Empire in the 2nd century*

were part of the land. They could not be sold as individuals or as slaves. But when the land was sold or changed hands, the serfs went along with the land.

Suppose we look at two peasants in ancient Rome. We are in a place known as Carsoli, in central Italy. It is located about 50 miles east of the city of Rome. It is the year 350. Our two farmers are surrounded by acre after acre of golden, ripening wheat. They talk of the good old days of the Roman Empire. They think back to happier times when they were young.

Ask yourself why the Roman peasants looked back to the past. How had the changes in the empire affected them?

# Carsoli, 350

"Why are you so angry today?" asked Horace. "It's a beautiful day. The wheat is high. We're going to have a great crop!"

"We're going to have a great crop," mocked Antonio. "Whose crop is it going to be? Not too long ago, each of us had his own land.

We were citizens of Rome, and we were free! Now we're nothing but miserable tenants who can't even leave the land."

"Don't get so upset," replied Horace. "Things could be a lot worse. Our landlord isn't too bad. He protects us, and we're still working on Roman soil. Don't forget, we do get to keep part of our crops."

"Who needs him?" asked Antonio angrily. "If the enemy had ever come, we could have protected ourselves. The Roman army would have rescued us from the barbarian invaders."

"There are too many barbarians around these days," replied Horace. "And you know as well as I that you can't trust the army anymore."

"That's one point I'll agree with. You can't trust anyone," said Antonio. "In the old, glorious days, things were different. Remember how powerful our armies were, and how they crushed the tribes around us? People from all over the world learned to speak Latin because it was *our* language!"

"That's your trouble, Antonio. You live in the past. Times have changed. You may be right about Rome in the good old days, but the world doesn't stand still. Why can't you understand that? It's our job in life to be tenant farmers. Accept it. I don't expect you to be happy about it, but this is the way things are!"

"Maybe I do think too much about the past," said Antonio thoughtfully. "But what's wrong with remembering the power and wealth of our country? I'll never forget the first time my father took me to the city of Rome. There were great buildings, fountains, wide streets—all marvels of engineering. The people seemed happy. They busied themselves at their jobs. They weren't worried about barbarians."

"You mean they didn't seem worried," said Horace. "You were a child. How could you tell whether people were happy or unhappy, worried or unworried?"

"Child or not, even you have to admit that Rome had great playwrights, poets, and orators who stirred the imagination of the people. I'll never forget them."

"No, don't forget any of it," said Horace, "but wasn't there another side of the coin? It wasn't all beauty and poetry and good looks. There was the cruel treatment of Christians and Jews. Haven't you overlooked the suffering and starvation of the poor?

The emperors put on a big show, but you know they weren't interested in poor people."

"You have a point there," said Antonio. "Remember when taxes began to get impossible to pay? Well, I thought of giving up the farm and moving to the city of Rome. But so many men there were out of jobs and begging for scraps of food. I looked at them and realized that on the farm I had always had enough to eat. I came back to my life on the land. I have suffered, but I must admit that I have never been hungry."

"Now you're starting to sound more like yourself," said Horace. "I think that you're beginning to see that we must accept our future. Our lives will be spent on the land. We'll have to work hard, but we'll live!"

"I really don't disagree with you, Horace. It was just impossible for me to accept the laws that forced us to stay on the farm even when we weren't making a living. Now this. We're tenant farmers. We're no longer free! Our lives are no longer in our hands! Is this living?"

"Calm down, please," pleaded Horace. "If some of the other farmers hear you, we may not be able to live out even this miserable existence."

"How could this happen to loyal, trusting citizens of the greatest empire in the world?" asked Antonio quietly. "Where has it all gone? Why do filthy ragged savages roam everywhere? Where is the glory that once was Rome?"

"Try not to be so bitter," said Horace. "Perhaps some day we will be free again!"


## UNDERSTANDING THE STORY

**A.** *You can see that Horace and Antonio have different ideas about many things. Decide who made or might have made the remarks that follow. Write H for each statement that Horace made or might have made and A for each statement that Antonio made or might have made.*

1. I hate my life as a tenant farmer.
2. I remember how good it was to be a free citizen of Rome.
3. The landlord protects us and lets us keep part of our crop.
4. A person should accept things as they are.

5. There were lots of things wrong with Rome.
6. Even though life can be hard for a tenant farmer, at least you don't starve.
7. How could a great country like Rome be in such trouble?
8. Some day we will be free again.

B. *Decide whether the following statements are true or false. Write T for each statement that is true and F for each statement that is false.*

1. Rome was beginning to fall apart by the 4th century A.D.
2. Horace disliked the life of a tenant farmer.
3. Antonio thought about the days when he was a free farmer.
4. A free farmer could never become a serf.
5. The landlord protected Horace and Antonio and let them keep part of the crop.
6. Antonio said that people should accept things as they are.
7. Horace and Antonio complained that, although they worked hard, they were starving.
8. Antonio was surprised that a great empire like Rome was in such trouble.

C. Which of the two men, Horace or Antonio, would be more comfortable living in the United States today? Explain.

## ACTIVITIES AND INQUIRIES

1. Use each of the following key terms in a sentence.
   barbarian            slave                  savage
   tenant farmer        serf
2. Look at the map of the Roman Empire on page 4. Compare it with the map of present-day Europe on page 424. List five modern countries whose lands were once part of the Roman Empire.
3. Look for pictures of ancient Roman buildings, roads, aqueducts, and works of art. Bring them to class. Be prepared to talk about what the pictures tell you of life in ancient Rome.
4. Go to the library and look for information on the life of women in ancient Rome. List the facts you find about Roman women. What differences do you see between the lives of women in ancient Rome and those in present-day America? What similarities do you see?

# 2. The Feudal Arrangement

*Serfdom, as we have seen,* started in the last years of the Roman Empire. It lasted for over a thousand years in Western Europe, and many centuries longer in Eastern Europe. The period that followed the fall of the Roman Empire is called the Middle Ages, or the medieval period. It lasted from the 5th century through the 13th century, or until the beginnings of modern times.

During the Middle Ages, the serfs were under the complete control of the lord of the manor. The lord was a nobleman, a member of the upper class. After his death, his title of baron, earl, count, duke, or prince was passed on to his eldest son. The manor was a sizable piece of land that was farmed by the serfs. These serfs were treated either well or badly according to the wishes of the noble. He could be kind or brutal, pleasant or nasty. In any case, there was little the serf could do about it.

In our story we see another view of the noble's control of his serfs. We are in the home of a family of French serfs. It is a single room about 15 feet long. In this small space the family cooks, eats, and sleeps. The room is dark, smelly, and smoky from the wood fire. The dirt floors are dusty in hot weather. They are muddy in the rain and snow. The walls are thin; they are mud that has been plastered over twigs and branches. Somehow, the family lives here.

See if you can decide whether the parents should be grateful for what the noble has done. Who do you think is right, the husband or the wife? Why?

## Talcy, 954

"This is going to be the most exciting day of our lives," said Louis to his wife, Helene. "At last, our daughter, Estelle, is to be married, and we have our noble lord Pierre to thank."

"Thank him?" replied Helene. "You must be out of your mind. He finally did approve the wedding, but the marriage tax is very high."

"I still feel we should be grateful," said the husband. "After all, he could have refused permission, as he did for Charles' daughter. He might even have charged two to three times as much for the wedding tax."

"Why did he approve this marriage? I'll tell you why," argued Helene. "Our daughter is marrying a man from this manor. She is going to stay right here and work alongside her husband. Later on, their children will help with the work. In heaven's name, what did our noble have to lose?"

"You forget how kind and thoughtful he is to us," said Louis. "He isn't nearly as cruel as some other nobles in the province. He seldom beats us. He allows us to keep part of the crops we grow. His taxes for the use of his mill, wine press, and tools aren't really too high. We have to work for him only 15 days of each month."

"Why should we have to turn over a share of our crops, and work so hard for him? We have hardly anything left for ourselves. He may be better than some nobles, but the whole system is still unfair."

"I'll tell you why we pay," said Louis, angrily. "We couldn't get along without him. He protects us, takes care of us, and makes important decisions. We could not have had this marriage without him. It's time for the wedding. Let's all go to the chapel, and while there, let us pray for the health and happiness of our noble lord."

"You pray for him," said the wife. "I'll pray for a happy life and more freedom for our daughter and her husband!"

## UNDERSTANDING THE STORY

A. *Helene had strong feelings about many things. Tell which of the statements below describe her thinking.*
   1. We should thank our noble lord for our daughter's marriage.
   2. The wedding tax is too high.
   3. The noble lord had little to lose when he approved the marriage.
   4. Our noble lord is kind and thoughtful.
   5. The taxes are not really high.

6. Taxes leave us little for ourselves.
7. Our noble lord protects us.
8. Pray for a happy life for the newlyweds.

**B.** *Match each question in Column A with its answer in Column B.*

COLUMN A

1. When did serfdom begin?
2. How long did the Middle Ages last?
3. Who owned the land of the manor?
4. For what did serfs pay taxes?
5. What did the noble get from his serfs?
6. For what did Helene and Louis need the noble's permission?
7. How did the noble benefit from the marriage?
8. What does Helene pray for?

COLUMN B

(a) Part of their crops
(b) For their daughter's marriage
(c) More freedom
(d) From the 5th century through the 13th century
(e) The lord of the manor
(f) In the last years of the Roman Empire
(g) For use of the lord's mill, wine press, and tools
(h) The daughter and her husband would both work on the manor.

**C.** Imagine that Helene and Louis' lord is running for president of the United States today. Would you vote for him? Explain. Would Helene and Louis vote for him? Explain.

## ACTIVITIES AND INQUIRIES

1. Use each of the following key terms in a sentence.
   lord            manor            serf
   noble           Middle Ages
2. Look for pictures of medieval homes and people. Bring them to class. Be prepared to talk about the differences between the lives of the nobles and the serfs.
3. Pretend that you are Louis. An old friend from another manor meets you. He tells you that his noble lord is very fair. What would you tell him about your noble lord? Explain.
4. Imagine that you are Helene. Would you agree with what your husband, Louis, said? Explain.
5. Helene and Louis give us different pictures of life on the manor. Which one is giving a truer picture? Explain.

# 3. Crusaders at the Walls

*The life of the serf* was dull and boring. There was little to look forward to except a wedding or festival. The serf's life changed very little from day to day. There was no place to go. The world of the serf was limited by the boundaries of the manor.

In 1095 something happened that would bring a great change into the lives of many serfs. Pope Urban II called for a *Crusade* (krew-SADE), a campaign to capture the city of Jerusalem from the Moslem Turks. Jerusalem (jeh-ROO-sa-lem) was a holy city for Christians, Jews, and Moslems. It was very important to Christians, since it was the city where Jesus preached and died.

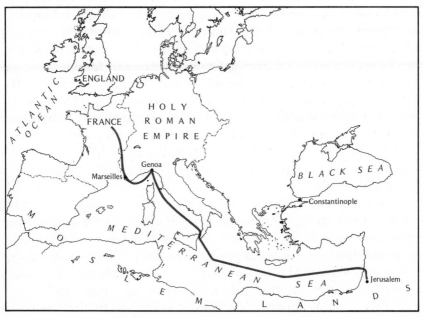

*Route of French Crusaders to Jerusalem*

Thousands of serfs from Western Europe joined the armies of the Crusade. This was their great chance to leave their little world behind them. They saw things they had never believed existed. They did things they had never dreamed possible. They threw away the chains of serfdom on the land for the chance to serve in a nobleman's army. Those who lived to return to their homes would never again work in the narrow prison of the manor.

In this chapter, two peasants discuss their problems and their feelings. Ask yourself whether you would have joined this Crusade. How would you have felt as you stood before the walls of Jerusalem?

# Jerusalem, July 1099

"At last, we're camped just outside the walls of Jerusalem," said John to his friend Robert. "For months we fought to reach this city, and now it's almost ours. Soon we'll be on our way home."

"Not so fast," said Robert. "We've been marching and fighting for almost four years. This is a hard life and I'm tired of it. Suppose we capture the city. Then what will happen? We may have to stay on. I don't think we'll ever get home to see our families!"

"Why are you so discouraged?" asked John. "The city is ours. You can see the Moslems are getting weaker. They have courage, but don't forget that the one true God is on our side. The fight will be over very quickly. We'll be back home before you know it!"

"Before I know it? I'll never know it. It's all such a waste of time and human life. Even if I do get home, what useful purpose will it all have served?"

"Don't be a fool!" insisted John, his voice rising. "We have learned more in this short time than in all the other years of our lives. Our friends on the manor will never believe what we have seen and done. Think of our great adventures, the tastes of strange foods and spices. Have you forgotten the sights and sounds of different peoples, of great cities, works of art, churches?"

"True," said Robert, "but has it been worth the pain and suffering? I often wonder, Why am I fighting these people? Our

*"The fight will be over very quickly."*

leaders tell us that the Moslems are infidels who torture and kill our fellow Christians. But I don't believe that these people are guilty of all the bad things that are said about them."

"Our Savior died here. It is our duty to capture the city of Jerusalem for all future Christians. You must believe this," added John.

"I am sorry. I want to believe," said Robert. "But there are other things. I am very disappointed in the actions of many men on our side. They seem much more interested in looting the places they visit than in capturing the Holy Land for our religion. In our travels we were often cheated by our fellow Christians. We have risked our lives, and—"

"The attack has started!" shouted John excitedly. "The enemy are fighting well, but we are pushing them back. Thousands of Moslems are running in wild panic. I told you we would be in Jerusalem very soon!"

"You're right! The Moslems are running for their lives! Bodies are piling up on the walls and in the streets. Hundreds of our men are being killed. Their bodies fall all around. All I can smell is blood and burning flesh. I can barely hear your voice over the screams of the dead and dying! I'm going to be sick!"

"My God! The slaughter!" screamed John. "But the city is ours!"

"Would our Savior give us his blessing this day?" cried Robert.

## UNDERSTANDING THE STORY

**A.** *Number the events below in the order in which they took place.*

Thousands of serfs joined the Crusader armies.

Jerusalem was captured by the Christians.

Jesus preached and died in Jerusalem.

Pope Urban II called for a Crusade.

The Moslems fought very hard.

Jerusalem became a holy city for Christians and Moslems, as well as for Jews.

John and Robert were cheated by fellow Christians.

**B.** *Tell which of the statements below are true.*

1. Serfs led very interesting lives.
2. Pope Urban II asked for a Crusade to capture Jerusalem.
3. Serfs did not join the Crusades.
4. John felt that God was on his side.
5. Robert enjoyed the great adventures of the Crusade.
6. Robert and John had been marching and fighting for almost four years.
7. John said that the Crusaders would take Jerusalem.
8. Many people died in the attack on Jerusalem.

**C.** Imagine that John and Robert were asked to serve in the recent war in Vietnam. Who would have served more willingly? Write two sentences explaining your answer. How would the other one have felt about the war? Why? With which one of the two do you agree? Explain your answer in one sentence.

## ACTIVITIES AND INQUIRIES

1. Look at the map of Europe during the Middle Ages on page 11. This map shows a route Crusaders took from France to the Holy Land. Draw the map in your notebook in outline form. On your map show the routes that a Crusader would have taken from each of the following places:
   *a.* England—show the route with a dotted line.
   *b.* Holy Roman Empire—show the route with a solid line.
   *c.* Genoa—show the route with a broken line.
2. Pretend that you are John. You are talking to your friends on the manor about your adventures on the Crusades. Write three sentences describing these adventures. Include the exciting things you saw and did on your travels.
3. Imagine that you are Robert. You have just come home from a Crusade. Your friends have heard from John about his experiences. Now they are eager to hear from you. Write three sentences telling of your experiences. Is your story going to be like John's? Explain.
4. Look at the illustration on page 13. Describe what is happening. Write your own title for this picture.
5. Pretend that you are a Moslem. List the reasons why you feel that Jerusalem should be defended against the Christians.

# 4. Training to Be a Knight

*The Crusaders we saw* in the previous story had once been serfs. Joining the Crusade was their chance to escape from the small world of the manor. The serfs were followers. A smaller group of men were the leaders in battle. These were the knights, the professional fighting men. They lived to fight. They were members of the upper classes—of the nobility. Their training and education prepared them for lives as knights in the service of a noble lord.

The center of the knights' years of training was the castle. It was a world far different from that of the serfs. There was no backbreaking work for the knights. They did not live in fear of a lord of the manor. They did not live in broken-down little houses. Their home was the castle. It was a fortress of defense against the enemies of the noble.

Before the Crusades, these castles were very simple buildings. They were stone towers, square in shape. The tower was encircled by a single or double wall and a *moat* (a trench or hole filled with water). In the East, however, the Crusaders saw castles that were much stronger and more easily defended. Why not copy them? The new castles of Europe were built very much like those the Crusaders had attacked on the way to the Holy Land. These new castles were on hills. Wall after wall circled many rounded towers, or turrets. Defenders could lean over the walls and throw tar and fire on their attackers.

The English castle that we are visiting is in the city of Salisbury (SALZ-berri). The castle has many features the Crusaders brought back from the East. It is well built and has many defenders. We overhear two squires—young men who are training to become knights. Ask yourself why it is so important to them that they become knights. Why should it have been so hard to become a knight? What are the duties of knights?

# Salisbury, 1130

Two squires are dueling playfully with sticks in the castle court-yard. Around them are other squires polishing helmets, swords, and shields. Knights are practicing their skills of war. In the distance, archers are shooting their arrows and foot soldiers are drilling. It is very noisy.

"It won't be long now, Malcolm," said Donald. "Our dreams will soon come true."

"How can you be so sure?" asked Malcolm.

"I overheard Baron Chester say that we are ready," answered Donald.

"Ready for what?" asked Malcolm excitedly. "Do you remember exactly what he said?"

"Don't get so excited, Malcolm. Of course I remember. He said, 'Malcolm and Donald are ready for the big step.'"

"There you go again," said Malcolm. "He didn't say 'to be knights' or 'for knighthood,' did he? Then how can you be so sure what he meant? He probably saw you listening and made the whole thing up. Maybe he's testing us. He wants to see how we'll act when we hear things like that."

"Malcolm, I hate to say this, but I don't think you're ready to be a knight! Knights are sure of themselves. They know what they are supposed to do and they do it! If this were a test—and I didn't say that it is—you would fail!"

"Sorry, Donald, but don't I have a right to be nervous? My father, the Earl of Salisbury, brought me to this castle when I was a child of seven. Baron Chester took me in and made me a page. I learned to ride and handle a sword. That was great. But then after a few years, I had to spend all my time in the kitchen. I scrubbed and cleaned in the kitchen. I waited on tables and did as I was told. Can you tell me how waiting on tables helps you become a knight? Did they have to treat me like a common person? Did they think that I was a serf? Did you ever see a knight working in a kitchen? At last, when I was 15, they made me a squire. Big deal!"

"Slow down, Malcolm, it wasn't all that bad."

"Every time I wasn't exactly perfect, someone slapped me,"

continued Malcolm, not hearing Donald's remark. "They pulled my ears; they even knocked me down!"

"Didn't I have to do the same things?" interrupted Donald, growing angry. "Wasn't I beaten and knocked around at least as much as you? Do you think that I liked being hit on the head any more than you did? Malcolm, we suffered all these years because we knew that we were preparing."

"Preparing for what?" asked Malcolm.

"To be a knight, you fool!" snapped Donald. He swung at Malcolm with his wooden sword and knocked him down. "A knight must be strong and fearless. He must do what he has to do and stay loyal to his lord. Our training here has made us strong. We can stand up to pain. We have learned to do a lot of things we hated."

"You must be much stronger than I am," said Malcolm as he picked himself up. "There were times when I felt like running away. But where could I go? Can you imagine what my father would have said to me? How he would have beaten me!"

"You are stronger than you think," said Donald thoughtfully. "Ask yourself why they made you a squire when you were 15. You helped the knight, Sir Sydney, and he thought well of you. You learned to handle a sword, a lance, and even a battle-ax. You haven't done badly in your practice fights, your tournaments. You aren't doing badly now!" Donald blocked Malcolm's thrust.

"How little you know," said Malcolm quietly. "Baron Chester has been threatening to send me home. He says I'm not tough enough. I'll never learn to fight like a true knight. Maybe he's right. A true knight laughs off pain. He loves to fight for his lord. And, if there's a lady to fight for, so much the better. But I feel pain and I don't enjoy fighting. Honestly, I ache all over!"

"Don't you think that I feel pain?" answered Donald. "That blow really hurt! Don't you think that I've had doubts? I'm a person, too. I live and breathe and bleed like everyone else. But I think I can hide my feelings better than you."

"Donald, am I good enough to be a knight? You forget that I've been a squire for a year longer than you. I'm 21, but you are only 20. Why didn't he knight me last year? Everyone else around here made it at that age. No, I know I'm just not good enough. They'd send me home in a minute if they weren't afraid of my father."

"Malcolm, keep quiet!" whispered Donald. "Let's agree that you aren't the best fighter in the world." Donald knocked Malcolm to the ground again. "But what else is there for you to do? Do you want to be a common serf? Can you see yourself, all covered with mud, plowing the fields? When the lord of the manor comes near, you put your face in the dirt. Your fellow serfs talk to you; the better people spit on you!"

"For once, you're right," said Malcolm with a small smile. "Perhaps I could be a priest. I would work with people, help them, pray with them. I would be a good person. Or I could become a monk. Get away from everyone, think, write, and pray. But, Donald, I don't know Latin. I can barely read and write English. I would have to go to a school. But I could learn."

"This is the life for you and me," said Donald. "Very soon you will be a knight. Believe me. This is what you must live for."

"Every night I have a dream. Baron Chester tells me that tomorrow is to be my day!" said Malcolm. "They bathe me in holy water. I put on a white robe. I pray all night. My sword is with me."

*"Soon you will be a knight."*

"Keep dreaming, Malcolm. We can dream together."

"At last," said Malcolm, "it is daylight. The priest comes. I hear mass and make my confession. He offers my sword to the service of God. I promise to defend the Christian faith."

Donald interrupted him and continued the story. "I kneel. Baron Chester hits me across the shoulders with the flat of his sword. He calls me Sir Donald. I'm a knight! I promise that I will never deal with traitors. I will never give bad advice to a lady. I will always go to mass. I will always remember holidays and festivals."

"I promise to do anything they ask," Malcolm added. "Oh Lord, let me be a knight!"

"Now," continued Donald, "I dream I am at a tournament. The best-looking woman in the whole kingdom is watching me. Wait, she waves at me! She throws her handkerchief to me! I fight for her—for her honor. I am a demon! I can't lose. Nothing stops me! My lance throws the other knights off their horses. They haven't a chance. I'm too strong and fast for them!"

"If only it could be true," added Malcolm.

"There's more," shouted Donald. "We are fighting with battle-axes. I go wild; I crush them all! I am young; I am a knight!"

Suddenly Baron Chester shouted to them. "Donald! Malcolm! Come over here. Quickly—don't keep us waiting!"

## UNDERSTANDING THE STORY

**A.** *You can see that Donald and Malcolm have many differences of opinion. Decide who made or might have made the statements that follow. Write D next to each statement that Donald made or might have made. Write M next to each statement that Malcolm made or might have made.*

1. I heard Baron Chester say that we are ready to become knights.
2. You're ready to be a knight when you are sure of yourself.
3. Baron Chester made me a page.
4. Knights don't work in kitchens.
5. A knight must be strong and fearless.
6. I felt like running away from the castle.
7. I'll never learn to fight like a knight.
8. Nothing can stop me from becoming a knight.

**B.** *Malcolm and Donald were educated to become knights. Compare their education with your own. Write S for each statement that is similar to education in the United States and D for each statement that is different from education in the United States.*

1. It took a knight a long time to complete his training.
2. Knights had very few teachers.
3. Knights were taught how to fight wars.
4. Knights began to train in early childhood.
5. Knights were trained to build up their bodies.
6. Knights-in-training had to wait on tables and work in the kitchen.
7. Usually only upper-class people could be trained for knighthood.
8. Knights were taught good manners.

**C.** Which of the two young men would be a better knight? Explain. Whom would you prefer to have on your side in a fight, Donald or Malcolm? Write two sentences.

## ACTIVITIES AND INQUIRIES

1. Look at the illustration on page 19. What do you think would be a good title for this illustration? Identify the people in the picture. Do you think Donald's dream came true?
2. In the Middle Ages knights wore armor. Bring in pictures of knights dressed in armor. Be prepared to talk about the purposes of each part of the knights' armor. Today, soldiers wear uniforms. What differences do you see between the armor and uniforms? What similarities?
3. Read the description of a castle on page 16. Using this information, try to draw a picture of a castle. Be prepared to tell how you would defend this castle.
4. Imagine that you are being placed into a time machine. You are being sent back to the days of Malcolm and Donald (12th century). Would you want to train to become a knight? Explain your answer. Could you use this training in the 20th century?
5. You have a choice: You can live in the 12th century or in the 20th century. Which would you choose? Why?

# 5. The Emperor and the Pope

*The Crusades gave many people* of Europe a chance to break out of the confines of their narrow lives. The pope started the Crusades, but he knew that there would be no victory without the military help of the powerful kings and nobles of Europe.

A few years earlier, there had been a serious argument between the pope, Gregory VII, and the Holy Roman Emperor, Henry IV. Henry, a national leader, challenged the great authority of the Church. He argued that he should appoint the pope and the bishops of the Church because he was the emperor. Gregory, of course, refused to accept this. He said that he was all-powerful in anything concerning religion and the Church. These were Church decisions, and he would make them.

Henry tried to show how strong he was. He said that Gregory was not fit to be pope and ordered him fired. Gregory would not budge. He ordered Henry excommunicated—which deprived him of the sacraments of the Church.

The climax of this struggle came at Canossa (ka-NOSS-ah), in northern Italy. See if you can understand why Henry acted as he did. What did this mean to the Church and to the power of kings and nations?

## Canossa, 1077

"What's everyone doing in front of the castle on a freezing day like this?" asked Carla. "I have never seen a crowd this large. Why is everyone so tense and restless?"

"Don't you know that Pope Gregory is inside the castle?"

replied Joseph. "We have heard a rumor that Henry IV, the Holy Roman Emperor, is going to meet with the pope today."

"That's great. I'd like to see them, but I have work to do," said Carla.

"Don't leave now. I've heard that something unusual is going to happen today. We shouldn't miss it," said Joseph. "This may be our one chance to see both an emperor and a pope. Who knows what may happen when they face each other. After all, emperors and popes have been enemies for hundreds of years!"

"Why should emperors and popes dislike each other?" asked Carla. "A king rules a country, and a pope rules the Church."

"It's not as simple as that," replied Joseph. "You see, it's a question of power. Pope Gregory feels that only he should appoint men to important jobs in the Church. I agree with him!"

"Well, Henry is the Holy Roman Emperor. Why shouldn't he appoint whomever he wants to positions in the Roman Catholic Church?" asked Carla.

"No, the pope is right. The Church should control the Church. The Church exists for God and all his people. The emperor is only one person," answered Joseph angrily. "When an emperor or king goes too far, the pope must punish him. That's why I feel that the pope did the right thing in excommunicating Henry for his error."

"How terrible for Henry! I really feel sorry for him," said Carla. "Without the salvation of the Church, he is doomed to burn in hell. He is a man without hope. How long will it be before the people in the empire turn away from him?"

"I think he's had this punishment coming to him," answered Joseph. "But I also agree that this makes his position very difficult. Some of the nobles are saying that his excommunication frees them from their vows of loyalty to him. That's why he is coming here today. He hopes that he can work out his differences with Pope Gregory."

Suddenly there was a shout from the crowd.

"What's happening?" cried Carla. "Why is everyone screaming and yelling? I can't see a thing. Wait! There's a man dressed in sackcloth. He's not wearing shoes. He's walking through the snow. It's Henry!"

"You're right!" answered Joseph excitedly. "Without his fancy clothes, he looks like one of us. Now he's standing in front of the

*"I bet he will have to stand in the freezing snow for a long while."*

castle steps. He must be waiting for the pope to come out and speak to him. I bet he will have to stand in the freezing snow for a long while before Pope Gregory speaks to him. Suffer, Henry, it's good for you!"

"What do you think Henry wants most," asked Carla, "his salvation or his empire?"

"Why not both?"

## UNDERSTANDING THE STORY

**A.** *Write* T *for each statement that is true and* F *for each statement that is false.*

1. There was a disagreement between Pope Gregory and Emperor Henry.
2. A pope would never excommunicate an emperor.
3. Emperor Henry said that Gregory could be pope for as long as he wanted.
4. Emperor Henry went to Canossa for a long rest.
5. The pope and the emperor were meeting because they were friends.
6. Emperor Henry begged forgiveness by walking barefoot in the snow.
7. Carla said that the emperor was right in his argument with the pope.
8. The people of Canossa were very excited by the visit of Pope Gregory and Emperor Henry.

**B.** *Complete each of the sentences below by writing the missing word or words.*

1. Henry IV was the ———— Emperor.
2. Henry felt that he should appoint the ———— and the ————.
3. Carla did not want to wait to see Henry IV and Pope Gregory because she had ————.
4. A king rules a ————. A pope rules the ————.
5. Henry IV went to ———— to work out his ———— with Pope Gregory.
6. Henry IV was dressed in ————.

7. Carla was worried that Henry IV would ——— without the salvation of the Church.
8. Joseph thought that Henry IV would have to stand in the snow for ———.

C. Who do you think would win an argument today between a pope and an emperor? Why? Would an emperor be worried about excommunication today? Explain.

## ACTIVITIES AND INQUIRIES

1. Go to the library and find material for a report on either Pope Gregory VII or Emperor Henry IV. Add to your report an explanation of why you chose to write about one man rather than the other.
2. Look at the illustration on page 24. Describe what is happening. Write your own title for the picture.
3. Imagine that you are Pope Gregory. Write down your thoughts as you watch Emperor Henry approach.
4. Imagine that you are Emperor Henry. Jot down your thoughts as you walk barefoot in the snow.
5. Talk to a Catholic priest. Ask him if excommunication is still used by the Catholic Church today.

# 6. A Monk's Story

*As you have seen, central governments* were weak during the Middle Ages. Feudal nobles fought with each other for land or glory. The life of a poor person, especially a serf, was worth very little.

In the middle of all this confusion, the Catholic Church stood solid and strong. It was well organized. Each person knew his or her job. The Church offered people a proper way of life, a path to follow from birth to death to heaven. Kings and nobles were encouraged to be less cruel. Work was praised and blessed. Marriage was a sacrament—an oath that could not be broken.

It was a blessing to care for poor people, widows, and orphans. Hospitals to heal the sick were opened in many towns. The church or cathedral was the center for everyone. Most villagers were baptized there, and most were buried in the churchyard. The older people would gather on Sundays (after services) for talk and gossip. The young went to see and be seen. The church might even be used as a storage center for grain, or hay, or wine.

All education and training of the young took place in church or monastery schools. Art was often brought by the villagers to the church to beautify the house of God. As we shall see, the monks in monasteries were often artists in their own right.

In this story we look in on a monk in a monastery in the French city of Dijon (dee-ZOHN). A monastery was a place where a man lived away from the problems of life of the rest of the world. Often the rules and regulations of the monastery were strict. The monk promised to follow a life of poverty, chastity, and obedience. He gave up everything he owned (poverty), and he promised never to marry (chastity). He agreed to obey the rules of his order or group of monks

(obedience). Ask yourself why a young man would be willing to give up so much. Why does he find it difficult to follow
the rules of the monastery?

# Dijon, 1131

At last sunlight comes into my lonely little room. Soon I will
leave my cell and join my brother monks in prayer and breakfast.

It will be cold outside, but I can't wait to feel the earth in my
hands. My job today will be to pull weeds from the vegetable
patch. It is backbreaking work, but I love it. Bend down, dig up the
whole weed. Bend and dig, bend and dig; never stop, keep moving. The sun is warm on my head and back. I am out of doors in the
sight of God.

I must keep working, working. I must forget my life in the
village. I must forget my friends. Why do I hear their voices? Why
can't I talk to them? What a fool I am! There are no voices. There's
no one here! Six months in this monastery! Six months I have been
alone. I am alone with over a hundred brother monks.

Why can't I talk to anyone? Why did we vow never to talk to
each other unless we get special permission? Is that why I keep
hearing voices? No, I know that there are no voices here. God will
help me; he will make me strong. I must pray now.

Why did I come to this monastery? I could have become a
knight. Wouldn't I be more proud to be Sir Denis instead of Brother
Denis? No—I hate fighting. I can't kill anyone. I get sick to my
stomach just thinking of blood! Or I could have been a rich merchant. I could have bought and sold anything and everything that
rich people want. No—I have no use for money. It means nothing
to me. I enjoy being poor!

Would I be happy as a village priest? I'm not sure. If I had my
own church, I could talk to people and work with them. I could
help them understand life and death, with the words of God. I see
myself giving the blessed sacraments. I baptize, confirm, and
marry their children. I give them Holy Communion and the last
rites when they die. Yes, I thought about being a priest for a long,
long time. But these are troubled times. There is killing and stealing. The weak are pushed around by the strong. The strong are

overcome by those who are even stronger! People just don't seem to care for each other.

I'm not one of those strong ones. I am not strong enough to push others around. I cannot help poor people because I myself am weak. Yet I want to do God's work. I know that, if I cannot do it in the outside world, I can help in the monastery.

This is my world. In this monastery I know exactly where I am and what I must do every day. I do what I am supposed to do. There are rules for each hour of the day. Everything is planned for me, but I do have time to think and pray. Here, I will atone (make up) for the sins of my youth.

I am not lazy or afraid to work. No one wastes time in this monastery. I work hard because it is God's will. I love my farm-work, and I am beginning to enjoy copying Latin and Greek books. My lettering is better now. I am learning to decorate the pages with little drawings. I never thought that I, Brother Denis, could be an artist! Now my life has meaning! This is real! I work at my own pace; I do as much as I can. I will not let myself feel tired! I think only of my work. I help myself, but I am useful to God and to the people.

There's the bell for breakfast. O Lord, help me through the day, the months, the years. Help me do your work in this monastery. Help me to stay silent today. I promise I will not say one word —even if another monk speaks to me! Do not let me break any of the rules.

I pray that you will help me to forget my life out there in the village. Let my mind be clear of worldly things.

## UNDERSTANDING THE STORY

**A.** *Write* T *for each statement that is true,* F *for each statement that is false, and* N *for each statement that is not mentioned in the story.*

1. During the Middle Ages central governments were stronger than the Church.
2. All monks were weak people.
3. The Church gave people a path to follow from birth to death to heaven.
4. Church buildings were used only for prayer.

5. All people during the Middle Ages were Catholics.
6. Brother Denis vowed never to speak without special permission.
7. The Catholic Church took no interest in the sick and the poor.
8. Brother Denis could not learn to draw pictures in the books he copied.
9. All monks in the Middle Ages took vows of silence.

B. *Would Brother Denis agree with or disagree with these statements? Write A for each statement that he would agree with and N for each statement that he would not agree with.*

1. I became a monk because I did not want to get my hands dirty.
2. I don't care if I never speak to anyone.
3. I would rather be a monk than a soldier or a businessman.
4. I don't mind being poor.
5. I should have been a village priest.
6. Too many monks waste time in this monastery.
7. The monastery will help me to help people.

C. Do you think Brother Denis made a wise choice when he entered the monastery? Explain. There are still monasteries in the world today. Would you be willing to join one? Why or why not? If Brother Denis were alive today, what other jobs would be open to him?

## ACTIVITIES AND INQUIRIES

1. Pretend that you are Brother Denis. Write a diary telling about one day in your life in the monastery.
2. Draw a picture of a monastery from what you have read in this chapter. Bring in a picture of a monastery from the library. Compare it with your drawing.
3. Brother Denis is sworn to silence. Pretend that you are his father or mother. Write a letter to him asking about his life in the monastery.
4. Imagine that you are Brother Denis. Answer your parent's letter.
5. List five reasons why the Catholic Church was so important to most people in Europe during the Middle Ages.

# 7. A New Life in the City

*During much of the Middle Ages,* as we have seen, life was very orderly and very predictable. However, there were challenges to this neatness and orderliness. In an earlier chapter, you saw how a ruler challenged the great power of the Church and what happened when he did.

Many thought that the arrangements between serf and noble would last forever. But there were also challenges to the great powers of the nobles. Serfs were unhappy and restless. As the Crusaders learned, there was another world outside the manor. Serfs now looked to the towns. In the 13th century, these towns became magnets for many serfs. Some serfs bought their freedom. Others simply ran away from the manor. All were looking for a new life.

Former serfs were attracted by the openness and variety of jobs offered by the towns. However, the great differences between life on the manor and that in the town could be both exciting and terrifying.

In this chapter, a serf who has bought his freedom faces the dangers and pleasures of the new life in an English town. Ask yourself whether he made the right decision in leaving the manor and going to the town. Would you have stayed in the town under the conditions he describes?

## Leeds, 1230

Has it only been seven days since I left the manor to come to Leeds? Everything seems such a blur. So much has happened in one short week. I paid the lord of the manor for my freedom, and I had such strange feelings. It was strange that he was happy to trade a little money for my lifetime of work and service. Perhaps, he won't miss my crops and tax payments.

The devil with Lord Cecil and his manor! What do I care what happens to him? I have my own life to think about. Did I do the right thing in coming here? I remember stories about this town when I was a child. They said it was a lively place. There was much to do and many people to meet. A person might not become rich, but there were many jobs. Work hard, they said, and you will live well as a free man. Get away from the slavery of the manor. Be free. Live!

My chance came. Exactly one week ago, I turned my back on the manor. I told myself that now my life would begin. I walked and walked for two days. I was so tired I could hardly move. At last, there it was—Leeds, the city of my dreams. I couldn't wait to get through the main gate. What marvelous sights would I see? Then it hit me. The first thing I saw was a gallows for hanging criminals. Each street I walked down seemed worse than hell itself. Everything was covered with garbage. Rats, pigs, and dogs were fighting over scraps of food that were thrown from windows. Some of this horrible garbage bounced off my head. I couldn't stand the smells that came from the rotting garbage, slaughterhouses, and stables.

Men were dragging carts through the narrow, filthy streets to pick up dead bodies. I made the mistake of looking at the faces of some of the dead. Now I can't get their tortured, ravaged faces out of my dreams. I asked some people what was happening. They said that the dead had been cursed by evil demons! They all had that same tortured look. Will I be next?

Night is falling. It is the worst time for me. I am afraid. The room is hot and stuffy. I feel as though I am going to choke to death. I'd like to go outside for a walk, but I don't dare to. People warned me that there are robbers hiding in the shadows. There is no one to protect me. I have no friends, and I can't afford to buy a weapon.

I thank God when daylight comes. I like to walk through the crowded marketplace, and watch the people working at their trades. I see them making helmets, saddles, coats of armor, spurs, and swords. Others are dyeing cloth or melting gold and silver and making cups and jewelry. There's a fair almost every day. People come from all over to buy these wonderful things.

The manor was never this interesting, but I was safer there.

*"I like to walk through the crowded marketplace and watch the people working at their trades."*

Often, I long for the smells of the soil and the harvest. My home was small, but I never felt shut in. I miss my friends and relatives. How I wish I had someone to talk with!

Enough of this dreaming. I must stop thinking about days past. The manor is dying; there's nothing there for me. This is where I am going to stay. There is excitement and liveliness here in Leeds that I never saw on the farm. There are thousands of people doing great things. There are people to meet and people to know. I will make friends with many of them; I will find a woman to love.

I am going to learn a trade and earn enough to live well. When I marry, I am not going to have to ask Lord Cecil for his approval. My children will be free. I am not afraid any longer. There is much more life than death here.

I will live and die a free man.


## UNDERSTANDING THE STORY

**A.** *Complete each of the sentences.*

1. The growth of towns helped make serfs unhappy and ———.
2. Some serfs bought their ———. Others ——— from the manor.
3. Many said that if you ——— hard, you would live well in the town.
4. One thing you saw when you entered a town was that streets were covered with ———.
5. Men were dragging carts to pick up the ———.
6. People worked at their trades in the crowded ———places.
7. A free man believed that it was better to learn a ——— and stay in the town than to go back to the ———.


**B.** *Compare life in a town in the Middle Ages with life in your city or town today. Write S for each statement that is similar to life in your town and D for each statement that is different from life in your town.*

1. The town has a gallows where criminals are hanged.
2. The streets are covered with garbage.
3. Men with carts collect the bodies of people who have died.
4. People are afraid to go out at night.

5. Many people go to the town to learn trades.
6. The town has crowded marketplaces where people work at their trades.

C. If you had a choice, would you live in a big city or on a farm? Explain. If you had lived during the Middle Ages, would you have chosen life in a town or on a manor? Why?

## ACTIVITIES AND INQUIRIES

1. Look at the illustration on page 33. Describe what is happening. Write your own title for this picture.
2. Imagine that you are standing on the roof of the tallest building in Leeds during the Middle Ages. Make a list of what you see.
3. Bring to class pictures of your town or city. Compare these with pictures of the medieval town. Does your town or city have anything in common with the town of the Middle Ages? Explain.
4. Imagine that you are a health inspector. List all the dangers to health and safety that you find in a town in the Middle Ages. Compare these with the dangers in your city or town today.
5. Pretend that the former serf asks your advice about staying in the town or going back to the manor. Write down what you would tell him.

# 8. The Guild System

As you have seen, towns offered new and exciting lives for many former serfs. Towns were also centers of business and trade. There were many chances to find jobs. However, there was (as today) much competition for good jobs and businesses. There were also problems such as making good-quality products and seeing that people acted fairly in buying and selling.

These problems were solved by forming *guilds*. Each guild was a group of persons who made the same product or carried on the same business. Guilds were the forerunners of today's unions. The guilds' rules were strict and often harsh. Boys and young men worked for many years to develop the skills needed to become masters of a craft. Many persons were never able to become masters, however, even though their work was as good as that of the masters.

In this story two young Italian men meet in the main square of Venice. One of them, a shoemaker, tells his friend of the path he is taking to become a master craftsman. See if you agree with his plan. What other way might he have chosen?

## Venice, 1254

"Congratulations, Sebastian. In a few hours you and Sophia are going to be married. She is a fine woman," said Enrico.

"Thank you, Enrico. I know I am lucky," replied Sebastian. "Now my dream of going into business for myself will come true."

"What does this have to do with getting married?" asked Enrico.

"It's very simple," answered Sebastian. "My future father-in-law, Luigi, is a rich master shoemaker. He has much to say in his guild. Thanks to him, my masterpiece has been approved by the guild masters. He's even promised me enough money to open my own shop!"

"It looks like you're really on your way! Marrying a master's daughter is something I never thought of doing. But is this what you want to do with your life?"

"Are you serious? I've spent the last ten years of my life working as an apprentice and journeyman in my future father-in-law's house. For seven years I slaved from six o'clock in the morning until nine o'clock at night, six and a half days a week. My reward was eating at the master's table and sleeping on the kitchen floor!"

"Why did you do it? You got no pay and the working conditions were horrible," said Enrico.

"It was a chance to learn a trade and someday become a master shoemaker," replied Sebastian. "It was what I wanted, even though my father made the arrangements. Three years ago, I finally became a journeyman. Now I earn a small salary."

"I understand all that," said Enrico. "But why is your future father-in-law, Luigi, so important to you? You speak of him so much. Have you forgotten about his daughter, Sophia, your bride-to-be?"

"I'll tell you why Luigi is so important to me," answered Sebastian. "Many of my friends will be journeymen for the rest of their lives, even though they are just as good shoemakers as I am."

"Why can't they become masters without marrying the master's daughter?" asked Enrico.

"The guild masters say that if there are too many masters with too many shops, there will not be enough work to go around."

"Now I understand why the guild has rejected many master-pieces lately," nodded Enrico. "But do you think it's fair? Why should the guild make such serious decisions? If a man wants to be master of a craft, I say let him! Why shouldn't he make and sell whatever he chooses?"

"I'm not so sure you really understand," said Sebastian. "The guild does more than pass or fail those who wish to become masters. It protects its members from shoemakers who don't live in town. Do you remember what happened last year when a shoemaker from Padua (PAD-yoo-uh) tried to open a shop here?"

"Yes, I remember," said Enrico. "He opened his shop very close to my home, and I was happy to give him my shoes to repair.

The next thing I knew, he was gone. It didn't make sense to me that he was forced to leave. He was a good man and a good worker. He had a large family to feed."

"Once again, you don't understand what a guild is all about," answered Sebastian. "That shoemaker from Padua could not join our guild. He did not have permission to open a shop here in Venice. We did not need another shoemaker to take business away from our guild members. Our people have many children to feed, too. They must come first!"

"Why did the guild burn his goods and drive him out of town?" asked Enrico. "He was a good man. He need not have been treated so cruelly."

"Very simple," said Sebastian. "No outsider has tried to open a shop since that time. They have been warned. They know how we treat them!"

"Why are you so hard on outsiders when you are so easy on your own members?" asked Enrico.

"You're wrong again!" replied Sebastian. "There is no difference in treatment. The guild is as strict with its own members. No merchant can sell goods cheaper than anyone else. No shop can be kept open longer than any other. All shoes must be of the same high quality. A member who breaks these rules will have his goods burned and his shop closed down."

"How can you live and work in such fear?" asked Enrico.

"Very easily," said Sebastian. "I'm no fool. I will follow every rule and regulation of my guild. I'll stay out of trouble, and I will enjoy being a master craftsman in my own business."

"Are you going to tell Sophia why you are marrying her?" asked Enrico.

"Once again, I am not a fool."

## UNDERSTANDING THE STORY

A. *Sebastian and Enrico make many different statements. Decide who made or might have made the following remarks. Write E for each statement that Enrico made or might have made and S for each statement that Sebastian made or might have made.*

1. My future father-in-law is a rich master shoemaker.
2. I worked as an apprentice and journeyman for ten years.

3. I never thought of marrying a master's daughter to become a master myself.
4. Many of my friends will be journeymen all their lives.
5. Let a man make and sell whatever he wants.
6. The guild protects its members from outsiders.
7. A member who breaks the rules has his shop closed down.
8. Why did the guild drive away the shoemaker from Padua?

**B.** *Tell which statements are true.*

1. It was very difficult to become a master craftsman.
2. Guilds were formed by men who made a certain product.
3. Every man in a guild became a master.
4. Sebastian was an apprentice before he became a journeyman.
5. Sebastian was marrying Sophia only because he loved her.
6. Enrico felt that a man should be able to make and sell whatever he wanted.
7. Many masterpieces were rejected by the guild.
8. The guild never punished its own members.

**C.** Would Sebastian be a successful businessman in today's world? Explain. Would we be better off today if we had the strict regulations of the guild system? Explain your answer.

## ACTIVITIES AND INQUIRIES

1. Visit a local union office or write to a union. Find out how a person becomes a member of the union. What are the benefits of being a union member? Report your information to the class. Be prepared to talk about how the union is like a medieval guild. How is a union different from a guild?
2. Imagine that you are a business person in your city or town. Make a list of the rules of the medieval guilds that you think would help business people today. List the rules that you would not like to follow. Explain the reasons for your choices.
3. Pretend that you have just become a guild master. Make an outline of all the things you had to do to move from apprentice to journeyman to master. Was it worth your effort? Explain.
4. Imagine that you are one of a class group arguing whether guilds should be brought back today. Which side would you take? Why?

# 9. School Life

*As the Middle Ages drew to a close,* there were more and more chances to escape from a boring, narrow life. As we have seen, many people went to the towns to make their fortunes in trade and business. Some years later, their sons were searching for other ways to spend their lives.

Some of these young men went to places of learning called universities and studied to become doctors, lawyers, and priests. Universities were located in cities and towns all over Western Europe.

At Bologna (bol-LOH-nyah), in Italy, the setting of this story, the university was started by a group of students, and this became the model for the student university. In Bologna the students were in control. They paid the teachers and hired and fired them. Other universities, such as the one in Paris, were run by teachers, who were in control of their operation.

In this letter, a student at the University of Bologna writes to his father about university life. Ask yourself whether you would have enjoyed attending this university.

## Bologna, 1260

DEAR FATHER,

I really appreciated the advice you gave me when I left for school. I do try to study hard and stay out of trouble. I keep myself clean and avoid the cold and damp air. But surely you can't believe that life at the university is easy and full of fun. You write that you would rather study here than work at your job. You seem to think that all we do is make life difficult for our teachers and annoy the people of Bologna.

Don't you think that we should have the best teachers? Shouldn't our teachers come to class on time? Shouldn't their lectures be interesting and helpful? Yes, professors know that they can lose their jobs if their lectures are dull and boring. This keeps them on their toes. You would be surprised at the number of professors who are anxious to get jobs here under these conditions.

It is not true that we waste time and fool around. I get up at four o'clock each morning—hours before you do. Can you imagine taking notes at a lecture at five in the morning, before you have had breakfast? All day, I have classes, debates, recitations, and lectures. That's not all, Father—I have a recitation most evenings after supper. I still have to find time for study at night to memorize my lecture notes. Believe me, by the time I crawl into bed at night, I have had a full day and an evening of hard work.

No, this is not like living in a fancy inn. I wonder how you would feel sitting on the floor of a cold room for hours at a time. I strain my eyes reading hand-copied books. Sometimes I can just about stay awake. Yes, if you would like to learn speech, logic, arithmetic, geometry, astronomy, music, and many other subjects, you could join me here. There are some men your age studying at the university.

I am sorry, Father, if I sound disrespectful. I want you to understand the life I lead here. Please don't think that I'm discouraged. The life is hard, but it's worth it to me to suffer a bit and get my degree. I have learned a great deal, and I have started to question and think. I don't always agree with my professors, but I realize that I still have much more to learn.

I know that you do not like to think of a university as a place where people argue with one another. But I am trying to find the answers to many puzzles. You have faith in things as they are. I recognize your beliefs, but I must know more. I must find new paths, and I must understand.

Father, please realize that I am very grateful for your sending me to a university that teaches me to disagree with you.

Your loving son,
PETER

# UNDERSTANDING THE STORY

A. *Write* T *for each statement that is true,* F *for each statement that is false, and* N *for each statement that is not mentioned in the story.*

1. Students at the University of Bologna hired their teachers.
2. Peter, the student in the story, never had evening classes.
3. All the students did their homework every night.
4. Peter's father said that he preferred work to study.
5. All the professors at the University of Bologna were at least 40 years old.
6. Peter often sat on the floor of a cold room for many hours.
7. Students at the University of Bologna studied music, astronomy, geometry, and many other subjects.
8. Peter always agreed with what his professors said.

B. *Complete each of the sentences below.*

1. The University of Bologna was started by ————.
2. Young men went to universities to study to become ————.
3. If a professor's lectures were boring, he could ————.
4. Peter attended a lecture before ————.
5. Peter strained his eyes reading ———— books.
6. Peter had learned ———— at the university.
7. Peter was trying to find the answers to ————.
8. Peter was grateful to his father for sending him to ————.

C. Imagine that Peter is a visiting student in your school. What would he say is similar to his school in the Middle Ages? What would he say is different about his school?

# ACTIVITIES AND INQUIRIES

1. Write down your daily school program. Compare your school day with that of Peter by writing his program alongside yours. Would you trade any part of your school day for his? Explain.
2. Pretend that you are a student at the University of Bologna in 1260. Your friends write to you and ask if they should become students there. What would you write back?
3. Imagine that you are Peter's father. Write a letter to Peter answering the one in the story, which you have just received from him.

# 10. Joan of Arc

*Think back to the story of the emperor* and the pope. Emperor Henry had a difficult time with Pope Gregory. However, the power of the kings and their countries grew greater. By the 15th century the Church still played a major role in European affairs, but it was no longer all powerful.

By the 14th century wars were no longer local affairs between nobles. Entire nations were involved in endless killing. The war we are talking about in this chapter was fought between England and France and was called the Hundred Years' War. It dragged on for 116 years, from 1337 to 1453. First the French, then the English, looked like winners.

In the last part of the war (1421–1453), the English had the French on the run. Fortunately for the French, a peasant girl, Joan of Arc, insisted that she heard strange voices. Only she could hear these voices, and their message was very clear. Joan was told by her voices that it was her duty to lead a French army against the English.

Joan faced many problems. How could she convince the French leaders that her voices spoke the truth? How could she get them to permit her to lead an army into battle? Would the soldiers follow her? What would be her plan of battle? What would happen if she did not win? Somehow, she convinced the French of the truth of her voices. She, the uneducated young girl, was given an army to lead.

In 1429 Joan's army defeated the English and ended their siege of Orleans. The English were driven from north central France. However, the next year Joan was captured by the English.

Joan of Arc was held prisoner in a small tower in the city of Rouen (ROO-ahn), about 90 miles northwest of Paris. She was burned at the stake in the city square. The ungrateful king of France, Charles VII, did not try to save her.

As you read, ask yourself whether you would have followed this young, untrained girl into battle. How did Joan's
actions encourage the French to be more loyal to their
nation?

# Rouen, May 1431

The English are in an ugly mood today. They curse and wave
their fists at me. Now rough hands take hold of me and tie me to
the stake. Soon my executioner will set fire to the straw. I will be
burned alive!

As I silently pray to my maker, my whole life passes before me.
How strange that I, a peasant girl who cannot read or write, was
chosen by God to achieve a miracle. How strange that I was chosen
to save France!

How well I remember those difficult days. For nearly 100 years,
England and France had been locked in a bitter war. Most of France
had already fallen into English hands. There was talk that the king
of England would soon be crowned king of France. This would
happen when the English captured our city of Orleans. Most
French people expected the city to fall at any moment.

It was then that I first heard the voices—voices that urged me to
lead the French to victory at Orleans. I remember trying to run
from those voices because they made me afraid. But no matter how
I tried, the voices continued to speak to me. Finally I asked for a
meeting with the French leaders.

How they howled with laughter when I explained my mission!
"You, a girl, are going to lead an army of men against the English?"
said one. "Go home and milk your cows," said another. "We men
will protect you." But the voices would not let me go home.
Finally the leaders decided that I should be given a chance.

How amused the army captains were to see me dressed in a
man's armor and riding a horse. But the common soldiers loved me
and they swore to risk their own lives to protect mine. Soon we
grew from a small band into an army. When the smoke of battle
had cleared, we had chased the English from Orleans.

Now those who once had mocked me stood in line to congratulate me. I was asked to be at the king's side in the cathedral in

Rheims as he was crowned king of all of France. My voices had not deceived me after all.

But just as my Savior had once carried his cross, mine was also being prepared. The English captured me, put me on trial, made fun of my voices, and condemned me to death. My followers have all deserted me in my hour of need. Yet I stand before my maker unafraid, and not quite alone.

The flames are now beginning to rise. The pain is unbearable—I bite my lips to keep from crying out. In my last moments on earth, I beg forgiveness for my torturers. My life is about to begin.

God save France.


## UNDERSTANDING THE STORY

**A.** *Write T for each statement that is true and F for each statement that is false.*

1. The Hundred Years' War lasted for 116 years.
2. Joan's army defeated the English at Orleans.
3. Joan of Arc fought to save England.
4. Joan of Arc was burned at the stake by the French.
5. Joan of Arc could neither read nor write.
6. The common soldiers would not follow Joan into battle.
7. Joan was at the king's side when he was crowned king of France.
8. Joan died bravely.


**B.** *The following questions refer either to England or to France. Write E for each statement that has to do with England and F for each statement that has to do with France.*

1. Joan was captured by the army of this country.
2. Joan fought for this country.
3. Joan and her army defeated the armies of this country.
4. Joan convinced the people of this country that her voices were real.
5. Joan helped to crown the king of this country.
6. This country did not try to save Joan in her hour of need.
7. This country tried Joan and found her guilty.
8. Joan was burned at the stake by this country.

**C.** Would the president of the United States let a 16-year-old girl who hears voices lead our army? Explain your answer. Would you follow Joan of Arc into battle? Why or why not?

## ACTIVITIES AND INQUIRIES

1. Look at the map of France below. In your notebook, draw an outline of the map. On your map mark the cities where Joan (*a*) was born (*b*) defeated the English (*c*) saw the king crowned (*d*) died.

*France in 1431*

2. Imagine that you are a French soldier fighting at the side of Joan of Arc. In class be prepared to describe an interview with Joan. What was there about Joan of Arc that made her a great leader?
3. Pretend that your class is going to hold the trial of Joan of Arc. You are her lawyer. Prepare her defense. Now imagine that you are her accuser. Prepare the case against her.

"Well, what do you think, Jack?" asked Mr. Miller.

"I'm not so sure. All this stuff happened a long time ago. But it's not boring, as I thought it would be."

"What do you mean?"

"The Roman Empire broke up. No one was really running things. There was no strong government telling people what to do," said Jack.

"You mean people were doing whatever they wanted?"

"No. There was no strong central government, but there were many small ones. It's what you called feudalism. There were nobles fighting and protecting their own land. Then the nobles with the best armies would fight other nobles and take over some of their turf."

"What does this sound like?" asked Mr. Miller.

"The strong are always pushing the weak around," answered Jack. "I can see it all around me almost every day."

"That's good, Jack, but aren't you forgetting about most of the people during the Middle Ages?"

"That puzzles me, Mr. Miller. Many of them weren't free. The serfs were almost slaves. They couldn't leave their land. The nobles and knights really pushed the poor serfs around!"

"Why did they let themselves be pushed around?" asked Mr. Miller.

"What choice did they have? They didn't own land, and they needed somebody strong to protect them. There was no strong government, not even a police department. What could they do? They turned to the lord of the manor. He said, 'I'll protect you —just spend your life working for me!' Sounds like a protection racket to me!"

"You're right, Jack, this situation couldn't last. It was a hard life for the poor. What do you see yourself doing in those days?"

"I know one thing, Mr. Miller. I would never have been a serf. I'd have run away, joined a crusade, gone to a town. I'd have done anything to get away from the manor! I think I'd be a knight. Fighting all the time sounds like fun. That code of chivalry was really something. I would be traveling around, crusading; and I'd meet lots of beautiful women!"

"Sounds like life in the army would be just the thing for you!" laughed Mr. Miller.

"Except that a knight doesn't start at the bottom of the ladder," added Jack. "One thing bothers me, though. You can get hurt —even killed. I don't think that this knight business is for me. There doesn't seem to be much purpose to it."

"Then have you thought of becoming a priest or a monk?"

"Not really," answered Jack. "It would be good to help people, I suppose. But you don't see me copying manuscripts all day or preaching a sermon, do you? I know that the Catholic Church held things together in the Middle Ages. And it gave some of the kings a lot of trouble. The Church held its ground for a long time. But it's just not the life for me."

"How can we be sure what you might have done in those days?" asked Mr. Miller. "The way you're going, I can almost see you lecturing in a medieval university! Or you might be a master in the furniture makers' guild! What do you think was the number-one problem during the Middle Ages?"

"People worried about making a living. That's it! They wanted to live," said Jack excitedly. "They weren't that different from us! But there was one thing that made them different from people today."

"What's that?" asked Mr. Miller.

"They thought so much about life after death. Some of them seemed to worry more about heaven and hell than about life on earth," added Jack very quietly. "When did people start thinking more about life on Planet Earth? When did they start thinking more about today?"

"Don't stop looking, Jack. The answers are in the next unit!"

# The Renaissance—
# Modern Times Begin

"Mr. Miller, you know how I hate those big words," complained Jack. "What did you call this period we're studying?"

"Take it easy, Jack," said Mr. Miller. "It's not that hard. The word is 'Renaissance' (REHN-uh-sahns)."

"No way, Mr. Miller. That's a big word!"

"You can call it a rebirth or a revival, Jack. You'll soon see what I mean."

"A rebirth? How can anything be born all over again? That's impossible! What does this 'Renaissance' have to do with me?"

"People started to be interested in learning once again. Like you, Jack, they wanted to know more about today—*now*. They wanted to know about life on earth. They wanted to live. One big difference, of course, was that their *today* was 400 or 500 years ago."

"Didn't people always care about themselves?" asked Jack. "Didn't they look around them to see what was going on?"

"Yes, but their world was different from ours," answered Mr. Miller. "The Renaissance opened people's eyes. They saw new things. They wrote, painted, and traveled. They wanted to find new places. They were not satisfied with the old ways of doing things."

"I'm looking for new things, too. Am I a Renaissance person?" asked Jack in a puzzled voice.

"Not exactly, Jack. You're not coming out of the Middle Ages. You know that you are a person. You know that your life on earth has to give you a great deal. The people of the Renaissance had to find themselves, and they had to learn about life on earth."

"How did they do all that, Mr. Miller?"

"Why not read the unit on the Renaissance? Perhaps you can become a Renaissance person!"

# 1. A Writer Tells It As It Is

*In the final story of Unit I,* we saw how the nations of Europe were becoming stronger. People were drawn to the flags of their own countries. They were beginning to feel proud of their own countries and their leaders.

Other changes were taking place as the Middle Ages were coming to an end. People had been taught that life on earth was not as important as life after death. By the 14th and 15th centuries, however, this outlook was changing. Many people were living better. They were looking forward to a good life on earth rather than later.

This excitement and interest in "now" was described by writers called humanists. They stressed the importance of life for human beings. The humanists got many of their ideas from reading ancient Greek and Roman books, which are referred to as the *classics.* The Greek and Roman scholars had said that people should be the measure of all things.

The humanists were excited about finding the classics. They felt as though they were being born again. This rebirth or revival of interest in people and the classics is called the Renaissance.

In the story that follows, Petrarch (PET-rark), the first Renaissance humanist, is visited by Boccaccio (boh-KAHT-choh). Petrarch lives in the city of Padua, in north-eastern Italy. Through the window he can see the clock on the cathedral of Padua. See if you can understand why both Petrarch and Boccaccio are really Renaissance humanists. Are their ideas and thinking really so different?

# Padua, 1351

"Hello, Petrarch," said Boccaccio. "How is the poet laureate (LOR-ih-at) today?"

"Not too bad, Boccaccio, not too bad," answered Petrarch with a big smile. "You are a real friend. You remember that I was named the greatest poet in Italy. You know, it's been ten years since my big day."

"What a thrill it must have been," said Boccaccio. "But where do you go from here? Have you thought of new worlds to conquer, new things to write?"

"Wait a minute," said Petrarch. "Isn't my poetry good enough for you? I am where I want to be! Why should I change now?"

"I was hoping you would say something else," said Boccaccio quietly.

"What do you mean?" asked Petrarch.

"Why don't you write about what's happening in Italy and in the world?" said Boccaccio. "There's so much going on around you. Don't shut your eyes to pain and dirt. There are fires and floods. Write about them! There is crime in the streets. Death is all around us. Don't hide from it. People laugh and cry. Some are born, some leave us. Why do you run from the truth? Where are you? Why do you stand on the sidelines? Why don't you write so that people can understand you?"

"What do you mean 'understand me'?" snapped Petrarch. "Many of my poems are written in Italian. Most people can't read Latin, but they know their *own* language!"

"That's not enough, Petrarch!"

"You're jealous, Boccaccio! Do you think that your poems are as good as mine?"

"I told you before that you were our greatest poet," said Boccaccio quickly. "You wrote all those poems to your friend Laura. The words are beautiful. Your thoughts belong in heaven. But you never let yourself go. You never say what you really feel deep down inside of you. Yes, you loved Laura. You missed her when she was away."

"Stop it, Boccaccio! Stop it! You know that Laura is dead. I wrote about her death in my own way. In my poems I cried for her. Yes, I cried and cried. I remembered her beauty, her gentle look, her fair face. I miss her. I'll never forget her. Isn't that enough?"

"I'm sorry that she's gone," said Boccaccio. "I think I know how you must feel. But you can say more—much, much more. Why don't you tell it all in Italian? Why don't you write a story about Laura? Why don't you tell about the plague of 1348? Why don't you write about how Laura and thousands of others died? Poetry isn't everything, you know."

"Why do you torture me like this?" asked Petrarch in great anger. "Can't you understand that I don't want to write anything but poems about Laura. I don't want to write a story about the plague. I don't want to write about death and dying. I can't write about blood and boils and the smells of corpses."

"Why is it so hard for you to think and write about ugliness and suffering? I did it in my *Decameron*. Death and sin are parts of life. Even Petrarch cannot escape from that. Look at your Laura. Did she close her eyes one night and go off to heaven with a smiling face? No, she died a horrible death. In three days the plague made her old and ugly!"

"Enough!" cried Petrarch. "I know what you want me to do —and I won't do it. You want me to write as you do. You want me to tell how Laura's beauty turned to dust. You want people to read about her agony. I won't do it, Boccaccio! I can't!"

"Of course, you can. Why don't you start writing what people want to read?"

"I write what I think people should read," answered Petrarch grimly. "I write what I want to write. I choose my words carefully. I won't write everything I think and know. Look at your *Decameron*. Your stories are a disgrace. They're crude! They're filled with ordinary people working and having fun. This is not my way. This is not me."

"How can you be so sure?" asked Boccaccio. "People are people. They live, they die, they are human. Isn't that what humanism is all about? Aren't you a humanist? Where are your feelings? Why are you so far above everyone? Come down to earth!"

"How dare you say that I am not a humanist? You're the one who's not a humanist. You say the individual person is important—well, where do I fit into your picture? Why can't I write about love and life as I see and feel them? All right, Boccaccio, I cannot feel and smell and touch exactly as you do. I cannot write exactly as you do. Does that mean that I'm not as human as you?"

"Petrarch, why do we have to argue this way? I know that we are both humanists. You are right! Each of us must think and write in his own way. A writer must write what he feels, as long as he doesn't hurt anyone. Each of us is different; bravo for that! But we do agree about many things. Your poems and my *Decameron* are written in the language of the Italian people. Yet we both love the classics. You found the Latin speeches of Cicero. I translate Homer into Latin."

"I wonder," said Petrarch quietly, "will people remember me for my Italian poems or my classical translations?"

"They will remember you as a humanist and a human being," answered Boccaccio.

## UNDERSTANDING THE STORY

**A.** *Tell which statements are true.*

1. In the Middle Ages most people felt that life after death was more important than life on earth.
2. Living conditions were becoming better by the 14th and 15th centuries.
3. Ancient Greek and Roman writers wrote books that were called humanities.
4. The Renaissance was a time of a rebirth of interest in people.
5. Boccaccio was called the first Renaissance humanist.
6. Petrarch was a great poet.
7. Boccaccio wrote the *Decameron*.
8. Petrarch felt that Boccaccio's stories did not have enough love and adventure in them.

**B.** *You can see that Boccaccio and Petrarch had different ideas about many things. Decide who made or might have made the remarks that follow. Write B for each statement that Boccaccio made or might have made and P for each statement that Petrarch made or might have made.*

1. It was very exciting to be named poet laureate.
2. You are the greatest poet in the world.

3. Why don't you write about what's happening in the world?
4. Do you think your poems are as good as mine?
5. In the *Decameron* I wrote about death and sin.
6. Why don't you write about the plague?
7. A writer should say what he wants as long as he doesn't hurt anyone.
8. Why can't I write about love and life as I see it?

C. Imagine that Petrarch and Boccaccio are writing today. Whose book would you rather read? Why? Whose book do you think the school would like you to read? Explain. Which writer might be most popular today? Why?

## ACTIVITIES AND INQUIRIES

1. Fill in the blanks in the sentences with one of the following key terms.
   Renaissance          classics
   poet laureate        humanists
   Both Boccaccio and Petrarch showed interest both in human beings and in the great books of the past. They were men of the ———.
   The ——— were writers who wanted to know a great deal about people and how they lived.
   The ancient Greek and Roman writers left us books that are called ———.
   A country's best poet is sometimes known as the ———.
2. Go to the library. Prepare a report on either Petrarch or Boccaccio. Explain why you selected the person you wrote about.
3. The following was written by one of the writers in the story. Read the passage and decide if it was written by Petrarch or Boccaccio. Explain your answer.

   I stood on the mountaintop. The time to leave was near. I saw other mountains. Then sensed the sea and the waves. I was angry with myself. Why was I still interested in things around me?

# 2. An Artist Looks at Life

*We have seen that the writers* of the Renaissance were beginning to write about people as they really were. They were emphasizing the importance of people's lives on earth. They were concerned with humanity's feelings and its everyday problems. Artists also realized that each person was different from every other person. They started to paint men and women as real men and women, not as dull, blank figures. The artists of the Renaissance painted pictures of people who seem able to move and to feel. The artists were able to do this because they had studied the human body and learned a great deal about how people moved. How did people really look when they did certain things? How did they look when they were happy, sad, tired, satisfied?

Renaissance artists discovered new ways of drawing the world around them and of working with light and shade. But they never forgot about beauty, and their works are attractive to our eyes.

In our story Leonardo da Vinci (leh-oh-NAR-doh da VEEN-chee) is walking across St. Peter's Square in Rome. Suddenly, he sees another artist, a follower of the old methods of painting. This older artist feels that the subject of a painting is very important. The people in a work of art are of secondary value. See if you can understand why Leonardo is so upset by this man's ideas about art. Is Leonardo right that art should deal with things as they are?

## Rome, 1490

"Bruno, I hear that you are saying bad things to many people about my paintings," said Leonardo angrily. "If you don't like my work, I can understand that. But why haven't you spoken to me? Why do you complain to everyone who will listen to you?"

"Calm down, Leonardo," replied the older artist. "I admire much of what you paint, but there are also many things that I don't like. Art should be a reflection of our religion and our connection to God. Your work is not religious. It's too worldly."

"That's not what you really mean," said Leonardo. "You know very well that most of my paintings are of religious subjects."

"Yes, but somehow your religious subjects are not really religious," Bruno replied.

"Nonsense! What you can't get through your head is that I try to paint real people. I want to feel real flesh and blood on my canvas," said Leonardo. "I want people to look at my paintings and believe my figures live and breathe, that they are not sticks that look alike."

"I am sorry, Leonardo, but that is not what art is all about," answered Bruno. "If I want to see real people, I walk down the street. I do not look at a picture on a wall just to see men and women. I want to see pictures of holy subjects, stories from the holy Bible, reminders of our Lord."

"I do all this and more," replied Leonardo. "I paint what you call 'holy subjects.' But I refuse to believe that every man and woman should look exactly the same as every other man and woman. Is every person thin, sad, and worried looking? Have you never seen happy faces and plump bodies? Is everyone in life worried, unnatural, unreal?"

"Leonardo, holy subjects need saintly people. People in pictures have looked and posed in the same way for centuries. It is a terrible sin to paint religious subjects with saints who look like ordinary people. Follow the customs of the past, I always say, and you will never go wrong."

"No, no, I must paint a person as I see and understand the person," said Leonardo. "This is the way I see myself as an artist. My art is my own. I paint as I see things through my own eyes."

"You're becoming more and more difficult," said Bruno. "You must understand that if a person's eye sees what you call beauty and reality in a picture, that's all the person will see. How can the soul of the holy person be seen? The mind is blocked from understanding the true purpose of the picture. The person does not see the religious meaning of the painting."

"Not true, Bruno—the eye is the window to the soul. You must see human beings in all their beauty and ugliness. Then you will understand what the soul is really like."

"Why is the human body so important to you?" asked Bruno.

"Bruno, admit it. You're afraid of the human body," replied Leonardo. "Your soul is in your body, isn't it? Wait, I think I understand your feelings about the body. You don't know enough about it to paint it properly! What do you know about how your body works and functions? I have cut and worked on muscle and bone to discover how people move. I have seen what is inside a person. To paint the outer person, you must know what is inside."

"Sinful insults," shouted Bruno. "Does the pope know what you think and how you act? You are a danger and a disgrace to your Church!"

"Why don't you study real people?" said Leonardo, disregarding Bruno's insults. "Watch them at work and at rest. Observe them in the streets, in the fields, in their homes. Don't just look at them—make sketches of everything that you see."

"Do you always have to be so insulting?" continued Bruno. "I do look at people. I observe them, but I don't sketch them. And I don't ask them to pose for me. My art does not deal with people who live today. Once again, I must repeat, because you will not understand, we are here to paint holy subjects."

"Bruno, if I didn't know you so well, I would say that you are a fool! Where is your curiosity? Why aren't you interested in how people's faces show their feelings? Have you ever really looked at my painting 'The Last Supper'? Did you see the looks of horror, anger, sadness, unhappiness, and fear that I painted? Which of these might you have felt at the Last Supper of our Lord? What is my painting of Mona Lisa trying to tell you?"

"Never mind about my curiosity," said Bruno. "A painting of the Last Supper is not supposed to be a study of human character. It is a painting of our Lord and his apostles at the Passover seder. No, I haven't looked that closely at their faces. I will not let my mind wander from what I believe should be the purpose of the picture. 'Mona Lisa'—what's that got to do with religion?"

"Bruno, no matter what you say, you must look around more. You must want to discover more. What's wrong with you? Have you never wondered how a bird flies? What the organs of our bodies do? Where wind and clouds come from? Why cracks appear in walls? Why there are seashells on mountaintops? What happens when a person yawns or sneezes? Why a person dies of old age? What do you know of life, of people, of war, of death?"

"You ask too many questions," replied Bruno. "But can you answer one for me?"

"Try me," said Leonardo.

"All right. For me, anything and everything in life begins and ends with God. What is the meaning of life for you?"

"For me," said Leonardo thoughtfully, "it is searching for the answers to my questions."

## UNDERSTANDING THE STORY

A. *Write T for each statement that is true, F for each statement that is false, and N for each statement that is not mentioned in the story.*

1. Renaissance artists saw that each person was different from every other person.
2. Renaissance artists were the greatest the world has ever seen.
3. Renaissance artists were not interested in the human body.
4. Most art museums in the United States show only Renaissance paintings.
5. Leonardo da Vinci never painted religious subjects.
6. Bruno felt that art should deal only with holy subjects.
7. Leonardo wanted the people in his paintings to look alive.
8. The art of Leonardo is not as popular today as it was during the Renaissance.
9. Leonardo painted "The Last Supper."

B. *Tell which word or phrase makes each statement correct.*

1. Bruno felt that Leonardo's paintings were too (a) worldly (b) fancy (c) large.
2. Leonardo wanted you to think that people in his paintings (a) looked like sticks (b) lived and breathed (c) all looked exactly alike.
3. According to Bruno, holy subjects needed people who looked like (a) ordinary people (b) kings and queens (c) saints.

4. Leonardo believed that the human body was something to (a) be afraid of (b) study in great detail (c) cover up.
5. In his painting "The Last Supper," Leonardo painted people who (a) showed their feelings (b) all looked like him (c) looked as if Bruno had painted them.
6. Leonardo was interested in (a) copying the art of the past (b) becoming famous (c) learning the truth.
7. The most important thing in Leonardo's life was (a) getting to heaven (b) being the best artist in the world (c) finding the answers to his questions.

C. 1. Leonardo's paintings are worth a lot of money today. Why do you think this is so? Would you spend thousands, even millions, of dollars for a painting by Leonardo? Explain your answer.
2. If you could find a painting by Bruno, would you want to own it? Why? Might a painting by Bruno be worth a great deal of money? Explain.

## ACTIVITIES AND INQUIRIES

1. Go to the library. Find copies of Leonardo's paintings. Ask yourself if Leonardo was a great painter. Explain your answer.
2. In addition to his paintings, Leonardo also made many drawings of his ideas for new machines. Go to the library. Find sketches of Leonardo's ideas. Report to the class on what you learned about Leonardo.
3. Visit an art museum. Look for paintings by other Renaissance artists. How is Leonardo's work different from that of other artists? How is it the same?

# 3. A Scientist Challenges the Past

*Renaissance writers and artists* changed their views of people. They wrote about and painted real people in the real world. So too, in the 16th and 17th centuries, daring men of science had new ideas about the world. They challenged what ancient writers and the Catholic Church had said about the earth and the sun. These scientists looked around them. They observed nature, saw how people lived, and learned that the earth moved around the sun.

They asked questions and searched for answers. Sometimes they found the answers. If they did not, they kept searching. One of these searchers for truth was Galileo Galilei (gal-ah-LAY-oh gal-ah-LAY-ee), who made several important discoveries.

In the selection that follows, Galileo is about to appear before the *Inquisition* (in-kwih-ZISH-un) to explain his discoveries. This court seeks to uphold the teachings of the Church. Galileo will be given a choice of life or death. If he insists that the earth moves around the sun, he will die. If he denies what he knows to be true, he will live. Given these same choices, what would you have done? How can Galileo be so sure that he is right and that the teachings of the Church are wrong?

## Rome, 1633

To think that I have come to this! If I do not admit that I am wrong, I will be executed! I will be remembered for all time as a heretic who denied the truth of the teachings of his Church. Yet I, Galileo Galilei, have always been faithful to my Church and to the discoveries of science. Now I am told that I cannot believe in both science and God.

The Church says that the earth is the center of the universe. I know better. I have read and tested the theories of Copernicus (ko-PUR-ni-kus). A hundred years ago, he proved by mathematics that the earth moves around the sun. I made my own telescope because I wanted to test his ideas. People asked how the astronomy of the Bible could be wrong. It was an insane idea to think that the teachings of the Church have been false for so many centuries. But my eyes did not betray me. Copernicus was right. The earth is not the center of the universe. How excited I was when I saw the rings of Saturn, the moons of Jupiter, and the countless stars of the Milky Way. These were my eyes, my telescope, making my discoveries!

We know the things we can see and prove. Is there any other possibility? There cannot be. Perhaps I was wrong to think that I could know more than the great scholars of my Church. If it is true that we are made in God's image, then we must be at the center of the universe. Are there not mysteries and spirits that we cannot understand? Only God knows all. The leaders of his Church can explain the meaning of life to us.

That is what I am supposed to believe. But in my heart of hearts I know that there is much to be discovered and explored. No one, not even the holy Church, knows the answers to all the mysteries!

If we are to find the answer to the riddle of the universe, we must never stop looking. We must experiment and experience as much as we can. Blind faith is not my way of life. I cannot accept whatever I am told simply because it has been said by the Church.

When I wanted to find the speed of falling objects, I dropped some weights from the top of the Leaning Tower of Pisa (PEA-zah). I experimented, I saw, and I made my conclusions.

The other day I heard an argument in the street. Five grown men were arguing about the number of teeth in a horse's mouth. The horse was standing right there, but no one thought of opening the animal's mouth and counting its teeth. In fact, no one even looked at the horse! This argument went on for over an hour. I suggested checking the horse's mouth, and I was rewarded by being pushed rudely aside. There was no conclusion to the argument. The people went away confused and angry. Is this the way to learn the answers?

Enough of these wandering thoughts! I must make up my

mind. I know that I can have faith in my God and still search for answers. The Church fathers do not agree. They say I must give up my search for learning, destroy my book, agree that the sun moves around the earth. They want me to stop my experiments and accept the ways of God and of the Church.

I don't want to accept blindly, but if I am to see another sunrise, I must give in. I must pretend to believe. I will call the guard to tell them that they have won. I wonder—is it better to live a lie than to die and face the unknown?

## UNDERSTANDING THE STORY

**A.** *Write T for each statement that is true and O for each statement that is an opinion.*

1. Galileo was the greatest scientist of all time.
2. Galileo looked through his telescope to see planets and stars.
3. Galileo should not have looked beyond the earth.
4. The Inquisition should not have tried Galileo.
5. Galileo studied the speed of falling objects.
6. A scientist should do whatever he thinks best.
7. Galileo wondered why he had to lie to the Inquisition.

**B.** *Match each item in Column A with its description in Column B.*

| Column A | Column B |
|---|---|
| 1. scientist | (a) instrument used to study planets and stars |
| 2. Inquisition | (b) person who studies the planets and stars |
| 3. Copernicus | (c) building where Galileo tested the speed of falling objects |
| 4. telescope | (d) tried to prove that Copernicus was right |
| 5. Leaning Tower of Pisa | (e) person who searches for answers |
| 6. heretic | (f) put Galileo on trial |
| 7. Galileo | (g) proved mathematically that the earth moves around the sun |
| 8. astronomer | (h) person who denies the teachings of the Church |

C. Imagine that you are Galileo. You are accused of heresy by the Church. Would you act in the same way that Galileo did? Explain your answer. Are there people today who, like Galileo, are placed on trial for their ideas? Explain.

## ACTIVITIES AND INQUIRIES

1. Draw a cartoon of Galileo sitting in his prison cell. What is he thinking? Make up a title for your cartoon.
2. Imagine that you are a lawyer. Would you rather defend or prosecute Galileo? Prepare your case.
3. Go to the library. Prepare a report on another scientist of the Renaissance. Why was this person not placed on trial?
4. Pretend that you are Galileo. You have been arrested. Write a letter to a friend explaining why you acted the way you did.

# 4. Europe Discovers America

*You have seen how scientists* were discovering things about themselves, about life and death. They found new things about the earth and the heavens. Other brave men, at the same time, also had a dream about the earth. They said that by sailing west from Europe, one would reach the Orient —India and China, and the Spice Islands.

Christopher Columbus and other great sea captains sailed to the west hoping to make that dream come true. But the continents of North and South America blocked the way to the riches of the Orient. Instead Columbus found the New World of the Americas. He thought that he had reached India, however, and naturally called the people Indians. He never found the gold, silver, spices, and precious stones of the Orient. But his discovery of the New World made his four trips worthwhile.

In this story, Queen Isabella of Spain thinks back over her years as queen. She has strong memories of Columbus and his dreams. See if you agree with her selection of the most important act of her reign. Was she really responsible for the creation of the Spanish Empire? Were North and South America really a New World?

## Seville, 1504

The other night, my son Charles asked me what I thought had been the most important or best act of my service as queen of Spain. I brushed him aside with a brief remark about there having been so many good things. Actually, though, I simply was not prepared to answer at that point.

Now I wonder. This is the twentieth year of my reign as queen. So many things have happened. Marrying Ferdinand was impor-

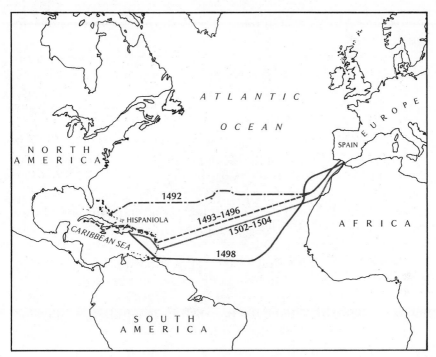

*Columbus' four voyages of discovery*

tant and exciting. We did many good things for Spain. Sometimes, though, I think I was a bit unhappy about our life together. Who can deny the importance of driving the Jews and the Moors out of our country? We united Spain and we made her into a truly Catholic country. The Inquisition keeps it that way. We have ruled firmly and well. The nobles may not be too happy, but our nation is strong.

Yes, we have done so many things for Spain. In my mind, though, one thing always seems to come first. I am proudest of my support for Christopher Columbus. When he first came to see us in 1486, I knew that he was a man to believe in. He was a most convincing charmer. He could make a believer of almost anyone. He insisted that by sailing about 3,000 miles to the west from Spain, he would come to the gold, silks, and spices of India, China, and the Spice Islands.

I believed in him from the beginning, even though my commissioners would not accept his plan. They insisted that the ocean was too wide to sail across to Asia! Anyway, with the war going on against the Moors in Granada, there simply wasn't money for expeditions.

Columbus never gave up! He returned five years later, and I believed in him even more strongly this time. But what demands he made upon us! I think that if it had been anyone but Columbus, I would have had him thrown into jail without another thought.

The nerve of Columbus! There he was begging support for his voyage to the unknown, but still insisting that he be named "Admiral of the Ocean Sea"! He wanted 10 percent of all of the profits and had to be viceroy of all islands he discovered. That ridiculous man went on and on. In April 1492 I finally agreed to what he wanted. Why did I do it? He wanted too much. But somehow I knew that he would make some great discoveries. And he was such a charming man!

He never found the Spice Islands or China and India. He never found much of the wealth he promised either, but he discovered a New World. There were new people, new places—all claimed in the name of Spain. What if the people he called Indians really were not Indians? No matter—they were different from anyone we had ever met or read about.

I read his detailed letters with pleasure and worry. How he suffered! His food was poor; the crew was hard to control. He often wrote that the natives were dangerous and the climate was bad. But I always knew that he would succeed, and he did. We gave him a hero's welcome on his return to Spain!

Four times he sailed from Spain. He found many islands and the coast of South America. He even named a colony after me on the island of Hispaniola. Yes, he did much for Spain and the world.

Why then did I approve of his arrest and imprisonment after his third voyage? Why did I believe the stories told by jealous liars? Perhaps he wasn't the best leader in the world, but why should that be so important? What if he did not find all the gold he had promised? Was there ever a man more dedicated to his purpose and to his queen?

I am so happy that he was given a fourth chance to sail to the New World. I wonder what great stories he will tell me when he returns this time. What new wealth will he bring back for me? For his sake and mine, I pray that he finds a passage to India. Even if he finds nothing, I will welcome him. Please God, have him hurry back to Spain. I want so much to see him again. I know that I do not have too many months left on earth.

What have I, Isabella, accomplished in a lifetime? I am the mother of the empire of Spain.

## UNDERSTANDING THE STORY

A. *Tell which of the following statements are true.*

1. Columbus believed that the earth was round.
2. Columbus thought that he had sailed to India.
3. Columbus married Queen Isabella.
4. Ferdinand and Isabella united Spain.
5. Isabella never trusted Columbus.
6. Columbus was given the title Admiral of the Ocean Sea.
7. Columbus discovered the New World.
8. Columbus had excellent food and good crews on all of his voyages.

B. *Read the following statements. Tell which of the facts, events, or beliefs were results of Columbus' voyages.*

1. People now knew that China and India were in the Atlantic Ocean.
2. People knew that they could sail across the Atlantic Ocean.
3. Columbus believed that the islands he discovered were the Spice Islands.
4. Spain developed a great empire in the New World.
5. People no longer believed that the earth was flat.
6. Much gold was found in the New World.

C. Imagine that Columbus is alive today. He wants the government of the United States to pay for his exploration of the planet Mars. Would you want the government to pay for his trip? Explain your answer. Would you go along? Why or why not? Which do you think takes more courage: the voyage to the New World or the exploration of Mars? Explain.

## ACTIVITIES AND INQUIRIES

1.  Look at the map of Columbus' voyages on page 65. Copy the map in your notebook. Draw a line showing the route you would have followed from Spain if you had been Columbus. Compare your route with the ones that Columbus took.
2.  Pretend that you are Columbus at the court of Queen Isabella of Spain. Write a letter to the queen. Explain why you want her to help you make your voyage to the Indies. In your letter underline the ideas that you think would be most convincing.
3.  Pretend that you are Queen Isabella. Write a letter to Columbus. Tell him what you think of his idea of sailing west.
4.  Go to the library. Read more about Columbus' voyages to the New World. Be prepared to talk about one of them in class.
5.  Imagine that you are one of the crew sailing with Columbus on his first voyage. Make a drawing of your ship. Write a diary describing your experiences on one or two days of your voyage.

# 5. An Empire Is Born

*The 16th century was the age* of exploration. By 1507
Ferdinand Magellan's ships had sailed around the world. A
few years earlier, as we have seen, the New World—North
America, the Caribbean islands, and South America—had
been discovered.

This New World was talked about a great deal in the
towns and on the farms of Europe. Centuries before, serfs
had been able to leave the manor and go to the towns. Now
here was another chance for unhappy but brave people to
make a fresh start 3,000 or more miles from home.

European governments and businessmen also urged
people to leave their homes in Europe and settle in faraway
places. These settlements were called colonies. Here in
North America, many settlers suffered and died from starvation or disease. Life was harsh and difficult. Only the
strongest could live through the freezing winters. The natives were often unfriendly or hostile.

There was another side to the coin: the European side.
Europeans encouraged the setting up of these colonies for
their own profit. Colonies were places where raw materials
not found in Europe could be obtained. Colonies were also
places to sell the goods made in Europe. This system of using
colonies to increase a European country's wealth was called
mercantilism (MUR-kan-til-izm).

In the following conversation, the chief adviser of King
Charles II of England reminds the king of the importance of
the colonies to England. He has suggestions for making
these colonies more useful to England. See if you understand how Lord Clarendon proposes to use the colonies. Do
you agree with his ideas? Was it fair to use the colonies for
England's benefit?

# London, 1663

"Your Majesty," said Lord Clarendon, "you understand that a great country like England cannot live without trade. We must buy and sell without a stop, or we will die. Please let me explain my ideas about trade."

"Clarendon, you are right," Charles II replied. "But I do not want to think about foreign problems at this time. It's less than three years since I became king, and I must be concerned first with what's going on in England."

"Sire, I appreciate your feelings," said Clarendon. "But surely you realize that more trade with our colonies will improve business here in England. Better business will naturally make people hap-

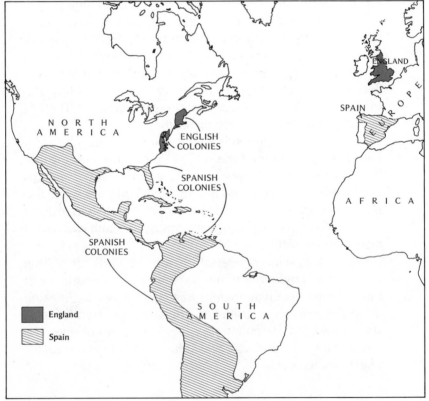

*English and Spanish colonies in the New World in the 17th century*

pier. If people are doing well, my king will be more popular. You will have less to worry about."

"Lord Clarendon, I truly appreciate your interest. You are my most trusted adviser. I value your advice above all others, but my mind is not on foreign matters. And I am not afraid of the people's opinion!"

"Your Majesty," continued Clarendon, "I beg to differ with you. These are not foreign matters. What the colonies do or do not do with buying and selling concerns us at home. The colonies are growing valuable things, but they are not shipping them to us. For example, last year the colonies of Virginia and Maryland grew almost 7 million pounds of tobacco. Very little of this passed through English ports. I ask Your Majesty, is this fair? What are our colonies for? They are cheating us!"

"Agreed, agreed," said Charles wearily. "It sounds unfair. But it does not seem a matter of great importance to me. Suppose the colonies send their products where they choose. What of it? We're still doing very nicely. Look at the strange foods that are coming here. Most people never even knew they existed! How many knew about potatoes, corn, squash, citrus fruits, chocolate, peanuts? I could go on and on. Need I mention the spices, coffee, and tea from the Orient!"

"Sire, I must disagree with you. True, we are getting a variety of products from the New World and from India. But the most important are gold and silver. The more gold and silver we take in, the richer our country will be."

"Any fool knows that!" answered the king angrily.

"Please, it is not my idea to annoy you," said Clarendon. "Is it not true that the foods you mention must be paid for? Is it not true that they must be paid for in gold and silver?"

Charles nodded at the mention of gold and silver. Clarendon continued. "More and more silver and gold are leaving the country than are coming in!"

"I see. We must do something about that," said Charles quickly. "But what shall we do?"

"Your Majesty, my suggestion is that we change our Navigation Acts. And we must strictly enforce them this time."

"I'm listening," said King Charles, "but my time and patience are growing short. Please don't test me!"

"Quickly, then," said Clarendon, "we must have acts that will not allow the colonies to use any but English ships. Sugar, cotton, tobacco, and ginger must be shipped only to England or to another English colony. Only England may ship goods from another country of Europe to an English colony."

"Good, good," smiled the king. "But aren't the people who live in the colonies English? Didn't they come from England? Don't they have the same rights as English people? How can you force them to trade only with England?"

"Your Majesty, you are absolutely right!" answered Clarendon. "But why do we have colonies? Colonies exist for us! We allowed those people to leave England. They built homes on our lands. True, some of them suffered, but they realized the risk they would be taking in the New World."

"Clarendon, why are you so one-sided? Colonies do not exist only for us. I want the colonists to be happy and well. You must stop picking on them. How many times must I tell you that they are still citizens of England!"

"I agree, Your Highness, I agree," said Clarendon quickly. "We will not forget our colonists. Let's look at my plan once again. Suppose we in England can buy all the raw materials we need at low prices from our colonies. And suppose that we sell our manufactured goods to them at a high profit. Then, Majesty, gold and silver will roll into England! We will be rich!"

"And the colonists, Clarendon?" asked the king angrily.

"I have not forgotten them, Sire. How could I?" asked Clarendon, bowing slightly. "England is getting richer every day, and the colonies grow rich with us! Soon England will pay a higher price for colonial goods. We might even sell them our products at lower prices! If England does well, the colonies do well. How can they lose?"

"There's no stopping you, is there?" asked King Charles. "Are you forgetting that all is not perfect in this world? Let's see what could go wrong with your plan. Suppose our people in England make poor-quality goods. The colonists will not buy them. Or suppose our people make goods the colonists don't want or can't use. Once again, they won't buy! Now our people are left with things no one wants!"

"Your Majesty, the colonists need goods from Europe. They must buy."

"True, Clarendon. They must buy from someone. Suppose the

French and the Dutch make the same products. Suppose they make them better and at lower prices! Then the French and Dutch move in. They grab the markets in our own English colonies. Say good-bye to all that gold and silver!"

"Sire," said Clarendon with great excitement, "that is exactly the point! No one else can take our markets if we enforce our Navigation Acts. The markets are ours! The Dutch and the French cannot grab our markets! The colonists must send their materials only to us. They can buy only from England. The gold and silver will be ours, I tell you, Your Highness!"

"If this plan is followed, I can see that England will one day control the trade of the world!" laughed King Charles.

## UNDERSTANDING THE STORY

**A.** *Complete each of the sentences below.*

1. By 1507, ——— ships had sailed around the world.
2. Settlements in the New World were called ———.
3. Colonies provided ——— materials that could not be found in Europe.
4. Under ———, colonies were used to make European countries richer.
5. Spices, coffee, and tea were shipped to Europe from the ———.
6. According to the ———, English colonies were to ship goods only in ——— ships.
7. Lord Clarendon said that England must ——— the Navigation Acts.
8. The king was worried about what might happen to the ——— in the colonies.

**B.** *Lord Clarendon and King Charles II had different ideas about the colonies. Decide who might have made the remarks that follow. Write KC for each statement that King Charles made or might have made and LC for each statement that Lord Clarendon made or might have made.*

1. England will die without trade.
2. Before I think about colonies, I must think about what is happening here in England.
3. Our colonies are not shipping their best crops to us.

4. Everything shipped to England from foreign shores must be paid for with gold or silver.
5. The people who live in the English colonies are English.
6. Colonies exist to make us rich.
7. Why should England take poor-quality colonial goods?
8. England will one day control the trade of the world.

C. Imagine that Charles II is the president of the United States. Lord Clarendon is his adviser. What areas of the world might these two men pick out to turn into American colonies? Why would they do this? Do you agree with them?

## ACTIVITIES AND INQUIRIES

1. Look at the map on page 70. England and Spain and their colonies in the New World are shown. Draw an outline of the map, including the colonies. On your map, draw lines showing the routes that ships might have taken from England and Spain to their colonies.
2. Imagine that you are an English colonist in America in the 17th century. Write a letter to a relative in England telling about your life in America. What things would you ask your relative to send you? Why?
3. Explain the meaning of the cartoon below. Who is speaking? Who do you think drew the cartoon, a colonist or an English person? Why?

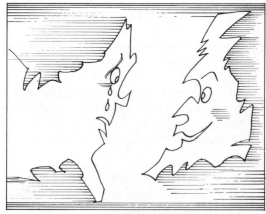

"Don't cry. Aren't we all English people?"

# 6. A Monk Rebels

*This unit is concerned* with change. We have seen how people looked at themselves differently in art and writing. Scientists and explorers opened new worlds. Old ways of thinking were challenged; many questions were asked.

The Church was also being challenged during this period. The pope and other Church officials often had to yield to the power of strong kings. Some people asked serious questions about priests. Were they necessary to speak to God? Were they always completely honest with those who prayed in their churches?

Martin Luther was a monk who seriously felt that many things in the Church were wrong and had to be changed or reformed. For example, he said that the sale of *indulgences* (pardons for sins) should be stopped. He believed that one could not substitute indulgences for the faith of the people. Finally he could stand it no longer. In October 1517 he nailed 95 *theses* (ideas to be debated publicly) to the door of the church at Wittenberg, Germany. These theses were printed and read all over Europe. People were excited and upset. The authority of the Church was challenged. Perhaps the Church did not have an absolute control over everything that was right and true.

In the letter that follows, Martin Luther expresses to a friend his feelings about religion and the Church. See if you understand and agree with Luther's feelings about the Church. Do you think that he was really trying to reform the Church? Or was he anxious to become a very powerful man?

# Wittenberg, 1526

DEAR KURT,

I am terribly sorry that I have not been able to answer your letter of several months ago until today. You can guess that I have been very busy.

You ask me many questions that are very difficult to answer. Why did I leave the Church and become its enemy? There is so much to say and so much to explain that I would never finish this letter to you. I know that you are unhappy with what I have done, but they left me no choice. Believe me, Kurt, when I say to you that all I wanted to do was to make a few changes. My Church had strayed from the path of true religion. My job was to reform it, to bring it back to its real purpose. All I wanted was that people be saved from sin and find salvation by having faith in God. Faith was the answer, but they would not listen to me, a poor monk!

I write to you, Kurt, as my oldest and dearest friend. I will never forget the fun and good times of our childhood. It was a simple life; we were very poor. But our fathers worked hard in the mines to feed and clothe us. There was always food on the table; that and the fresh air and the mountain beauty were all we needed to live. Remember how we loved the snow and hated and feared the fog? Remember how we talked of the future? We decided to leave our beloved mountains and study law.

In those early days, I honestly had no desire to follow the religious life. Then it happened! In July 1505 I was thrown to the ground by a bolt of lightning! For the first time, I saw death. I was afraid that this was the end for me. I cried out, "Saint Anne help me! I will become a monk." That moment of intense fear passed as death went on its way.

That promise to my father's saint saved my life. I could not back away. I had to become a monk. My father and your father protested—they cried and argued. It was no use. I had to do it!

I joined the Augustinians. If I say so myself, I was a good monk. I would find salvation through my faith and obedience. I prayed and starved and froze. I went to Rome and crawled on my hands and knees up the 28 steps in front of the Lateran Church. I prayed for a dead relative on each step. But I was not sure of the value of what I had done.

Why am I recalling all of these things to you, Kurt? I want you to try to understand that these were things in my life that had to be done. They were out of my hands. In my own way, I was happy with the simple, harsh life of the monastery. I thought it was God's will that this was where I would spend the rest of my days. But it was not to be. I was ordered to teach Bible classes at the University of Wittenberg. What of it, you might very well ask. When I started preparing my lectures, I began to understand what God meant in his Bible.

Now I saw that the Bible was the written record of our God. There were his words for all to see. I asked myself, How can the people read and understand his divine words? They are written in Latin! Most people cannot read Latin. The answer came to me at last: Translate the words of God into the language of the people. I knew then that I must rewrite the Bible in German! Each person must be able to read and explain the meaning of the stories of God's Bible as he or she wishes. No one needs the help of a priest to understand the Bible!

I knew something else. I knew that God did not want the money or the lands of sinners. I do not have to tell you that salvation cannot be bought. I saw Tetzel selling indulgences, and I exploded. What right did he have to sell salvation? What right did he have to speak for the pope and the Catholic Church? Then I realized—Tetzel was their appointed representative!

I understood then that people do not need priests to speak to God for them. God speaks and listens to all. Why should a person ask forgiveness for sins through a priest? Worst of all, why should we pay someone to be forgiven by God? This is not the way of God! You cannot sell religion!

I went up to the church and hammered a list of 95 theses onto the front door. You did not approve; you felt that I was going too far too fast. I must disagree with you, dear friend. The holy Church and its leaders had gone too far. They had lost sight of the true meaning of God and religion. They forgot that they must be absolutely pure, honest, and sincere. Perhaps every priest and bishop cannot be a saint, but each one must set an example of godliness and decency. They should care about people. They should be priests first and politicians last! A priest must be loyal first to God, not to a nobleman—not even to a king!

Now we come to your question about the "good life." Yes, you are right, Kurt. Perhaps I am a bit unfair in my feelings that people on earth should lead a simple life. You feel that a person is entitled

*"I went up to the church and hammered a list of 95 theses onto the door."*

to many pleasures. I should lead my life, and you should follow yours.

I am not so sure that you understand about life and my feelings about it. You think that I am in favor of a dull, boring existence. Not so! Give away your fancy clothes, your foreign spices, and your profits from business. This will force you to think more of God. Your life will not be dull. You will be much more aware of the world around you, just as you were when we were young. Stop all of this overeating and drinking. Think more of other people's needs!

Put a stop to wanting so much that we do not need and we will stop war and senseless killing. You write that my attacks on the Church have led to war and bloodshed. You wonder how I can justify all of this fighting when I say that I am a man of peace. This is an excellent question about a situation that I hate. You know that I detest killing. The fighting must and will stop. First, princes and kings will have to stop hiding behind the pope and the Church. They must stop using the Church as an excuse for fighting against Protestant noblemen. These princes want the Protestants' land and money. Soon, I hope, all people will understand the importance of the simple life. Fighting will stop, and peace will be with us.

No, I do not feel that I am a revolutionist. All I want is a church that will help people to develop faith in our God. Some day, the Catholic Church will realize that it is not the only voice of God. There are other voices and other ways.

My wife, Kathie, joins me in sending our sincerest wishes for your peace and happiness.

Your friend,
MARTIN LUTHER

## UNDERSTANDING THE STORY

A. *Write T for each statement that is true and F for each statement that is false.*

1. Martin Luther became a monk.
2. Luther felt that it was wrong to sell indulgences.
3. Luther never talked about his opinions in public.
4. Luther never left the Catholic Church.

5. Luther wanted to reform the Catholic Church.
6. Luther liked the simple life of his monastery.
7. Luther did not teach classes in the Bible.
8. Luther felt that he was a man of peace.

B. *Martin Luther had strong feelings about many things. Tell which statements you feel Martin Luther made or might have made.*

1. Salvation cannot be bought.
2. People need priests to speak to God for them.
3. People need priests to ask God's forgiveness for their sins.
4. While every priest cannot be a saint, he must be honest, sincere, and decent.
5. People should think more of God.
6. People should dress in fancy clothes and live and eat well.
7. Religion must help people believe in God.
8. The Catholic Church should not be the only Christian church.

C. Martin Luther dared to challenge and change the Catholic Church. Suppose that Luther were alive today. Would he challenge religion in America? Why? If your answer is "yes," how would he do it? Do you think he would succeed? Explain.

## ACTIVITIES AND INQUIRIES

1. Look at the illustration of Martin Luther at Wittenberg on page 78. What do you think would be a good title for this drawing? Why? What does it tell you about the type of man Martin Luther was?
2. Make a list of the things in your life that you think should be changed. Give reasons for your choices.
3. Go to the library. Prepare a report on another Protestant reformer of the 16th century. How was his thinking similar to that of Martin Luther? How was it different from Luther's thinking?
4. Imagine that you are Martin Luther's friend Kurt. You are a loyal Catholic. Answer Luther's letter.

"Well, Jack?" asked Mr. Miller.

"Okay, okay, it wasn't so bad," answered Jack. "I have to admit that I learned something. I never knew that artists and writers had much to do with what went on around them."

"Of course," replied Mr. Miller. "They see things and have feelings. Other people can learn from them."

"Mr. Miller, Leonardo was really something! Imagine cutting open dead bodies just to be able to paint them better!"

"It was more than painting, Jack. He was trying to understand."

"That's true," said Jack. "There are a lot of things Renaissance men like Leonardo tried to understand. They were searching. They were looking for answers. I guess they wanted to find out what life was all about."

"How did the Renaissance writers fit into the picture?" asked Mr. Miller.

"They had the same feelings as the artists," said Jack, with a smile. "They wrote about what was going on around them. They tried to write so that people would want to read their words."

"Did you see any differences between Petrarch and Boccaccio?" asked Mr. Miller.

"I think Petrarch was in touch with what was happening. But Boccaccio really knew what life was all about," added Jack. "Boccaccio is much more into everyday problems. Boccaccio could get along very well in today's world. Come to think of it, Mr. Miller, there's room for Petrarch, too!"

"We can let them into our world without too much trouble, I suppose," added Mr. Miller. "But Galileo might have a little difficulty. Why do you think that his ideas were attacked?"

"I know that Galileo wasn't an artist or a writer. He was a scientist," answered Jack thoughtfully. "He was searching for truth. What he found upset many people."

"What truth did he discover?" asked Mr. Miller.

"It's very strange," replied Jack. "Galileo and other scientists saw that the earth moved around the sun. Why didn't people believe him? He could prove that he was right."

81

"Why do you think they wouldn't believe him?" asked Mr. Miller.

"I guess that people didn't want to believe that they were living on just another planet," said Jack thoughtfully. "One day they were the center of the universe. Suddenly they were living on just another hunk of rock in the heavens!"

"What else did they discover?" asked Mr. Miller.

"Explorers found lots of places that people in Europe never even heard about," answered Jack. "Columbus dreamed of getting to India and China by sailing west. He might have made it, but America was in the way! The poor guy thought that the natives here were *really* Indians. He didn't know that they were native Americans, not the people of India!"

"Didn't the Europeans show a lot of interest in the New World?" asked Mr. Miller.

"Right, Mr. Miller. It didn't take them long to set up colonies. The Spanish and Portuguese got here first. But soon the English and the French were in the race. They all took over big chunks of land for themselves."

"Where does the Protestant Reformation fit into all this?" asked Mr. Miller.

"Everything was changing," said Jack slowly. "Not everyone was happy with the Catholic Church. Martin Luther had his ideas of how Christians should pray to God. Just as today, nothing stays the same. By the way, Mr. Miller, wasn't government changing, too?"

"Good thinking!" smiled Mr. Miller. "Let's take a look at England."

# Unit III

# England—The Beginnings of Democracy

"Democracy, democracy!" Jack said. "Why do we have to hear so much stuff about democracy?"

"How can you ever hear too much about democracy?" asked Mr. Miller.

"Why should I care about democracy outside the United States?" asked Jack. "We have a democracy. Isn't that enough?"

"Well, Jack, what does democracy mean to you?"

"Come on, Mr. Miller. I know that democracy means that the people rule."

"Oh, you mean that the people all get together and pass laws."

"Now you're saying impossible things!" said Jack. "I know that there are too many of us to do that. We elect people who make our laws for us. You would say they represent us."

"That's great, Jack! What else do you know about democracy?"

"No one person can take over. No person can become a dictator or a tyrant," replied Jack. "It's just not possible under our Constitution!"

"Where do you think all of this came from?" asked Mr. Miller.

"Oh, we had a revolution about 200 years ago. We beat the English and won the right to govern ourselves."

"Believe it or not, Jack, but we owe a lot to the English. Many years before our Revolution, the English kings ran their government. They controlled their people. The king's power was total, or absolute. His word was law. He ran a one-man show."

"There must have been a lot of changes," said Jack thoughtfully. "How did the English kings lose their power? How did England become a democracy? And what does that have to do with the United States?"

"Slow down, Jack," smiled Mr. Miller. "Read the unit on democracy in England. You'll soon see how it all happened."

# 1. Forcing a King's Hand

*In our unit on the Renaissance* we saw that many changes were taking place in Europe in the arts, in the sciences, and in religion. People wanted to know more about themselves and the world around them. They looked and studied and realized how little they really knew. There was so much more to discover. For example, how should large numbers of men and women be governed? Should people accept the decisions of kings merely because they were kings? Should any one man on earth be all-powerful?

In the early 13th century, England was ruled by King John. We should not be surprised that he didn't care about the average English man and woman. His control was total. A person lived or died because of a nod of the head or a wave of the hand by John. You may be surprised, however, that even the nobles or upper classes were afraid of the king. He was unpredictable. His ideas changed from day to day. The nobles' lives, lands, and fortunes were in the king's hands.

In 1215 the English nobles refused to stand any longer for John's mistakes and taxes. They insisted that there must be limits to what an English king could do. They forced John to sign the *Magna Carta* (MAG-nuh KAHR-tuh), the Great Charter. The powers of the king were no longer absolute.

In this story four English nobles and a Frenchman discuss King John and the Great Charter. Ask yourself why King John agreed to sign away some of his powers. Did he do the proper thing? How did the Magna Carta help the common people of England?

# Egham, 1215

*(A Frenchman enters the dining room of an inn. The room is hot and noisy. The Frenchman hesitates for a moment. Then he walks over to a table where four English noblemen are eating dinner.)*

PHILIPPE. Good evening, gentlemen. May I join your group?

BARON HOWARD. Yes. Please sit down. Your speech and clothes tell us you are French. It isn't often that English barons have a chance to speak to a Frenchman. Join us for dinner.

PHILIPPE. Thank you very much. *(He pulls a chair up to the table. After several minutes of exchanging introductions, the Frenchman is still not sure of how to begin. He is a stranger in a foreign land, yet he wants to ask his hosts about recent events in England.)*

PHILIPPE *(hesitating)*. What's this I hear about your good King John?

BARON ROGER. What do you mean, "What's this I hear?" There are so many things he's done. Who knows where to begin with our *good* king? If we wanted to talk—

PHILIPPE. I meant about John and the Magna Carta. *(He pushes a pitcher of ale toward the English barons.)* What is it all about?

BARON ROGER. A better question might be, What's King John all about? He's dug himself into a deep hole. He did too many things unworthy of a king. John *had* to sign the Magna Carta.

PHILIPPE. Well, what did he do?

BARON REGINALD. You name it and he has done it. Murder? He did away with his nephew! Divorce? He's your man! Why not marry someone else's fiancée?

BARON ROGER. Yes, and the man he took the woman away from was his best friend. How do you like that?

PHILIPPE. I don't like it one bit. But shouldn't kings have more power and rights than people like ourselves?

BARON EDWARD. Maybe kings should have more power, but there have to be limits on what anyone can do. Because a man is a king is no reason to let him do whatever he pleases. He had no right to raise so many taxes and try to force us to pay them.

PHILIPPE. But didn't he need the money to fight his wars?

BARON ROGER. Yes, he needed money, so that he could lose more land and more men to your French armies.

BARON HOWARD. And don't forget the run-in he had with Pope
   Innocent III!
PHILIPPE. What was that all about?
BARON REGINALD. It was a mess. The question was, Who was to be
   Archbishop of Canterbury, the most important churchman in
   England? Innocent took a firm position and insisted upon his

*"John had to sign the Magna Carta."*

own choice. King John had other ideas and refused to listen to the pope. But Innocent answered him by cutting English people off from all the blessings of the Catholic Church. Then to be certain that John understood him, he also excommunicated our beloved king. John could no longer be a member of the Catholic Church. But that didn't scare John. I guess he figures that he's doomed anyway!

BARON HOWARD. There's nothing like using force to solve a problem. Innocent asked your king to invade England. That made John see the light. He backed off and accepted the pope's archbishop.

PHILIPPE. Your King John doesn't sound like a good person. *(Philippe looks carefully around the crowded room and whispers to the Englishmen.)* Why didn't you get rid of him?

BARON ROGER *(angrily)*. Careful, Frenchman! He is our king. We are pledged to support him. But he went too far. He had to understand that there is a moral law. There are certain things that even kings cannot do!

BARON REGINALD. We had to show him that we have rights. If he had not agreed, then we would have gotten rid of him.

PHILIPPE. But how does the Magna Carta put the king in his place?

BARON HOWARD. I'll try to explain. Let's take taxes. Taxes can be ordered only by the king's Great Council, not by the king himself. He can ask for taxes, but the Council must approve them. And the barons are the Council.

PHILIPPE. Suppose the king controls the Council?

BARON ROGER. The Magna Carta takes care of that too. We have made certain that every one of the barons will be called to meet at a certain time in a certain place for a definite purpose. We will meet 40 days after getting the call for the meeting.

PHILIPPE. Is that all?

BARON ROGER. If we are to be fined, only people of our own class —our peers or equals—can fine us.

PHILIPPE. Sounds great, but haven't you forgotten the common people?

BARON REGINALD. Absolutely not! There's something for them too. Suppose a merchant, a free peasant, or even a serf does something wrong. Now he may be fined only according to how serious his crime is. His neighbors will decide on the fine. But no

one can take a freeman's land or a merchant's goods. Nor can
they take a serf's farm tools.

PHILIPPE. That's a great step forward! Let the punishment fit the
crime. But don't take away a man's ability to support himself.

BARON REGINALD. Wait, there's more. Trials will be held as soon as
possible. And no free peasant can be sent to jail without being
tried by his equals.

PHILIPPE. Is there more?

BARON HOWARD. A great deal more! We have just mentioned only a
few things. But these few give all English people more liberty as
well as protection from an evil tyrant like King John.

BARON EDWARD. Wait, don't forget that a widow does not have to
marry again if she does not want to.

PHILIPPE. And the Church?

BARON EDWARD. The Church shall be free. The king may no longer
interfere. Nor may he interfere with the running of our great city
of London!

PHILIPPE. I have to admit that I am impressed. You have come a long
way toward freedom. One thing, though: I still don't agree with
you about keeping King John. He's no good—

BARON EDWARD. You still don't understand! John could easily have
been pushed off his throne. But then, what would we have had?
We would have had total war. This way we have peace and we
have our king in a corner. He wants his throne. We want our
rights. We both have what we want.

BARON HOWARD. If John goes too far, we have our Magna Carta to
straighten him out. It's all written down to keep him in his place.
We have him where we want him.

PHILIPPE. I am not so sure. Suppose he does not keep his word?
What then?

BARON ROGER. He will not dare break his written promises to the
English nobles. But if he does, we will march against him—even
if it means civil war. Don't worry about us.

BARON HOWARD. We may have trouble. But I know that many years
from now people will remember the Magna Carta.

*Postscript.* In 1216, a year after signing the Magna Carta, King
John refused to honor it. The nobles, with the help of the son of the
king of France, marched against John. He retreated to the north of
England where he died on October 19, 1216.

## UNDERSTANDING THE STORY

**A.** *Write T for each statement that is true and O for each statement that is an opinion.*

1. The Magna Carta was the best thing that ever happened to England.
2. King John did not care for the English people.
3. English nobles should not be afraid of a king.
4. English nobles forced King John to sign the Magna Carta.
5. The Frenchman in the story felt that kings should have more power than ordinary people.
6. The English nobles should have asked the common people to help them replace King John.
7. Guilty people were to be punished according to the seriousness of their crimes.
8. According to the Magna Carta, a merchant's goods and a serf's tools could not be taken away as punishment.

**B.** *Which statements show how the Magna Carta started England on the road to democracy?*

1. The king alone could not order new taxes.
2. Every baron had a chance to become king of England.
3. The size of fines to be paid was decided by the guilty person's peers.
4. Trials of accused people were to be held as soon as possible.
5. The king could interfere with the Church.
6. English people were given freedom and protection from evil kings.
7. Widows could be forced to marry again.
8. People would be tried by members of their own class.

**C.** The English are very proud of the Magna Carta. It limited the powers of the king. Does the United States need a Magna Carta to limit the power of the president? Explain.

## ACTIVITIES AND INQUIRIES

1. Imagine that you are one of the barons responsible for writing the Magna Carta. Your job is to make a list of the powers of the king that hurt the people. List these powers.
2. Look at the illustration on page 86. Describe what is happening. Write your own title for the picture.

# 2. The Right to Rule

*A year after he signed the Magna Carta,* John died (1216). He had been a bad king. He is remembered chiefly because the Magna Carta had been forced upon him. The English people now knew that law was more important than the king.

Something was still missing from the English government, however. There was no representative group of people who would meet, discuss, and pass laws. At last, in 1265, Simon de Montfort called together a *parliament.* For the first time, representatives of the minor nobles were able to meet with others. In 1295 King Edward I called together a group called the Model Parliament. This group served as a model for later Parliaments. Edward's Parliament included bishops, barons, knights, and town representatives. Later the first two groups formed the upper house of England's Parliament, which is now called the House of Lords. The last two groups became the lower house, or the House of Commons.

In the story of Joan of Arc, we saw how the Hundred Years' War raged during the 14th and 15th centuries. The English Parliament used this war as an excuse to increase its power. It insisted once again that kings must get the approval of Parliament to raise new taxes. (Wars cannot be fought without a great deal of money.) The Hundred Years' War was followed by a bloody civil war between two groups of Englishmen. This war was called the War of the Roses. At last, in 1485, Henry Tudor, a member of the house of Lancaster, became King Henry VII, and the power of Parliament was once again limited by a strong ruler. In fact, during his last 20 years, Henry called a meeting of Parliament only once! Parliament had become a rubber stamp; Henry VII controlled it completely.

Elizabeth I was the last of the Tudors. During her rule (1558–1603), the Renaissance came to England. She was a very powerful ruler who had the good sense to ask for the approval of Parliament and the people.

Now we turn to the subject of this story, James I. The first of the Stuart kings, he came to England from Scotland. He was crowned a few weeks after the death of Elizabeth. At first James was very popular, but his popularity soon dimmed when the people saw how weak and peculiar he was. He insisted that he ruled by divine right. It was God's will that he be king of England. He was certain that whatever he did was right. He never thought he might be wrong. However, English people found it hard to accept James' disregard for Parliament and English common law.

James writes to his adviser, Buckingham, and expresses his feelings about England and his rule. He wonders why he is not popular.

Ask yourself why James' idea of divine right made him unpopular. Is there such a thing as the divine right of kings? Why was the creation of Parliament so important to English democracy?

## London, 1612

DEAR BUCKINGHAM,

Perhaps you can explain to me why so many Englishmen hate me. I was brought down from Scotland to rule England. Believe me, it was not my idea to leave Scotland. I was happy there; the people appreciated me.

Here in England, I have studied and worked hard to be a good king. I have had a new translation made of our holy Bible. What was my reward? That fool Guy Fawkes sets a murderous charge of blasting powder in the Parliament building to blow my body to pieces. People call it the Gunpowder Plot, but I call it the King James Plot.

Evil men wanted me dead so that they could replace me with a Catholic king. They didn't care whether I was good or bad. They did not like my religion. But God would not allow me to die. Thanks to him, the plot was discovered. I asked Fawkes how he could plot to kill so many innocent people. The wretch replied, "A

dangerous disease required a dangerous remedy"! *I* am dangerous! I who work and sweat for my English people! I knew I was
right when I ordered all Catholic priests out of England. They were
all plotting against me. Not one of them could be trusted!

For years I heard that King Henry IV of France called me a wise
fool. It hurt to be called a fool, but I kept the hurt to myself. No
doubt you heard what happened to poor King Henry last August.
He was stabbed to death! Now who is the fool? Tell those people
out there that fools do not live too long on the throne of kings!

You say that some Englishmen dislike me because I insist I have
been placed on the throne of England by God. But is it not obvious
that this must be so? Could I have lived through the Gunpowder
Plot? Did not God protect me against last year's plague in London?
People were dying all around me, but I lived. It was God's will.

Is it not clear that I am God's messenger on earth? It is my duty
to carry out his wishes. Anyone who argues with what I say and do
is denying God. You cannot dispute what God says. If you do, you
lack respect for God, and you know that that is blasphemy! That is
why all those who plot against me must die. They must be tortured, they must be hanged, they must be quartered! Oh, how I
would love to do that to all of those traitors in Parliament. I talk to
them, but they do not listen.

You write that people in England want laws to be passed by
Parliament. They object to my issuing *proclamations* (announce-
ments) without the consent of Parliament. They say this is not
the way things are done in England. They accuse me of being
a dictator and a tyrant because I must do things my own way in my
own time. Tell the English people that they do not know what it is
like to deal with members of Parliament. They are impossible.

Members of Parliament try to tell *me*, the king of England, what
to do. They refuse to accept my divine right to be king. They seem
to think that they have as much power as I do. The fools keep
looking back to Magna Carta, as though I should be guided by
what happened 400 years ago. Why should I have to worry about
raising money? Why should I have to ask Parliament for taxes?
Why does Parliament have to meet at all?

Why won't they let me spend as I please? Why can't I decide
how much the government of England needs? When Elizabeth was
queen, she threw money around. She bought jeweled swords for

her lover. Who had the nerve to tell her to stop, or even to question her? Why do they pick on me? Why can't they trust me the way they trusted Elizabeth?

I think, Buckingham, that Parliament too often forgets who is king. Well, I am the king. I have the right to make decisions and to tell my people what to do. I did not want wheat wasted in making starch. I forbade it. I felt that there were too many buildings in London. I ordered that no more be built. What's wrong with my ordering that all Englishmen take an oath of allegiance to me? Are they afraid to show their loyalty to their king? I insist upon it!

Do you remember the scene at the palace in 1610 when Francis Bacon unrolled a petition from Parliament? The thing was four feet square, and he could scarcely handle it. I was sorry, but I could not help laughing. Parliament wanted me to stop issuing my own proclamations. Parliament is afraid that my orders will become as strong as the common law.

It was all nonsense, but I pretended to agree. I am sure that you will agree that a king's proclamations are necessary in times of emergency. Where there is danger, shall I wait for laws of Parliament? Should the king not have the power to govern his country in any emergency? And you know, Buckingham, there are many emergencies in a king's life!

Chief Justice Coke said that the common law is above both Parliament and the king. I refuse to accept that decision. I have said it many times, and I will say it again: The king is above Parliament. The king must be above the law.

I shall judge all, but none may judge me.

God be with you.

JAMES I

King of England

## UNDERSTANDING THE STORY

**A.** *Write* T *for each statement that is true and* F *for each statement that is false.*

1. In England, a group of people who meet and pass laws is called a Parliament.
2. The first Parliament was called by Simon de Montfort.

3. In the Model Parliament, there were three houses: the rich, the poor, and the nobles.
4. Under Henry VII, Parliament met at least ten times a year.
5. Queen Elizabeth I asked Parliament to approve her requests for taxes.
6. King James I said that a king was never wrong.
7. James was killed in the Gunpowder Plot.
8. James felt that he was more important than Parliament.

B. *Do you think that King James would have agreed or disagreed with the statements below? Write A for each statement King James would have agreed with and N for each statement he would not have agreed with.*

1. The king rules because God wants him to rule.
2. Guy Fawkes was right in saying that King James was dangerous.
3. I am happy to be a Catholic king.
4. I am God's messenger on earth.
5. I really enjoy working with the members of Parliament.
6. It is only fair that I ask Parliament for tax money.
7. Parliament is always picking on me.
8. All Englishmen must swear that they are loyal to the king.

C. Would King James be successful as a president of the United States today? Explain. How do you think Congress would deal with him?

## ACTIVITIES AND INQUIRIES

1. Go to the library. Prepare a report on a ruler of England such as Edward I, Henry VII, Henry VIII, or Elizabeth I. Compare that king or queen with James I. Who was a better ruler? Why?
2. Pretend that you are Lord Buckingham. Write a letter to King James I. Explain why so many Englishmen hate him.
3. Bring in pictures of England in the 17th century, particularly of London. Be prepared to describe what you see. Was King James right that there were too many buildings in London? Explain. Try to find out why there were so many buildings in London.
4. Imagine that you are a member of Parliament at the time of James I. What do you think of your king? Why? Do you agree that your king is above both Parliament and the law? Explain.

# 3. A King Is Executed

*James I died in* 1625. Few English people were sorry. Many hoped that his son, Charles I, would be a successful replacement. Charles worked long hours, did not waste money (as his father had), and even looked like a king. But the job of being a successful king was simply too much for him. Before long, the people knew that he could not and would not understand them.

Charles believed even more strongly in divine right than his father had. He could not stand anyone who opposed him. He fought constantly with Parliament. For their part, the members of Parliament did not trust him. Charles' wife was a Catholic, and Parliament was afraid that Charles would convert to Catholicism and possibly turn England away from the Protestant faith.

For a period of 15 years, Charles struggled with Parliament. It refused to obey him. In return, he did not permit it to sit. In fact, for 11 years, he did not call Parliament at all. He ruled on his own, without the approval and support of Parliament. But he was able to raise enough money to keep his government going, fight wars, and live the way kings were expected to live.

By 1640 Charles was forced to turn to Parliament for money. In return for taxes, he agreed that the Parliament would meet at least once every three years. It could not be *dissolved* (sent home) unless it agreed. But Charles would sign anything without the slightest intention of keeping his word. He even personally tried to arrest the leaders of the House of Commons who were against him. Parliament now knew that Charles would not obey the law. Promises were empty words.

A civil war followed (1642–1645). The army of the king (the Cavaliers) was defeated by the forces of Oliver Cromwell (the Roundheads). The king was finally captured, tried, and sentenced to die.

In this story, we find King Charles preparing to face his executioner. Ask yourself whether Charles really had to die. What, if anything, was accomplished by his execution? Was Charles really a *martyr* (a person who gives up his or her life for a noble cause)?

## The Tower of London, January 1649

"What time is it, Father?" asked King Charles.

"We have plenty of time," said the priest. "Have no fear."

"Fear!" replied Charles. "Don't be a fool. I am the king of England. I will not be afraid . . . not even when I walk up to the head-chopper. I know that I will soon pass through the gates of heaven."

"Perhaps, sire, you might have been better off if you had been a little afraid."

"Afraid of what? I was—I am—the king. I am God's representative on earth. God walked beside me; he guided me."

"We are all human," said the priest. "We all make mistakes. Can you not understand that even a king cannot be perfect?"

"You are right, Father. Perhaps, I have made a few mistakes. But do I belong in jail because Parliament would not agree with me? Shall my neck feel the ax because Parliament would not give me the money to hold court? Were they not traitors when they refused me the money to fight the war against Spain in 1627?"

"Sire, you must have known that Parliament represented the English people. You should have been more understanding. Why couldn't you give in—at least some of the time?"

"You are like all the rest of them!" answered the king angrily. "To you, I am just an ordinary man. To Parliament, I was sometimes less than a man. It needed someone to push around. There I was, the king of England, and it treated me like a fool. It made things as difficult as possible for me to reign. Parliament never listened when I asked for something."

"Your Highness, please do not excite yourself."

"You are right. I will try to calm down. You want me to admit that I made some mistakes in my lifetime. I confess that I have been thinking of my life during the past week. Each year passes before me in review. I think—where did I go wrong? Where were my mistakes? I was—I am—a king. I was sent by God to do a job. Perhaps I was too sure of myself. Perhaps I kept myself too much apart from my people. But then I could never get too close to anyone. Perhaps I listened too much to my advisers. I thought that Buckingham and the others wished me well. . . . Now, I wonder—"

"Think of how you might have changed your feelings about Parliament," suggested the priest. "Could you not have tried to get along better with some of the members? Could you not have understood that all men are jealous of their rights? Would you be feeling the ax if you had been willing to give in a little here and there?"

"But, Father, I gave and gave. I promised and promised. What more could I have done? They were interested only in driving a hard bargain. Shame the king; push his face in the mud! Did I not agree to the Petition of Right?"

"Yes, and it was the high spot of your rule as king. Was it so difficult to agree to these things?"

"Of course not," said Charles. "I agreed with Parliament. I would never order a man imprisoned without a fair trial. But they would not believe me! They would not trust me! They would not accept my promise to do these things. They had to write it all down and take those powers away from me! Why did they have to make a long list of the rights of Englishmen? Habeas corpus (HAY-bee-us KORE-pus), where an accused person must be charged in open court, sounds important. But is it necessary? Bail or freedom for a prisoner brought to court on a writ of habeas corpus? Ridiculous! All that does is encourage more crime. Steal and be free! Is this to be the basis of English law?"

"Do you really mean all that, Your Highness? I'm sure that you know as well as I do that these are guarantees that must be given to every free Englishman. Innocent men must be kept out of jail; all must be given a fair trial. This is a nation of laws, not of men. Your promise was not enough! Men come and go. They say and do different things from year to year, from day to day. The law remains. It is our God-given right!"

"Your God-given right!" shouted the king. "A listener might think that you were going to lose your head, and that I was the priest. I can see that it's a waste of time talking to you. I could not even levy a tax without the approval of Parliament."

"Your Majesty, talking to me is not a waste of time. I understand how upset you are. You have gone through life feeling that people—especially those in Parliament—were using you. You fought constantly. You were—are—the king. Did it never occur to you that you could ever have been wrong about Parliament—just a little wrong?"

"Members of Parliament are power grabbers," said the king. "They fought me and I fought back. Would I be here if they weren't out to steal my powers? Who are Cromwell and all the others? Did they fight me to protect Englishmen? No sir, they are rebels, traitors! They are mad for power. They have overthrown the king, the monarchy, the representative of God on earth! And Cromwell is the worst of the lot. I would not want to be Cromwell when he tries to get into heaven!"

"Your Highness has a way of turning things around. You signed the Petition of Right. You knew very well it said that tax bills had to be passed by Parliament. How then could you expect to raise money when you dismissed Parliament? You would not let it meet for years."

"I refused to meet with traitors," said the king.

"But you promised," replied the priest.

"If you promised me a happy day on earth tomorrow, should I believe you? I promised Parliament what it wanted to believe."

"Sire, I give up. You are the king. You will do as you wish," said the priest wearily. He got up to leave the cell.

Suddenly there was a harsh shout from outside the cell. "Get ready, Your Highness! Your time has come!"

Charles looked at the priest. "Will you stay with me, Father? I am cold and weary."

"I will stay, if you wish."

"What happens today is against the will of God," insisted Charles, for the last time.

"No," thought the priest. "Today a tyrant loses his head."

## UNDERSTANDING THE STORY

A. *King Charles and the priest have many different points of view. Decide who made or might have made the remarks that follow. Write KC for each statement that the king made or might have made and PR for each statement that the priest made or might have made.*

1. I am not afraid to die.
2. No person is perfect.
3. Parliament represents the English people.
4. Members of Parliament are power grabbers.
5. You should have tried to get along better with Parliament.
6. No person should be sent to jail without a fair trial.
7. Habeas corpus encourages crime.
8. Keep innocent people out of jail.
9. Cromwell is a rebel and a traitor.

B. *Match each item in Column A with its answer in Column B.*

COLUMN A

1. habeas corpus
2. James I
3. Charles I
4. civil war in England
5. Cavaliers
6. Oliver Cromwell
7. Roundheads
8. Petition of Right

COLUMN B

(a) followers of the king
(b) Roundhead who became ruler of England
(c) fought between Cavaliers and Roundheads
(d) right of an accused person to hear charges against him
(e) granted right of habeas corpus
(f) father of Charles I
(g) English king who lost his head
(h) followers of those against the king

C. Some people today say that we have so much crime because our leaders are too weak. They are said to worry more about the rights of accused criminals than the rights of the victims. Would Charles I serve as a good model for the leaders of our country in the fight against crime? Explain your answer.

## ACTIVITIES AND INQUIRIES

1. Use each of the following key terms in a sentence.
   bail              Parliament         writ
   habeas corpus     petition
2. Go to the library. Prepare a report on either the Cavaliers or the Roundheads. Would you be willing to fight for that side? Explain.
3. Look for pictures of Cavaliers and Roundheads. Bring them to class. Be prepared to talk about why they dressed and looked different from each other.
4. Imagine that you are present at the trial of Charles I. You are Charles' lawyer. Prepare his defense. Now pretend that you are Charles' accuser. Prepare the case against him.
5. Suppose Charles had been told that his life would be spared if he agreed to certain things. Write down what you think those things might be.

# 4. The Glorious Revolution

*Soon after Charles I* was executed, the monarchy and the House of Lords were abolished. The government of England was changed to that of a free *Commonwealth*. In theory it was a republic, but in reality the army was in control. Oliver Cromwell was the head of the army. Therefore, he was the ruler of England. He was the man who had crushed and executed Charles because he was a tyrant. Now Cromwell turned around and did some of the things for which Charles had been put to death. Cromwell became the Lord Protector—a military dictator. He believed, as the English kings had, in his divine right to rule. He felt that God had called upon him to rule England.

After Cromwell died, the people were happy to see a king once again. Charles II, son of Charles I, became king. Parliament went back to its usual pattern of struggling with the king about money matters.

Charles II was followed by his brother James II in 1685. He was sincere and honest, but also narrow and stubborn. He was very much like his father, Charles I. He had no idea what people wanted and never tried to find out. He had decided to become an absolute ruler and restore the Roman Catholic Church to England. But the English people found these two things unacceptable. They would not agree to be ruled by an all-powerful Catholic king.

Leaders of Parliament felt that drastic steps had to be taken. In 1688 they asked William of Orange (the Netherlands) to come and rule England. William was married to James' Protestant daughter, Mary, and was acceptable to the English people. William landed in England and defeated James' armies. William and Mary were offered the English crown as equal rulers. This marked a very important step in the march of English democracy. Parliament had shown that it had the rights to crown and remove the crown of the country's rulers.

In this chapter, William and Mary discuss with John Locke their feelings about coming from the Netherlands to rule England. Locke was a famous writer who had opposed James II. Ask yourself why William and Mary were willing to come to England. How did their becoming king and queen affect the theory of divine right? Why is this change in the English government called the Glorious Revolution?

## London, 1690

"Sire," said John Locke, "I must tell you how much I appreciate your allowing me to come back to England with you."

"It's nothing at all," replied William of Orange. "After all, this is your home. You were forced to leave England by bloody King James. Besides, I am happy that you can advise me about things here in England. This is my first visit, you know."

"I'm sure that Queen Mary can give you all the help you need about England," said Locke. "As for me, you summed it up when you said 'Bloody King James.' Without your protection, there would have been one less loyal Englishman on this earth. He meant to kill me—along with all other protesters!"

"Yes, I'm told that he killed at least 300 men," said the king. "They said that he enjoyed watching prisoners being tortured."

"And don't forget the thousand or more shipped off as slaves to the West Indies," added John Locke.

"I don't think that King James cared at all about England and the English people!" laughed William.

"William, do you really care about England?" asked Queen Mary, as she entered the room. Locke wisely left by another door.

"How can you ask me a question like that?" William said. "Would I have left my beautiful home in Holland to come to this God-forsaken land if I didn't care?"

"You certainly would, William. You certainly would. Power is your life—power and money. England is where you can find both. What an easy way you found to line up an ally against your enemy, France!"

"Nonsense," replied the king. "I came to England because I was asked to come by Parliament. I forced no one to accept me!"

"Accept you? Force you?" asked Mary. "Whom do you think you are talking to? You are king of England because I am the queen! I am the daughter of King James. Without me, you would be the third-rate king of a fourth-rate nation!"

"All right, then. You are the queen. But do you have to talk at me as though I'm an outsider? I am at least your equal on the throne. Your friend John Locke is always talking about liberty and equality. Why don't you start by practicing a little equality with your husband?"

"You may complain about John Locke all you want, but without his ideas, I doubt that you would ever have been asked to be king of England."

"Mary! Now you want me to say that Locke put me on the throne! You seem to forget that he wasn't even in England. He lived under my protection in Holland. I agreed to permit him to return to England."

"Don't be a fool, William. I am talking about his ideas. His brilliant mind found an acceptable excuse for you, a foreigner, to become ruler of England. That's why you are here!"

"You're going soft in the head!" shouted the king, his face purple with anger. "His ideas may be interesting, but they are not why I am here in England.

"All right, Mary, call your hero Locke back into the room. He's probably right outside the door listening."

John Locke entered the room. "Your majesties, did I hear my name mentioned?" he asked.

"Yes, John," said Queen Mary. "Perhaps you can help clear up a disagreement that the king and I are having. Why were we asked to come and rule England?"

"Your highnesses, may I explain? The people of England cannot allow any part of their government to be too strong. No one branch can do solely as it pleases. We cannot accept the tyranny of the Parliament, nor can we accept the tyranny of the crown. James had gone too far. We could not permit this. He had to go."

"Then," said Mary, "you are encouraging revolution, are you not?"

"No, I am not encouraging a revolution," said John Locke. "I am merely describing one that has already taken place. The king of England went far beyond the powers given him by the English people. He abused the people's trust. Therefore, it was only fair that he lose his right to be king."

"Well spoken, Locke," said King William. "But where does this leave us?"

"It's very simple, Your Majesty," replied Locke with great patience. "James' powers were taken from him and given to you and Queen Mary."

"Then," said the queen, "this means that we have all the powers of my father, King James. Now we can do whatever we wish to do."

"I'm sorry to say no, you may not, Your Highness," replied Locke. "That would defeat the purpose of the revolution. Surely you remember the limits you placed upon your powers when you took over the throne?"

"We signed the paper willingly. Have we signed away too much of our power?"

"Not too much of your power," said Locke. "But just enough so that the people and the Parliament will not permit you to go too far."

"Are you sure that we haven't signed our lives away?" asked the queen.

"Not at all, Your Majesty. You merely agreed that Parliament will have certain powers. It will prevent all future kings and queens from going too far. The Bill of Rights passed last year says that you cannot interfere in elections for members of Parliament. You cannot stop members from arguing with one another or having a debate. Now only Parliament has the power to tax and keep up the army. The English now have guarantees of jury trial and fair bail while waiting for trial. People may not be thrown in jail unless they have been found guilty in a court open to the public's ears and eyes."

"What you are saying, John, is that Parliament has as much power as we have. We are not as powerful as the kings and queens who once ruled this great country. It is a shock, but we will live up to our agreement. We can survive with it. But don't you really think that some future ruler of England will feel that the Parliament has gone too far?"

"No, Your Majesty," answered John Locke. "Parliament cannot go too far, and neither can the crown. Each part of the government has been given some powers by the people. The Parliament and the crown have an agreement with the people to use their powers wisely. This is called the social contract. The powers that have been given can be taken back. Anything else is tyranny! This country will not stand for a king, or even a Parliament, that has gone too far!"

"This is a glorious country," said King William. "It deserves a glorious revolution!"

"I see that you are beginning to appreciate our England," said the queen. "Now do you understand that we are protecting the lives and happiness of future generations of English men and women?"

"Yes, I understand," said William.

"Your Majesty now sees that he too is part of the revolution!" said Locke.

## UNDERSTANDING THE STORY

**A.** *Write T for each statement that is true, F for each statement that is false, and N for each statement that is not mentioned in the story.*

1. Cromwell was the best ruler that England ever had.
2. Cromwell was both Lord Protector and military dictator of England.
3. Cromwell was the last king of England.
4. The leaders of Parliament asked William and Mary to rule England.
5. A queen should never have the same power as a king.
6. The rule of William and Mary was part of the Glorious Revolution.
7. John Locke was an American adviser to William and Mary.
8. Queen Mary felt that William agreed to become king of England because he loved the English people.
9. Locke believed in liberty and equality.
10. Locke was the most important English writer of all time.

**B.** *The Glorious Revolution was a big step forward on the road to democracy. Tell which statements show how in the Glorious Revolution England became more democratic by limiting one-man rule.*

1. Cromwell became a military dictator.
2. Parliament chose the new king and queen.
3. William and Mary were elected by the English people.

4. John Locke could speak freely to William and Mary.
5. No one part of the English government could become too strong.
6. The Bill of Rights protected the liberties of English men and women.
7. The king and queen decided how long members of Parliament could debate.
8. The king and queen could not interfere in elections for members of Parliament.
9. Jury trials, fair bail, and habeas corpus were rights of the English people.
10. The social contract was an agreement between John Locke and William and Mary.

C. The United States form of government borrowed many ideas from the English form of government. Make a list of ideas that were borrowed from England.

## ACTIVITIES AND INQUIRIES

1. In our story John Locke speaks of a social contract—an agreement between government and the people. Write a contract between the people of the United States and the government.
2. Here are a few statements taken from the English Bill of Rights.

> It is not legal to raise taxes without the permission of Parliament.
> English people may send petitions to the king.
> Keeping a standing army in time of peace without the permission of Parliament is against the law.
> Bail and fines should not be so high that people cannot pay them.

   Why are these rights important to democracy? How would the lives of Americans be different if the English people had not gained these rights?
3. Pretend that you are William of Orange. You can become king of England if you sign the Bill of Rights. Write down your true feelings. Be ready to explain.
4. Imagine that you are Mary. Your father has lost his throne as king of England. How do you feel about your husband signing an agreement with Parliament, the enemies of your father?

"Why did they chop off a king's head?" asked Jack excitedly. "We don't do that to presidents we don't like. That's a little scary!"

"Were English kings like our presidents?" asked Mr. Miller.

"Oh, I see," answered Jack. "The kings were there for life. Nobody elected them, but they gave the people and Parliament a hard time. I guess that they had to keep the kings in line somehow. Still, sending your king to the chopping block—"

"What were the English people afraid of, Jack?"

"I know what happened," said Jack thoughtfully. "The nobles and the Parliament would say, 'You, king, you're going too far! Who do you think you are? Take it easy. Listen to the people once in a while!' "

"Great, Jack. So all you need is a Parliament to make sure the king doesn't do it all himself."

"It's not so easy, Mr. Miller. Those kings thought they had been given their jobs by God himself. They called it divine right. I guess they felt that nothing and nobody could stop them. But the nobles stopped King John."

"How did they do that?" asked Mr. Miller.

"I think you once said that 'money talks,'" said Jack. "King John needed money. The English nobles said, 'You want tax money? You have to ask us for permission. But first, sign this little piece of paper—this Magna Carta!'"

"Yes, Jack, King John certainly did agree to a lot of things. But there was something missing in the English government."

"Right, Mr. Miller. They had to set up a Parliament to pass the laws. Parliament battled the king. I remember they wouldn't let James do whatever he wanted. They wouldn't let him be a dictator. They showed him who was 'boss'!"

"Now do you have an idea why they killed Charles I?" continued Mr. Miller.

"I suppose it was a little different," replied Jack slowly. "Charles would sign anything; he would promise anything. He was a liar. I think he felt that kings didn't have to keep their word. He thought he was above the law. Laws weren't for kings. They were for ordinary, plain folks! Charles signed the Petition of Right, but everyone knew that he didn't believe in rights for other English people! I don't know, Mr. Miller. Maybe he deserved to die. But wait a minute. Parliament threw out James II; they didn't kill him."

"What does that tell you about revolutions, Jack?"

"I think I get it. There are revolutions and there are revolutions. Some revolutions happen quietly, without people being killed. The English Revolution of 1689 was like that."

"Do you remember what John Locke said about revolution?" asked Mr. Miller.

"Locke said that people get together and give a government the right to rule them. But suppose that government doesn't do its job. The people aren't too happy with it. Then the people will pick someone else to run the country. That's really revolutionary!"

"What's the connection with the Glorious Revolution?"

"Well," said Jack, "Parliament would be like the people in John Locke's story. They felt that James II was not doing his job. So they threw him out and called in William and Mary."

"Could they be sure that William and Mary would do their jobs?" asked Mr. Miller.

"No. Parliament had William and Mary sign the Bill of Rights. That gave the English Parliament a lot of power. It gave the English people a lot of things that you need for a democratic government."

"Does this sound familiar to you, Jack?"

"Yes. That's what must have happened to us in our own American Revolution. The English government broke its contract with its colonists in America. And our people here wouldn't stand for it! Bang! We fought for our freedom. Anyway, we do owe the English a lot. Their ideas help make our democracy work. I don't know where we'd be without them!"

"Well spoken, Jack."

"Did revolutions take place in other countries, too?" asked Jack.

"You bet. Now read the unit on France. Their revolution was quite different from the one in England."

# France—The Beginnings of Democracy

"Oh, come on, Mr. Miller. I asked a simple question about other revolutions. I didn't say that I wanted to read all about what happened in France."

"Why not, Jack? The French Revolution is exciting. You'll be able to see how people rose up and threw a government out."

"Isn't studying about the English Revolution enough?" asked Jack.

"No, because the French Revolution is quite different from England's Glorious Revolution," answered Mr. Miller. "In France it's a revolution of violence and bloodshed. A whole system is turned upside down and inside out."

"Okay, maybe the French Revolution is interesting. But how about those French words? You know I have enough trouble with English."

"Don't worry, Jack. I promise that the few French words won't bother you at all. Watch your word list grow."

"All right, Mr. Miller. Bring on the French Revolution. Where do we start?"

"With Louis XIV. Then you can read the rest of the unit on France."

# 1. The Sun King

*In Unit III we saw how* the English Parliament challenged the power of the king. Their struggle lasted for almost five centuries. One result of the Glorious Revolution of 1689 was that the king could not rule without the help of Parliament. The kings and queens of England were no longer the *sole* (only) rulers of their country. Death and taxes were too important to be decided by one person.

In this unit we move to France. The absolute power of the French king was challenged by the Parisian *Parlement* (parliament) during the 17th century. Actually, the Parlement had little power. It was not representative of France, as the English Parliament was representative of England. But the French also were eager to limit the king's power to set taxes. Wars cost a great deal of money, so taxes were very high.

A revolt against the French monarchy was fought during the 17th century (1648–1653). The revolt was called the *Fronde*. The name means slingshot. It was taken from the gadget that children in the Paris slums used to toss mud at passing coaches. The mud annoyed the noble riders in the coaches, but it never stopped them from using the streets of Paris. So too the revolt of the Fronde was annoying, but it did not stop the kings of France from doing as they pleased. The Fronde was a failure. No limits were to be placed upon the absolute powers of the kings of France until the end of the 18th century.

In 1643, Louis XIV, a child of five, became king of France. For the next 18 years, the real ruler of France was Cardinal Mazarin. When he died in 1661, the people were shocked that Louis XIV himself took control of the French government. He decided that he would be his own prime minister. For the next 54 years Louis XIV was at the center of

*The palace of Versailles in the late 17th century*

Europe, its wars, its life. In fact, this period has been called the Age of Louis XIV.

Louis was the greatest of the absolute monarchs. (Absolute monarchs had total control of their countries' affairs.) Louis was called the Sun King. He looked and acted like a king. He loved praise and flattery and was very fond of pictures and statues of himself. He believed he was the greatest of all rulers—a king of kings.

Louis insisted on moving the French court ten miles from Paris to Versailles (ver-SIGH). Louis disliked Paris. He hated the narrow streets and was afraid of the crowds of people. He never forgot his fears during the Fronde, when he was at the mercy of the mob. He had to get out of Paris, no matter what the cost.

At Versailles, he built a palace worthy of a sun king. It was the finest palace in the world. It took over 30 years to build, and as many as 35,000 people worked on it at one time. Hundreds of people lost their lives on the project. No one knows how much Versailles cost. Louis made sure that he destroyed the records of expenses before he died.

In this story two young nobles meet at Versailles. They talk about life at the court. We can see how everything revolves around the thoughts and actions of the king.

Ask yourself why most of the nobles of France were at the court of Versailles. Why was Louis called the Sun King? Did he deserve the title?

## Versailles, 1691

"Count Chaumont!" called Count Rideau as he recognized a familiar face in the crowd that filled the great Hall of Mirrors. Rideau walked quickly to greet his old friend. "When did you arrive at Versailles? I see that Louis finally forced you to come here. How do you like it?"

"It's great to see you again, Rideau," said Chaumont as they greeted each other. "It's been a long time. How do I like it? That's a fine question coming from you. You warned me about how dull and boring it was here. Remember how you kept writing me not to come because it wasn't my kind of life?"

"I suppose," said Count Rideau, "you felt that I was trying to hide the truth from you. You must have had the idea that I would not want to share the fun of Versailles with my best friend."

"No, Rideau. I believed you. I admit that I did have some doubts about your stories at the beginning. But why would you have wanted to keep me away from here? Now I'm sure that it was for my own good. I've been at Versailles only three days, and already I wish I were back home!"

"Now you realize that everything they say about Versailles is true. You can be happy here if you can learn to do exactly as you are told. You'll find plenty to eat and drink. There are many good-looking women. Keep your eyes open. But stay away from the gambling. You can lose your shirt. The king will pay for the gambling losses of his closest friends. But you are far removed from that position."

"Thanks for your good advice," said Chaumont. "Tell me, do you see the king very often? You've been here for three years. Are you at all close to him now? Will he talk to me?"

"Slow down—not so fast," said Rideau, laughing. "One question at a time. Only the most powerful nobles are close to the king.

That doesn't include people like you and me. I haven't even reached the high position of handing the king his shirt or pants. The best I've been able to do so far is watch him wash his face a few times. Oh, and once I saw him put on his wig. Only his favorites can actually hand him his food. I have never gotten that close. But can he eat!"

"I'm sorry," said Chaumont, "but I must confess that I just don't understand what you're talking about. What's the big deal about handing the king his underwear and watching him dress? Who wants to watch him eat or bring in his food? We're not servants. We're nobles! This is ridiculous!"

"Chaumont, you have to understand that Louis isn't just the king of France. He is the sun and the moon and the stars! He is the center of everything in our world. We nobles are here to honor him, to do everything to make him happy."

"Does being dressed and undressed by his nobles make him happy?" asked Chaumont.

"You'll find out," answered Rideau. "There is a set way of doing everything at court. These things please the king. He likes doing exactly the same thing at the same time each day. This is his life. You'll see; someday you'll be happy to do things for the king you now think are so silly. Who knows, someday he may even speak to you! But don't expect it; he's not a great talker. Some claim he says so little because then he won't have a chance to say the wrong things.

"Do you know that he has been his own prime minister since Mazarin died? He tries to do too much. Not even the 'Grand Monarch' can run a country as large as France all by himself. He wants to know everything, sign everything."

"With all the parties and games going on around here, when does the king find time to govern?" asked Chaumont.

"Don't let appearances fool you," said Rideau. "Yes, he loves all the parties and rituals of Versailles. But he spends a good eight hours a day on the business of running the country. Believe it or not, he is a hard-working king."

"Isn't he afraid of making mistakes?" asked Chaumont.

"My dear Chaumont, the king makes no mistakes. He is the all-powerful ruler. He is the image of God on earth. He thinks of himself as the greatest of men—and we nobles agree. That's why he took the sun as his emblem. Our King Louis XIV is the source of our light and life!"

"But that's blasphemy!" cried Chaumont. "That's disrespect for God—to compare Louis with God! After three years in Versailles you are a stranger to me. I don't understand you. You were my closest friend, and now—"

"Chaumont," said Rideau coolly, "I am very sorry that I disappoint you. Three years is a long time. But what I said is what the people at court are saying. They are not my ideas. Someday soon you too will understand. You will change. You will learn your place here. This will be your entire world. You too will say that Louis is a great king. You will see his pockmarks and his warts, but you will learn to love him!"

"Please forgive my shouting at you," said Chaumont. "I would like to think that I will never change. My mind will always be open. But suppose you are right. I want to be myself, to be a person. Should I ask for permission to go home?"

"Ask, but you are now a member of this court. There is not much chance that you will be given permission," answered Rideau. "You may visit your home, but this is where you will spend the rest of your life!"

"Thank you for your patience," said Chaumont, much more calmly. "I must learn to accept things here. But, if Louis is such a great king, almost a god, why doesn't he save the poor people from starving?"

"We know very little about life in the outside world," replied Rideau. "That's not our concern. Don't worry. Louis will take care of the people. Chances are that you know much more about what's going on in the rest of France than I do. Tell me what you know."

"Well," said Chaumont, "Louis is a great spender. Taxes are very high. People say that the money goes in and out of the royal treasury faster than you can say 'Sun King.' But the spending isn't all personal. Let's not forget all of his wars. It's hard to think of a time when France, or should I say Louis, was not at war! Why does he have to fight war after war? First he wins some land and then he loses some land. He is bleeding our country to death!"

"Louis fights for the glory of France," replied Rideau. "We will not let any nation push us around. Why should we? We are great!"

"Yes, but does he have to fight the world?" responded Chaumont. "Doesn't France have enough land of its own? Don't we have enough problems? I could understand why Vauban built fortresses on our frontiers. I am all for defense, but do we always have to attack? Who needs the Spanish Netherlands? Why should we make secret deals with the English?"

"Think of it, Chaumont, if you had had great generals like Condé and Turenne, what would you do? Wouldn't you attack? Why shouldn't France become even more powerful?"

"Yes," answered Chaumont, "a great country knows how to live in peace with her neighbors. A great king understands that his first responsibility is to his people. He doesn't send them to die in wars. He doesn't bleed them of all their money!"

"What you are saying about our king makes sense to you as a newcomer to Versailles," said Rideau, speaking quietly once more. "But wait. You'll soon be caught up in the life and death of Versailles. The king will be the center of your world. You will accept whatever he does and whatever happens here. This is all you will know. You will change, believe me. I did. You will respect and appreciate Louis. He is human. He may not be perfect, but he is the very best king that Europe has ever had!"

"You mean that he is the best king that France has at this moment," said Chaumont, also very quietly. "Perhaps he is strong enough to hold our country together during his lifetime. But what will happen to France and Europe after he dies? Who will pay for all of his waste, for his extravagance? Who will account for all the people's suffering?"

Rideau thought for a moment. "We will all pay, I suppose. France cannot afford another Louis XIV."

## UNDERSTANDING THE STORY

**A.** *Which statements show that Louis XIV had complete control over France?*

1. Louis XIV always asked the peasants for advice.
2. The revolt called the Fronde did not affect Louis' actions.
3. Louis liked to be called the Sun King.

4. Louis spent as little money as he could.
5. Most French nobles were forced to live at Versailles.
6. Louis believed in democratic government.
7. Louis was his own prime minister during much of his rule.
8. Louis felt that he was the image of God on earth.

**B.** *Chaumont and Rideau have many different ideas. Decide who made or might have made the following remarks. Write C for each statement that Chaumont made or might have made and R for each statement that Rideau made or might have made.*

1. Louis finally forced you to come to Versailles.
2. I wish I were back home.
3. Only the most powerful nobles ever get close to the king.
4. Why should you want to see the king get dressed?
5. Someday Louis may speak to you.
6. We were brought to Versailles to limit our power.
7. The king is a big spender.
8. Louis fights wars for the glory of France.

**C.** Imagine that Louis XIV is alive today. How would life be different for all of us if Louis were president of the United States? What changes would Louis have to make to be a successful United States president?

## ACTIVITIES AND INQUIRIES

1. Imagine that you are Chaumont. Write a letter to a friend. Describe how you feel about your new life at the palace of Versailles.
2. Pretend that you are Rideau. You have found Chaumont's letter. You know that the king sees all mail before it is sent from the palace. What changes would you make in the letter to protect your friend Chaumont?
3. Look at the illustration of Versailles on page 111. Describe the palace and its grounds.
4. Suppose that you were able to spend a day at the palace of Versailles in the days of Louis XIV. Write a diary describing that day at Versailles.

5. Why is Louis XIV shown in this way in the cartoon? Explain what the noble means by the question. Pretend that you are the other noble. Answer the question.

*"But what happens when the sun sets?"*

# 2. The Age of Reason

*In 18th-century France there were* men who fought against the evils of their country's government. Their weapons were ideas and words, not swords and guns. These men did not fight in a revolution, but their words caused others to die for freedom.

These men were called the *philosophes* (FILL-oh-soffs). They were writers and thinkers who asked that all people be treated fairly. All should have the same rights. They demanded that the nobles and clergy give up their special privileges. Taxes should be fair. No one man, such as a king, should have total power over the lives of the French people.

All people were important. All had something to offer to France. You can see that these writers were challenging the absolute power of the king and the privileged classes. They said that a man did not deserve to be king of France simply because his father had been king. He had to earn the right to be king.

The *philosophes* would not accept anything unless there was a very good reason for it. People must think for themselves. They must use their minds. They must understand what they are doing and why they are doing it. This is why the 18th century is often called the Age of Reason.

In this story two writers, Voltaire (vol-TAIR) and Jean Jacques Rousseau (roo-SEW), are discussing their philosophies. They are searching for truth. As you read, ask yourself how their ideas are different. How did these ideas set the stage for a revolution? How do they help to make the 18th century an age of reason?

# Paris, 1768

Voltaire and Rousseau meet at a gathering of writers in an apartment in Paris. The two men have been enemies for many years. Rousseau is jealous of Voltaire's success as a playwright. Voltaire resents Rousseau's fame. Rousseau is very sensitive about anything said or written about him.

"How are you, Rousseau?" asked Voltaire. "It's been many years since I last saw you."

"I'm still alive, but no thanks to you, Voltaire!" answered Rousseau.

"How can you talk this way?" grinned Voltaire. "We were never friends, but we both fight for freedom and equality. Aren't you against privilege for the nobles? Don't you hate prejudice as much as I do? Would you allow a person to give you an opinion without facts?"

"You talk about prejudice and making up your mind without facts," angrily answered Rousseau. "Well, how about your own little prejudices? Don't you think that I've heard about your nasty remarks about me? My friends tell me that you're jealous of me. You can't stand my success. You think that you're the number-one writer of France. You won't let anyone praise me. Isn't there plenty of room for more than one good writer? Don't you know that I've called you 'great'? You're a genius—"

"Just a minute, Rousseau. Don't let your mouth run away with you, as usual! I hear things, too! Sure, you said I was a genius. But, then, did you have to add that I had an 'evil soul'?"

"What's so terrible about that?" smiled Rousseau for the first time. "You write like a genius. You have a great mind. Your soul or what is inside of you is something else. Let's just forget it. I like so much of what you have written. I think you speak from your heart. To me, you *are* the Age of Reason. You think; you challenge; you annoy people. You try to destroy evil. You see something that you don't like, and you go after it. You cannot stand anything that is not fair, that is not just."

"Why, thank you, Rousseau. I think that if I weren't 74 years old, I could really begin to like you. Yes, I've tried to crush tyranny.

I can't stand anything unfair or unjust. I am against torture, unfair laws, unreasonable government."

"I agree with you absolutely," replied Rousseau. "We are both against privilege and prejudice. How well you said it in your story *Candide*. How well you pointed out that this is far from the best of all possible worlds. But I must disagree with you about one thing. I think you are too strong in your arguments against religion, but that's your opinion."

"I am against anything that cannot be proved," said Voltaire forcefully. "Superstition is fear of what you don't know. Superstition should not exist! My mind—my reason—tells me that there is a God. But I cannot know what he is. To change the subject—I never quite understood what you meant by 'back to nature.'"

"I have tried to tell everyone that life is too complicated today," answered Rousseau very seriously. "People should live more simply. They should get out of the cities. You know that city life is dirty and artificial. So I am suggesting that we get away from crowds and noise. And get rid of our silly clothes!"

"Do you mean," said Voltaire, "that we should give up all our pleasures? Are we all supposed to go back to living in the woods? Rousseau, I can't see you living as naked as Adam in the Garden of Eden."

"No, no, Voltaire. There you go again, twisting what I say. I want us to live happily. How can we be good to ourselves in today's world? There are times when we should get away from other people. All I'm saying is that we should make some changes in our life-styles from time to time. Perhaps, I should have said 'when we can.'"

"I'm sorry, Rousseau, but I like all of my pleasures. I enjoy the simple and the complicated ones, and, I dare say, so do you!"

"No one of us can always do what he preaches," added Rousseau softly. "I'm a human being, too. As for your books, I've read them all. But I don't see much about democracy—people choosing their government. You believe in democracy, don't you? Why don't you let people rule themselves?"

"No, I don't think that most people are able to govern themselves," answered Voltaire. "They are not ready for that big step. We can have a king, but we must not let that king go too far. Others should share his powers. Have you looked at the government of England?"

"Very reasonable, Voltaire. But, as usual, you miss the point. Where does government come from? Free people come together to make a contract. All of us can't run a government. So we must choose a few people to do the job for us."

"How do the people know whom to choose?" asked a puzzled Voltaire.

"You lack faith in people, Voltaire. We will know when the time comes. We may make mistakes, but then we'll make changes. We'll find others to run our country. You must have faith; you must believe."

"Faith in people!" shouted Voltaire. "You shock me. You are talking revolution. You sound as though you want to overthrow the government! I am not against rights for the people. Make them all equal before the law. Give them fair trials. Lower their taxes. Abolish serfdom. But by all means keep the king!"

"Do you remember what I said in my *Social Contract?* 'Man is born free, and everywhere he is in chains.' All people—all men and women—must throw off their chains! They must be free again! If that means the king's head, so be it!"

"I can't agree with you, Rousseau. But we are not really that far apart on most things. Changes are coming. As long as I live, I will never stop attacking everything I think is bad. People must know the truth. They must understand."

Rousseau answered, "And I will not stop until all our people have liberty, equality, and fraternity!"

## UNDERSTANDING THE STORY

A. Write T *for each statement that is true and* O *for each statement that is an opinion.*

1. The *philosophes* wanted all people to be treated fairly.
2. Rousseau and Voltaire were the greatest writers France ever produced.
3. The *philosophes* wanted people to think for themselves.
4. People today do not spend enough time using their brains.

5. Voltaire was against anything that was not fair or could not be proved.
6. Rousseau felt that 18th-century life was too complicated.
7. Cities in the 18th century were as dirty as those of today.
8. Voltaire did not want to throw out the king.

**B.** *Tell which item below makes each statement correct.*

1. The weapons of 18th-century French *philosophes* were (a) guns and swords (b) ideas and words (c) pens and typewriters.
2. The *philosophes* said that (a) nobles should give up their special privileges (b) kings should have more power (c) England and France should become one nation.
3. Making up your mind without knowing the truth is called (a) prejudice (b) contract (c) being fair.
4. Rousseau and Voltaire (a) were good friends (b) wanted the poor people to rule France (c) were both writers.
5. Rousseau's idea of "back to nature" meant that (a) people should go back to living on farms (b) people should live more simply (c) all cities should be destroyed.
6. Voltaire believed that (a) a king must not go too far (b) every person could be a king (c) the government of the United States was the best in the world.
7. Rousseau wrote (a) *The Social Contract* (b) *Candide* (c) *The Right to Live.*

**C.** Imagine that Rousseau and Voltaire are alive today. Whose ideas would interest you more? Why? Whose ideas sound like those of the people in our time? Why?

## ACTIVITIES AND INQUIRIES

1. Use each of the following key terms in a sentence.
   liberty              Old Regime              *philosophe*
   fraternity           prejudice
   equality             Age of Reason
2. One of the passages on page 123 was written by Rousseau, the other was written by Voltaire. Decide who wrote each passage. Choose statements to prove that you are right.

> Reason moves slowly. The roots of prejudice are deep. I may not agree with what you say, but I will fight for your right to say it.
>
> The people must decide who should govern them. The people may have any kind of government they want. Democracy is the best kind of government.

3. Imagine that Voltaire is going to be tried by a French criminal court. Because of what he has written, Voltaire is accused of treason against the government. Would Rousseau defend him? If yes, how would he defend him? If no, why not?
4. Suppose that Rousseau is going to be tried by a French criminal court. He is accused of treason against the government because of his writings. Would Voltaire defend him? If yes, how would he defend him? If no, why not?
5. Pretend that a copy of Rousseau's *Social Contract* has fallen into the hands of the king of France. You are the king's chief adviser. He asks you to read *The Social Contract* and to write what he should do about it. Should he *ban* it (stop it from being sold)? Should he copy its ideas? Explain why you think you have given the king good advice.

# 3. The Revolution Begins

*Earlier we saw that Louis XIV* was a great king in name and in deed. He ruled as he wished. Who would dare to tell him that he was wrong? He was followed by his great-grandson, Louis XV, who ruled from 1723 to 1774. He tried to continue Louis XIV's system of government but had little success. He sat at councils, yawned a great deal, and often dozed. He was not interested in doing the work of a king. In fact, just about everything bored him! The government of Louis XV was weak, corrupt, and divided. Yet somehow the monarchy survived.

The people of France were growing more and more dissatisfied, however. Average people played no part in government, were taxed unfairly, and were looked upon as inferior to the so-called upper classes. France was a nation of inequality and privilege. French society was divided into three classes, or estates: the high clergy (First Estate), the nobility (Second Estate), and the remainder of the people (Third Estate). The Third Estate included peasants, workers, professional people, the lower clergy, and members of the middle class.

The first two estates made up about 2 percent of the people but controlled the lives and fortunes of the other 98 percent. The high clergy and nobles had little in common with the average French person. They were exempt from the worst of the direct taxes, were tried in special courts, and were even given different punishments. This system was called the *Old Regime* (old way).

The vast majority of the French people were peasants. True, they were better off than peasants in Germany, Italy, Russia, Poland, or Spain. But the French always worried about famine. A poor harvest would bring with it hunger, illness, and death. Hardly a year passed without a shortage of grain in some part of France. It was difficult to ship extra grain from one part of the country to the area in need. Taxes on the peasants were extremely high and unfairly collected. Many nobles decided to collect feudal taxes that had been overlooked for generations. All in all, the peasants felt *exploited* (used).

When Louis XV died, it was obvious that France needed a king with the ability and personality of a Louis XIV. Louis XVI was not that king. He was timid and slow. He was more interested in hunting and locksmithing than in learning how to rule France. He too slept through many council meetings. He could not get himself to give a definite opinion and stick to it. His opinions were often those of the last person he had spoken to. He neither looked nor acted like a king. Obviously he was not the man to deal with an emergency.

The emergency was real. There had been a series of bad harvests. Bread was scarce, prices were high. When factories closed, many French workers lost their jobs. In 1789 Louis XVI found himself badly in need of money and decided to call the *Estates General,* the representatives of the three estates, into session. Many people expected great things from these representatives. *Petitions* (lists of grievances) were drawn up. There were demands for equal taxation, freedom of speech and press, and the abolition of special privileges and feudal dues.

A major question was how the three estates would vote. The Third Estate insisted that each person was to be given one vote. The nobles said that each estate was entitled to exactly one vote. But the Third Estate had its way. It met by itself and said that it was now the National Assembly—the representative of all of France!

In this story, we find that the people of Paris were determined to storm and capture the prison called the Bastille (bah-STEEL). The Revolution was well underway.

Ask yourself why the people felt that it was so important to capture the Bastille. What should Louis XVI have done about its capture? Why were the people of France justified in revolting against the French monarchy?

# Paris, July 14, 1789

"What's it all about? I've never seen the streets so crowded," said Jeanne. "Where's everyone running to?"

"Haven't you heard?" George replied. "We're going to capture the Bastille!"

"Capture the Bastille? How can you possibly imagine yourself doing such a thing? It's not just a prison—it's a fortress. Soldiers are defending it. Those thick walls with cannons on top have to be too much for a mob without guns. You'll all be killed—and for what purpose? What a waste!"

"We won't all be killed. What you say is plain nonsense," said George impatiently. "I am not fool enough to want to die. I say that we can take the Bastille. There are thousands of us against a few hundred of them. We are not a mob. We know what we want and nothing will stop us. Besides, when those soldiers see all of us coming at them, they'll give up without a fight! Don't be surprised if they come over to our side."

"Come over to our side?" asked Jeanne. "I don't understand what's going on. What is *our* side? People are running around screaming and yelling. 'Hurray for the Revolution!' 'Liberty and Equality' are on everyone's lips. What's it all about? I'm completely confused!"

"Jeanne, where have you been during the last few months? You act as though you've been asleep or away in America. Haven't you heard about the Revolution? Don't you understand that everything in France is going to be changed? Things will never be the same again!"

"Change . . . revolution . . . things will never be the same," repeated Jeanne. "You are right about one thing—I don't understand. No, I haven't been asleep, but I certainly don't pay attention to politics. I do my work, take my few francs, and try to survive. I've always felt government was for the king and the nobles. I am a worker, a member of the Third Estate. I was born poor and I will die poor. That is my destiny. Money and privileges are for the nobles. They are born to have good things. I am born to—"

"Born to what?" shouted George. "To starve, suffer, and die! And for what? So that those nobles can enjoy life? They all have a great time—at your expense! Doesn't it bother you that you are treated unfairly? Don't you care that no matter how hard you work and slave you will always be poor? Aren't you ashamed always to be under someone's heel? Do you enjoy bowing to and being pushed around by the nobles? Aren't you as good as they are? Don't you want to be free?"

"George, I see your point. I am beginning to understand. Of course, I am not happy with my life. But I always thought that this was the way things had to be. I never dreamed that things could be changed. I never realized that it wasn't fair."

"You are crazy! This is not a matter of fair or unfair. This is a case of absolute right and wrong. This is a case of crude privilege. Those people live off your suffering. They laugh at you. They spit at you. Sorry, Jeanne, there goes a group of my friends on the next street. I've got to be with them."

Close by, people were shouting—"On to the Bastille!"; "Save the political prisoners!"; "Kill the nobles!" George started to leave but changed his mind.

"Oh, what's the difference. I'll go along with the next bunch. Perhaps you'll join me. It's more important that you understand. You have to realize what they have been doing to you. By the way, how do you like the taxes you pay?"

"Oh, come on, George," answered Jeanne, laughing a bit. "No one likes to pay taxes, but everyone does. It's a part of living."

"No, Jeanne, you come on. Not everyone pays taxes, and even when they do, some don't pay all of their share. Do you realize that the nobles and the higher clergy don't even pay a land or income tax? They get away without paying the poll tax (a head tax paid per person). And those privileged people pretend that they never heard of other taxes too! It's a great life, isn't it? The people with the least money pay the most taxes. Those vultures of the upper classes use us!"

"Perhaps they would pay their fair share if asked," said Jeanne.

"No, Jeanne, it's not that simple. There's more. Do you know why I came to Paris from my little farm a few years ago? I just couldn't survive. Do you have any idea what the peasants have to sacrifice to work their land? Do you realize how unfair their tax burdens are? How would you like to neglect your own crops to help the noble with his harvest? How would you feel having to work on his roads? And when he went hunting, I was supposed to smile when his horses trampled my crops! I sold my land five years ago. Would you believe that I had to pay the noble almost one quarter of what I got out of it? For what!"

"I knew that peasants had a hard life, but I didn't realize it was anything like that," said Jeanne. "I thought that feudalism had been done away with in most of France."

"True," said George, "but no one ever thought of wiping out feudal taxes and services. These taxes stayed and broke our backs. Do you know that I had to have my bread baked in the noble's oven? My grain was ground in his mill. My grapes were pressed in his wine press. I had no choice. You don't think that he did those things for us because he was a decent person. He taxed us and he taxed us until there was almost nothing left for us to give." He started to walk away.

"Let me walk with you toward the Bastille," said Jeanne. "All right, I am beginning to understand. A lot of things in France have been wrong. Many nobles have been treating us unfairly. We poor people have been in a bad spot. But what are we going to do about it? Capturing the Bastille isn't going to stop the nobles from pushing us around. It won't cut our taxes."

"Wrong again, Jeanne. It will all help. We have to show those loafers that we mean business. We are going to the Bastille because it is a symbol of the rotten government of France, the Old Regime. It is the place where they put away the political prisoners. When the Bastille falls, the government and the king will know that things must change. They must make changes or they will die —their blood will flow through the streets of Paris! You will see!"

"I don't understand what you mean by 'political prisoners,'" said Jeanne.

"It's very simple and nasty," replied George. "The king can put anyone in jail for as long as he wants. There's no hearing, no trial, and no sentence. People are sent to the Bastille to rot. Their only crime is that someone in power doesn't like them!"

"Aren't you exaggerating?" asked Jeanne. "Don't you think that most of the prisoners in the Bastille are really criminals? Perhaps a few are what you call political prisoners. Why free these convicted men? They may be dangerous."

"You are still confused," said George angrily. "I give up." He started to move away rapidly, but Jeanne kept up with him.

*"The Bastille is ours! The Revolution has begun!"*

"I've heard that there are dungeons far underground where hundreds of innocent men are rotting away," George said. "I have also been told that there is a storage place where thousands of guns have been hidden away to be used against us. I am telling you for the last time that this place, this Bastille, must fall tonight!"

"George, I'm with you. Let me stay with you," said Jeanne. "But what about the king? Why don't we tell him about the things we don't like and ask him to make changes?"

"We've begged and we've begged," said George breathlessly, as he slowed down his pace. "He won't listen. Believe me, after the Bastille falls, he'll listen, or off goes his head. Here's the Bastille now."

"Look!" cried Jeanne, "there are thousands of people here! They have all kinds of weapons. But I still say that they are no match for the trained soldiers of the garrison. Look, the draw-bridge is down. Our people even have cannons. Everyone is rushing into the Bastille. People have been shot. I can't stand the sight. Why did I listen to you? Why did I come here? I feel sick."

"Victory! The Bastille is ours! Jeanne, don't be upset. We have won. I told you that we could capture it! The Revolution has begun! Let's show the nobles what we think of them. Kill the soldiers!"

Shouts of "Kill them all!" "Show no mercy!" "They drew the first blood!" "Let their blood join ours!" are heard.

"I wonder who really won tonight?" thought Jeanne. "Was it Revolution or was it Death?"

*Postscript.* The revolutionists found seven prisoners in the Bastille: four counterfeiters, two lunatics, and an alcoholic. Only one of the seven was a political prisoner.

## UNDERSTANDING THE STORY

**A.** *Match each item in Column A with its description in Column B.*

| COLUMN A | COLUMN B |
|---|---|
| 1. the Bastille | (a) head tax (paid per |
| 2. Estates General | person) |
| 3. liberty, equality, fraternity | (b) included all persons |
| 4. revolution | except high clergy and |
| 5. nobles | nobles |
| 6. Old Regime | (c) people who had many |
| 7. Third Estate | privileges |
| 8. poll tax | (d) prison in Paris |
| | (e) the nobles and high |
| | clergy and their |
| | privileges |
| | (f) slogan of the |
| | Revolution |
| | (g) representatives of the |
| | three estates called into |
| | session by Louis XVI |
| | (h) a great change |

**B.** *Write T for each statement that is true, F for each statement that is false, and N for each statement that is not mentioned in the story.*

1. Louis XIV was a great king.
2. Louis XV was also a very successful king.
3. The taxes paid by the French people in the 18th century were as high as those of today.

4. There were three estates, or social classes, in 18th-century France.
5. Most of the people of France were peasants.
6. The voting in the Estates General was fair: Each man had one vote.
7. The Third Estate included most of the people of France.
8. French peasants used good-quality seed and farm tools.
9. Louis XVI called the Estates General because he needed money.
10. Most French peasants were as bright as most French nobles.

C. Read the last paragraph of the story (the postscript) once again. Many would say that the people of Paris did not have good reason to storm the Bastille. Do you agree? Explain. How would George answer this question? What reason would he give?

## ACTIVITIES AND INQUIRIES

1. Imagine that it is 1789. You were a political prisoner in the Bastille in Paris. You have been set free by the revolutionists. You are asked to write a newspaper article telling why you were in prison and what prison life was like. Write the article.
2. Bring pictures to class of buildings and streets of 18th-century Paris. Draw a picture of the streets of Paris, including the Bastille and surrounding areas.
3. Draw a picture of what you think the inside of the Bastille looked like.
4. Imagine that you are George. Write a letter to your former lord. Tell him why you feel that he did not have the right to collect taxes from you. Pretend that you are the noble. Write a letter answering George.

# 4. The Reign of Terror

*The French Revolution was well* on its way. Which path would it take? Could Louis XVI live through the changes it would bring? Could the revolutionists live with the British solution, both Parliament and a king?

At first it seemed that Louis would be able to keep his crown. He said that he accepted the Declaration of the Rights of Man, which was inspired by the United States Declaration of Independence. All men and women were to be considered equal. The class lines created by birth were to be erased. The constitution of 1792 ruled that the king would stay on his throne. But the real power was to be in the hands of a legislature—a lawmaking body.

Those were great days in the lives of the French people. The surprise was that so much had been done with so little bloodshed. The Revolution seemed a great success. Then in 1792, the scene changed. France was thrown into a war with the great powers of Austria and Prussia. The new French government was in deep trouble.

Louis XVI did not really accept his new role as a not too powerful king. He hoped that European kings would win the war against France and rescue him. This was an idle dream. The French government was overthrown by the more *radical* (extreme) group called the Jacobins (JACK-oh-bins). Louis was found guilty of treason—plotting with the enemies of France.

The new Jacobin government was in a very dangerous situation. It was fighting a war against powerful enemies. At the same time, it was fighting its enemies within France. It felt itself surrounded. It trusted no one—including its own members. The Jacobins' answer was to start the *Reign of Terror* (rule of death). Over 500,000 French people were accused of being traitors. They were thrown into the overcrowded jails. From 3,500 to 4,000 were executed at the guillotine (GHEE-oh-teen). Others were shot to death or were drowned on boats that were sunk in the Loire River. What were their crimes? They were suspected of not being completely loyal to the revolutionary government of the Jacobins.

In this story we meet Robespierre (ROBZ-pih-aihr), who planned the Reign of Terror. Now he himself has been sentenced to die by the same blade that had killed so many other "enemies" of France. He writes in his diary of his days of glory. He recalls the men he worked with and against whom he plotted.

Ask yourself why Robespierre felt that the Terror was necessary. Did the leaders of the Terror destroy themselves? Could there have been a French Revolution without the Terror?

# Paris, July 27, 1794

What a ridiculous way for Maximilien Robespierre to end his life! A few days ago I was the leader of the revolutionary government. I was the head of the Committee of Public Safety. Now the "head" will lose his head. And for what? My enemies never understood what I was trying to do. They insisted that I wanted nothing but power. They even had the nerve to say that I wanted to become a dictator. What nonsense! They forget that in the National Assembly I was the champion of democracy. I was the one who worked to win the vote for all Frenchmen!

My dream was to make France a republic that would be fair, honest, and just. Was it my fault that I found that people had to die so that France could live? They call me a killer—I, who could not even bear the thought of death. They have no idea what happened many years ago when I was the judge of a criminal court. I actually resigned, left the job, because I could not send a convicted criminal to his death!

Life is sacred to me. It hurt me to send people to the guillotine. But I had to do it. France had to be cleansed and purified of all those who stood in the way of fair government! All the people who were not with us were against us. They were the suspects; they were the guilty ones! It was the only way I knew to make the Revolution live. Yes, people had to die for a better life for the good people of France. The end justifies the means!

Thoughts race wildly through my mind. I am perspiring. I cannot stand the pain in my jaw. Why did they have to shoot me? Can it be that I, the great Robespierre, am afraid? How will I act when I climb those stairs to the guillotine? Will I be able to make it on my own? I remember how the king behaved. There was a man who never looked or acted like a king during his lifetime. He was timid, always afraid. He never made a decision on his own. He was a slow thinker and doer! I thought they would have to carry him to the scaffold. But no, this was his greatest moment! Imagine, Madame la Guillotine bringing out the best in our King Louis!

I can see Louis now. He refused to let the soldiers take off his outer clothes. He would not even let the soldiers tie his hands. Yes, he died bravely. He had a strange dignity in death that he never had in his lifetime. I can still hear the mob screaming, "Long live the nation! Long live the Republic!" Then a soldier held up the king's head for all to see. For a moment, I wondered whether his life might have been spared. Was it a mistake to kill the king? No, that was no mistake. The king had to die. He may have been a fool, but he stood for all the evils of the absolute monarchy. He *was* the Old Regime in all of its evil ways.

Soon I will join those who gave their lives for the cause. How I wish they were with me now! But no—do I really want them here? I am confused. I wonder whether Marat would have defended me. Would he have taken my side? Or would he have joined the rest of the rabble and sent me to the guillotine?

I know the answer. He hated everyone in authority. He thought of himself as a great scientist and felt that no one recognized his talents. Too bad! He was no democrat. In his own way, he wanted to help the poor people, but he would not have given them any power. I have to laugh now, in spite of my troubles, when I think of people calling *me* cruel and ruthless. They do not remember when Marat called for 270,000 heads! He would solve all problems by killing and killing and killing. Too bad that he did not have the honor of dying by losing his own head to Madame la Guillotine! Stabbed while taking a bath! What a poor way to die!

There is one other I think of often. I remember meeting Danton

*"Soon I will join those who gave their lives for the cause."*

before the Revolution. What a kind man he was. And he was one of the strongest men I have ever known. He had a neck like a bull, with a head to match! And those piercing eyes: They seemed to look right through you! No wonder they called him Hercules and Atlas!

Danton was the best speaker I have ever heard. He could turn an audience upside down. Ah, how the Revolution changed him. A good man became cruel and harsh. I admit that I was afraid of him. He challenged me. I was afraid of losing my head as well as my job. I accepted his challenge. I sent him to the head chopper before he could get to me. Yet he was not all bad. He tried to help the poor. He worked hard to get feudal dues abolished.

I was too clever for him. I accused him of making secret deals with the nobles and get-rich-quick types. I wonder now if he really did those things.

Danton, I laughed when you said that you would break that guillotine before long, or you would lose your own head to it. I guess that you were tired of all the killing. I knew then that you were a dead man; you had to lose your head. But I did not laugh as I watched you climb the stairs to the knife. I admired the way you stood there and said, "Show my head to the people. It is worth it!" You were right; I can admit this now in my secret diary. I was shaken when you shouted, "Robespierre will be next!"

How right he was. That was only four months ago! I, Maximilien Robespierre, was called the "apostle of terror" by the people who should have known better. I, who hated and feared death, became a killer. Now I am about to die by the same instrument I used to save France. Is this fair?

I cannot stop my mind from wandering. Oh, if only I could sleep a little while. How can I? My jaw hurts so much. Soon there will be no pain at all. I see myself in a tumbril (cart) that is being drawn to the Place de la Revolution. I see the scaffold with the guillotine. It looks hideous, monstrous! The crowd is huge. People are screaming for my head! Why do they hate me so? I am afraid. I am weak. O Lord, please do not let me faint. I must be strong.

Somewhere I have read, "If you live by the sword, you will die by the sword!" For me, I would say, "If you feed the guillotine, it will chop you too!"

## UNDERSTANDING THE STORY

**A.** *Complete each of the sentences below.*

1. The French Declaration of ——— was inspired by the American Declaration of Independence.
2. According to the Constitution of 1792, the king ———.
3. Louis XVI hoped that his fellow kings would ——— him.
4. The moderate French government was overthrown by the radical ———.
5. The period when 500,000 French people were accused of being traitors was called the ———.
6. The man who created the Terror was ———.
7. Robespierre was the head of the Committee of ———.
8. Two other radical leaders were ——— and ———.
9. Robespierre was called the "apostle of ———."

**B.** *Write T for each statement that is true and F for each statement that is false.*

1. The Reign of Terror was a time of peace and quiet.
2. Louis XVI died bravely on the guillotine.
3. Robespierre sent many people to the guillotine.
4. Robespierre felt that it was a mistake to execute the king.
5. Marat was stabbed in his bathtub.
6. Danton was a poor speaker.
7. Robespierre was afraid that he would not die bravely.
8. Robespierre believed that the end justifies the means.

**C.** Pretend that Robespierre is alive today. Once again, he wants to become a leader of a country. Which country today would welcome his leadership? Why?

## ACTIVITIES AND INQUIRIES

1. Go to the library. Prepare a report on a modern-day revolution anywhere in the world. What similarities do you see to the French Revolution of the 1790s? What differences do you see?
2. In the library find material on the part played by women in the French Revolution. Tell the class about your findings.
3. Look at the illustration on page 135. Describe what is happening. Write your own title for this picture.

# 5. Napoleon's Rise to Power

*We have seen how France* lived in fear of the guillotine. But the Terror could not last. The people turned against violence and the radical Jacobins. The government became less extreme. It fell into the hands of the middle class. But many French people were still not satisfied. They felt that they should go even further and bring back a king. The Royalists (those who favored the king) were especially strong in Paris.

During October 1795, the Royalists of Paris were ready to make their move against the democratic government of France (called the Convention). Paul Barras (bah-RAS), the president of the Convention, asked a young Corsican general to defend the government. The young general was Napoleon Bonaparte (na-POLE-yun   BO-na-part). He quickly ended the Royalist revolt by firing artillery shells into the crowd at close range. The streets were filled with the dead and wounded.

From this time, Napoleon was the man to watch in France. He was a man of action, one who seemed to know what to do in difficult situations. He was counted on to crush the enemies of France in foreign lands. Why not let him do the job *in* France?

In this story Barras and Lucien Bonaparte talk about their plan to make Napoleon Bonaparte the *first consul* or leader of France. You will see how the *coup d'etat* (koo day-TAH), the plot to put him in power, almost failed.

Ask yourself why they felt that Napoleon could be a successful ruler of France. Were they right in turning to one man to rule their country? Why did Lucien Bonaparte talk of the possibility of a Jacobin takeover?

# Paris, November 9, 1799

"Barras, this is it!" said Lucien Bonaparte excitedly. "This is the day we have been waiting for."

"If all goes well," replied Barras, "your brother, Napoleon, will be the first consul of France. He will control the government."

"What do you mean, 'If all goes well'?" asked Lucien. "We're putting him in control, and that's that! You are not backing down at this point. We need your help, but this is no time for weaklings! Do you have any doubts?"

"Slow down, Lucien. Don't be so nervous. How could I have any doubts? You forget very quickly. Who gave your brother, Napoleon, his first push into power? Who asked him to come to Paris in 1795 to put down the rebellion? Who put him in charge of the army?"

"Yes, Barras, and who crushed the rebellion? He stood up to the mob! He was not afraid to shoot them down! He's a brilliant organizer. He is brave and fearless. Remember how he drove the British from Toulon in 1793? Do you know any other 24-year-olds who have been made brigadier-generals?"

"True, Lucien, but you are his brother. Remember that I was the first stranger who saw his talents. I sensed what he could do even though people thought that he was a revolutionist. You forget very quickly that your brother, Napoleon, was a Jacobin! He was a friend of Robespierre."

"I know, I know," replied Lucien, impatiently, "but that was a long while ago. If he were a Jacobin today, would he have a chance to become ruler of France? A Jacobin's life isn't worth a penny on the streets of Paris! Napoleon's job is to save us from the Jacobins."

"Lucien, you are wrong. It was only five years ago. He was in jail right after the Robespierres were executed. People knew that Napoleon was a Jacobin—a radical! He could just as easily have lost his head!"

"Don't tell me that you saved his life!" Lucien shouted angrily. "Are you going to tell the mob that Napoleon was a Jacobin?"

"I didn't say I saved his life!" replied Barras. "You know that I will never tell anyone that Napoleon was once a radical. And let me remind you of one more thing. His name was crossed off the list of

French generals in September 1795. I rescued him by giving him his big chance against the Parisian mob. I had faith in him. I knew that he could be trusted. His radical days were long past. Wasn't I the one who introduced him to Josephine? Would I have done that if I didn't really trust him?''

"Barras, someone would think that you were honest and could be trusted. I trust no one, not even you, where money and power are concerned!'' said Lucien Bonaparte.

"How can you talk that way to me?'' said Barras angrily. "I am as honest as any man in politics!''

"All right, Barras, let's say that you saved Napoleon. Let's stop arguing. You gave him his big chance in spite of a few mistakes he had made in his younger years. But many others also saw that he was going to be a great leader. Look what he did in Italy. He won brilliant victories in the north, while other French generals were losing to the Austrians.''

"Why stop there?'' continued Barras. "Remember how easily he beat the Austrians in 1797? We gained control of Belgium and the left bank of the Rhine. I could go on and on. He is a military genius! There's no doubt about it. He isn't afraid to try new battle plans. Men are happy to fight and die for him. He is a natural leader!''

"Good,'' said Lucien excitedly. "We agree. Napoleon will be first consul. You'll see. There will be no trouble.''

## The following day

"What's the problem, Lucien?'' asked Barras. "I thought that things were going well for us.''

"Not too well, Barras. At first, everything seemed almost too easy. The Council of Elders went along with the plan, and Napoleon was made commander of the soldiers of Paris. But now the Council of 500 looks doubtful.''

"I don't understand,'' said Barras. "You are the president of the Council. Keep control. Don't let them spoil our plan. Don't lose your nerve.''

"I'll do my best. Watch me,'' said Lucien Bonaparte.

Lucien took his seat in the council chamber.

"I recognize Napoleon Bonaparte. He has a few words to say to you."

Several deputies rose and began shouting: "Don't let him speak! He's a liar! He's a traitor! Down with the tyrant! Death to Napoleon Bonaparte! Throw him out of here! Throw him out of France! Kill the dictator! Outlaw him!"

Deputies rushed at Napoleon. He fainted. At Lucien's order, soldiers rushed in, surrounded Napoleon, and carried him out of the building. When Napoleon recovered, he spoke to the assembled soldiers. He was nervous and unable to control his emotions.

"Soldiers of France," said Napoleon, "our country is in great danger! We must protect France from the Jacobins. Otherwise, once again, death and destruction will tear apart our beloved France! I beg you, help me to save our nation. Together, we can make our France even greater—"

Napoleon's face was bleeding where he had nervously scratched it with his fingernails. Lucien Bonaparte rejoined Napoleon. He realized that his brother's speech was having no effect upon the soldiers. He then decided that he must speak to them.

"You know me. I am the president of the Council of 500. I am Lucien Bonaparte, Napoleon Bonaparte's brother. I tell you he is right. We need a new government, a government that can be trusted. I know that many of the deputies are plotting against us. They refuse to let us speak. They insist on running things in their own corrupt way. I ask you, soldiers of France, to protect us from those traitors! Clear them out of the hall! Give Napoleon a chance to lead you, to show you what he can do!"

Lucien pointed his sword at his brother. "I swear I will kill my own brother if he attacks the liberty of the French people!"

"A great speech, Lucien," said Barras. "You've done it! They're rushing into the council hall! They're throwing the deputies out! They are running from the bayonets! Look, some of them are jumping out the windows! We've won! We've won!"

"Yes," said Lucien, "we will have a new government for France. The Revolution is finished!"

"Perhaps," replied Barras, "the Revolution has just begun!"

*Postscript.* Barras resigned from the council to smooth the way for Napoleon's takeover of the government. Barras was never given another job by Napoleon.

## UNDERSTANDING THE STORY

**A.** *Tell which statements show that Napoleon was a great general.*

1. Napoleon fired artillery shells at a crowd of Royalists in 1795.
2. Napoleon drove the British from Toulon in 1793.
3. Napoleon had been a radical Jacobin.
4. Napoleon defeated the Austrians in 1797.
5. Napoleon was a great leader of soldiers.
6. Napoleon was a friend of the Robespierre family.
7. Napoleon knew what to do in difficult military situations.
8. Soldiers were happy to fight and die for Napoleon.

**B.** *Lucien Bonaparte and Paul Barras have many different ideas. Decide who might have made the following remarks. Write PB for each statement that Paul Barras made or might have made and LB for each statement that Lucien Bonaparte made or might have made.*

1. I asked Napoleon to come to Paris in 1795 to put down the rebellion.
2. Napoleon was a great 24-year-old brigadier-general.
3. Napoleon's job is to save France from the Jacobins.
4. He is a military genius.
5. I introduced Napoleon to Josephine.
6. I am as honest as any man in politics.
7. Our country is in great danger.
8. Give Napoleon a chance to lead the people.

**C.** Imagine that Paul Barras and Lucien Bonaparte are running for political office in the United States today. Which one would you vote for? Why? Which one has a better chance of winning? Why? Would you trust either of them? Explain.

## ACTIVITIES AND INQUIRIES

1. Use each of the following key terms in a sentence.

   Jacobin        first consul        tyrant
   radical        *coup d'état*       dictator
   royalist       traitor

2. Imagine that you are a member of the Council of 500 in 1799. You are against Napoleon's taking over as first consul. Prepare a short speech against Napoleon.
3. Prepare an answer in favor of Napoleon's being given the job.

# 6. Formula for Success

*After Napoleon became first consul* of France, he increased his control over the country, and he was very popular with the people. But he was not satisfied. In 1802 he asked for an election to allow him to remain first consul for life. He won by a vote of 3.5 million in favor to 8,000 against! He was now king in everything but name. Finally, in 1804, his dream came true. As the pope watched, Napoleon crowned himself emperor of France.

During these years he was very busy fighting wars against the major nations of Europe. In this chapter we visit with Napoleon immediately after the Battle of Austerlitz (OS-ter-litz). This was probably his greatest victory. Empress Josephine's congratulations were entirely justified.

Ask yourself why Napoleon seems upset about Josephine's remark about "work to be done at home." Why did Napoleon feel that his activities were really part of the Revolution? Was he really a revolutionist?

## Paris, December 1805

DEAR NAPOLEON,

The glorious news has come of your great victory over the Austrians and Russians at Austerlitz! How happy I am for you and for France! I can hardly believe that all this has happened exactly one year after you crowned yourself emperor of France. What a marvelous anniversary present! Congratulations.

Perhaps now you will have more time to spend with your lonely empress. France needs you too! There is so much work to be done at home. This is your chance to make France the best and freest country in Europe. Do you remember how you once said that you were a child of the Revolution? You have already made France the strongest country in Europe. Now you can turn to the other things.

We miss you terribly. Please come home very soon.

Much love,
JOSEPHINE

## Austerlitz, December 1805

DEAREST JOSEPHINE,

Thank you for your good wishes. You are very kind and thoughtful. It was indeed a great victory. As you say, it was quite an anniversary present!

Alexander of Russia and Francis of Austria helped quite a bit with their stupidity! They thought they had me cut off. Instead I led them into a beautiful trap. I cut off their armies completely! One moment they thought they had an easy victory over Napoleon. The next thing they knew they were completely crushed. My cleverness and battle plans are too much even for good generals. What could the Russians and Austrians expect? Their little "game" cost them over 20,000 soldiers!

So much for the battle. You say that France needs me, that there is so much work to be done. I agree. There always is. But I think, Josephine, that you miss the point. What was my first and most important goal? I had to remove the threat to France of our enemies on the outside. Surely you understand that France could never be safe while surrounded by powerful armies. Yes, we can breathe more easily now!

Now I can return to France to finish the work I have started. Somehow, I have the feeling that you do not realize how much I have already done. My purpose has been to build a France where the people can enjoy the good things the Revolution did. For example, the laws of France must be fair for all citizens. Do you remember what the laws were like when I became first consul in 1799? Laws were different in every part of the country. It was a terrible mess. I had the laws rewritten and reorganized. Now we have the Code Napoleon. There is one set of laws for all of France! The punishments for robbery are the same in Marseilles (mar-SAY) as they are in Paris.

Do you know that I myself wrote the laws dealing with marriage, divorce, and property? Lawyers could learn a lot from me. I suppose that I did not go as far as you would like. You, like every other wife, are still under the authority of your husband. But that is the way things should be! I do not think that the Revolution was fought to give women equal rights! I also do not feel that labor unions and strikes should be permitted. Wasn't the Revolution fought to protect private property?

Let's not overlook the schools. They were under the control of the Catholic Church. Now, with my changes, they are the business of the state. And you know who runs France these days! Education is very important to me. I want France to have bright, informed citizens. But, most of all, I want good soldiers who will be loyal to me. That is what I see as the purpose of French education.

Do you recall the money situation? The French people had lost faith in the money and credit of France. I fixed that. I set up a Bank of France. Only that bank can print money now. I reorganized the tax system. My agents do the collecting now. They are honest, and their collections come to my government in Paris. In fact, everything comes to and goes from my government in Paris. I must know everything that is going on all over France. I appoint all the mayors of cities and towns. And I choose the heads of all of the districts in France. That way they know that I am the emperor. I am in charge! I take the responsibility for everything that happens in government in all of France.

I am proud of the things I have done. Do you know of any other country that has a Legion of Honor? The revolutionists stopped giving medals and decorations. I (and you) know that people want to be honored for the good things they do. They want to be recognized; they want their friends and relatives to know. So I created the Legion of Honor. Would you believe that the men are thrilled to be members! They belong to the legion and to each other. Most of all, they belong to me—their emperor. They will always be loyal to me!

Josephine, my dear, I am sorry if I am boring you with these "great" things of mine. I will stop now. I promise you that I shall be home next month. I will tell you then more of my life on the field of battle. You will hear much more about my plans for the future of our beloved France. I shall tell you of my plan to control the continent of Europe. I want to do so much more for my people. But I must do it my way. I am the emperor!

I cannot wait to see you again.

> With love,
> NAPOLEON
> Emperor of France

## UNDERSTANDING THE STORY

A. *Which statements show that Napoleon had improved the living conditions of the French people?*

1. He crowned himself emperor of France.
2. He fought war after war with foreign enemies.
3. He had the laws of France rewritten so that they would be the same for all the people of France.
4. He permitted unions and strikes.
5. He made the tax system fairer.
6. He had the Code Napoleon written.
7. He favored equal rights for women.
8. He organized the Bank of France.

B. *Write T for each statement that is true, F for each statement that is false, and N for each statement that is not mentioned in the story.*

1. Napoleon was the greatest general in history.
2. Napoleon won many battles for France.
3. Napoleon always wanted to be president of France.
4. Napoleon himself wrote the laws on marriage and divorce.
5. The Code Napoleon is a better system of laws than the Constitution of the United States.
6. France would have had a new Reign of Terror if it had not been for Napoleon.
7. Napoleon was against people owning property.
8. Napoleon felt that the purpose of French education was to provide him with loyal soldiers.

C. If Napoleon were alive today, would you consider him a great man or a dangerous man? Why? American generals had a good deal of trouble fighting in Vietnam. Do you think that Napoleon could have helped them? Explain.

## ACTIVITIES AND INQUIRIES

1. Go to the library. Prepare a report on any one of Napoleon's great victories. Try to understand his plan of battle.
2. Imagine that you have the job of preparing a report card on Napoleon's accomplishments. Mark him pass or fail in the areas listed below. Write a sentence explaining the reasons for each grade.

equal rights for women
equal rights for rich
   and poor
fairness of taxes
rights of labor unions
private property rights
representative government
Legion of Honor

money and banking
education
organization of French laws
government leadership
military skills
organization of local
   government

3. Imagine that you are Josephine. Answer Napoleon's letter to you.
4. Pretend that you are a soldier in Napoleon's army. You fought at Austerlitz and other important battles. Write a letter to your family in France. Tell them what it is like to be a soldier in Napoleon's army.
5. Look at the map of Napoleon's empire on page 149. Copy the map in your notebook. Now look at the map of present-day Europe on page 424. List five modern countries that once were part of Napoleon's empire.

# 7. "General Winter" Beats Napoleon

*After the Battle of Austerlitz, Napoleon* continued to beat his enemies. The French empire grew. By 1810 the empire extended from the North Sea to the Bay of Naples and eastward to the Adriatic. His brother Joseph was king of Spain, brother Jerome was king of Westphalia (Germany), and brother-in-law Murat was king of Naples (Italy). Only Britain remained unbeaten.

Napoleon thought that he had a clever idea to defeat the English. He would not allow their goods to enter any port on the continent of Europe. This was called the *Continental System.* Naturally the British made some rules of their own. They insisted that no *neutral ship* (a ship from a nation *not* at war) could enter a European port unless it stopped first at a British port. Before long, European countries were losing trade and business. On the other side of the world, the Americans were caught between the rules of the English and the rules of the French. By 1812 the United States would be drawn into a war with England. Three thousand miles of ocean could not protect our country from Napoleon's dream of world empire!

Most countries found Napoleon's Continental System too hard to follow. They closed their eyes to the smuggling and the chances of losing their ships. Napoleon was disturbed and angry, but Russia's complete disregard for his system enraged him. After all, Czar (ZAR) Alexander I was supposed to be his *ally* (friend)! Napoleon decided to teach the czar a lesson. He would invade Russia with a large army and crush the Russian forces. In June 1812 Napoleon crossed the Russian border. He hoped for a quick victory, but the Russians had other ideas.

In this chapter see how Napoleon's dreams of empire

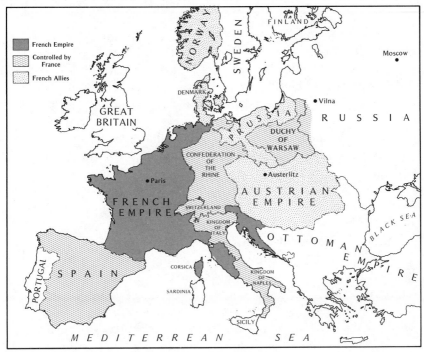

*The French Empire in 1810*

were smashed by Russia's plans and the freezing weather.
Two French officers on the battlefront near the city of Vilna
(VILL-na) tell what they think went wrong.

Ask yourself why Napoleon wanted to invade Russia.
Was the Russian invasion a mistake? Would the empire of
Napoleon have lasted if Napoleon had not insisted on in-
vading Russia?

# Vilna, December 1812

"Stop!" shouted the French soldier on guard duty. "Who goes
there?"

"Captain Menton, Ninth Dragoons."

"Give the password," said the guard.

"I don't know the password," said Menton, shivering. "I've

lost my men. I've lost everything. If you don't believe me, shoot me. I have nothing to live for."

At that moment Captain Darcy rode up. "It's all right, corporal. I know this man. I will be responsible for him." The two men recognized each other immediately. Darcy led Menton to a small tent. It was little shelter from the below-zero cold and high winds.

"Am I glad to see you again!" said Menton, still shaking. "How long has it been?"

"It seems a hundred years ago," replied Darcy. "Actually, it's been five years since I last saw you. It was at the Battle of Friedland."

"Those were glorious days," said Menton, now warming up a bit. "How happy we were! Napoleon took us from one victory to another. I honestly had a strange feeling that we could never lose as long as Napoleon was our emperor!"

"How little do we know what is going to happen to us," said Darcy thoughtfully. "Who would have thought that Napoleon and the great armies of France could be crushed by the Russians?"

"Not crushed by the Russians, Darcy. We were beaten by 'General Winter.' Napoleon had never fought under these conditions. How could he have known what the weather would be like? All I can remember are my men freezing to death. Every morning, at dawn, I'd see a dozen men I thought were still asleep. I'd try to wake them up. But their bodies were frozen stiff. They were dead! But it wasn't Napoleon's fault!"

"Not his fault?" said Darcy angrily. "You forget that Napoleon is the great leader, the great planner. He is supposed to know everything about war. He must be prepared for every possibility. He should have known about the weather. Surely he could have learned the facts about the Russian winter!"

"That may be true," replied Menton with some hesitation. "But he could not have known that the Russians would not fight battles. How could he have predicted that they would retreat and retreat into this huge country? At last we fight a battle at Borodino. We win, and—"

"We lose," finished Darcy. "Napoleon doesn't cut off the Russian retreat. The rest of their army gets away. We had lost 150,000 men to 'General Winter'. Perhaps we lost fewer men than the

Russians in the fighting, but how could our dead and wounded be replaced?''

"What a great speech Napoleon made to us at Borodino," continued Menton, as though he were alone. "I can still hear him saying, 'Soldiers, here is the battle you wanted. Victory depends on you. We need one victory—'''

"To make up for all my past mistakes," finished Darcy once again. "I will say it once again. Napoleon did not prepare for this Russian war. He should have realized that the Russians might retreat. He should have planned for feeding and supplying an army that could not live off the land. He should have had enough soldiers to replace the sick and wounded. If he could not do these things—and I say that he could not—he should never have come to Russia. A great leader must know that there are certain things he cannot do. Napoleon thought that nothing was impossible for him."

"I suppose that you are going to blame him for the Moscow fire," said Menton.

"Menton, what difference does it make? It's a terrible mistake that we are here. It is not my fault, and it is not yours. Yes, it was our leader's responsibility to care for his men. He didn't do it because he couldn't. The fire is just the worst example of his weaknesses! Fire is a weapon of war."

"We came to Russia for the greater glory of Napoleon and France," muttered Menton. "The Russians starved us, froze us, and burned us out of the shelter of Moscow!"

"There's not much glory in our starving and freezing to death, Menton. I wonder how many of us are left? Where are they all now? Dead—and for what? Did we have to be used to feed Napoleon's dream? Did he have to try to conquer the world? Didn't we have enough?"

"Ah, but what a dream," said Menton. "All of Europe would have been Napoleon's. Europe would have belonged to France—to us! The world could have been ours!"

"Be thankful that you are still alive," answered Darcy thoughtfully. "Empires, like dreams, fade away—and die."

# UNDERSTANDING THE STORY

**A.** *Tell which item in each sentence makes each statement correct.*

1. By 1810, the French empire extended from the North Sea to (*a*) Naples and on to the Adriatic Sea (*b*) Finland and Poland (*c*) Sweden and England.
2. To defeat the English, Napoleon tried (*a*) the Continental System (*b*) an invasion of Russia (*c*) an invasion of England.
3. A country that was drawn into the fight between England and France was (*a*) Mexico (*b*) the United States (*c*) Canada.
4. In 1812 Napoleon and his army invaded (*a*) England (*b*) Austria (*c*) Russia.
5. In Russia, Napoleon and his army were beaten by (*a*) rain and fog (*b*) "General Winter" (*c*) bad supplies from France.
6. The Russians used fire as a weapon of war when they burned (*a*) Moscow (*b*) Leningrad (*c*) Kiev.
7. Napoleon's dream was to (*a*) conquer Europe (*b*) become president of the United States (*c*) put the son of Louis XVI on the throne of France.
8. The person in the story who thinks highly of Napoleon is (*a*) the corporal (*b*) Menton (*c*) Darcy.

**B.** *Tell which statements Captain Darcy would agree with.*

1. Napoleon and his armies were crushed by the Russians.
2. The French were beaten by "General Winter."
3. Napoleon should have known what to expect in Russia.
4. Napoleon could not have known that the Russians might retreat.
5. We came to Russia for the glory of Napoleon and of France.
6. It's a mistake that we are in Russia.
7. Did Napoleon have to try to conquer the world?

**C.** General William Sherman, a famous American Civil War soldier, said, "War is hell!" Would Napoleon have agreed with him? Explain. If war is "hell," why do we continue to fight wars?

## ACTIVITIES AND INQUIRIES

1.  Pretend that you are Captain Darcy. Write a letter to your family in France. Tell how you feel about Napoleon.
2.  Imagine that you are Captain Menton. Write a letter to your family in France. What would you tell them about Napoleon?
3.  Hitler invaded Russia in 1941, many years after Napoleon. Write down the lessons that Hitler should have learned from Napoleon's invasion of Russia.
4.  Why are two French officers talking about Moscow? How does the cartoon explain why the French lost in Russia? The two officers are making a sad joke. What do they really mean?

*"At least it was warm in Moscow!"*

"Now that's what I call a revolution!" said Jack excitedly.

"What do you mean?" asked Mr. Miller.

"They chopped off the heads of Louis XVI and Marie Antoinette," replied Jack. "The French didn't fool around! People fought and died; blood flowed in the streets!"

"Is that what makes a revolution?" asked Mr. Miller.

"Well, it's one part of it," smiled Jack.

"Was that all that happened?" continued Mr. Miller.

"Oh, I know what you want me to say. You want me to say that there was a big change in France."

"And what was that change?"

"In the old days, France was ruled by kings like Louis XIV. He was an absolute ruler. He ran the whole show, and he ran it his way!"

"How did the French people feel about their kings?" asked Mr. Miller slowly.

"I guess you would say that the French people were unhappy," replied Jack. "Somebody had to pay for the spending of the kings. Why not put it all on the poor French peasants? They made the peasants pay all those unfair, stupid taxes. The nobles pushed the peasants around. The people were fed up with kings like Louis XVI. They wanted a government of their own."

"Were the people right?" asked Mr. Miller.

"You know they were right," said Jack. "Isn't that what democracy is all about? That's why Louis XVI and a lot of other people lost their heads. Remember when Rousseau said that everyone should have 'liberty, equality, and fraternity'? I think he said it best."

"And where was Voltaire in all this?" added Mr. Miller.

"Well, I guess he was right in there too. He wanted everyone to have a fair chance. He was against privilege. He hated prejudice."

"Then was the Revolution a success?" asked Mr. Miller.

"That's not easy to say," Jack replied. "It went on for a long time. There were lots of good changes. The unfair taxes and the special privileges of the nobles were wiped out. The French people even had their own Declaration of Independence. They called it the Declaration of the Rights of Man. But I think that they just didn't know where to stop. Things got bloodier and bloodier."

154

"Sounds dangerous," said Mr. Miller.

"I guess that's what makes some revolutions so exciting," said Jack. "Marat, Danton, Robespierre—all were working for a better France. But it was their idea of what would be good for France. I admit they had plenty to worry about. There were foreign enemies. And the nobles couldn't wait until they got their lands back. Robespierre and his crew trusted no one—not even themselves."

"It's easy to think you have a lot of enemies when you have so few friends," said Mr. Miller thoughtfully.

"Sure, Mr. Miller, but France had to have somebody who could be trusted. The people got tired of all the killing. That's when Napoleon was called in."

"Did he stop the violence?" asked Mr. Miller.

"I suppose that the French would say 'yes,'" answered Jack.

"And what would you say, Jack?"

"He stopped the fighting in France, but then the rest of the world was at war," said Jack very seriously. "He crushed the Jacobins at home, but he took on just about all the other countries of Europe."

"How could he do that?" asked Mr. Miller.

"He didn't ask people if they wanted to be freed," answered Jack. "He just decided to fight and conquer the rest of Europe. And, you know, Mr. Miller—he almost made it!"

"What happened, Jack?"

"Napoleon was a great general, Mr. Miller. I'm not sure, but maybe he was the best ever. But he made one mistake. He went too far out of France and tried to conquer Russia. Those Russians were just too much for him. They wouldn't fight his kind of battle. He couldn't beat 'General Winter.' Napoleon wasn't exactly a pushover after that, but he was a loser."

"Well, Jack, what does it all mean?" said Mr. Miller with a smile.

"Revolutions can be rough," answered Jack slowly. "A lot of people can get hurt. I think you just have to know where to stop. Napoleon tried to go too far, to do too much. He forgot that people should be able to decide things for themselves."

"What happened to the people in the countries Napoleon conquered?" asked Mr. Miller.

"I'm not sure, Mr. Miller. I haven't read that yet. But I can guess that they wouldn't be happy ruled by a king who didn't care about them. Napoleon got them started thinking about themselves. They'd want to be free! People would want their own nations!"

"Excellent thinking, Jack!" said Mr. Miller approvingly. "Now you are ready to find out more about nations and nationalism. Let's see what the Congress of Vienna thought about nationalism. Then you can read the rest of the next unit."

# Nationalism

"Mr. Miller, the word 'nationalism' (NAH-shun-al-izm) puzzles me."

"What do you mean, Jack?"

"Well, 'nationalism' has the word 'nation' in it. And I think I know what a nation is."

"Good, so far—and what is a nation?"

"A group of people want to have their own government," answered Jack. "They want to live together."

"Why would they want to do that?" asked Mr. Miller.

"I suppose they feel that they have some of the same interests," said Jack thoughtfully. "Maybe they speak the same language or belong to the same church or religion. Of course, it's easier if they live near each other."

"Excellent, Jack," smiled Mr. Miller. "You've hit it this time. There are many reasons why people would want to live in their own nations. Then why did you say you were puzzled?"

"Okay, let's say the people who live in a certain place want their own nation," said Jack excitedly. "They want to be together. They feel they belong together. Why shouldn't they be free to do it? Why should anyone stand in their way?"

"Jack, read the unit on nationalism and find out!"

# 1. The Plot to Turn Back the Clock

*Napoleon had been defeated.* He was shipped off into exile on the island of Elba in the Mediterranean Sea. His enemies hoped that this would be the end of Napoleon. But somehow he escaped, and for a time known as the Hundred Days, he won battle after battle. His moment as the great conqueror had passed, however. The Battle of Waterloo was his final defeat. This time, he was sent far away to the island of Saint Helena in the South Atlantic Ocean. There he spent the rest of his days.

Now that Napoleon was gone, the scene shifted from the battlefield to the meeting room. Kings and ministers of the

Europe in 1815

major powers of Europe met in Vienna, Austria, from 1814 to 1815. They redrew the map of Europe. Their goal was to "turn back the clock" to the "happy days" before the French Revolution and Napoleon.

Let us see how they proposed to return to those "good old days." Here, we sit in on a meeting of Czar Alexander I of Russia, Prince Metternich (MET-er-nick) of Austria, Viscount Castlereagh (KAS-ul-ray) of Great Britain, and Talleyrand (TAL-ih-rand) of France. They are discussing the past and the future of Europe.

Ask yourself why they wanted to turn back the clock. Do you think that it was possible to turn back the clock? How did they try to prevent the rise of another Napoleon?

# Vienna, June 1815

CASTLEREAGH. There is one thing we can all agree on. Things have changed in Europe.

TALLEYRAND. Things, things—I'm not so sure I know what you mean. Aren't we back where we started before the Revolution? Haven't we turned back the clock to the good old days? Change has been wiped out!

CASTLEREAGH. Don't be a fool, Talleyrand. (*He raises his voice slightly.*) Things can never be the same. We can try, but the French Revolution and Napoleon will always be with us.

METTERNICH. Don't say that! Thank God, Napoleon is gone. We've shipped him off to Saint Helena. I could not sleep if he were as close as Elba. Put the man on a battlefield and you never know what might happen. He took boys and gave them guns. Somehow he won ten battles in twenty days! That man is dangerous!

TALLEYRAND. I still dream of his escaping and rallying the mobs around him once again. What a nightmare! Never again will a man rise from nowhere and become an emperor, as Napoleon did. Only those born to be kings may be kings!

(*Czar Alexander enters the room. He listens to Metternich.*)

METTERNICH. You are right for once, Talleyrand. It was clever of us to choose old Louis, the dead king's brother, to sit on the throne of France. There is no question about his being the legitimate ruler. It was a blessing that there was at least one real Bourbon left in France.

ALEXANDER. Not clever, Metternich—we were not clever at all. We are lucky that Louis happened to be available. The clever thing was to make it look as though the French people were calling Louis back to the throne. What fools they were! Now he is Louis XVIII. Stupidly, he thinks that he was made king of France by the grace of God!

METTERNICH. He looks like a fool and acts like a fool. But he is the king of France. And that's it! Revolutions are over! There will be no more changes in the governments of Europe. The common people will never rule our nations. They will never be given a chance to get control. We must keep the mob in its place! Legitimacy—inherited rank and privilege—is the answer! We must never forget that!

CASTLEREAGH. I repeat: You cannot turn back the clock! We can *try* to hold back the hands of the clock. We can *try* to prevent changes. But gentlemen, the world is not the same. It can never be!

METTERNICH *(angrily)*. Wrong again, Castlereagh! We are going to keep things exactly the way they are. We will insist upon it! Everything we have done here in Vienna has one goal: Keep things as they are. The present order will remain forever. We have made revolutions impossible!

TALLEYRAND *(places a map of Europe on the table)*. Look at this map of Europe. The countries of our continent are all locked in. There is simply no room for change. No new nations can ever rise. Notice how Italy has been broken up into many states; each is weak and helpless. And don't forget how cleverly we've divided Germany! There are now 38 weak states, and they're really controlled by Austria. No, there will never be a united Germany!

CASTLEREAGH. I wonder—are we really all that clever—Belgium ruled by Holland, Norway ruled by Sweden? Do you honestly think that all of this is going to last forever?

ALEXANDER *(in a commanding voice)*. Gentlemen, I have a simple suggestion that will make all of this last forever. We must protect our thrones through definite action. I hear too much talk about how things can never change. To prevent revolutions, I propose a Holy Alliance of the kings of Europe. Let the people try to revolt. We will crush them without a second thought! We must be sure of ourselves. We must work together. We must fight together to keep things from changing!

*(Talleyrand and Metternich seem pleased and excited by Alexander's suggestion. Castlereagh's expression does not change.)*

CASTLEREAGH. You once said that kings were put on their thrones because God wanted them there. Then why do you need an alliance?

METTERNICH. Castlereagh, you know better than that. God helps us, but he does not fight our wars. We must never permit the world to be ruled by men like Napoleon. This is the best of all possible worlds for us! Let us keep it that way! My government will support Czar Alexander's proposal for a Holy Alliance!

CASTLEREAGH. England cannot become part of your alliance. It is not to our advantage to support one side or the other.

ALEXANDER. Nonsense! Who suffers from change? We who have created legitimate governments are the ones who must pay. Look what happened to your own country, Great Britain, during your American Revolution! Those little colonies made the great British empire look almost idiotic! And have you forgotten what the Americans did during the last years of the wars with Napoleon? What did they call it?

CASTLEREAGH. The War of 1812. Your Highness, no one likes to lose. But we have to face the facts. The world changes no matter what we try to do. We cannot stop the movement of time. It is not in England's best interest.

METTERNICH. Tell me, Castlereagh, if your king lost his throne, what would you do? Would you whine and complain? Wouldn't the king of England be better off to have all the other kings to help him?

TALLEYRAND. Do you think that those who have once tasted freedom will forever be satisfied with rule by others? We must always be alert and prepared!

CASTLEREAGH *(for the first time his face reddens with anger).* Enough of this talk of freedom and revolution! Britain may help, but she will not be part of your plan! *(He quickly walks out of the room.)*

ALEXANDER. He simply does not understand. God's will is that the governments are not to be changed. We must protect our God-given rights! If we do not help each other, we are lost!

TALLEYRAND. I wonder—is it not too late? Can we keep the seeds of nationalism and freedom from growing forever?

## UNDERSTANDING THE STORY

A. *Write T for each statement that is true and F for each statement that is false.*

   1. Napoleon was exiled first to the island of Elba and later to the island of Saint Helena.
   2. Most of the leaders at the Congress of Vienna felt that everyone, rich or poor, should benefit from the French Revolution.
   3. Many of the leaders at the Congress of Vienna tried to turn back the clock.
   4. Metternich and Talleyrand worried about Napoleon returning to Europe.
   5. Metternich said that the common people should rule.
   6. Castlereagh said that the world would never be the same.
   7. "Europe must change" is a remark that Talleyrand might have made.
   8. The Holy Alliance was proposed by Czar Alexander.
   9. Castlereagh said that England would not join the Holy Alliance.

B. *Tell which statements show that the Congress of Vienna tried to control the future of Europe.*

   1. Only legitimate kings can rule.
   2. Never let Napoleon come back to Europe.
   3. We will have revolutions every year.
   4. We have made revolutions impossible.
   5. We have made Italy into one strong state.
   6. There will never be a Germany.
   7. Belgium will be ruled by Holland.
   8. Sweden will be ruled by Norway.
   9. The Holy Alliance will crush every revolt.

C. Imagine that Germany and England go to war. England is defeated. Germany now attacks several other countries and also defeats them. The United States then goes to war against Germany and wins. Should the United States use the ideas of the Congress of Vienna in dealing with Germany? Write a peace treaty between Germany and the United States. Use the ideas of the Congress of Vienna.

## ACTIVITIES AND INQUIRIES

1.  Look at the map of Europe after the Congress of Vienna on page 158. Copy the map in your notebook. Now look at the map of present-day Europe on page 424. Make a list of countries that were not free in 1815 but later became independent.
2.  Pretend that you are an American newspaper reporter at the Congress of Vienna in 1815. Interview Czar Alexander. Write a newspaper article telling why the czar feels he must have a Holy Alliance.
3.  Interview Castlereagh. Write an article on why he is against the Holy Alliance.
4.  Look at the cartoon below. Why are the hands of the clock being pushed backward? Do Metternich and Talleyrand really

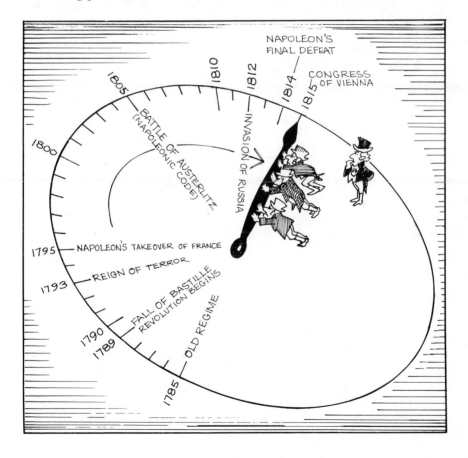

believe that they can go back to the days before the French
Revolution? Explain.

5. Use each of the following key terms in a sentence.

exile                    reactionary              Holy Alliance
reaction                 legitimacy               nationalism

6. Castlereagh stands alone several times in our story. He does
not agree with the other three men. Tell which statements
Alexander, Talleyrand, and Metternich would accept, but
Castlereagh would reject.

   *a.* We must have a Holy Alliance.
   *b.* We must turn back the clock.
   *c.* It is not in Britain's interest to join an alliance.
   *d.* The world can never be the same.
   *e.* There will be no more revolutions in Europe.

# 2. The Dream That Would Not Die

*We have seen how the seeds* of nationalism and revolution were planted by the French Revolution and Napoleon. The diplomats at the Congress of Vienna thought that they could uproot these ideas. They tried to turn back the clock, but they failed. They stopped progress for a few years, but that was all. The people of Europe were to have their own nations. They refused to be ruled by foreign kings. They insisted on the right of self-government. They remembered the words of the American Declaration of Independence and the French Declaration of the Rights of Man. Governments could not be forced upon people; they must be allowed to make their own choice.

The changes made by the Congress of Vienna were supposed to last forever. How wrong the diplomats were! Within a few years, nations that had been imprisoned within the boundaries of others were fighting for their freedom. Here is the roll of honor:

1821, Greece: Revolution failed, but independence from Turkey was granted in 1829.

1830, France: July revolution overthrew King Charles X. This led to rule of Louis Philippe, ''the bourgeois (bour-ZWAH) king.''

1830, Belgium: Gained independence from Holland.

1848, France: Louis Philippe *abdicated* (resigned) under pressure. Louis Napoleon elected first president of the Second French Republic.

1848, Austria and Hungary: Revolutions broke out in Hungary, Bohemia, and Vienna itself. (Metternich's home in Vienna was burned.)

The revolutions were crushed, but peasants were freed from feudal taxes.

*Italy in the 19th century, before unification*

Italians also were struggling for independence. An upris-
ing in Naples in the 1820s was crushed by Austria. In 1848
King Charles Albert of Sardinia attacked the Austrian armies.
Eventually he was badly beaten, and he abdicated as king.
Revolutionists led by Giuseppe Mazzini (mat-ZEE-nee) and
Giuseppe Garibaldi (gar-uh-BAL-dee) were successful at
first in Milan and Venetia, but were not strong enough to
keep control.

In this story, Garibaldi writes about his experiences and
feelings as he fought around Rome in 1849. Ask yourself

why Garibaldi and Mazzini felt so strongly about Italian nationalism. Why did they want to create an Italian nation? How did the views of Garibaldi and Mazzini differ on the subject of Italian nationalism?

# A ship off Sardinia, August 1849

DEAR MAZZINI,

My dear friend, what can I tell you at this point in our lives? How can I ever forget your words when you left Rome? You realized that all was lost, even though I insisted that I would stay a while and fight on. How right you were when you said, "I feel rage rising within me at the triumph of brute force over right and justice!" What else is there to say? What else is left to do but think of fighting still another day!

I am sure you heard that we were crushed and scattered by the soldiers of France. I never thought that Louis Napoleon would order his soldiers to fight against my Red Shirts in the streets of the Holy City. But Pope Pius IX called for help and Napoleon answered. He turned our fight to build an Italian nation into a holy war to protect the pope. He forgets that the pope is not merely the head of the Catholic Church. He is the ruler of the Papal States—of states that must belong to the Italian nation and people!

My Red Shirts fought bravely. Many gave their lives without complaint for the cause of the Italian nation! Was it a waste? I do not really know! We fought off the French soldiers for over two months. Finally, their numbers and training were just too much for us. I was lucky and escaped capture. But Anita, my beloved wife, is dead! The whole business was too much for her. She was completely exhausted. She could stand no more punishment. Perhaps she is better off, wherever she is!

Giuseppe, I swear by all that is holy to both of us that I will avenge her death! There is only one way. There is only one reason for my living now. I must free the people of Italy from their slavery. We Italians will have our own nation, our own rulers. Let's throw out the Austrians! The pope must give up the Papal States! We must do something about Louis Napoleon! It will be soon,

Giuseppe, soon! Do not be discouraged by our failure. I will win! I will win for Anita and the people of Italy!

I am sure that you agree that we must continue the fight. We cannot give up—we cannot stop now! I know that you are as dedicated as I to the cause of Italian freedom. But there is one thing I do not understand about your thinking. You keep saying that Italy must be free and independent. Then you go on to say that she must have a democratic government. Let the people rule, you say. Fine—but what if the people are not ready to govern themselves? What if the people know nothing about making their own laws at this time?

How many successful democracies do you see in Europe? What difference does it make what kind of government Italy has, as long as it is Italian? Charles Albert of Sardinia was a good king and a fair man. But he has been forced to abdicate.

Enough of Charles. Let's talk about his son, the new king, Victor Emmanuel. Will you agree to support him? Can't you see that we must have someone in a high office to whom we can turn? Victor Emmanuel can be the head of a united Italy! Encourage all Italians to rally to the flag and crown of Sardinia!

Giuseppe, back in the old days, you were the fighter, the conspirator! Nothing bothered you. You had one purpose in life: the creation of the nation of Italy. Remember your slogans—"Unity and independence"; "Liberty, equality, and humanity." Remember how you swore an oath to your brotherhood of Young Italy? Your life was to be given to the cause of Italian independence. Here's our chance, Giuseppe; let's gain our independence first! Liberty and equality will follow!

I know that you are discouraged. You have a right to be. But please, don't give up the fight now. Do you remember how you talked about remaking the map of Europe? It's not too late. You will still have your chance. Italy and Anita need you! Join with me once again in the fight to make Italy free!

I have no idea when we will meet again. But I pray that it will be on an Italian battlefield!

Italy will live again!

Your friend in freedom,
GIUSEPPE GARIBALDI

*Postscript.* Garibaldi did return to Italy. In 1860 he conquered the Kingdom of the Two Sicilies (the island of Sicily and the kingdom of Naples on the mainland). He could have become the ruler of the kingdom. Instead, he encouraged the people to vote to join Sardinia. In 1861 the Italian parliament named Victor Emmanuel king of Italy.

## UNDERSTANDING THE STORY

**A.** *Write T for each statement that is true and O for each statement that is an opinion.*

1. Garibaldi worked to create an Italian nation.
2. Garibaldi was the greatest Italian leader who ever lived.
3. The diplomats at the Congress of Vienna failed to turn back the clock.
4. Garibaldi's Red Shirts fought bravely in Rome.
5. Garibaldi should not have taken his wife along when he went to fight in Italy.
6. Mazzini wanted a democratic government.
7. A democratic government is better than any other kind.
8. Mazzini had a slogan, "Liberty, equality, and humanity."

**B.** *Complete each of the sentences below.*

1. The people of Europe insisted on the right of self-————.
2. The American Declaration of Independence is often compared with the French ————.
3. Garibaldi and Mazzini both felt strongly about Italian ————.
4. Garibaldi's Red Shirts were defeated by ————.
5. Mazzini said that Italy must be free and ————.
6. Garibaldi said that it made no difference what kind of government Italy had as long as it was ————.
7. King ———— was to be the head of a united ————.
8. Mazzini said that his life would be devoted to Italian ————.

**C.** Imagine that you are fighting for the independence of an African country today. Would you prefer your army to be led by a man like Garibaldi or a man like Mazzini? Why? Which man, Garibaldi or Mazzini, would be more successful as president of the new country? Why?

## ACTIVITIES AND INQUIRIES

1. Look at the map of Italy before unification on page 166. Draw this map in your notebook. Indicate on the map the territories mentioned in the introduction and the story.
2. Go to the library. Prepare a report on one of the following: Cavour, Victor Emmanuel, Young Italy, the Carbonari, the Red Shirts.
3. Imagine that you are Mazzini. Answer Garibaldi's letter to you. Tell him how you feel about the future of Italy.
4. Draw a cartoon showing Mazzini and Garibaldi working to turn a group of Italian states into an Italian nation. What is the title of your cartoon? Why are Mazzini and Garibaldi having such a hard time? What advice would you give Mazzini and Garibaldi to help them build the Italian nation?

# 3. Iron and Blood

*By 1870 Italy was a unified nation.* The dreams of Mazzini, Garibaldi, and many others had come true. The Germans had a similar dream. But there was a difference. There was not even a hint of democracy in the vision of Otto von Bismarck. This master planner of the German nation believed that the people should be ruled with an "iron hand." The state of Prussia would lead and the other German states would follow.

In this chapter we see that Prussia has just defeated

*Germany before and after unification in 1871*

France in the Franco-Prussian War (1871). The leaders of
the two countries, Louis Napoleon (Napoleon III) of France
and Prince Otto von Bismarck (BIZ-mark) of Prussia meet at
Sedan, France after the final battle.

Ask yourself why Bismark wanted Prussia to fight a war
against France. What difference do you see in the per-
sonalities of Napoleon III and Bismarck? Why was German
unification so important to Bismarck?

# Sedan, 1871

*(Louis Napoleon thinks to himself before meeting Bismarck on the
battlefield.)*
Where did I go wrong? What a fool I was to let myself be
dragged into war with Prussia! That Bismarck! He had only one
thing on his mind: Prussia must win. Prussia must be all-powerful,
no matter what the cost! I didn't understand what he meant by
"iron and blood," but, alas, now I do. Nothing must stand in his
way. Bismarck will stop at nothing. War and death are his tools.
Whoever gets in his way is crushed!

I felt that he was pushing France into war, but how could I do
anything about it? Was I supposed to look like a coward? Could I be
a weakling? I should have known that his Ems Dispatch was a trick
to force me to declare war against Prussia. The scoundrel cleverly
changed the words of the telegram. We French thought that our
ambassador had been insulted by the king of Prussia. At the very
same time, the Prussians thought that the French had insulted
their king! How could Bismarck fail to create a war?

It's all so clear now. We were used. The war against France
brought all the German states rushing to Prussia's side. German
honor must be upheld—but why at my expense? Now I see that
Bismarck used me to bring all the German states together!

Now it's done and I'm the loser. How could I have been so
stupid? My dreams of greatness are all down the drain! Where did I
get the idea that I could build a great French empire? Why did I
have to try to copy my uncle, Napoleon I? I was a Napoleon—how
could I fail? I would show the world what a Napoleon, an emperor,
could do! The people of France would believe in me. They would

follow me wherever I led them! I was the great man. Failure was impossible. Today, France; tomorrow, the world!

Why can't I be a great general as my uncle Napoleon Bonaparte was? Why can't I stand the sights and smells of the battlefield? Why am I bothered by blood and death? I am a weakling!

I could have been the greatest leader of this century. I knew all the mistakes my uncle made. I was going to avoid them. I made up my mind never to fight all the strong countries of Europe, as he did. I would pick a weak country here, a soft one there. It worked for a while. I built up France's empire in West Africa, Asia, and the South Pacific. I was doing well. It was all so easy.

I admit that it was a mistake to push my nephew Maximilian into Mexico. I didn't think the United States would get so angry about his being there. What business was it of theirs?

There were other glorious days. I remember when I was chairman of the 1856 conference ending the Crimean (cry-ME-un) War. We made those Russians squirm! What a moment of greatness! France was once again the leader of all Europe!

But after that things went downhill. I have a peculiar feeling that I might have been better off if that Italian assassin's bullet had killed me in 1856! I would not have become involved in war with Austria. Imagine *me* fighting on the side of little Sardinia! Then I was worried about Prussia fighting on the other side against France. I got out of that war fast! Oh, that devil Bismarck! And that was 12 years ago. But we couldn't avoid fighting each other forever, could we, Bismarck?

Here he comes now! How stuffy and coarse he looks! Look at that ridiculous uniform! I must pull myself together. I must not let him see that I am bitter and unhappy. I am a loser, a dreamer of broken dreams. But I must act the part of the emperor of France. I will give him nothing! He will have to kill me first!

*(Bismarck thinks to himself before he meets Louis Napoleon.)*
This has to be the greatest day of my life! Louis Napoleon and France have been crushed by my Prussian war machine. I have the backing of every German state. Now nothing stands in the way of the unification of Germany. It has taken me many years, but Germany will be a nation at last. The king of Prussia will be the king of all Germany. And I did it!

To be more honest, I did it with the help of Louis Napoleon.

He's a fool trying to act like an emperor. Did he really think that he was a great man and a great leader? Did he imagine that he could defeat Bismarck and Prussia on the battlefield?

Yes, Germany owes Louis Napoleon a great deal. His greed and dreams of empire made him a pushover for me. I changed the Ems telegram to make it read as though the Prussian king, William, had snubbed the French ambassador. I knew that Louis Napoleon would have to uphold the honor of France. I knew that he couldn't allow himself time to think. After all, an emperor worthy of the name Napoleon would bother to check the facts.

A weakling is sensitive about his honor. A fool is easily insulted. Louis Napoleon was very touchy and willing to fight. Perhaps he was afraid that people would find out the truth about him. Well, it's too late for you now, Louis Napoleon. They know what you are—a boastful, hollow shell. Yes, I pushed him into war; yes, I used him. But I had to do it for the greater glory of a united Germany.

It was a bloody war. We lost many men, but it was worth it! General von Moltke did a great job of leading our army. His organization and planning were excellent. Louis Napoleon's battle plans were out of date. He was finished before he started!

This is the end of the trip. The goal, a German nation, is in sight. It has taken me a long time to get to this point. Iron and blood, iron and blood—that was the way to do it! Nothing could stop me!

Yes, Louis Napoleon, I've crushed you. Now, I'm going to make you pay! You must suffer. I'll teach you that no Frenchman can stand up to a Prussian.

Here he comes now. Look at him in his fancy uniform with all those medals. Look at that mustache! He must spend hours in front of a mirror! Yes, he's a fool all right—a clumsy fool! Why doesn't he look at me? His eyes are blank. He's staring at the sky.

"Ah, Prince Bismarck," said Napoleon III, "you have never looked better. This situation is a little unpleasant, but I am very happy to see you."

"Your excellency," answered Bismarck, "it is a pleasure to see you. I have looked forward to this meeting for a long time!"

## UNDERSTANDING THE STORY

**A.** *Tell which statements are true.*

1. Bismarck was a strong believer in democracy.
2. Prussia defeated France in the Franco-Prussian War.
3. Bismarck played a great part in the unification of Germany.
4. Louis Napoleon believed in "iron and blood."
5. Louis Napoleon had dreams of a great French empire.
6. Bismarck used the Ems Dispatch to push France into war.
7. General von Moltke led the French army.
8. Louis Napoleon was not a great general like his uncle, Napoleon I.


**B.** *Louis Napoleon and Bismarck had different ideas about many things. Decide who made or might have made the remarks that follow. Write LN for each statement that Louis Napoleon made or might have made and B for each statement that Bismarck made or might have made.*

1. I could have been the greatest leader of the century.
2. Iron and blood are what I used to win.
3. He is a fool trying to act like an emperor.
4. I know that I'm the loser. How could I have been so stupid?
5. Why couldn't I be a great general?
6. I pushed him into war.
7. It was a bloody war, but it was worth it.
8. I built up our empire in Africa and Indochina.


**C.** Imagine that the Soviet Union is looking for a new leader. Would the Soviet Union want a man like Bismarck or a man like Louis Napoleon in the job? Explain. Would the United States pick either man? Explain.


## ACTIVITIES AND INQUIRIES

1. Look at the map of Germany before and after unification on page 171. Draw a map of Germany before unification. Then draw a map of Germany after unification. Make a list of the differences in the two maps.
2. Imagine that you are Bismarck. Write a letter to the king of

Prussia. Tell him about your victory at Sedan. What does this
mean to German unification? What does this mean to the king
of Prussia?

3.  Pretend that you are the king of Prussia. Write an answer to
    Bismarck's letter.

4.  Imagine that you are a reporter at the battle of Sedan in 1870.
    Your job is to interview Louis Napoleon and write an article for
    your newspaper. Write the article.

"Did those men at the Congress of Vienna think that they could stop the clock?" asked Jack. "Did they really think they could stop people from being free?"

"What do you think, Jack?" asked Mr. Miller.

"I think they were serious. Metternich and Talleyrand, Czar Alexander and Castlereagh wanted the world to go back to the days before the French Revolution. They wanted the kings to run the show. Down with people's rights! Who cares about people?"

"How could they go back to the days before the French Revolution?" asked Mr. Miller.

"They shouldn't have done it, but there was no one to stop them. Metternich and the others thought they had the answers. They pushed back the boundaries whichever way they wanted. They had Holland running Belgium. Norway lost its freedom to Sweden. They even put another King Louis back on the throne of France!"

"Was that so terrible?" asked Mr. Miller.

"It doesn't sound like much to us a hundred years later and thousands of miles away in the United States," said Jack. "But the people of Europe had to have felt terrible. They had rights. They had feelings. They wanted to be free. They wanted their own nations. Talleyrand and Metternich and the czar wouldn't let them. And then, they even formed a Holy Alliance to stop any revolutions!"

"You're right, Jack."

"Look what they did to Germany and Italy—chopped them up into small states," added Jack. "I guess they figured the states would never get together to be nations."

"How did Italy and Germany become nations?" asked Mr. Miller.

"It was a long, tough fight," answered Jack very seriously. "Look at Italy. Mazzini and Garibaldi worked hard to push out the Austrians. The pope had to give up most of his lands."

"What happened in Germany?" asked Mr. Miller.

"Bismarck did most of the work," answered Jack. "'Iron and blood.' Austria and France never had a chance to stop Bismarck and Prussia!"

"Very good, Jack, but where is the freedom you were talking about? Bismarck was certainly no democrat!"

"Well, I admit that I was a little mixed up, Mr. Miller. Now I can see that freedom means a lot of things to a lot of people. Nationalism is a kind of freedom, isn't it? You have your own nation. You are free. You are on your own, like the people of the United States!"

"True, Jack, but aren't there other freedoms?"

"Sure. Let's look at our own country. I live in a democracy. I'm a person and I have a lot of rights and freedoms. I can try to be as good as anyone else. Isn't that what freedom and equality are all about?"

"Right, Jack. We had our own American Revolution. We won our freedom from England. And we also have our Constitution and Bill of Rights. But did you know that a good part of the way we live comes from another revolution?"

"Not another revolution, Mr. Miller!"

"Yes, Jack, the Industrial Revolution. Why not read the following unit to find out what I mean?"

# The Industrial Revolution

"Tell the truth, Mr. Miller, haven't we had enough revolutions?"

"Believe me, this is an entirely different kind of revolution."

"Sure, everything is always different," laughed Jack.

"I know how you feel," said Mr. Miller. "Do you remember what we said about revolutions?"

"I guess so. Revolution means a big change."

"For example?" asked Mr. Miller.

"Well, it could be a change in government. There were big changes in the English and French governments," said Jack.

"Do you remember the Commercial Revolution?" asked Mr. Miller.

"Sure, Mr. Miller, but it wasn't as exciting as other revolutions. People learned that the earth was round. Explorers found new continents. A new world was open for living and trading."

"And that's not exciting?" laughed Mr. Miller.

"Oh, I know lots of things were going on. Maybe I missed it because there wasn't any fighting," added Jack. "I didn't mean that it wasn't important. Now I see. There are all kinds of revolutions."

"I think you're beginning to see that wars don't always make revolutions," said Mr. Miller. "Great changes in how people live and work and think are revolutions too."

"Right, Mr. Miller. Didn't the Renaissance change the way people thought about themselves? Bring on the Industrial Revolution! Where do we start?"

"Let's start with England."

# 1. The Steam Engine

*We saw how the English* and French revolutions changed people's views about government. People were not willing to be ruled by kings who were born to power. They began to believe in themselves. They felt that they should select their own rulers. But these new rulers would stay in power only as long as the people wanted them. And life would be freer for all people. Each person was as good as any other.

In the 18th century another revolution got underway. It too made great changes in the way people worked and lived. The *Industrial Revolution,* which began in England, spread to many other countries. Today it is still spreading and changing. It is not a revolution of battles or wars, of land or nations. It is a revolution of how and where things or goods are made.

At the beginning of the 18th century, England was a nation of farmers. Only one person out of every four lived in cities. Products such as cloth were made in the farmers' cottages. The entire family took part in manufacturing. The wife and children combed and spun the wool or cotton. The husband did the weaving. (The spinning wheel and hand loom had been used for centuries.) This work-at-home production was called the *domestic system.*

By the end of the 18th century, however, farm families were no longer spinning and weaving in their homes. Cloth was made in factories by machines. But there still was a problem: where to find the power to run the machines. The answer was found in James Watt's steam engine.

In this story James Watt writes a letter to a person who does not understand what steam power can do. Ask yourself whether Watt had good reason for being angry. Was the Industrial Revolution possible without the steam engine?

# Birmingham, 1780

DEAR GEORGE,

I have heard that you are telling people that England could have existed without James Watt. "What did he do? He was no inventor. He built a steam engine, but anybody can build a steam engine. What was wrong with Newcomen's steam engine? It puffed; it had lots of power. All Watt did was copy Newcomen."

George, let's be honest. I never said that I alone invented the steam engine. You know as well as I do that the ancient Greeks made a steam engine. But it was a toy; it could not make a machine run. Yes, Tom Newcomen made an engine many years before I did—and, by God, it worked! But all it could do was pump water out of the mines. That's where I did my part. I took Tom's engine and made change after change! No matter what you think, it wasn't easy. I worked on the steam engine until it had the power to drive the machines in the factories. I used coal to power the steam engine. And you know how rich England is in coal! We have enough coal to power millions of machines.

What did I do for England, George? I made it possible to use steam. I gave factories the power they needed to make cloth and iron and steel. Yes, I made it easier and cheaper to run the coal and copper mines.

Do you remember what it was like when factories used the rushing waters of a river or a pond to drive the machines? What did you do when there wasn't enough water? What happened when there was no rain? Did you bring your own buckets of water when the wheels would not turn?

Perhaps you would like to go back to the old days. Hitch up your horses and let them turn the power wheel. Find out what it means to depend on horses. How much cloth do you think the machines run with horsepower can produce?

You simply do not understand that steam is always there. You never have to worry whether there is enough water. You don't have to build your factory near water. My steam engine never gets tired, as your horses do. It never gets hungry. Do you know that my engine has the power of 20 horses? In fact, I have even made a few engines with the power of 80 horses! Imagine having 80 horses indoors for each of my engines! Can you see what this means?

James Watt's steam works, Birmingham, England

My engine never sleeps. It makes those factory wheels turn faster and faster. Each turn of the wheel means more goods and cheaper goods! That means money for the factory owners. It means lower prices for the buyers. It means more money for all of us. England's wealth is greatly increased. And don't forget the jobs the engine creates for all the workers in the new factories!

Yes, George, England could have lived without a James Watt. But could we have had an Industrial Revolution without my steam engine?

Some day, you'll see. They will call my steam engine the greatest invention of all time.

Your friend,
JAMES WATT

## UNDERSTANDING THE STORY

**A.** *Write T for each statement that is true and O for each statement that is an opinion.*

1. James Watt was the greatest inventor of all time.
2. The Industrial Revolution is still spreading and changing.

3. The Industrial Revolution is a revolution of how and where things are made.
4. Products made in factories are much better than those made in people's homes.
5. At the beginning of the 18th century in England, the entire family took part in making goods.
6. Watt's steam engine used coal.
7. Watt's steam engine helped increase the production of clothing, iron, and steel.
8. Steam power is the best kind of power.

B. *Which statements show how the Industrial Revolution changed the lives of the English people?*
1. Most cloth was now made in factories.
2. The spinning wheel and hand loom were widely used.
3. Steam power rather than water power turned England's machines.
4. Horses turned the power wheels in England's new factories.
5. Factory owners made higher profits.
6. Prices of factory-made goods were always higher than prices of home-made goods.
7. There were many new jobs for workers in the factories.

C. Imagine that James Watt did not develop the steam engine. Neither did anyone else. Imagine too that the Industrial Revolution never took place. Write a short paragraph telling how different your life would be if there had never been an Industrial Revolution. List some of the items you use every day that were made possible by the Industrial Revolution.

## ACTIVITIES AND INQUIRIES

1. What does the illustration on the facing page tell you about the steam engine? How could one steam engine be more powerful than 20 horses?
2. Go to the library. Prepare a report on another inventor whose machine helped make the Industrial Revolution. Among those you might choose from are John Kay, Richard Arkwright, Samuel Crompton, Edmund Cartwright, Eli Whitney, and James Hargreaves.
3. Make drawings of one or more of these inventions. Be prepared to explain how the invention works.

# 2. Farm or Factory?

*As you have seen, before* the Industrial Revolution, people made goods by hand at home. This was called the domestic system. Then the scene shifted to factories with machines. Farm people flocked to the factories in the towns and cities. No special skills were necessary to work in those factories. The workers repeated the same operations over and over, thousands of times each day. The machines did the thinking and planning for them.

Factory workers in cities often lived in filthy rooms in overcrowded slums. They worked in dark, airless factory rooms where they were in constant danger from the unguarded machinery. They worked as long as there was light. Often they could barely see what they were doing. The pay was low, but it was more than they could earn on the farm. Many of the workers in these factories (and even in the mines) were women and children.

In this story a young girl of 14 returns to her family home on an English farm. Ask yourself whether she should stay on the farm. Did she make the right decision? What would her life have been like if she had stayed on the farm?

## Harrowgate, 1842

"Susan, welcome back from Manchester," said Joyce. "It's great to see you again. Are you going to stay home with us for a few months?"

"I'm glad to see you, too," said Susan. "It's been such a long time since I left home. No, I'm just visiting for a short time. I am not going to stay here."

"Why not?" asked Joyce. "You look terrible. You're as skinny as a stick. Your clothes hang on you as though you're a scarecrow!"

"Stop it, Joyce," said Susan angrily. "You don't look so great yourself, but you don't hear me talking about how ugly you are. I've been sick for the past few weeks. How do you expect me to look?"

"Please don't be angry, Susan. I just want you to be well and look healthy. Stay with us for a few weeks, and you'll be yourself again."

"I am myself. This is the real me," answered Susan quickly. "I have no intention of staying for more than a few weeks. I never want to feel the way I felt when I lived here on the farm. My mind was a blank. My life was empty. I was so lonely and sad! All that I had to look forward to were the endless days and nights on the farm. There were chores to be done from before sunrise to after sunset. Chores and more chores every day—365 days a year. There was no end to my work. And I was so bored!"

"It may be lonely here," said Joyce quietly. "Yes, you may do the same things all during the year on the farm. But the farm isn't at all like a factory. You don't repeat the same movements minute after minute, hour after hour, day after day. Talk about being bored!"

"Joyce, you just don't understand," said Susan. "The thing that's so great about factory work is that it is not boring for me. I like it!"

"We have different ideas about boredom," laughed Joyce. "Let's forget about being bored, if we can. Look around you. It's clean here. The air is sweet and pure. The blue sky is up there to see—not just to dream about. It's not blotted out by the smoke from hundreds of factory chimneys. The water is good. There are no epidemics here in the country. You may not make any money, but I guarantee you that you will live twice as long!"

"Joyce, you will die of boredom on the farm. The city may not be clean, but it has life. There are lights, good times, excitement. There are people—real people. We can talk, go out, have fun. I'm alive in the city, Joyce. I'm dead here!"

"Look at you, Susan. You tell me that you're having a good time! I feel sorry for you. You look as though you're just this side of the grave. Face it. That factory work is killing you! How many hours do you work a week: 72, 84, 104? When do you have time for all that fun you talk about? You have less time off than you had on the farm. Do you think we don't know what goes on in those factories? Do you think we don't know what happens to girls who work in the cities?"

"Stop preaching at me!" interrupted Susan.

"No, I won't," continued Joyce. "Do they let you work at your own pace? Do they beat you if you slow down? Is there light and air? Whose fault is it if you get hurt on those dangerous machines? Don't you try to tell me that there's excitement and pleasure in working in a filthy room—100 girls squeezed into a space where 15 would be a crowd! What happens when you try to talk to another girl? And suppose they did let you talk. Could you hear anyone over the clatter of the machines?"

"Wait a minute," interrupted Joyce. "Don't let your feelings about cities and factories run away with you. I never said that the factory was paradise. Sure it's hard work, and there are dangers. But we work only 60 hours a week. Life in the factory is much easier now. They hardly ever beat us. There's more light in the factory than you think. Anyway, we usually stop work when the sun goes down. Yes, some girls do get hurt, but don't accidents happen on the farm? I'll never get hurt if I am careful. Girls get hurt because they get careless. They forget to keep their eyes on the sharp blades and the rough edges. You have to be alert every second. And, don't forget, I get two free meals a day!"

"What do they give you to eat?" snorted Joyce. "Garbage, that's what—and not too much of that! How much time do you get to eat: 15 minutes? Every extra minute spent eating means less cloth made by your beautiful factory. The bosses aren't going to lose profits so that you can eat your food in peace and quiet. Free meals? You know as well as I do that those meals come out of your pay. If they don't, they come out of your hide!"

"You still miss the point," continued Susan, refusing to give in. "Things are getting better every day. Besides, I'm away from home. I can earn money and I can save some. I'm on my own. A woman with money finds it easier to get a husband. You should know that!"

"No, Susan, I don't know! What are you earning? Is it one penny or two pennies an hour? How much can you save from all of that? You are living in a world of make-believe. You'll never have any money. You get a husband? What will you look like in a few years? What man will have you with or without money?"

"Let's not talk about good looks," said Susan angrily. "I suppose that you're going to tell me that working on a farm makes a girl better looking!"

"Maybe not, Susan, but at least I won't choke to death. I'll always have plenty to eat. I can get a good night's sleep after being out in the fresh air all day. I may not meet too many people, but the ones I do meet will be honest and trustworthy. I know that I won't be robbed walking down some dark, crooked alley in a filthy city."

"You won't be robbed," said Susan, "because you won't be going anywhere. Someday you may learn that people really live in the city!"


## UNDERSTANDING THE STORY

**A.** *Tell which of the statements are true.*

1. Under the domestic system, goods were made in factories.
2. No special skills were necessary to work in a factory.
3. Many factory workers lived in crowded, filthy homes.
4. Most of the factories were bright and airy.
5. Workers often stayed on the job until it was too dark to see the machines.
6. A large number of the workers in factories and mines were women and children.
7. Susan was not going to go back to work in the factory.
8. Susan said that she enjoyed her work in the factory.


**B.** *Susan and Joyce have different ideas about many things. Decide who made or might have made the following remarks. Write S for each statement that Susan made or might have made and J for each statement that Joyce made or might have made.*

1. I'm not going to stay here. There's too much work on the farm.
2. A woman with money can find a husband.
3. The air is pure and you can breathe here on the farm.
4. The city is full of excitement, fun, and lots of people.
5. They don't give you enough to eat at the factory.
6. You don't repeat the same job endlessly on the farm.

7. It's hard work, but we work only 60 hours a week in the factory.
8. You will live twice as long on the farm.
9. I never said the factory was paradise.
10. I won't be robbed walking down a dark street in a filthy city!

C. Pretend that you have just graduated from high school. You are offered a choice of jobs. You can work on a farm in the country or you can work in a factory in the city. Which would you choose? Why? What differences would you expect to find between Susan's factory and your factory? What differences would you expect to find between Joyce's farm and your farm?

## ACTIVITIES AND INQUIRIES

1.  Imagine that you have the job of preparing a report card on the working conditions in Susan's factory. Grade each of the items below pass or fail. Write a sentence explaining the reasons for each grade. How can the failing grades be raised to passing grades? How can the passing grades be raised to excellent grades?

| wages or pay | light and air | living quarters |
| hours of work | space in the factory | labor by women |
| safety of ma- | vacation and | and children |
| chinery | holidays | air pollution |

2.  Pretend that you are a member of the British government in the 19th century. Write a report telling how working conditions in the factories can be made better.
3.  A newspaper reporter visited a typical factory in 1842, the year our story took place. Read his description and answer the questions that follow.

> There are 1500 people working in the factory. Most are under 15 years of age. Some, not yet seven years old, are barefoot. All start work at 5:30 A.M. They do not finish until after 7:00 P.M. The children are small for their age. They are weak looking, and many are crippled. They are beaten with a heavy strap by the foreman. This makes them work harder. They have never been to school.

Imagine that you are a health inspector. You visit the factory. Make a list of all the violations you find. Why do you suppose parents sent their children to work in factories like this one?

4. Visit a factory. Compare this factory with those you read about in question 3.

5. Look at the cartoon below. Who is Joyce? How do you know? Who is Susan? How do you know? Imagine that you are Joyce. Why does she say, "This is the way to live"? Imagine that you are Susan. Why does she say the same thing—that her way of life is better than her sister's? Do you agree with Susan or with Joyce? Why?

*"This is the way to live!"*

# 3. Power to the People

*You may have thought that* the Industrial Revolution would have given the people an even greater feeling of equality. There could have been wonderful opportunities for all people to share in the profits to be made in the new factories. Actually, just the opposite happened.

A new "nobility" now controlled the daily lives of the workers. These new "nobles" were factory owners and businessmen. They were interested only in how much money they could earn for themselves. They hired people to work under bad conditions for the lowest possible wages. Workers who could not or would not work in a 19th-century factory were easily replaced. There was always a large supply of labor to replace the dropouts on the assembly lines.

Some workers were willing to labor under these brutal conditions. Others felt that they were being *exploited* (used) by the bosses. These workers could not accept their poverty and suffering. They had to do something to improve their lives. They felt that they too should enjoy some of the benefits of the Industrial Revolution.

Many different ideas were offered to give workers a larger share of the profits. In this story we see two English factory workers comparing their ideas and feelings about their boss (the capitalist), the factory, and their jobs. Ask yourself how you would have felt as a worker in their factory. Why does Kevin feel that Conrad's ideas go too far? Do you agree? How might the factory owner have answered Conrad's suggestions for taking over the factory?

# Liverpool, 1870

"How can I explain my feeling about the capitalist system?" said Conrad. "I hate it."

"Never mind how you feel about it," interrupted Kevin. "What is it?"

"'What is it?' Where have you been hiding? It's the system you're living under. Rich people own and run the factories and businesses so that they get even richer! They use us. They exploit us! The rich get richer, the poor get poorer."

"Exploit—is that the only word you know?" asked Kevin. "Why don't you use simple words? Can't you understand that some people are meant to be rich? Poor people like us work for the rich. We are paid money for our work. What's so bad about that?"

"That's exactly my point, Kevin. Why should some people be rich? Why should greedy capitalists decide how much to pay us? They always pay us less than we're worth! Why must they use us? Why should they profit from the sweat of our broken backs and hands? Break out of your chains, Kevin. Throw them in the capitalists' faces!"

The capitalists have the money and know how to use it," said Kevin, who refused to get excited. "They have the imagination and the nerve to try out new machines and make new products. You see, Conrad, I know who I am: I'm a worker. I'm poor. Perhaps someday I will earn more. Right now, I know that I don't have the money or the know-how to be a factory owner. I'm for hire. The capitalist puts me to work. He pays me. I can eat and my family can live. What more could I want?"

"How can you be satisfied with so little?" asked Conrad. "I tell you that you are being used by the capitalists. You come back and tell me that it's perfectly all right for you and me to be poor while others are rich. Do you mean to tell me that you don't want us to live as well as the capitalists? Aren't we as good as they are? Don't we eat and breathe and have feelings? Don't we bleed when we are injured? What's wrong with you, Kevin? Where are your feelings?"

"A man who is smarter than I am deserves to live better than I do," answered Kevin evenly. "No, I don't want to live like the rich. Yes, I am happy the way I am. I know that if I work harder I will earn more money. Let the capitalist get rich. I don't want what he has."

"And I tell you, Kevin," said Conrad, "I want *all* of the capitalist's money. I want *all* of his profits—not for myself alone, but for *all* of you workers. I want the true value of what I make with these hands! The money is mine! It is ours! The capitalists and their families deserve nothing! How can you be willing to work for whatever money they decide to pay you? Why should you let yourself be ground down by the capitalists' heels?"

"All right, Conrad, I admit I'm not completely satisfied. I never said I was. But I know what I can do, and I know what I can't do. I'm a worker, not a boss. Sure I want more money. Who doesn't? Yes, I want better working conditions. I wouldn't mind fewer hours of work in a cleaner place. I'll even admit that I have a dream. Someday, if I can save enough money, I want to open my own shop. But can't I make you understand that I don't want to own or run the factory?"

"Fool! I never said that you would own the factory by yourself!" shouted Conrad, his face as red as a beet. "Can't you see that your work in the factory should give you a share of the profits? The factory is yours *and* it's mine. It should not belong to the capitalist. All of us who work in the factory should own it. The capitalist controls the factory because he's lucky. He happened to have had a little money with which to get started in business. The capitalist may believe it, but we know that God did not decide who would be the owner of the factory. It was just chance!"

"How many times do I have to tell you that I don't want anything to do with owning his factory," said Kevin a little angrily. "The owner worked hard to set it up. He put his money, his brains, his sweat into it. He built it from nothing into a giant. Doesn't he deserve the fruits of his work?"

"He deserves nothing!" said Conrad with great feeling. "We'll take it from him! Soon it will all be ours! The day of the capitalist is over! Power to the workers!"

"And who will run the factory without him?" asked Kevin.

"We'll run it together," answered Conrad. "We'll choose our own leaders. They'll run it for us. We'll all share in the profits. Don't worry. We know as much as your capitalist pet!"

"And who will make sure that our leaders will do a better job than the capitalist? Who will make sure that they are honest? How will we know if we are getting our fair share? No, Conrad, I don't trust your leaders any more than I trust the capitalist. But I know what the capitalist can do. I know that I can work for him. I'm not sure I want to be bossed around by men who used to work alongside me. Their hands will become soft, and they'll never want to go back to real work. You and your friends dream of running factories. Do you really care about making things?"

"You must have a little more faith in me, Kevin, my friend," said Conrad in a low, intense voice. "A new day is coming for the worker. We will take over! The profits belong to the worker!"

"I wonder," said Kevin quietly, "if you want to take over the factories or the world?"

## UNDERSTANDING THE STORY

**A.** *Write T for each statement that is true, F for each statement that is false, and N for each statement that is not mentioned in the story.*

1. Factory owners hired workers at the lowest possible pay.
2. Nineteenth-century factory workers were the best the world has ever seen.
3. In the 19th century it was hard to replace factory workers who left their jobs.
4. All workers in the 19th century were happy with their jobs.
5. Some workers felt that their bosses were taking advantage of them.
6. Conrad said that all workers should share in the profits of their work.
7. The capitalist system offers the best way to run the factories of our country.
8. Conrad was against the capitalist system.
9. Kevin felt that all workers should be paid exactly the same amount of money.

**B.** *Tell which item makes each statement correct.*

1. The new "nobles" of the Industrial Revolution were the (*a*) workers (*b*) factory owners (*c*) members of Parliament.
2. Conrad said that (*a*) the rich got rich on the labor of the poor (*b*) workers should not run the factories (*c*) everyone should be very poor.
3. Kevin understood that he was always going to be (*a*) a rich man (*b*) a worker without much money (*c*) a foreman.
4. "Break out of your chains" was a remark made by (*a*) the factory owner (*b*) Kevin (*c*) Conrad.
5. Kevin knew that if he worked harder, he would (*a*) be a factory owner (*b*) marry a rich woman (*c*) earn more money.
6. Conrad felt that the factory owner's money should be given to (*a*) the workers (*b*) the government of England (*c*) anyone who asked for it.
7. Kevin's dream of success was to (*a*) open his own factory (*b*) stop working (*c*) open his own shop.
8. Conrad believed in (*a*) more income for the capitalists (*b*) .more income for the workers (*c*) more income for the farmers.

**C.** Imagine that you are working in a factory today. Kevin and Conrad are also working in the factory. Each one wants to become the president of your local labor union. For whom would you vote? Explain. Would you rather not vote for either Kevin or Conrad? Explain.

## ACTIVITIES AND INQUIRIES

1. Use each of the following key terms in a sentence.

   | exploit | capitalism | profit |
   |---------|------------|--------|
   | boss    | capital    | wages  |

2. Read the two passages below and answer the questions that follow.

   > Workers are cheated. They must work long hours because this is what the bosses want. The bosses control the factories. They also control the lives of the workers. Working conditions are getting worse. The revolt of the working class draws closer.

   > People want the best for themselves. They will compete with others to get ahead. They will work hard to

succeed. The smartest and hardest working people will do best. They will succeed because they are selling the best products at the lowest prices. Everyone will benefit.

With which of the two paragraphs would Kevin agree? Why? With which paragraph would Conrad agree? Why? With which do you agree? Why?

3. Imagine that you are a newspaper reporter. Your job is to interview Kevin or Conrad. What questions would you ask? How would your questions be answered by Kevin or Conrad?

4. Now suppose that the factory owner has asked you, the reporter, for a chance to answer Kevin or Conrad. What are the main points that the owner makes in his interview with you? Do you agree with the owner or with the worker? Why? If you agree with neither, explain your answer.

5. Imagine that you are Kevin. Write a diary of one day in your life as a factory worker. Include all the important and unimportant things that might have happened to you. Now imagine that you are Conrad. Write an account of one day in your life. Whose diary do you think might be more interesting? Why?

# 4. The Assembly Line Today

*Through the years, working conditions* in factories were much improved. It became legal for workers to organize into labor unions. Workers learned to act together. They bargained with the bosses as a union or group. When necessary, they stopped work and went on strike. They encouraged people to *boycott* (stop buying) the product. They used the power of their votes to get favorable laws passed.

But many workers were still not happy to be working in a factory. While the pay and hours were often good, the workers were tired of doing the same thing hundreds or even thousands of times each day. They grew bored. They did not have a feeling that they were really making something. Their part of the production process was too small to mean anything to them.

Some workers found that they were uncomfortable with so many people in the same room. Others did not like to obey rules made by someone else. The hours and conditions of work were decided for them. They could not be late, and they had to work a fixed number of hours.

In this story two English workers are talking about their factory. Ask yourself why one worker is so strongly against this type of work. What are his objections to working in this factory? Why is the other worker not unhappy about working in the same factory?

## Birmingham, 1970

"How do you like working at Acme Motors, Ed?" asked Joe.

"I don't know how to answer, Joe. I'm mixed up about it," replied Ed. "The money isn't bad—though I could use more."

"Who couldn't?" laughed Joe.

"But I don't know if I'll ever get used to this routine," added Ed.

"But Ed, everyone has a routine or a schedule of work," replied Joe. "It doesn't matter whether you work on a farm, in a store, or here. You've got to know what you're doing and when you're going to do it."

"Yes, Joe, but the factory is different. I have to be here at the same time every day. I could use a little more sleep. I have to keep doing the same things each day. Why should I hurry to be here? It's the same stuff day after day. And you know what happens when you're late a few times!"

"Work starts at eight," said Joe. "And everyone has to start at the same time. Otherwise the factory couldn't operate."

"Wait, there's more, Joe. Why do I have to work as late as everyone else? Some days I'm just too tired to put in a full day. Here I am, tired as a dog, dragging myself along! Why do I have to punish my body this way?"

"Suppose the boss let you off an hour or two early," answered Joe. "Can you see what would happen? Dozens of others would ask for the same deal. And what would happen to the assembly line? There could be a breakdown without enough workers!"

"Who in blazes cares what happens to their stupid assembly line? Let it break down!"

"If it breaks down and the factory stops, there goes your job and mine along with it!"

"Okay, Joe, okay. Why did you ask me how I felt about working here? You don't care. You just like to hear yourself talk."

"Oh, cool off, Ed. You're just tired. After another month or two your hours will fly by."

"You can say what you want, but it's still a drag to me," said Ed tiredly.

Joe didn't seem to hear Ed's last remark. "The pay is good here. It's the top wage in the industry. Our union has done a terrific job! We're working a six-hour day with time and a half for overtime. You've got morning and afternoon breaks. You've got nine paid holidays, and you even get your birthday off! And don't forget your two-week vacation with pay!"

"Great," said Ed with disgust. "You forgot the wage tie-in with the cost of living."

"Right, Ed. Why can't you be serious? Why do you pass it all over? I suppose you'd be thrilled to work 18 hours a day for a few cents!"

"Tell me more," laughed Ed.

"Okay. Imagine that you're living in the bad old days," said Ed seriously. "You can't keep body and soul together. You and your family are starving. One fine day, you open your mouth to complain to your foreman. 'Get out!' he says. 'Pick up your pay. You're through!' "

"Come on, Joe. With or without the union, we're all dead in this factory anyway."

"You still don't see it," continued Joe. "Okay, complain today. Can anyone fire you without good cause? Do a good job, keep your nose clean, and you've got no problems."

"Haven't you forgotten one thing?" asked Ed.

"What's that?"

"Seniority, Joe. There's always the union and seniority. Say they don't sell enough cars. Some of us have to go. It's last hired, first fired! It's my head that will roll first around here!"

"Can you think of a better way?" asked Joe.

"Sure, Ed. Have you heard of ability—and skill? But maybe you're right. What kind of skill do you need to work in this factory? You win. I lose!"

"Don't talk this way, Ed."

"How should I talk?" Ed said angrily. "Maybe you can do the same thing hour after hour. I can't! I'm tired and bored!"

"Pull yourself together! Maybe it's boring, but you don't have to think about what you're doing. You just keep doing it. And the money keeps rolling in!"

"Where's the feeling of really making something?" asked Ed, a bit more calmly. "We're supposed to be making cars here. But I don't know what I'm making. I hardly know what I'm doing! All I ever do is tighten bolts. I tell you, Joe, it's getting to me! I feel out of everything. I'm nothing!"

"That's just not true, Ed. You are important. You are somebody. Your work is one step in the making of a car. It may be a small step, but somebody has to do it or else there'd be no car!"

"All right, then, why do I have to do such a small thing?" asked Ed. "Thousands of times each day I tighten a bolt or cut a piece of metal. Over and over and over. Why can't I do other things? I'd rather do many things a hundred times, not one thing a thousand times. I'd be more interested. I'd be more relaxed. I could almost enjoy myself. I could think about myself and what I'm doing. I could be important!"

"This is a factory, Ed. There are over a thousand of us working under one roof. The supervisors divide the work. Each of us has one thing to do each day. This way we become specialists. We know exactly what we're doing. We make fewer mistakes."

"But who wants to be a specialist in turning a screw or tightening a bolt?" asked Ed. "We've got a strong union. Let's make a few changes around here. Call a meeting of all the men and women in our group. We'll divide up the work. Each of us will do a job he or she wants to do. We'll exchange jobs as often as we think it will help us. We'll all be happier and healthier. We'll produce more. We'll make very few mistakes! We'll turn out better cars!"

"Impossible!" cried Joe. "They'd never let us do it! Talk about this to the others, and we'll all get fired! Count me out!"

"I thought you were a man, a friend. Now I know that I couldn't trust you to bring me the right time!"

"You're upset, Ed. You'll feel better in the morning."

"These pains in my head and stomach aren't going to go away by morning! I can't stand this grind. I can't stand some of the people I work with. And I'm not sure I can stand talking to you!"

"Ed, you've made your point. Maybe the union can do something for you. I'll bring your suggestion to the union. Change may be what we need in this factory. Give them a chance. Let them try to work something out with the owners. Don't quit now!"

"All right, Joe, I'll try to stay. Unions and bosses are learning that workers are people. We are individuals. We're not all the same."

## UNDERSTANDING THE STORY

**A.** *Complete each of the sentences below.*

1. Many persons were unhappy about working in a ———.
2. Every worker must have a ——— of ———.
3. They encouraged people to stop buying their ———.
4. "Our union has done a terrific job to help the ———."
5. "How can you do the same thing hour after ———?"
6. "All I ever do is ——— bolts."

7. "I make a small part of the ———— car."
8. "Seniority means that the ———— hired is the ———— fired."

**B.** *Write T for each statement that is true and F for each statement that is false.*

1. Some workers were uncomfortable because of overcrowding in the factory.
2. Joe thought that Ed would get used to the work in the factory.
3. Ed enjoyed going to work at the same time each day.
4. Joe felt that every worker on the assembly line should work the same number of hours.
5. Ed was tired of doing the same things over and over.
6. A specialist keeps working at the same job, or part of a job.
7. Specialists make many more mistakes in their work than people who do not specialize.
8. Ed wanted to enjoy his work.

**C.** Imagine that a factory like the one in the story opened near your home. Would you apply for a job there? Why or why not? Who would you want to be your foreman—Ed or Joe? Explain your answer.

## ACTIVITIES AND INQUIRIES

1. Speak to a member of a labor union. Ask him or her to read the story and give you an opinion about it. Report your findings to the class.
2. Turn back to the report card that you prepared for activity 1, page 188. Now grade the factory in this story. What does your report card tell you about the working conditions in the two factories? Do you think that Ed might have been happier if he had known about the factory where Susan worked? Explain.

"I think I get it, Mr. Miller. This Industrial Revolution changed the way everyone lived."

"What do you mean, Jack?"

"Most people used to live and work on farms," said Jack thoughtfully. "They grew their own food. They made their own cloth at home. That was the domestic system."

"What made them change, Jack?"

"It was those new machines. People invented machines that made spinning and weaving go much faster. James Watt used coal for his steam engine—and there was the power to turn the machines!"

"Good, Jack, but what did that have to do with people?"

"That's easy. The owners had to put all their machines somewhere. So they built factories in the cities. Then they had to have people to run those machines. Why not use the people on the farms—especially the women?"

"Why would a person leave a farm to go to a city?" asked Mr. Miller.

"Maybe a lot of people weren't happy or doing that well on the farms. The cities were out there with their new factories. Why not try that kind of life?"

"Do you think that's enough to get people to change?" insisted Mr. Miller.

"People always want to earn money, I guess," said Jack. "Some parents shipped their young children off to factories. Sure the factory was a miserable place, but the work was something almost anyone could do."

"What could the workers do about conditions in the factories?" asked Mr. Miller.

"I don't think they could do too much at the beginning. But there were a lot of workers in those factories. They got together to improve things. Laws were passed to cut the number of hours of work. Some of the dangerous machines were covered."

"Then the workers were satisfied?"

"Who's ever satisfied, Mr. Miller? A few workers became capitalists, the owners of factories. And I guess that some dreamed of taking over and running the factories themselves."

"That still leaves most of the workers," said Mr. Miller.

"Right," added Jack, "and they just kept on working. Some joined unions. Lots of workers were bothered by their jobs. The lucky ones got better jobs. But they all needed the money. Sometimes, their children, like me, had a chance to move up in life."

"How did they get to move up?"

"Well, after a while, almost everyone got the right to vote. There was more education for more people," said Jack slowly. "Maybe we won't get rich, but there's that chance—that dream. The chance for equality is there. You just have to grab it. You may not have the most money, but you can be as good as anyone else!"

"Do you see how the Industrial Revolution did that for you?"

"Sure, Mr. Miller. The Industrial Revolution made life more open. People moved around more. They could see more. They could do more—and they could want more."

"Excellent, Jack. Do you know that there are people in other parts of the world who want the same things we have?"

"I can imagine, even if I don't know," replied Jack. "But what does that have to do with me?"

"You'll see, Jack," said Mr. Miller. "Why not find out by reading the unit on imperialism?"

# Imperialism

"Mr. Miller, you said that people in other parts of the world want the same things we have," said Jack.

Mr. Miller nodded. "That's right, Jack."

"But isn't it true that, up until a short time ago, we knew very little about those people?"

"I suppose so," answered Mr. Miller.

"Then," said Jack, a look of triumph on his face, "those people probably knew very little about us."

"Very little," agreed Mr. Miller.

"Well, then, how could people in other parts of the world want what we have? After all, they know so little about us."

"Let's just say for now that we took an interest in people in other parts of the world," replied Mr. Miller. "There were many reasons for this. We, the people of the Western world, visited many places in Africa and Asia. I suppose we liked what we saw so much that we decided to stay awhile."

"And were the Asians and Africans happy to have us stay?" asked Jack.

"I'm afraid that they had little choice," answered Mr. Miller.

"But—"

"I know," Mr. Miller smiled. "You have many questions. But save them. Our first lesson on imperialism is about to begin."

# 1. The Englishman's Burden

*During the 19th century,* Germany and Italy joined England, France, Portugal, Spain, Belgium, and the Netherlands in the rush to gain control of large areas in Asia and Africa. When a strong nation takes control of a weak one, this act is called *imperialism.*

Why were Europeans so interested in Asia and Africa? Why were they prepared to spend fortunes to bring these continents under their control? Why were they willing to risk war to fly their flags in these far-off places?

Many people have tried to answer these questions. Some say that the industrialized countries needed Asia and Africa because of their supply of raw materials. They add that Asia and Africa provided them with cheap labor, a ready market for their goods, and the promise of great profit.

Others believe that hatred and competition among the great powers drove each to outdo the other in bringing new areas under their control. Nations feared that, if they did not gain colonies, they would become weak and would lose the respect of the other powers.

A few people maintain that a sense of duty drove nations to take charge of many of the peoples of Africa and Asia. Believing themselves superior, the Europeans brought Western civilization to the ''backward'' areas of the world.

Imperialism had both its supporters and its critics. In our story two Englishmen are having an argument over imperialism. One is a government official, and the other is a *missionary* (a person who brings Christianity to people in faraway places). Each believes that he has the right set of answers.

# London, 1834

"Oh, forget it," shrugged Lawrence. "Talking to you is a big waste of time."

"Be fair and stop complaining," smiled Roger. "You always were a bit too hot-headed. Now calm down, I say, and let's discuss this like grown men."

"What is there to discuss? You believe that England should take control of the lands and lives of Asian and African peoples, and I don't. It's that simple!"

"It's anything but simple," answered Roger. "Those aren't people. They are poor, dirty savages who need everything we can do for them."

"My, my, aren't we concerned," mocked Lawrence. "Since when is England in the business of helping the poor?"

"Lawrence, sometimes you annoy me. England has always helped her own poor. She has a duty to help others."

"Oh, and who assigns England this duty?"

"Why, the good Lord, of course," answered Roger. "You, an Englishman, should know that, Lawrence. We, the most civilized race in the world, have a duty to guide these poor devils. We must teach them our ways. It is our burden to do so."

"But suppose they don't like our ways?"

"Don't be a fool, Lawrence. They will welcome us with open arms. We will stop their wars. We will feed and clothe them. We will teach them to read and write. And, best of all, we will teach them to give thanks to our Lord for all of these blessings."

"And who will pay the bills for these blessings?"

"Why the English people, of course. And why shouldn't they pay? They will be paid back in full when Asians and Africans begin to buy English goods."

"How will those miserable people pay for our goods?" Lawrence asked.

"Their resources will be payment enough for now. Look, Lawrence," Roger continued, "we English are a great nation because it is God's will. If we are to continue to be a great nation, we must see our country grow. We need more room for our growing population. We need new markets for our goods. We need new bases for our navy. This is what must be done. God wills it so!"

"I swear, Roger," said Lawrence, "you sound more like a government official than a missionary. By the way, what do you suppose God wants us to teach those poor devils?"

"His word, of course," replied Roger, "and—"

"Yes," said Lawrence.

Roger smiled again. "And to act like Englishmen."

## UNDERSTANDING THE STORY

**A.** *Write* T *for each statement that is true,* F *for each statement that is false, and* N *for each statement that is not mentioned in the story.*

1. Powerful European nations gained control over lands and peoples of Asia and Africa during the 19th century.
2. Lawrence agreed that England should take control of Asian and African peoples.
3. It was God's will that Englishmen take control over Asian and African peoples.
4. Roger believed that Asian and African peoples needed help from the English.
5. The Asian and African peoples did not want the English to help them.
6. The English people would pay the cost for England's takeover of parts of Asia and Africa.
7. England planned to give her finished goods to Asian and African peoples.
8. Roger believed that the English were very special in the eyes of God.

**B.** *Tell which statements Roger would have made to explain the English takeover of parts of Asia and Africa.*

1. The English are not interested in the natural resources of Asia and Africa.
2. Asians and Africans are poor, dirty savages. They need everything the English can do for them.
3. God wants the English to help the Asians and Africans.
4. Asians and Africans may not welcome English help.
5. God wants England to have new markets and new military bases.
6. We English have a duty to teach Asians and Africans to be like us.

C. Imagine that the United States government has asked Lawrence and Roger for advice. The government is thinking about taking control of backward areas in Asia. How would each man advise the American government? Which man's advice would you like to see the government take? Why?

## ACTIVITIES AND INQUIRIES

1. Imagine that Roger has sent a letter to the English government. He is complaining about Lawrence. Write that letter.
2. The English government tells Lawrence that he must write a letter defending his opinions. Write the letter for Lawrence.
3. Who is making the statement in the cartoon below? What does the statement mean? Are the Asian and African really learning civilized ways? Would Roger or Lawrence agree with the cartoon? Explain.

*"Learning civilized ways is hard work!"*

# 2. Indian or Englishman?

*The West brought great changes* to the East. The nations of the East were *Westernized* (modernized) whether they liked it or not.

India, once a powerful empire, was easily taken over by

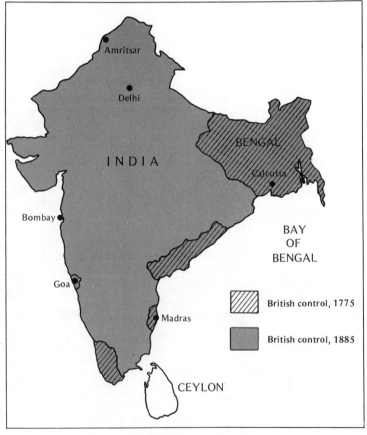

*India in 1775 and 1885*

the British. The Indian government had become weak and divided over the centuries. The government was disliked by many Indian people who began to look forward to the benefits of British rule.

The British made huge profits from India. India became known as the largest "jewel of the British Empire." The British used some of these profits to introduce reforms in India. Schools were built, the English language was taught, and a civil service was created. Indians who knew how to speak and write English and who knew something about European history could pass civil service tests and get government jobs.

Our story is about an Indian who is a successful civil servant. He has always felt proud of himself and loyal to the British. But he has just learned that something is wrong.

# Bombay, 1911

I, Akbar, am a native-born Indian. Everything I am I owe to the British. As a child, I was educated in British schools here in India. As a young man, I was sent to England to study law. Today I hold a high position in the Indian government, and I am paid very well.

Some of my countrymen are not happy that we are not ruling our own country. They often complain to me. I listen for awhile. Then I remind them that, thanks to the British, widows are no longer burned according to the old practice of suttee. We do not die off so quickly from hunger and disease. Can my people forget that the British have brought law, order, and industry to our country? In spite of my arguments, people usually look at me, shake their heads slowly, and walk away.

Yesterday one man listened to me and said, "Your face is Indian, but your heart is English."

I thought this over all day. Finally I had to admit to myself that I knew far more about the history and customs of the British than of my own India. Feeling a little ashamed of myself, I decided to buy some books on Indian history. I visited five bookstores, but there were very few books on Indian history. I am beginning to understand my countrymen's feelings.

# UNDERSTANDING THE STORY

**A.** *Write T for each statement that is true and F for each statement that is false.*

1. The search for raw materials and markets for goods led European nations to take control of areas of Asia and Africa.
2. England refused to take control of any part of Asia or Africa.
3. Akbar, the Indian in the story, hated the British.
4. The British sent some Indians to England to be educated.
5. All Indians were happy with British rule.
6. The English did some good things for India.
7. Some Indians began to think of themselves as British.
8. It was not easy to find a book about Indian history in India.

**B.** *Complete each of the sentences below.*

1. Akbar had a position in the ——— government.
2. The British said that they had brought ———, ———, and ——— to India.
3. Thanks to the British, fewer Indians died from ——— and ———.
4. A custom in India was to burn ———.
5. Akbar was told that his ——— was Indian, but his ——— was British.
6. Akbar knew more about the ——— and ——— of England than he did of his own country.
7. Akbar could find very few ——— on ——— history.

**C.** Imagine that Akbar approaches you for advice. He asks you to tell him why he is so disliked by his fellow Indians. He also wants to know what he should do to win the respect of other Indians. Answer his questions.

# ACTIVITIES AND INQUIRIES

1. Go to the library. Find pictures of 19th-century India. Also find pictures of 19th-century England. Study the two sets of pictures. How are they alike? How are they different?
2. Imagine that you are a British soldier stationed in India. Write a letter home telling about what your life in India is like.
3. Pretend that you are an Indian who has been sent to England to study. Write a letter telling about your life in England.

4. The caption of a cartoon reads, "Your face is Indian, but your heart is British." Explain the caption. Is this meant as a compliment or an insult? Draw the cartoon that goes with the caption.

5. Study the map of India on page 208. Tell which item below makes each statement correct.

   a. From 1775 to 1885, British control of India (1) increased (2) decreased (3) stayed the same.
   b. A city in British India was (1) Shanghai (2) Bombay (3) London.
   c. In 1775 an area under British control was (1) Bombay (2) Goa (3) Bengal.
   d. In 1775 a city under British control was (1) Delhi (2) Amritsar (3) Calcutta.
   e. An island off the southern coast of India is (1) Ceylon (Sri Lanka) (2) Bengal (3) Madras.

# 3. The Supreme Crime

*We now understand why some Indians* welcomed British rule. The British built roads, schools, railroads, and hospitals. They provided jobs for many Indians. Suttee, the practice of widows throwing themselves on the flames as their husbands' bodies were cremated, was outlawed. Killing female babies was made illegal. And the British sought to control thievery and murder.

But there were other Indians who disliked the British. These Indians were angry that the top positions in government were filled by the British. The schools taught European rather than Indian history. Indians said that many industries were owned and run by the British. They blamed the British for practicing racism by keeping Indians out of certain clubs, parks, and neighborhoods. They charged that the British caused much poverty in India by stealing the wealth of the country.

These people began to demand a greater voice in government. Soon they would ask for total independence. But how could the Indian people hope to force the British to leave India? The British had a strong army with modern weapons. At the same time, the Indian people were still struggling with backward customs such as the caste system. This system divided Indians according to skin color, jobs, and social class. It helped to keep the Indian people from becoming united and strong.

In our story an Indian named Mohandas Gandhi (GAHN-dee) has somehow managed to shape the Indian people into an army so powerful that even the mighty British are forced to respect it. How was it possible for him to do so much with so little?

# Calcutta, 1932

I am the chief secretary to the governor general of India. Last week, the governor general and I were waiting for the Indian leader, Mohandas Gandhi. In the past few years Indians have talked of no one else but this man. They say that one day he will free them from British rule.

The governor general was pacing back and forth. He was nervous about this meeting. Thanks to Gandhi, Indians were refusing to work in British factories or to pay their taxes. Some threw themselves across railroad tracks and tied up our trains. Our jails were filled with the rebels. We did not know how to deal with them.

It was Mr. Gandhi who puzzled us most. He was educated in our schools. He has been to England. He was a lawyer and could have lived a life of comfort and luxury. Instead, he went on hunger strikes and spent much of his time in jail.

There was a knock at the door. Mr. Gandhi was announced. He entered. He was short, thin, bald, and toothless; he wore a simple native robe and sandals.

The governor general blurted out, "Mr. Gandhi, what do you really want from us?" Before Gandhi could answer, the governor general jumped out of his chair and said, "We British have brought law, order, sanitation, and industry to your country. We have given you our best people and our finest ideas. All of this has been done at great personal cost to the British people. Yet you are not grateful. You refuse to cooperate with us."

The governor general had become red-faced. He pounded the desk. "For a hundred years we have done practically everything for you!"

Gandhi shook his head sadly. He replied, "That, sir, is the supreme crime that you have committed against my people!"

# UNDERSTANDING THE STORY

**A.** *Tell which statements are true.*

1. All Indians welcomed British rule.
2. India's backward customs made it easier for the British to gain control of India.
3. The British were afraid of Gandhi.
4. Gandhi asked the Indians to cooperate with the British.
5. Gandhi was educated in England.
6. Gandhi dressed like the British.
7. The British did many things for the Indian people.
8. Gandhi chose a life of poverty instead of a life of wealth.

**B.** *Tell which item below makes each statement correct.*

1. The caste system divided India by (*a*) age (*b*) skin color, jobs, and social class (*c*) education.
2. The Indian people hoped that Gandhi would (*a*) free them from the British (*b*) make them wealthy (*c*) bring industry to India.
3. Indians refused to (*a*) pay taxes to the British (*b*) go to jail (*c*) give up their jobs.
4. Gandhi was a (*a*) doctor (*b*) merchant (*c*) lawyer.
5. Gandhi spent a good deal of time (*a*) in jail (*b*) going to dinner parties (*c*) making treaties with the British.
6. Gandhi wore (*a*) British clothing (*b*) silk robes (*c*) Indian clothing.
7. The British claimed that they brought all of these to India except (*a*) sanitation (*b*) the caste system (*c*) industry.
8. Gandhi accused the British of (*a*) not allowing Indians to help themselves (*b*) teaching Indians how to rule themselves (*c*) teaching Indians to be proud of their own customs.

**C.** Imagine that the United States has been taken over by a foreign power. How would Gandhi advise Americans to behave? Would you follow his advice? Explain.

# ACTIVITIES AND INQUIRIES

1. Go to the library. Prepare a report on the life of Gandhi. Include Gandhi's plan for the Indian people after the British left India.

2. Pretend that you are a reporter. You are going to interview Gandhi. Write the questions that you would like to ask him. Answer these questions as you think Gandhi would have done.
3. You have been asked to interview the British governor general of India. Write the questions that you would like him to answer. Answer these questions as you think he would have done.
4. Study the table that shows living standards in India. It tells you about living conditions in India a few years after the British left. Answer the questions that follow.

**Living Standards in India, 1957**

| | |
|---|---|
| Earnings of average farmer | as low as 33 cents a day |
| Health | 20 percent of the people suffered from diseases caused by malnutrition |
| Life span | 26 years (average) |
| Infant mortality | 50 percent of the children died before age one |

Could an English person point to this chart and say that India would have been better off if the British had not left India? How would an Indian person answer this argument? Which argument do you think is the stronger of the two? Why?

# 4. The Final Sacrifice

*Gandhi's weapon, passive resistance,* was successful. He and his followers forced the British to grant the Indian people more self-rule. But Gandhi was not satisfied. He would settle for nothing less than complete self-rule.

When World War II broke out, the British asked for and received India's help. Two million Indians fought for the British. Indians worked in the new factories that were built to help the war effort. A new, more powerful India was being born. This India would demand independence from England, and would not take no for an answer.

But England was not India's only enemy. India was divided by the conflicts between its two leading religious groups, the Hindus (HIN-dooz) and Moslems (MAHZ-lemz). The Moslem minority feared living in a Hindu-controlled India. While the Hindus fought for independence, the Moslems looked for ways to separate themselves from the Hindus. The British stalled for time by playing one group against the other.

Finally the British could delay no longer. After almost a hundred years of control, they were forced to give up their brightest jewel. India was granted independence in 1947.

But what of the problems between Hindus and Moslems? Was Gandhi able to find a way to help these two groups to live in peace?

## New Delhi, 1948

There was great shouting and noise as India's leaders debated the future of the country. Now that the British had left, Hindus and Moslems were turning against each other. Our beloved leader, Mohandas Gandhi, had spoken out in protest against acts of violence by Moslems and Hindus. He now prepared to speak before a gathering of Hindu and Moslem leaders in the Indian parliament. He stood up; suddenly the room was quiet. Gandhi looked at his audience for a few moments. Then he spoke.

"I am here to remind everyone that I spent 25 years of my life in British jails because I believed in India. I did not ask our people to make sacrifices so that one day they would kill one another! Hindus and Moslems must learn to live together. Otherwise, India has no future."

There was silence. Gandhi sat down. He had risked the hatred of dangerous fanatics with this speech. But Gandhi had taken risks all his life. At last the meeting ended. Gandhi walked off by himself. He was deep in thought. His face was sad. He understood that the fight to bring the people of India together would be much harder than the fight to rid India of the British.

Suddenly there was a sharp noise like an exploding firecracker. It was a gunshot. Everywhere there was confusion and panic. Delegates scattered. A tiny figure lay slumped on the ground. It was our beloved Gandhi, murdered by one of his own people!

*Postscript.* Independence has not solved most of India's problems. Since independence, India has been *partitioned* (divided) into two countries, India and Pakistan. This division was necessary because Hindu and Moslem leaders wanted their people to live apart. Riots broke out soon after partition, and almost a million people lost their lives. The wounds have not yet healed. To this day, India and Pakistan are enemies. The most recent war between India and Pakistan was over East Pakistan, which now is the state of Bangladesh.

## UNDERSTANDING THE STORY

**A.** *Write T for each statement that is true and O for each statement that is an opinion.*

1. India should have solved all of her problems when the English left the country.
2. Hindus and Moslems turned against each other after the British left.
3. All Hindus and Moslems loved Gandhi.

4. Gandhi spent over 25 years of his life in British jails.
5. Gandhi was hated by many Indians.
6. Gandhi was shot by a man who loved India.
7. Gandhi was shot and killed by a fellow Indian.

**B.** *Look at the cartoon below. Tell which item makes each statement correct.*

1. The British commander really thought that India's problems (*a*) were over (*b*) were just beginning (*c*) were not too serious.
2. The men fighting are probably (*a*) Boxers (*b*) Hindus and Moslems (*c*) Englishmen and Indians.
3. Gandhi would probably have been happy that (*a*) the men were fighting (*b*) the British were wishing India "good luck" (*c*) the British were leaving.
4. Gandhi would probably have been unhappy that (*a*) the men

were fighting (b) the British were wishing India "good luck" (c) the British were leaving India.
5. The British were probably leaving because (a) they were bored with India (b) the Indians wanted them to leave (c) they no longer needed India as a colony.
6. What happened in India after the British left probably left the British commander (a) uninterested (b) happy (c) sad.
7. If an Indian had answered the British commander, he would probably have said (a) "Thank you" (b) "It's all your fault" (c) "Please don't leave."

C. Some important people have been assassinated in recent years. They include John F. Kennedy, Robert Kennedy, and Martin Luther King. Compare Gandhi with any one of these men. Write what both men had in common.

## ACTIVITIES AND INQUIRIES

1. Pretend that you are writing a movie script on the life and death of Gandhi. Write an outline for your script.
2. Imagine that you are a reporter at Gandhi's funeral. Write the questions that you would ask people. Then write the answers that you would expect to get.
3. You are interviewing the English governor general of India. Write what he would say about Gandhi's assassination.
4. Imagine that you are Gandhi's assassin. Write a letter explaining why you feel that Gandhi had to die.
5. Pretend that Gandhi is alive today. Write down the things he might say about modern India.

# 5. A Dance of Death

*For centuries Europeans had shown* great interest in China. China's beautiful cities, natural resources, great wealth, and its porcelains, silks, and teas made the Europeans' mouths water. China appeared to be very powerful, and the Europeans were careful not to push the Chinese too far.

Little was really known about China, however. Europeans did not know about China's vast problems. China was crippled by poverty, illiteracy, disease, and overpopulation. Laws favored the rich and hurt the poor. Secret terror societies planned to overthrow the government, which was weak and corrupt.

The Chinese had another picture of themselves. They thought of themselves as the proud bearers of the world's finest civilization. The Chinese agreed to trade with Europeans only after they had begged for the privilege. The Chinese showed little interest in European goods. They were even less interested in the power-driven machinery that was making the Western nations so strong. The Chinese believed that anything foreign was not worth having.

At first Europeans traded silver for Chinese goods. Later Europeans discovered that the Chinese would accept a new "currency": opium. The Chinese government became alarmed. Europeans were corrupting Chinese officials. Long after the Chinese government had outlawed the opium trade, some Chinese officials were accepting bribes to help smuggle opium into China. The Chinese people were being hurt. It was time to rid China of the Europeans.

Our curtain rises on 19th-century China. The Chinese people are preparing to defend themselves against an attack by the British.

# Canton, 1839

I am a Chinese official. I fear for my country. Giant ships, each one flying the British flag, are coming closer to the shore. Soon my people and those foreign devils will lock together in a dance of death. We must teach those barbarians a lesson they will never forget!

How I hate those fish-faced round eyes! They lie, they curse, and they stink from the evil odors of the things they smoke and drink! We Chinese are better than they are.

Yet I fear these people. We have invited them to leave our country. They refused to go. We told them that we had no interest in their barbarian goods. We have everything we need under the sun. Still, they begged to trade with us. We called them inferiors and made fun of their clumsy ways. They ignored our insults!

They protest that they have come here in the name of peace. But they have brought ugliness with them. These British have smuggled opium into China. They have made my countrymen suffer so that many beg to die. No longer will the Chinese people allow these foreign devils to bring their poison into our country. That is why the English have declared war against us.

The gunboats draw closer. Some of my countrymen are shouting cries of victory before the battle has even begun! I will wait awhile before I join them.

## UNDERSTANDING THE STORY

**A.** *Write T for each statement that is true and F for each statement that is false.*

1. Until the 19th century, Europe was not interested in China.
2. The Chinese believed that they had the greatest civilization in the world.
3. The Chinese did not want "barbarian goods."
4. The Chinese were fond of the British.
5. The Chinese wanted to trade with the British.
6. The British smuggled opium into China.
7. The Chinese believed that they had everything they needed and trade with foreigners was unnecessary.

**B.** *Complete each of the sentences below.*

1. Until the 19th century, Europeans knew little about ———.
2. Europeans thought that China was very ———.
3. Into the mid-19th century, China was still without power-driven ———.
4. The British ——— opium into China.
5. The British begged to ——— with China.
6. The Chinese called the British ———.
7. British ——— sailed into Canton harbor.
8. As our story ended, the British and the Chinese were preparing to go to ———.

**C.** The United States has a narcotics problem today. Most of the illegal drugs sold here come from foreign countries. How would the Chinese official in the story advise the American government to deal with the problem?

## ACTIVITIES AND INQUIRIES

1. Use each of the following key terms in a sentence.
   superior          barbarian              opium
   inferior          culture
2. Pretend that you are an English sailor spending some time in China. Write a letter home describing what China is like.
3. Imagine that you are Chinese. You are writing to your cousin who has never seen an English person. Describe what the English are like.
4. Below is part of a letter written by a Chinese emperor to King George III of England. Read it carefully. Then answer the questions.

> Yesterday your ambassador asked permission to trade in new areas of China. This cannot be done. I remind you that we have no need of your goods. We have everything we need within our own borders. You, on the other hand, need our teas, silks, and porcelains. Do not take advantage of our good nature. Be happy that we let you trade in the city of Canton. Tremblingly, obey!

What did the Chinese emperor think of the British? Why do you think he felt this way? Imagine that you are King George. Answer the emperor's letter.

# 6. "Foreign Devils, Go Home!"

*The Chinese fought the British* and lost. Stunned and confused, the Chinese signed treaties that opened the door to the British. It was not long before other countries made their demands upon China. France, Germany, Russia, and Japan were among the countries that helped pick the remains from the rotting body of China.

The Chinese resented Westerners. They claimed that Westerners took advantage of them. Westerners who committed crimes in China were tried in their own courts and were usually found innocent or given light sentences. Chinese laborers worked for less than European workers. Westerners grew rich amidst a sea of poverty in China.

The Chinese were also unhappy about other things. They resented their weak and corrupt government. The government was blamed for China's poverty and crime. People became impatient with the government's weak attempts to modernize China. They became even more upset in 1894 when China went to war with tiny Japan and lost. The time had come for the government to take action.

The government decided that China's problems could best be solved by driving out the foreigners. A group of Chinese organized for just such a purpose. The government gave them its full support. How did this group propose to rid China of foreigners? What plans did the group have for China? Could this group succeed?

# Peking, 1900

We, the members of the Society of Righteous and Harmonious Fists (the Boxers), are planning to storm the city of Peking. We must rid China of all of her foreign devils!

We are a proud people who refuse to suffer more insults and disgrace! No longer will we be treated as inferiors and laughed at in our own homeland. No longer will we permit Westerners to cheat us and steal from us. No longer will we let them commit horrible crimes against us and escape punishment.

The foreign devils have spread their poison throughout China. The British do as they please in Canton, Shanghai, and many other ports. Hong Kong now belongs to them. France, Russia, Germany, and Japan have also rushed in to pick our bones clean. China is a country in name only. We Chinese have become second-class citizens in our own country!

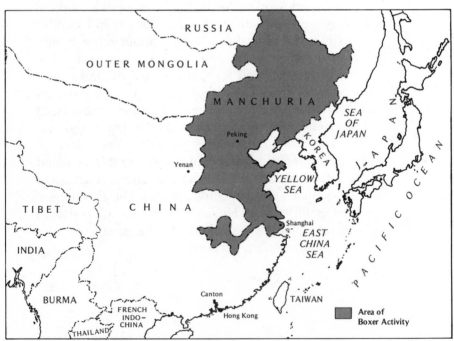

The Far East in the mid-19th century

We are determined to sweep away all that the foreigners have brought with them. We will destroy the telegraphs, railways, rifles, and guns. We will rid ourselves of all foreign ideas. Once again, we will travel the true path.

Death to all who oppose us! Death to the barbarian priests and ministers! Death to the women and children who belong to the foreign devils!

Armed with knives, we will run down the narrow streets. We will slit the throats of all who are not Chinese. Old people, women, and children—they will die with the rest! Our consciences are clear. We have come to strike terror into the hearts of our enemies. No act is too horrible for us to perform!

Our leaders tell us that the foreign dogs have united against us because they are so frightened. If we must fight all of them, so be it! Thousands of foreigners are massing to attack. We do not fear them or their weapons. The gods are with us. Today is our day of revenge! Long live China!

## UNDERSTANDING THE STORY

**A.** *Tell which statements express the goals of the Boxers.*

1. China must be rid of all foreigners.
2. China should learn from the West.
3. China should get rid of foreigners, but keep their telegraph and railways.
4. All foreigners, except women and children, shall be put to death.
5. China must use terror to free herself from foreigners.
6. China must free herself from the West and follow the old ways.

**B.** *The passage that follows is taken from a pamphlet written by the Boxers. Tell which item makes each statement correct.*

Terrible things have happened in China. Foreign devils have come with their teachings. Many Chinese have become Christians. The foreign devils have corrupted every official. They have brought their telegraph, railways, and guns. We must burn down the houses of the foreigners. We must restore our own temples. We will destroy all foreign goods. The gods are on our side.

1. Foreigners tried to teach the Chinese to become (*a*) wealthy (*b*) independent (*c*) Christians.
2. According to the Boxers, foreigners wanted the Chinese to be (*a*) corrupted (*b*) shot (*c*) rewarded.
3. An item that foreigners did *not* bring to China was (*a*) guns (*b*) railroads (*c*) tea.
4. What did the Boxers plan to do to the homes of foreigners? (*a*) burn them (*b*) rent them (*c*) paint them.
5. The Boxers hoped to rebuild (*a*) Christian churches (*b*) Chinese temples (*c*) railways.
6. What did the Boxers want to do to foreign goods? (*a*) destroy them (*b*) pay for them (*c*) steal them.

C. Imagine that a Boxer came to your school. Write down the things he would probably say about your country. How would you answer him?

## ACTIVITIES AND INQUIRIES

1. Imagine that the Boxers are asking your advice. They want you to tell them how to get the foreigners out of China. What advice would you give them?
2. Go to the library. Prepare a report on the battle that took place between the Boxers and the Western powers (the Boxer Rebellion).
3. Imagine that you are Chinese. You have just been told of the ideas of the Boxers. Which ideas do you agree with? Which ideas do you disagree with?
4. Study the map of China and the Far East on page 224. Tell which item below makes each statement correct.
   *a.* One of the regions of China affected by the Boxer Movement was (1) Shanghai (2) Manchuria (3) Hong Kong.
   *b.* A city where the Boxers rebelled was (1) Hong Kong (2) Peking (3) Canton.
   *c.* The country south of the Manchurian border is (1) Korea (2) Outer Mongolia (3) Macao.

   *d.* The Boxer Rebellion took place mainly in (1) southern China (2) western China (3) northern China.

   *e.* An island east of Mainland China is (1) Taiwan (2) Korea (3) Hong Kong.

5.  Write a caption for the illustration below. If the cartoon is correct, should the Boxers have hoped to defeat the armies of the West? Explain.

# 7. Sun Yat-sen

*The proud Boxers were downed* by a hail of bullets. The Chinese now were forced to take a good long look at themselves. Some began to ask if the Chinese themselves were the cause of their failure.

The government, known as the Manchu dynasty, led by an aging empress, became very nervous. After all, it had supported the Boxers. Now the government tried to introduce some reforms. It began to build Western-style schools and modernize the army. But it was too late. The Chinese were looking elsewhere for leadership.

It would take a very special person to awaken the Chinese and give them the will to face these terrifying problems. The Manchu government would stop at nothing to crush such a man.

## London, 1895

I am Sun Yat-sen. I love my country, but I fear for its future. Every day, foreigners insult my people. These outsiders grow rich on Chinese soil while my people can barely make a living. My country has been invaded and disgraced because China is governed by corrupt people. These officials have stopped every attempt to reform our laws and bring China up to date. They do not understand that the old ways are dying and they are doomed to die with them.

I went to London to raise money for my cause. My followers and I had decided that we must rid China of the Manchu rulers. We had to move China forward. For this, the government had a price on my head. I was thousands of miles from home, but I knew that dangerous enemies were close at hand.

I prepared to leave my apartment. There was a knock on the

door. "Enter," I said. Two men burst into the room and grabbed me. I was pushed into a waiting carriage and taken to the Chinese embassy. I was dragged to the basement and tied to a chair.

Later, a man appeared at the door. I had seen him before. He was the Manchu's ambassador to England. He walked up to me, looked into my eyes, and slapped me hard across the face. "You are the worst kind of traitor," he said. "You throw mud in your country's face while strangers attack her. You travel around the world and tell unspeakable lies about us. You are more dangerous than the barbarian!"

I spoke out through puffed lips. "One day, my people will again command the respect of the nations of the world. A true Chinese government will help them to grow strong and will free their minds. Your empress is not that government!"

The ambassador now whispered something to one of the men. Suddenly all but one rose to leave. One man was left behind to guard me. Was he my executioner? He stared at me for a long time.

At last he whispered, "I can get word to someone who will help you!" He loosened the ropes so that I could escape. He too had seen a glimpse of China's future. He was willing, as I was, to risk everything for it.

## UNDERSTANDING THE STORY

A. *Write T for each statement that is true and O for each statement that is an opinion.*
   1. Chinese officials stood in the way of reform.
   2. China would suffer as long as she followed the old ways.
   3. The government believed that Sun Yat-sen was its enemy.
   4. Sun Yat-sen told lies about China.
   5. A government run by the empress would never have been able to command respect from the nations of the world.
   6. One of Sun Yat-sen's captors helped him to escape.
   7. The man who helped Sun Yat-sen escape believed that Sun would become a great Chinese leader.

B. *Match each item in Column A with its answer in Column B.*

| Column A | Column B |
|---|---|
| 1. What happened to the Boxers | (a) Foreigners (barbarians) |
| 2. Person who wanted China to learn from the West | (b) London, England |
| 3. Person who was against reform and modernization | (c) Manchus |
| 4. Where Sun Yat-sen was kidnapped | (d) to raise money for his cause |
| 5. Group that kidnapped Sun Yat-sen | (e) Manchu empress |
| 6. What Sun Yat-sen was accused of | (f) defeated by the West |
| 7. Sun Yat-sen was thought to be more dangerous than these people | (g) speaking out against his own country |
| 8. Sun Yat-sen's goal in England | (h) Sun Yat-sen |

C. Imagine that Sun Yat-sen is visiting the United States today. List the things that he would like about this country. List the things that he would want China to copy. List the things that he would not want China to copy.

## ACTIVITIES AND INQUIRIES

1. Pretend that you are a reporter. Your assignment is to interview Sun Yat-sen. List the questions that you want to ask him. Write down the answers that you think Sun would give you.
2. Imagine that you are interviewing a Manchu. List the questions that you would like to ask. Write down the answers that you think he would give you.
3. Suppose that you are a follower of Sun Yat-sen. Draw a poster that will help explain some of Sun's ideas.
4. Sun Yat-sen has come to you for advice. He wants to know how he can begin to make China a more modern country. Write down your ideas.
5. Look at the illustration on page 229. Describe what is happening.

# 8. Kidnapped

*Sun Yat-sen's revolution* was a success. The Chinese overthrew the Manchu leaders and began to take the first steps toward becoming a modern nation. Most Chinese agreed that China must learn the ways of the "foreign devils" to be rid of them. But not all agreed on how this should be done.

Two groups began to compete for the leadership of China. One group, the Nationalists, was headed by a general named Chiang Kai-shek. The other group, the Communists, was headed by a peasant named Mao Tse-tung. At first, these two groups worked together to unify China. But soon, Chiang broke with the Communists and declared war on them. Watching this carefully, the Japanese rubbed their hands in delight and decided that this was the time to invade China.

As our story opens, the Japanese have just declared war on China. In spite of this, Chiang was determined to continue the fight against Mao's Communist army. Not all of his followers agreed with him. One, a young army marshal named Chang Hsueh-liang, tried to convince Chiang to stop his war against the Communists. Chiang was kidnapped by the young marshal. The ransom was to be the Nationalists' agreement to fight against Japan.

## Sian, 1936

I am Marshal Chang Hsueh-liang. I had General Chiang Kai-shek kidnapped yesterday and brought to my headquarters here in Sian.

Chiang was announced. We greeted each other and started talking. "Marshal Chang," he said, "you are playing with fire. I have fought against the Manchus, the European imperialists, and now the Japanese. But I tell you that China's greatest enemies are her own people who call themselves Communists."

"How can you speak this way when China is now being carved up by the Japanese?" I asked. "Chinese people will die fighting the invaders. Yet all you can speak of is your quarrel with the Communists. These men are loved by our people. They help us to work our lands, and they will soon risk their lives for us against the Japanese. I beg of you, make your peace with the Communists. Let us face the Japanese as one people!"

Chiang gave me an angry look. "I will not be lectured by you," he said. "You are a fool not to recognize the Communists for what they are. They will do anything to make people like them now. They say that they mean to make Sun Yat-sen's dream come true. They say China will be free of the foreign devils and cured of the disease of poverty. They claim they want to build a state where no one is poor. But all they really want is power for themselves."

"Generalissimo," I said, "it is obvious that we do not agree. Sadly, while we argue, the Japanese do us great harm. All of us—Communists as well as Nationalists—are Chinese first. We must all join as brothers and sisters and drive the Japanese out of our country. Promise that you will stop your war against the Communists and welcome them into your ranks."

Chiang shook his head. He replied, "This I cannot do!"

"Then, sir, you leave me no choice but to imprison you until you change your mind!" I replied.

Chiang looked up. In a soft voice he said, "My son, you fear the Japanese, who are but a disease of the body. To fight them, you are willing to join with the Communists, who are a disease of the soul!"


## UNDERSTANDING THE STORY

**A.** *Decide who made or might have made the remarks that follow. Write GC for each statement that Chiang Kai-shek made or might have made and MC for each statement that Marshal Chang made or might have made.*

1. I swear that I will rid China of all Communists.
2. The Communists are China's greatest enemies.
3. The Japanese are China's greatest enemies.
4. Many Chinese people love the Communists.

5. The Communists want power only for themselves.
6. We must join with the Communists to drive out the Japanese.
7. The Communists are a disease of the soul.
8. The Communists help the people by working on their land.

**B.** *Tell which statements show how China was affected by the war between Chiang Kai-shek and the Communists.*

1. Chiang was imprisoned by one of his own followers.
2. The Japanese shot Chinese women and children.
3. Chiang fought the Communists and the Japanese at the same time.
4. Chiang decided to trust the Communists. He gave them weapons to help fight the Japanese.
5. The Communists tried to get the Chinese people on their side by helping them work on their lands.
6. Chiang and the Communists agreed on most things.
7. The Chinese people were torn between their loyalty to Chiang and their good feelings for the Communists.

**C.** President Richard Nixon made a trip to Communist China in 1972. Imagine that before leaving on his trip to China Nixon asked Chiang Kai-shek for advice. Would Chiang have agreed that President Nixon should make the trip? Explain.

## ACTIVITIES AND INQUIRIES

1. Imagine that you are a reporter. Interview Chiang Kai-shek. List the questions you would ask him. Write down the answers that you think he would give you.
2. Pretend that you are interviewing a Chinese Communist. List the questions you would ask. Then, answer the questions as you think he would.
3. Read the quotes from *The Guide for Chinese Communist Soldiers* and answer the questions that follow.

> Speak politely.
> Pay fairly for what you buy.
> Return everything you borrow.
> Pay for anything you damage.
>
> Do not hit or swear at people.
> Do not damage crops.
> Do not hurt women.
> Do not mistreat captives.

Which of these rules should American soldiers follow? Why? Why did the Chinese Communist leaders want their soldiers to follow these rules carefully?

4. Imagine that you are a Japanese general who is fighting the Chinese. Which group would you rather see in power, the Nationalists or the Communists? Why?

5. How would the soldier in the cartoon below probably answer the farmer's question? How would Chiang Kai-shek answer the question?

*"But how can I ever repay you?"*

# 9. Civil War: Chiang Versus Mao

*Chiang agreed to stop* the war against the Communists and join with them in fighting the Japanese. But both sides continued to fight each other even as they fought the Japanese.

As the war dragged on, the Nationalists faced serious problems. They had to print paper money to pay for the war. This caused the value of money to drop and the price of goods to rise. People began to say that the Nationalist government was corrupt. Officials could be bribed to do favors for the wealthy. The government took food from the people and forced them to pay high taxes. The people became restless, confused, and unhappy under the Nationalist government.

In the meantime, the Communists were winning the support of the people by lowering land rents and helping the peasants to work the land. The Communists also gained the reputation of being fierce fighters against the Japanese.

When the war with Japan ended, people wondered how long it would be before the Nationalists and the Communists would be at each other's throats. As our story opens, Chiang and Mao are meeting in a last-minute effort to prevent a war. See if you can guess whether or not war will break out between these two and their followers.

## Chungking, 1945

Chiang entered the room. He was well-groomed. His uniform was hand-tailored, and his chest was covered with medals. Next Mao entered. His uniform was simple and badly in need of a pressing. He wore no medals.

The two men glared at each other. For 19 years they had been locked in a fight to the death. Both had bitter thoughts at the moment. At last, the two began to bargain.

Chiang said, "Now that the Japanese have been defeated, there is no need for you to keep your armies. You must send your soldiers home and turn their weapons over to China's real government, the Nationalists."

Mao replied, "I will be happy to join my army with yours if you give me and some of my generals a place in your government."

Chiang spoke quickly. "This I will not do!"

"All right, then," said Mao, "don't take me into your government. But I insist that you hold free elections and give up the powers that have turned China into a dictatorship!"

Chiang would have none of this. "My voice is the voice of the Chinese people. I govern in their name. For this reason, I consider my government to be a democratic one."

Both men were silent. Chiang thought: "Mao is a dangerous man. He kills landlords to give their lands to his followers. He encourages his people to steal from property owners. Soon no man who owns property will be safe from these jackals. If Mao has his way, those who have become rich by use of their wits and hard labor will be chased from China. The country will become a land of peasants!"

Mao stared with hatred at Chiang. Mao thought: "Look at the way he dresses. How many mouths could be fed with the money that uniform cost? While people starve, he and his wife sleep on silk sheets! How can he understand China's problems when he surrounds himself with landlords and bankers? But time is on my side. Chiang may have larger armies than I do, and, thanks to the United States, he will soon have the newest equipment. But his government is rotten. The Nationalists will be destroyed because they are their own worst enemies!"

The meeting was over. The two men faced one another. Mao filled his glass with wine. He raised the glass in Chiang's direction. With a half-smile he said, "Long live China!"

Chiang filled his glass, raised it, smiled, and said nothing. The two men drank their toasts in silence.

## UNDERSTANDING THE STORY

**A.** *Write C for each statement with which Chiang Kai-shek would have agreed and M for each statement with which Mao Tse-tung would have agreed.*

1. A leader should always be dressed well.
2. A leader should dress like those who follow him.
3. The Communists should turn their weapons over to the Chinese government.
4. Communist generals should be given positions in the Chinese government.
5. Free elections should be held in China.
6. People should take goods from property owners.
7. Landlords and bankers are useful people to have around.
8. The Chinese Nationalist government was corrupt.

**B.** *Look at the cartoon below and answer the questions on page 239 based on the story and the cartoon.*

*"Long live China!"*

1. Mao is thinking of a China that is led by (*a*) the West (*b*) the Communists (*c*) the Nationalists.
2. Chiang is thinking of a China that is led by (*a*) the West (*b*) the Communists (*c*) the Nationalists.
3. Mao and Chiang are really wishing each other (*a*) good luck (*b*) long life (*c*) bad luck.
4. According to the cartoon, the two men (*a*) have much in common (*b*) like each other (*c*) dislike each other.
5. Both men seem to agree on (*a*) their love for China (*b*) their taste in clothing (*c*) their enjoyment of drinking parties.
6. The cartoon shows that the two men (*a*) trust each other (*b*) distrust each other (*c*) are good friends.
7. According to the cartoon, the two men will probably (*a*) join forces (*b*) step down from power (*c*) continue the civil war.

C. Imagine that a group of Chinese have asked you for advice. They want to know which man they should follow, Chiang or Mao. What advice will you give them? Why?

## ACTIVITIES AND INQUIRIES

1. Go to the library. Prepare a report on either Chiang Kai-shek or Mao Tse-tung. Be prepared to tell the class how he came to power.
2. Pretend that you are a reporter. Interview Mao Tse-tung. List the questions you would ask. Write down the answers that you think Mao would give to your questions.
3. Imagine that Chiang has read your interview with Mao. How would he answer Mao's charges?
4. Pretend that you are an American reporter and are present at the meeting between Mao and Chiang. Write a newspaper article about your impressions of the two men.
5. Now imagine that you are a Chinese person who is present at the meeting between Chiang and Mao. Write down your thoughts about the two men. Be prepared to defend your ideas.

# 10. The Wind Cannot Read

*In spite of United States efforts* to bring Mao and Chiang together, in 1945 the Nationalists and the Communists once again declared war.

The Nationalists began with more troops and equipment. The Communists had a better-organized army and higher morale. Fighting was fierce, but when the smoke had cleared in 1949, the Communists were in control of the vast Chinese mainland.

Now the Chinese people waited to see how their new masters would behave. After centuries of corruption, poverty, and backwardness, would China at last find peace and prosperity? The Chinese Communists say yes. The Chinese professor in our story has another opinion.

## Peking, 1967

"Come in, Professor Lin. Please sit down. You remember me, of course. I was a student of yours only three years ago. Now I am the captain of a Red Guard unit. I am here to save you from your own errors."

Professor Lin recognized me immediately. "Of course, I remember you, Captain Chen. You were one of my brightest pupils. Together we explored the beauties of the ancient Chinese writings. I had great hopes for your future."

"I was very foolish once," I answered. "I did not understand that the only worthwhile results come from studying the thoughts of Chairman Mao. I have seen the light, and I am going to try to help you to do the same."

"My son," Professor Lin said, "I am an old man. I have seen much. Many who came before you have tried to change the ways of our people. Now it is your turn. I have seen you students beat old

people and burn temples and churches. You make war on everything old and foreign. Yet you succeed only in making all China
afraid of her young people."

"Professor Lin, I can have you beaten to death for those words!
Don't you understand that we, the young people of China, are
building a new land? We will no longer suffer at the hands of
landlords, warlords, and imperialists! Each day we win the fight
against hunger and ignorance! Soon the whole world will be at our
feet. I ask you to join with us, and help us to give birth to this
glorious future!"

The professor thought for a few moments. He replied, "Chen,
you cannot make a revolution with robots. You may imprison a
human body, but even you cannot control a person's thoughts!"

"Enough!" I yelled. "Guards! Take him away! There is nothing
more we can do with him!"

Two guards stepped forward. As he turned to go, Professor Lin
said to me, "Think back to that proverb that was your favorite and
mine as well."

Later I recalled the proverb: "The sign says do not pick the
flowers, but the wind cannot read."


## UNDERSTANDING THE STORY

A. *Decide who made or might have made the remarks that follow. Write*
   *PL for each statement that Professor Lin made or might have made and*
   *CC for each statement that Captain Chen made or might have made.*

1. I am here to save you from your errors.
2. Together we studied ancient Chinese writings.
3. Worthwhile results come only from thinking the thoughts of
   Chairman Mao.
4. You want to destroy everything old and foreign.
5. China is afraid of its young people.
6. We are building a new nation.
7. No one can control another person's thoughts.
8. Soon the world will be at our feet.

**B.** *Tell which statements show how China was affected by communism.*

1. People were asked to read ancient Chinese writings.
2. People were forced to go to temples and churches.
3. Some students beat up old people.
4. Westerners were chased out of China.
5. The Chinese government fed and educated its people.
6. The Chinese people were free to read anything they chose.
7. The Chinese government tried to control the thoughts of its people.
8. Chinese people were allowed to speak freely on any subject.

**C.** Imagine that a person who was born and brought up in Communist China comes to visit you. Write down the Chinese person's comments about life in the United States. Would this person want to stay here or go back to China? Explain.

## ACTIVITIES AND INQUIRIES

1. Go to the library. Prepare a report on life in Communist China today. Try to bring pictures of Communist China to class.
2. Imagine that you are visiting Communist China. Write a diary describing what you see.
3. Look at an American newspaper. Draw a line through every story that could not be printed in Communist China. Explain why you drew lines through these stories.
4. Imagine that Professor Lin is being placed on trial. You are the prosecutor. Prepare the case against him.
5. Now imagine that you are the professor's lawyer. Prepare the case in his defense.

# 11. East Meets West

*We are now going to be introduced* to the Japanese people. Most of them live on four islands off the coast of Asia. Together, these islands are just about the same size as California, but Japan's population is more than half that of the entire United States.

For centuries, emperors had ruled the Japanese people. Three hundred and fifty years ago, a powerful family by the name of Tokugawa (toe-ku-GAH-wah) won the right to help the emperor rule.

The Tokugawa family gained power only after they had defeated other powerful Japanese families. The Tokugawa were very jealous of their newly won power. They watched the other families carefully to make sure that none would try to challenge them. They made special rules for the Japanese people to live by. People were divided into classes. They were not allowed to marry outside their class or move up to another class. Of course, the Tokugawa were members of the highest class. One member of the family made all the important decisions. This person was known as the *shogun* (SHOW-gun), or commander in chief. His power was handed down from generation to generation in his family. Soon the shogun had more power than the emperor. The Tokugawa rule lasted for more than 250 years.

Europeans began to visit Japan in the 16th century. Many Japanese people welcomed these foreigners and were eager to learn from them. But the Tokugawa feared that foreigners would bring change to Japan. They chased the foreigners from the country. Some Dutch traders remained, however, and they helped to keep alive the desire of the Japanese for knowledge of the outside world.

By the 19th century, the Tokugawa were beginning to lose their hold on Japan. People began to resent the Tokugawa rulers. The Japanese wanted the emperor to rule.

**243**

They also wanted to better themselves and move freely from one class to another. They needed some outside pressure to help. This pressure was on the way.

In our story, Commander Matthew Perry of the United States Navy has just arrived in Japan. He is there on an important mission. How will the Japanese deal with Perry? Will his mission be successful?

## Tokyo, 1853

"Commodore Perry, a Japanese noble and his guards are here. He and his party want to come aboard ship and meet with you."

Perry gave orders for the Japanese group to be escorted to the bridge. An interpreter was sent for.

"May I ask the purpose of your visit?" said the Japanese noble, perhaps a bit too politely.

"By all means, sir," answered Perry. "I am here to ask you to stop torturing and putting to death shipwrecked American sailors."

To this, the Japanese said nothing.

"In addition," Perry continued, "my government asks that you open your ports to American ships so that our two countries can trade and become good friends."

"Perhaps," said the Japanese, "we will become even better friends if we do not trade with one another. We have our own way of life, and we do not wish to see it disturbed by outsiders!"

"But I believe that we have much to offer one another," Perry replied. "My government asks that I present you with gifts for your emperor. We think that these gifts will convince you that we can be of service to your people."

The Japanese nobleman waited for Perry to show him his gifts. Perry nodded his head and sailors brought out a sewing machine and a large model of a steam engine railroad train.

"We will show you how to use these things," said Perry, smiling. "You see," he repeated, "we do have much to offer you!"

The Japanese noble spoke in hard tones. "Once before—long before my time—foreigners came to our shores. At first they too wished only to trade. Later we learned that many of our people were being taught to pray to a false god. So we ordered the foreigners to leave. We see no reason to change that policy now!"

Perry looked uncomfortable. "I hope that this is not your final decision. My government understands that you must have time to think things over. I am returning to the United States, but I will come back soon. Perhaps by then you will have changed your mind."

The Japanese noble greeted this statement with silence. Suddenly he and his men stood and bowed politely. It was their signal that the meeting was over.

Perry watched in silence as the Japanese party left the ship. He had strong doubts that the Japanese would change. But as he turned back to his cabin, Perry saw some papers that had accidentally been dropped by one of the Japanese. Every sheet of paper was covered with drawings of parts of Perry's ship.

Suddenly Perry relaxed and smiled. He would have good news for his government after all.

## UNDERSTANDING THE STORY

**A.** *Write* T *for each statement that is true,* F *for each statement that is false, and* N *for each statement that is not mentioned in the story.*

1. Outsiders knew little about Japan until the middle of the 19th century.
2. Foreigners were forbidden to enter Japan because they were carriers of deadly germs.
3. Shipwrecked American sailors had been tortured by the Japanese.
4. The Japanese begged Perry for trading rights with the United States.
5. The Japanese were more interested in the sewing machine than in the railroad train.
6. The Japanese thought that foreigners would bring false gods to Japan.
7. The Japanese government immediately granted Perry's request for trading rights.
8. The Japanese made drawings of Perry's ship.

**B.** *The following statement shows how the Japanese felt about Perry's visit. Read it carefully. Then choose the item that makes each of the sentences that follow correct.*

> If we were to go to war with a foreign country today, we would face a very tough enemy. He would come with many ships and surround our shores. He would capture our ships. No matter how many of his ships we destroyed, the enemy would fight on.
>
> Japan cannot afford such a war. Our people would suffer many hardships and grow tired of fighting. Let us, therefore, have contact with foreigners. Let us learn from them. Let us study their science and inventions. Perhaps one day we shall be strong enough to wage wars with foreign countries and take land from them. We will give the land to our people.

1. The Japanese believed that foreign countries might one day (*a*) declare war against Japan (*b*) give them their products (*c*) torture shipwrecked Japanese sailors.
2. The Japanese thought that foreigners were probably (*a*) cowards (*b*) madmen (*c*) great fighters.
3. In case of war with a foreign country (*a*) the foreign country would suffer most (*b*) Japan would suffer most (*c*) neither would suffer great hardships.
4. Foreign ships were (*a*) better than Japan's (*b*) not as good as Japan's (*c*) not as fast as Japan's.
5. The person who wrote the above statement believed that Japan should (*a*) not have any contact with foreigners (*b*) have little contact with foreigners (*c*) have much contact with foreigners.
6. The Japanese should (*a*) stick to their own ways (*b*) learn the ways of foreigners (*c*) follow the religions of foreigners.
7. The Japanese should be prepared to (*a*) live in peace with foreigners (*b*) teach foreigners Japanese ways (*c*) go to war with foreigners.

**C.** Imagine that a space ship has landed in your country. People from another planet step from the ship. They ask that your country open its cities to the people of the other planet. These people also bring wonderful gifts, which no earth person has ever seen before. Should your country open its cities to these people? Explain your answer.

## ACTIVITIES AND INQUIRIES

1. Go to the library. Prepare a report on Perry's trip to Japan. See if you can find pictures of 19th-century Japan.
2. Imagine that you are an American sailor aboard Perry's ship. Write a letter home describing the Japanese people you have seen.
3. Pretend that you are a Japanese official who has just come from a visit aboard Perry's ship. Write a report about everything that you saw.
4. Assume once again that you are a Japanese official. The emperor wants your advice. He wants to know if Japan should open its ports to the United States. Advise the emperor, and explain why you advised him as you did.
5. Explain the cartoon below. Imagine that you are the person in the cartoon. Answer your own question.

*"Which one?"*

# 12. Imitation Is Power

*Perry returned to Japan* a year later and the Japanese agreed to a treaty. Soon other nations knocked on Japan's door, and the Japanese signed treaties with them as well. Many Japanese complained about these treaties. Japan was buying more from Westerners than it was selling to them. The Japanese were making up the difference with gold. Cheap foreign goods were driving Japanese industries out of business. The shogun was blamed and was forced to step down.

A new group came to power in Japan. This group believed that Japan must become a modern nation in order to stop the West from taking over the country. They decided that Japan would borrow the best ideas from the West. They modeled Japan's government, army, navy, industries, and agriculture after those of Western countries. However, this group kept most of the powers that it had taken away from the Tokugawa shogun. Once again the emperor ruled in name only. The Japanese government—made up of the emperor, a two-house legislature, and a constitution that gave people the right to vote for their leaders—was really a dictatorship of the few over the many.

We now visit Japan 40 years after Perry's ships first steamed into Tokyo Bay. An English professor is visiting Japan to study the Japanese school system. He has been brought to the office of Dr. Saito, a high school principal. The two men have just introduced themselves. Ask yourself what changes had taken place in Japan in 40 years.

## Tokyo, 1893

"Professor Blake, how can I help you?" asked Dr. Saito.

"Dr. Saito, I would be most pleased if you took me on a tour of your school."

"Why of course, professor."

The two men began their walk around the school. Classes were in progress and not a single student could be found in the hallways.

"Dr. Saito, do your students ever cause problems for your teachers?"

"I do not understand your question. If you mean are they late to school or do they misbehave, the answer is of course no. You see, only our best students can go on to high school. And they must work very hard to stay here."

"I notice, Dr. Saito, that your students dress like Westerners, rather than in the style of your country."

"Yes, Professor Blake, we Japanese are most impressed with your ways. We are not ashamed to admit that we have copied much from you. This is why in only 40 years Japan has become a modern nation."

"Dr. Saito, I cannot tell you how impressed I am by your factories, railroads, ships, and, of course, by your schools. Can you tell me how you have done so much in so short a period of time?"

"Professor, we are a poor country. We are only rich in one resource: our people. We work very hard, and we are not too proud to borrow good things when we see them. The best that the world has to offer has been brought to our humble land, and we continue to learn much from you."

"One thing troubles me, Dr. Saito. I noticed a map on your office wall. Unless I am mistaken, I saw a Japanese flag pinned on the northern part of China."

"Professor Blake, as I have said, we continue to learn much from you!"

## UNDERSTANDING THE STORY

A. *Tell which statements are true.*

1. The Japanese agreed to sign treaties with foreign countries.
2. Japanese students were noisy and difficult to control.
3. The students dressed like Westerners.
4. Only the best Japanese students went on to high school.
5. The Japanese fought foreign ideas.
6. Japan has many natural resources.

7. The Japanese were not ashamed to borrow foreign ideas.
8. The story tells us that the Japanese were interested in China.

**B.** *Tell which statements Dr. Saito would have said were correct.*

1. All students should be allowed to enter high school.
2. The Japanese people should not accept any foreign ideas.
3. Japan has learned much from foreign countries.
4. Japan should build railroads and factories.
5. The Japanese should never go to war with any country.

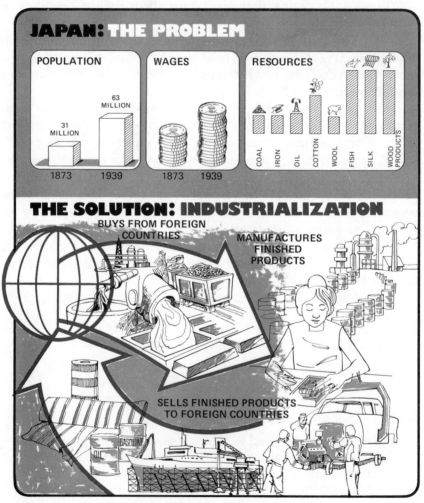

*Japan's economic problem and its solution*

6. The Japanese people are Japan's best resource.
7. The Japanese should begin to take over part of China.

C. Imagine that Dr. Saito has been asked to tell our president how to solve our problems at home. What advice would Dr. Saito give? Should the president follow this advice? Explain.

## ACTIVITIES AND INQUIRIES

1. Study the illustration on page 250. Use the information to answer the questions that follow.
   a. Why did the Japanese have to buy many things from foreign countries?
   b. What are some of the things that Japan bought from foreign countries?
   c. What are some of the things that Japan sold to foreign countries?
   d. Why do you think wages remained low in Japan?
   e. Was its rapidly increasing population good or bad for Japan? Explain.
2. Imagine that you went to Japan with Professor Blake. Write a letter home describing what Japan was like.
3. Pretend that a Japanese student is visiting your high school. What will the Japanese student like about your school? What will the Japanese student not like about your school?
4. Assume that you are Professor Blake. You must report on what you saw in Japan to the English government. Write the questions that you will be asked. Answer these questions.
5. Go to the library. Prepare a report on the role of women in Japanese life. Would an American woman find life difficult if she chose to live in Japan? Explain.

# 13. The Riches of Africa

*We now turn from Asia* to Africa. By the 19th century, much was known of Africa's coastal areas but little was known of its interior. Most people were afraid to explore the interior. They feared diseases, unfriendly natives, wild animals, jungles, swamps, and deserts. They also believed that anyone who dared explore the African interior would die a horrible death. For these reasons, Africa became known as the "Dark Continent." It was widely believed that the African interior was populated only by savage people who used all of their energies to survive in the wild environment.

In truth, however, Africa's interior had been the birthplace of a number of highly civilized groups of people. They had developed governments, laws, economies, religions, strong family ties, literature, arts, and other social traditions. There were a number of rich African cultures, but it would take years before outsiders would recognize them.

In the meantime, Europeans built trading posts along Africa's coast where they bought gold, ivory, and spices from native traders. Europeans were eager to explore the treasures of Africa, but fear kept them back.

In 1865 a missionary and explorer named David Livingstone went on an expedition to central Africa. Over the years little was heard from Livingstone, and rumors of his death soon spread throughout the Western world. Henry Stanley, a reporter for the New York *Herald,* was sent to Africa to search for Livingstone. The following are some highlights from Stanley's diary of the trip.

## Zanzibar, January 6, 1871

Here I am in Africa. What do I do now? I must organize an expedition. James Bennett, my publisher, has given me unlimited funds, but I don't know where to begin! I'm sure that this will be my toughest newspaper assignment.

## January 10

I have made great progress. At the advice of some American and Arab traders, I have begun to organize the expedition. I must buy thousands of yards of cloth, thousands of different colored beads, and several hundred pounds of brass wire. I will use these items to trade with the natives in the interior. I also need food, pots and pans, boats, donkeys, horses, guns and ammunition, medicine, and porters. I'd better get busy!

## Bagamoyo, March 21

Ready at last! I left Zanzibar on February 4 and sailed for Bagamoyo, 20 miles away. My party is now 192 persons, 22 donkeys, 12 goats, 2 horses, and a watchdog. We carry six tons of material and supplies. Now the adventure begins!

## April 3

The journey is turning into a nightmare. We are bogged down in rain and mud. Sickness is everywhere. The porters are coming down with malaria. Luckily we have quinine. My horse became infested with stomach worms and died. We are moving through a jungle. The smells are sickening. The bush slows us and tears our equipment loose from the backs of our donkeys. I can't wait to leave this place behind us.

## April 24

We have had good luck. A friendly chief sent us food in return for some of our cloth. The rains have stopped and we are moving nicely again. The scenery is beautiful. We are dazzled by wild flowers, sugarcane, Indian corn, cucumbers, eggplants, and beautiful trees against a background of giant mountain ranges. Best of all, I met an Arab trader who told me that he lived next to a white man in Ujiji. He said this man was old and had just recovered from a serious illness. I'm sure this man is Livingstone, and I am more determined than ever to find him.

## Makata Valley River, May 9

Bad luck again! The rains started once more. The men are tired. We can cover only a few miles a day. Someone in the group is stealing from us. I have had bad attacks of chills and fever. The donkeys keep getting stuck in the mud. They are beginning to die. My faithful watchdog has also died. Each day, more men come down with the chills. When the rains stopped, they were followed by blazing heat waves. The temperature rose to 128 degrees. One man died and another's legs were so badly swollen that he couldn't move them. Perhaps we'll find better luck in the next village.

## Mawapwa, May 22

Thank heaven for Mawapwa! The food is delicious and we are well rested. My only complaint is about insects. They are in my tent, my cot, my clothing, and in my hair. We are joining two Arab caravans and moving on.

## Tabora, June 23

What an adventure! We have traveled through 30 miles of desert. Then we passed through the lands of the Wagogo people. The Wagogo chiefs were greedy and demanded much wire, cloth, and beads before they would let us pass on. My porters tried to turn back and I had to threaten them with my pistol and my whip before they would move on. At last we reached Tabora. We have been traveling for three months and two days and we have come 525 miles from the coast.

## Malagarasi River, October 25

We have narrowly escaped death. The road to Ujiji was blocked by a bandit chief named Mirambo. He made war on the Arabs at Tabora and we were stranded there for many weeks. We have finally decided to take our chances and move toward Ujiji. I have 54 men left. Some deserted. Others fell sick. We stumbled into a grassy plain where we saw many wild animals. Herds of buffalo, zebra, giraffe, and antelope ran past us. At the river bank, I was about to dive into deep water for a refreshing swim when I saw a giant crocodile swimming beneath me! We stocked up with food and pushed forward. We have seen lions, leopards, elephants, and rhinos. Will we ever reach Ujiji?

## November 3

Great news! I met two men who had been in Ujiji eight days ago. They said they saw a white man dressed like me. His beard was white and he looked old and sick. It must be Livingstone! He is alive! My men have packed our supplies and we are about to complete the last leg of our journey. Next stop, Ujiji.

## Ujiji, November 10

We have made it! We completed a journey of 975 miles in 236 days. The men were overjoyed. We marched into the village and greeted the chief. My heart was pounding. I asked a native if a white man lived in the village. He pointed toward a hut.

I saw an old man wearing a blue cloth cap and gray tweed trousers. I walked toward him. I was now face to face with him. I wanted to hug him but I was afraid that I would frighten him. I removed my helmet and in a trembling voice said, "Doctor Livingstone, I presume?" He looked at me for a moment and smiled.

*Postscript.* Stanley's newspaper accounts of his adventures in Africa aroused tremendous interest around the world. Stanley told of great quantities of ivory, copper, cotton, copal, and many other resources. Europeans made a mad rush to explore and colonize the interior of Africa.

As for Livingstone, he refused to leave the jungle with Stanley. He chose instead to continue working in his beloved Africa. A year after Stanley found him, Livingstone died.

## UNDERSTANDING THE STORY

A. *Write T for each statement that is true, F for each statement that is false, and N for each statement that is not mentioned in the story.*

1. In the early 19th century, little was known about the interior of Africa.

2. The interior of Africa was the most dangerous part of the world.
3. Asia was called the "Dark Continent."
4. Europeans were afraid to explore the unknown parts of Africa.
5. Henry Stanley was a missionary who was lost in Africa.
6. David Livingstone was a newspaper reporter who searched for Henry Stanley.
7. Henry Stanley was the greatest explorer of the 19th century.

**B.** *Tell which statements by Henry Stanley encouraged Europeans to colonize Africa.*

1. Many of my men became ill with malaria.
2. I was dazzled by the sugarcane, Indian corn, and eggplants.
3. The temperature sometimes rose to 128 degrees.
4. There are large amounts of ivory and metals.
5. Natives will trade valuable things for cloth, beads, and brass wire.
6. There are many dangerous animals.
7. Many of the natives are very friendly.
8. There are bandits who rob and kill.

**C.** Imagine that you have a choice. You can go to Africa with Stanley to search for Livingstone, or you can stay at home. What would you do? Why?

## ACTIVITIES AND INQUIRIES

1. Use each of the following key terms in a sentence.
   Dark Continent                    missionary
   expedition                        reporter
2. Go to the library. Prepare a report on Stanley, Livingstone, or another African explorer.
3. Pretend that you are Stanley. You are looking for Livingstone but have not yet found him. Write a news report telling of your experiences.
4. Now assume that you have found Livingstone. Send a report to your newspaper telling how you found him.

# 14. The Treaty—Guns for Gold

*Europeans now raced into* Africa's interior. Countries sent agents to explore and claim territory. Often, several countries went after the same territories. Tempers flared and threats were exchanged. England and France almost went to war over a desert in the Sudan.

European countries finally decided that it was both foolish and dangerous to fight over Africa. They met in Berlin in 1884 and 1885 to set rules for the colonization of Africa. They tried to settle arguments and to divide Africa in a fair manner. They also tried to provide for free trade on African rivers. The only people not represented at the conference were the Africans themselves.

By 1900 Africa had been divided up among the countries of Europe. Much of Africa's territory was gained by treaties. In our story, a chief is about to sign a treaty with a European nation. See if you can understand why Europeans were more interested in making treaties than in using force. Why did the chiefs sign these treaties? Who will gain the most from the treaties? Why?

## Matabeleland, 1888

"Chief Bengula, I can't remember when I've had a more enjoyable time," said C. D. Rudd, a British agent. "The hunting and fishing have been excellent, and you are a wonderful host."

"Mr. Rudd," said the chief, through his interpreter, "it has been a pleasure to have you visit us. Please come back soon."

"Chief Bengula, I don't mean to upset you, but is it true that other tribes are preparing to go to war with you?"

"Mr. Rudd, my people are ready to defend their homeland against attack. Any attackers will find that we have sharp claws."

"Chief Bengula, I respect you very much. I would like to help you if you will let me."

"What do you have in mind?"

"My government is willing to supply you with guns, ammunition, and a gunboat. If you have these weapons, no tribe will dare to attack your people!"

"And what must I do for you?"

"Just put your mark ("X") on this piece of paper. This is your word that we will always be friends. In return for our help, you will give us the rights to all of the yellow rocks under your land. You will let us hire your people to help us to remove these rocks. You see, chief, you need our weapons, and we need the rocks under your land. So we need one another."

"You are indeed a good friend, Mr. Rudd!"

## UNDERSTANDING THE STORY

**A.** *Write T for each statement that is true and O for each statement that is an opinion.*

1. Chief Bengula was asked to sign a treaty.
2. Chief Bengula made a mistake by signing the treaty.
3. Mr. Rudd deserved to be promoted to a higher position because he got the chief to sign the treaty.
4. The chief gave away the rocks (minerals) under his land.
5. The treaty was signed in Africa.
6. The treaty was the best one Chief Bengula could get.
7. Mr. Rudd's country would supply Chief Bengula with guns and ammunition.
8. Chief Bengula could not read the treaty he signed.

**B.** *Complete each of the following sentences.*

1. Europeans wanted to sign —— with the Africans.
2. C. D. Rudd was a —— agent.
3. Chief Bengula thought the —— would attack him.
4. "If a tribe attacks us, they will find we have ——."
5. "We will supply your tribe with guns and ——."
6. "Just sign this —— with an 'X.'"
7. "We will have the rights to the —— under the ——."
8. "You need our ——; we need your ——."

C. Imagine that you are a United States president in the late 19th century. Would you send Mr. Rudd to arrange a treaty with an African nation? Explain. What would an American president want from an African chief? What would you give in return?

## ACTIVITIES AND INQUIRIES

1. Look at the cartoon below. Why is the European saying this? Is it true? Explain. If you were the chief, would you sign the treaty? Explain. What does the chief want? What do the Europeans want? Why do the Europeans bother with a treaty? Why do they not simply take what they want?

*"Chief, you drive a hard bargain."*

2. Imagine that you are Mr. Rudd. Write a letter to the head of your department at home. Tell him about your experiences with the African chief.

3. Now pretend that you have received the letter from Mr. Rudd. Are you satisfied with his work? Explain.

4. Suppose that Chief Bengula is being tried by a court of members of his tribe. He is accused of giving away tribal lands. You are given the job of defending the chief's signing of the treaty. Prepare his defense.

5. Imagine that you are accusing Chief Bengula of doing wrong by signing the treaty. Prepare the case against him.

# 15. Africans Learn to Obey

*Europeans took much from Africa,* but they brought a number of good things as well. They built schools, hospitals, roads, and railroads. They installed telephones and telegraphs, provided jobs, and put an end to the slave trade. Agriculture was modernized and industries were developed. But these things had to be paid for. The Africans paid with their hard work. They provided the cheap labor needed to make profits. They paid taxes from their wages. In addition, African chiefs were told to provide men to help clear jungles and build roads and highways. These men had no choice. They were forced to work.

Some colonists treated their people decently, but others treated their people cruelly. The worst colony was the Congo Free State. This area belonged to King Leopold II of Belgium. Leopold was concerned with one thing—making money. There were great profits to be made from ivory and rubber. Leopold hired companies to gather the rubber and ivory. He instructed them to use forced labor. Africans were beaten, crippled, tortured, and even killed for not gathering enough rubber. Women and children were held as hostages until the men returned with their quota. Men were forced to spend long periods of time in the forests in order to gather rubber. Some did not gather enough and ran away. Others were killed by wild animals.

In our story some African workers are staging a work stoppage. How do you suppose the story will end?

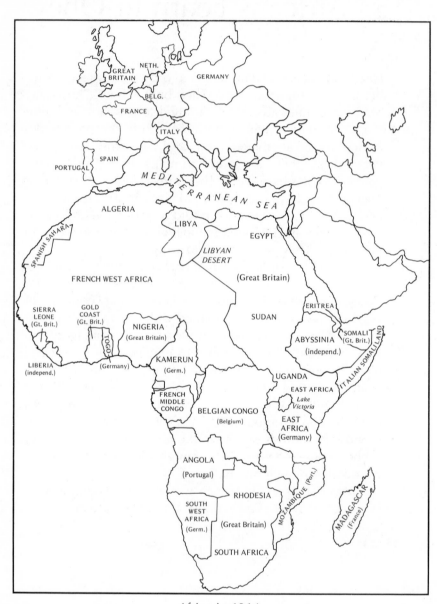

*Africa in 1914*

# Belgian Congo, 1903

"Mr. Hendricks, please come quickly. We have a terrible problem!"

"Yes, Smith, what is it?"

"Five natives are refusing to go to work. They are just sitting together and the others are watching them. I don't like it one bit!"

Hendricks quickly pushed through the crowd of natives, and Smith followed. He approached the five men who suddenly stopped speaking to one another and looked up. Their mouths were set defiantly, but there was a trace of fear in their eyes.

"All right, boys, rest time is over! It's time to go to work. Pick up your baskets and move out!"

One man stood and faced Hendricks. He was obviously the leader of the group. He nervously cleared his throat and prepared to speak.

"Sir, we do not wish to make trouble. We have tried to please you by working hard and you only force us to work harder. Each time you send us out for rubber, you ask that we bring back more. It takes us many days and much hard work to fill these baskets. We must sleep away from our families, and it is lonely and cold. We only ask that you—"

"Seize that man!" Hendricks cried. The man was immediately set upon by three armed men who tied his hands behind his back. The man began to scream with fear.

At Hendricks' command the man was pushed into a hut. The others gathered around, and wild eyed, they waited and listened.

They heard the man pleading and moaning. Suddenly there was a horrible shriek! Then another! Then silence. The natives picked up their baskets and ran off to the forest. The work stoppage was over.

Hendricks looked down at the dead native. He smiled and said to Smith, "Well, I gave him his wish. He'll never have to gather rubber again!"

## UNDERSTANDING THE STORY

**A.** *Tell which item makes each statement correct.*

1. This story takes place in (*a*) the Congo (*b*) Egypt (*c*) South Africa.
2. The Europeans got the Africans to work harder by (*a*) being kind (*b*) using force (*c*) paying more money.
3. Some natives refused to work because they (*a*) wanted more money (*b*) thought the work was too hard (*c*) wanted a five-day week.
4. Hendricks wanted to teach the native leader (*a*) how to collect rubber (*b*) how to speak English (*c*) a lesson.
5. The African colony where natives were most exploited and ill-treated was (*a*) Algeria (*b*) Cape Colony (*c*) Congo.
6. The natives complained that when they worked hard (*a*) they were made to work harder (*b*) they were paid less (*c*) nobody talked to them.
7. When Hendricks spoke to the natives (*a*) they did not listen (*b*) they were afraid (*c*) they refused to obey because he was a European.
8. After Hendricks killed the native leader, the workers (*a*) ran away (*b*) rushed back to work (*c*) refused to work.

**B.** *Which statements below might Hendricks have made?*

1. Natives must be afraid of us or they will not work.
2. We do not want trouble with the Europeans.
3. It takes us many days to fill our baskets with rubber.
4. I'll teach the natives a lesson they won't forget.
5. We are often away from our families; it is very lonely.

**C.** Pretend that you are the owner of a rubber plantation in Africa. Would you hire Hendricks as your foreman? Explain. You are a worker. How would you like to work with Hendricks as your foreman? Explain.

## ACTIVITIES AND INQUIRIES

1. Study the map of Africa in 1914 on page 262 and answer the following questions.

   *a.* France controlled (1) Nigeria (2) the Middle Congo (3) South Africa.

    *b.* Kamerun (Cameroon) was a possession of (1) Germany (2) Italy (3) Great Britain.

    *c.* Egypt was a possession of (1) Great Britain (2) Germany (3) France.

    *d.* Portugal controlled (1) Mozambique (2) Angola (3) Algeria.

    *e.* An independent African nation not controlled by a European country was (1) Liberia (2) Somaliland (3) Tripoli.

    *f.* Which country did *not* control lands in Africa in 1914? (1) France (2) Japan (3) Spain.

2. The caption of a cartoon based on the story is: "This will teach them a lesson!" Draw the cartoon.

3. Imagine that you are a Belgian. Your government has sent you to the Congo. Write a report describing what Hendricks did. What action would you recommend that the Belgian government take? Why? If none, explain why.

4. Assume that Hendricks is being tried for murder. You have been named the prosecuting attorney. Prepare the case against Hendricks.

5. Suppose that you were assigned to defend Hendricks. Prepare his defense.

# 16. The Minority Rules

*Many Europeans disapproved of* the cruel ways in which black Africans were treated. They looked for better ways than torture and fear to control the large native population. Greatly outnumbered by the black population, the white settlers in South Africa developed a system that guaranteed they would continue to be the controlling group.

Beginning in 1926 and continuing up to the present day, the white-controlled government has passed strict racial segregation laws. Black Africans must carry passes at all times. The penalty for not carrying a pass is a fine or jail term. Blacks are not allowed in certain buildings, parks, theaters, and libraries. These are reserved for whites only. The best jobs go to the whites.

Black South Africans, for the most part, are not taught the skills that would enable them to get better-paying jobs. They must obey strict curfew laws. They cannot travel around the country without the permission of the government. If a black African takes a job in a town away from his home, he cannot go home after his workday is finished. Black Africans also find it difficult to leave the country. If they leave South Africa without permission, they are by law forbidden to reenter.

The whites say that the black Africans are as much in favor of the separation of the races as they are. They say that only black Africans receive free education and low-cost housing and health care. They also claim that blacks in South Africa have higher incomes and better living conditions than blacks living anywhere else in Africa. The whites say that thanks to their policies South Africa is the richest and most highly developed country in Africa.

Many people predicted that there would be an explosion in South Africa. The first one came in 1960. Thousands of Africans left their passes at home and walked to the police stations to surrender for arrest. They hoped to force the government to stop demanding that they carry passes. Police fired on the marchers. A number of demonstrators were killed or wounded. The government, however, was not prepared to give up its tight control over the black population. Nor was it willing to give blacks the right to vote.

In 1976 black Africans protested once more. This time, it was against low pay and discrimination. Workers walked off their jobs. A number of blacks were shot and killed. Black leaders were jailed and kept in prison without trial. Others lost their jobs. Thus the South African government continued to control the black population through force and fear.

Many nations have criticized South Africa. The United Nations has passed resolutions condemning South Africa's policies. Even a small number of South African whites have been critical of their government. These people are usually silenced by prison terms or house arrest. In our story we find out why some South African whites disagree with their government. Ask yourself why the government refuses to change its policies. Is it wise for the government to continue these policies?

## Cape Town, 1970

"Mr. Jones, it is my duty to tell you that you are under arrest," said police officer Crosby. "Please come with me at once."

Jones and Crosby left the newspaper office. Jones was placed in a car and taken to the station house. He was escorted into a private room. An old enemy, Mr. Greene, awaited him.

"Well, Greene," said Jones, "I see that you've called the dogs out on me again."

"Jones, you're the worst kind of fool! Don't you understand that your newspaper articles are loaded pistols held against the heads of all the whites in this country?"

"As a newspaperman, it is my job to tell the truth. Why are you so afraid of what I write?"

"We've talked about this many times, Mr. Jones. You know as well as I that we whites are outnumbered by Africans by more than three to one. You also know what will happen to us if we educate them and let them work alongside us—or even mix with us. They'll demand more money and better housing. They will want to be able to vote! Once that happens, we'll have no choice except to leave this country. By God, if you can't see that, then you deserve to live in a country governed by these people!"

"Greene, open your eyes! Up and down this continent, Africans are demanding and getting a voice in government. If we whites have any future at all, it will be as partners with Africans, not as their masters."

"Jones, you're hopeless! It is useless to reason with you. But whether you agree with us or not, your attacks against the government must stop. I am therefore placing you under house arrest for the next two years. I will see to it that you never write for a South African newspaper again. The thoughts expressed in this room today make me tremble for the future of this country!"

Jones stared hard at Greene. "For the first time, we agree!"

## UNDERSTANDING THE STORY

**A.** *Write* T *for each statement that is true and* F *for each statement that is false.*

1. Many Europeans did not approve of treating African natives cruelly.
2. Jones was arrested because of what he wrote.
3. There are more whites than blacks in South Africa.
4. Greene will be happy when the natives have the right to vote.
5. More and more Africans are taking part in their government.
6. Jones feels that if whites have any future in Africa, it is as partners with the blacks.
7. Greene will leave South Africa if blacks get the right to vote.

**B.** *Tell which statements show how life in South Africa is affected by the white government's fear of the black population.*

1. There is little freedom of the press.
2. People cannot be arrested unless they are accused of committing a serious crime.

3. Police officers are equally fair to blacks and whites.
4. The government of South Africa does not wish to be criticized.
5. There are no more newspapers in South Africa.
6. Blacks and whites are not permitted to mix.
7. A newspaperman can be placed under house arrest.
8. There is no fear of the government in South Africa by either blacks or whites.

C. Imagine that you are a member of Congress. A bill has been introduced that will end the right of newspapers to criticize the United States government. Prepare to speak either for or against this bill. Can we have a democracy without freedom of the press? Explain.

## ACTIVITIES AND INQUIRIES

1. The caption of a cartoon is: "You're under arrest!" Assume that the person arrested is a writer or reporter. Draw the cartoon, using the ideas in the story.
2. Imagine that you are an American newspaper reporter in South Africa. You see what happens to Mr. Jones. Write your story so that it will be approved by the South African *censors* (those people who read all material and decide if it can be printed).
3. Now write another story about Mr. Jones so that it might not be approved by the South African censors.
4. Look at your local newspaper. Clip out all the pictures that you feel would not be permitted in South African newspapers. Explain why.
5. Read the following selection. It was written by Chief Albert Luthuli, a South African, who was awarded the Nobel Peace Prize in 1960. Then answer the questions by telling which item makes each statement correct.

> Here in South Africa white supremacy is worshiped like a god. The government claims that white men built everything that is worthwhile in the country. They are the only ones who can plan and build the cities, the industries, and run the farms and mines. Only they, the whites say, are fit to own and control

these things. Black people are only temporary vis-
itors in the cities. They are supposed to be fit only for
the dirtiest, least important jobs. Blacks are not fit to
share in political power. These ideas survive in South
Africa because the people who support them profit
from them.

a. The author of this selection wrote about (1) England (2)
   South Africa (3) West Africa.
b. According to many white South Africans, the only ones who
   could build the cities were (1) the blacks (2) the whites (3)
   members of special tribes.
c. Black people were considered (1) good city planners (2) the
   best politicians (3) fit only for the least meaningful jobs.
d. White supremacy was (1) insisted upon by both races (2)
   insisted upon by the blacks (3) insisted upon by the whites.
e. White rule survived in South Africa because (1) the United
   Nations approved of it (2) its supporters profited from it (3)
   black people preferred it.

# 17. Jomo Kenyatta

*While the government of South Africa* tightened its control over its black people, explosions were taking place elsewhere in Africa. World War II forced Europeans to use Africans as soldiers or factory workers in Europe. These Africans came in contact with Europeans and learned from them. They listened to speeches about freedom. They saw black Americans in uniform, bearing arms. Most of all, they watched Europeans fighting among themselves. Africans came to realize that their masters were not all powerful. These Africans would never again be the same. They returned to Africa with new ideas. They wanted what the whites had in Africa: good schools, good jobs, and good salaries. Most of all they wanted to be free people in their own country.

Jomo Kenyatta (ken-YAH-tah) was one of those African people who returned to their countries after having lived in Europe. Here is his story.

## Nairobi, 1974

You are Jomo Kenyatta and you believe that the price of freedom comes very high.

As a boy growing up in Kenya (KEEN-ya) you would cry with tears of anger because your tribe, the Kikuyu (kee-KOO-yoo), were no longer what they used to be. They and the other African tribes were pushed aside by European settlers, who took the best lands for themselves. A few thousand white farmers produced four times as much farm goods as Kenya's entire native population of 8 million. Secretly you admired the Europeans. They had worked hard to conquer crop and livestock diseases, insects, and dry spells. But you hated them as well. They and the settlers from

271

India controlled your country. They owned the best land and most of the industry. They ran the government. You swore that some- day you would help your people to become the masters of their own country.

You spoke often and well. People began to listen. You became a leader of the Kikuyu tribe. Soon money was collected to send you to England. Your backers hoped that you would win some rights for your people from the English.

You stayed away from your homeland for 15 years. You lived in England and traveled to other European countries. But you never forgot Kenya. You spoke, you pleaded, you demanded a greater share of government for your people. The English turned a deaf ear.

You returned to Kenya in 1946. Once again you became a leader of your people. You demanded the vote, the end of color discrimi- nation, and the return of some of the best lands to the native Africans. While you talked, many of your followers took an oath to kill Europeans or frighten them into leaving the country. These people called themselves the Mau Mau (mow mow). They ter- rorized both blacks and whites. They spilled the blood of women and children. Throats were slashed. They burned entire villages to the ground. All who did not go along with them were the enemy. Years of pent-up rage were now drenching Kenya with the blood of her children.

The Mau Mau never attacked you. This made the police sus- picious. They decided to arrest you. You maintained your inno- cence but did not resist. You were sentenced and imprisoned for seven years.

The war went on. It would last for almost ten years. At last the African fire burned itself out. The Mau Mau had killed 30 white civilians, almost 2,000 Africans, and 38 British security men. The Mau Mau dead totalled over 7,800.

The British got the message. They began to prepare Kenya for independence.

You were released from prison in 1961. Your party immediately chose you as its leader. Elections were held, and for the first time your people were given the right to vote. When all the votes had been counted, you learned that your people had elected you prime minister of Kenya. You thanked them by shouting, "I have snatched you out of the lion's belly!" Your people understood.

You decided that it would be best to forget the bitter past. You kept close ties with the British. You believed that your country still had much to learn from them. You tried to teach your people that independence is a responsibility. Independence means hard work. You invited all races to work together for Kenya's future. Your people listened.

You are Jomo Kenyatta, and you believe that the price of freedom comes very high. You were not afraid to pay that price!

## UNDERSTANDING THE STORY

A   *Tell which statements are true.*

1. Africans resented Europeans for having taken advantage of them.
2. All Africans were against using violence.
3. Kenyatta secretly admired Europeans.
4. Kenyatta spent many years away from his homeland.
5. The Mau Mau attacked Kenyatta.
6. The Mau Mau killed more whites than blacks.
7. The Mau Mau used terror tactics against both blacks and whites.
8. As prime minister Kenyatta threw the British out of Kenya.

B.  Pretend that your government is doing certain things that you feel are wrong. How can you make your feelings known to your government? What action would you expect to be taken as a result of your efforts?

## ACTIVITIES AND INQUIRIES

1. Go to the library. Prepare a report on the Mau Mau movement.
2. Pretend that you are a writer. Your assignment is to prepare a motion picture or television script on an African nation's struggle for independence. Who would your main characters be? Describe some of the major scenes in your script.
3. Go to the library. Prepare a report on the life and work of the leader of an African nation's independence movement.

4. Imagine that you are a British soldier who is fighting against the Mau Mau. Write a letter home describing your feelings about the Mau Mau. Why do you think they are so violent?
5. Study the table of lives lost in the Mau Mau conflict and answer the questions that follow.

### Casualties in Kenya in the Mau Mau Conflict, to 1960

|  | Persons Killed | | | Persons Wounded and Captured | | |
|---|---|---|---|---|---|---|
|  | Africans | Asians | Europeans | Africans | Asians | Europeans |
| Mau Mau | 7,800 | 0 | 0 | 7,850 | 0 | 0 |
| Security forces (soldiers) | 470 | 2 | 38 | 400 | 12 | 62 |
| Civilians | 1,315 | 20 | 30 | 0 | 0 | 0 |

*a.* The table shows losses in the Mau Mau conflict in (1) Europe (2) Africa (3) Kenya.
*b.* Most of those killed in the fighting were (1) Africans (2) Asians (3) Europeans.
*c.* The number of civilians killed in the fighting was (1) smaller than the number of soldiers killed (2) much larger than the number of soldiers killed (3) about the same as the number of soldiers killed.
*d.* The smallest number of those killed, wounded, or captured were (1) Asians (2) Europeans (3) Africans.
*e.* The number of Europeans killed and wounded in the fighting was (1) much smaller than the number of Africans (2) much larger than the number of Africans (3) about the same.

# 18. The End of Imperialism

*Much of Africa south of* the Sahara Desert is now controlled by black Africans. But independence has not brought an end to Africa's problems. In our story, four United Nations delegates are having a drink in the delegates' lounge. They are delegates from England, France, Belgium, and a new African nation.

See if this selection helps you to understand why modern-day Africa continues to face serious problems. Ask yourself whether the Europeans and the African can speak as equals. What changes had taken place in Africa by this time?

## United Nations, New York, 1976

ENGLISHMAN *(speaking to the African).* Really, my friend, your speech today in the General Assembly was a lot of rot! Don't you think that it's a bit foolish to blame us for the problems that you yourselves can't seem to solve?

FRENCHMAN *(also speaking to the African).* Have you forgotten that we always treated your people as equals? In our eyes, you were Frenchmen. My countrymen need not apologize for anything!

AFRICAN. I see that my Belgian friend has nothing to say.

BELGIAN *(angrily).* Oh, nonsense! We taught you a better way of life, and you kicked us out. You're just too dishonest to admit that you made a mistake. Admit it! You simply aren't ready to rule yourselves.

AFRICAN. So it comes down to that! "The poor, helpless, ignorant Africans can't manage without Bwana." You laugh at us because we fight among ourselves, because we suffer from poverty, disease, and dishonest leadership. But what of yourselves? How many times have Europeans made war against one another?

Have you solved your problem of poverty? Have you found a way to solve inflation? Are your leaders so very honest?

ENGLISHMAN. That's quite enough! You have a sharp tongue and a bright mind but a very poor memory. You forget that my country and not yours provided for your education. Were it not for Europeans, people like you would still be ignorant tribesmen living as your ancestors did.

*(At this, the Frenchman and the Belgian exchange smiles.)*

AFRICAN. You Europeans still think of yourselves as the finest creatures on earth. For over a century, you have pushed the people in Asia and Africa around. But today a new generation of Asians and Africans challenges you for the leadership of the world. Already you tremble before the might of the Chinese. You worry about competition from the Japanese. You have led us into the 20th century, but we will move into the 21st century under our own power! No, gentlemen, now that you can no longer take what you need from us, it is you who begin to stumble!

BELGIAN. Your future is bad government, hunger, disease, famine, and civil war. One day, you will look back with longing and realize that we brought you your finest hour.

AFRICAN. No, it is for you to look back! Your greatness is already behind you. Ours is soon to begin! Gentlemen, I bid you good day.

*(The African walks quickly away from the other three men.)*

ENGLISHMAN. What gall!

FRENCHMAN. You take him too seriously. He is hopelessly ignorant.

BELGIAN. Gentlemen, let us forget this bit of nonsense. I propose a toast. Let us drink to a bright future for our people everywhere.

*(The Englishman and the Frenchman are slow to pick up their glasses.)*

## UNDERSTANDING THE STORY

**A.** *Write T for each statement that is true, F for each statement that is false, and N for each statement that is not mentioned in the story.*

1. Today much of Africa south of the Sahara is controlled by black Africans.
2. Independence has solved Africa's problems.

3. The Belgians were the best colonial rulers.
4. The Frenchman says that the French treated the Africans as equals.
5. Most African nations were not ready for independence when they received it.
6. The African thinks that his countrymen can rule themselves without European help.
7. All African nations get along well with one another.
8. The British were the worst colonial rulers.

**B.** *With which of the statements would the African in the story agree?*

1. Western leaders are not honest about Africa.
2. Westerners treated Africans as their equals.
3. The West taught us a better way of life.
4. The West has not solved its own problems. How can it expect Africa to be different?
5. We suffer from poverty and disease.
6. African countries are just as powerful as European nations.
7. The West is afraid of the power of the Chinese and the competition of the Japanese.
8. One day Westerners will be called back to run Africa.

**C.** Assume that you are a visitor to the gallery of the United Nations General Assembly. You have heard the African, Belgian, French, and English delegates make speeches. Which of them impressed you most? Explain. Which of them impressed you least? Explain.

## ACTIVITIES AND INQUIRIES

1. Go to the library. Prepare a report on one of the new African nations. Include material on resources, population, climate, and outlook for the future.
2. Imagine that you are the United States ambassador to the United Nations. The African ambassador from a new nation speaks to you about American aid for his country. Prepare a list of questions you would ask this African representative. Write the answers that you would expect him to give about his country.
3. Pretend that you are a reporter. Interview the Belgian representative to the United Nations. Ask about Belgium's treat-

ment of the native population in the Congo before the Congo
gained independence. What will the Belgian say?
4.  Assume that you are a leader in the Congo today. Would you
    ever ask the Belgians to return and run your country? Explain.
5.  Look at the map of present-day Africa below and answer the
    questions on page 279.

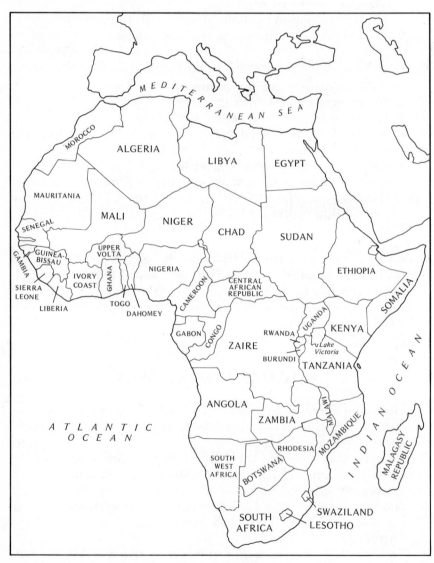

*Africa in 1976*

*a.* A nation in Central Africa is (*a*) Algeria (*b*) Zaire (*c*) South Africa.

*b.* The nation that is between Rhodesia and the Indian Ocean is (*a*) Zambia (*b*) Angola (*c*) Mozambique.

*c.* Angola has seaports on the (*a*) Atlantic Ocean (*b*) Mediterranean Sea (*c*) Indian Ocean.

*d.* Chad is south of (*a*) Libya (*b*) Zaire (*c*) Gabon.

*e.* The Sudan is (*a*) south of Egypt (*b*) on the Mediterranean Sea (*c*) west of Chad.

*f.* Countries without seaports are (*a*) Zambia and Nigeria (*b*) Tanzania and Rhodesia (*c*) Chad and Zambia.

*g.* Nations on the west coast of Africa are (*a*) Somalia and Tanzania (*b*) Algeria and Libya (*c*) Mauritania and Senegal.

*h.* Nations on the east coast of Africa are (*a*) Angola and South West Africa (*b*) Zaire and Sudan (*c*) Kenya and Tanzania.

"That wasn't bad at all," Jack said to Mr. Miller.

"Oh, do you mean you enjoyed learning about the Western powers and their colonies?" Mr. Miller asked.

"I wouldn't go that far. Still, it was kind of interesting to see how the colonies began to do their own thing. It almost reminded me of how my parents and I get along."

"How do you mean, Jack?"

"Well, my parents also tell me that they know best, and that I must follow their advice. And they brought law, order, and health into my life. But I understand that I must begin to make my own choices. Otherwise, I'll never grow up."

"In other words, Jack, your parents behaved toward you just the way the Western powers behaved toward their colonies."

"Not exactly. I'm not so sure that the Western powers really had the colonies' best interests in mind. And no matter how angry I get with my parents, I'm not going to drop bombs on them. I'll never use violence against them. In fact, that's what I really don't understand."

"What's that, Jack?"

"I don't understand how the colonies could just push the mother countries out of their lives."

"Perhaps the colonies are simply making their own choices," said Mr. Miller. "They too want to grow up. Maybe one day these countries will feel themselves truly grown up. Then they can be friendly with the Western powers."

"One thing is certain," said Jack. "They can never go back to what they once had."

There was silence for a moment as teacher and student thought over what had been said.

Jack broke the silence. "Mr. Miller, there is something else I don't understand. The Western powers had rough times with their colonies. How come they get along so well with each other?"

Mr. Miller smiled. "I think you are in for a big surprise in Unit Eight, Jack."

# World War I

"But I don't understand, Mr. Miller," said Jack. "How could the Western powers be so stupid? I mean, they were smart enough to take over giant countries in Africa and Asia. Why weren't they smart enough to keep out of one another's way?"

"They tried, Jack. They tried very hard."

"You mean they didn't want to go to war with one another?" Jack asked, a note of surprise in his voice.

"War was the last thing they wanted. In fact, to keep the peace each country built up its army and navy and prepared to go to war."

"What kind of crazy way is that to prevent a war?"

"Perhaps you're right, Jack," said Mr. Miller. "But don't be too hard on the Western powers. I think if you look carefully, you will find that there are still powerful countries that act this way today."

"I get it," said Jack. "You're telling me that World War I is a lesson for the way the countries in the world are acting today."

"More than a lesson, Jack. Perhaps it's a warning."

"Okay, Mr. Miller, I'm hooked. Let's find out why countries that didn't want a war were pushed into World War I."

# 1. Prelude to War

*As our first story opens,* a war between Germany and France has just ended (the Franco-Prussian War, 1870–1871). Germany won and signed a peace treaty with France. Two diplomats, a Frenchman and a German, are discussing the treaty.

See if you can understand why many people think the Franco-Prussian War was really the first step that led to the outbreak of World War I.

## Versailles, 1871

"For the last time, Poincaré (pwan-kah-RAY), why can't you listen to reason?"

"Schmidt, it is you Germans who are the unreasonable ones. You forced the war upon us. Now you push our faces in the mud and force us to sign this so-called peace treaty."

"Sir, I remind you that the French were the first to declare war. It was your Emperor Louis Napoleon, not our Prime Minister Bismarck, who swore to avenge his country's honor. Your government made a terrible mistake. Now the people of France must pay for it!"

"You make everything so simple, Schmidt. Even a lie sounds like the truth when it comes from your lips. We both know it was Germany that really wanted this war. We understand that it was Bismarck who tricked us into a war that we never even wanted. Louis Napoleon is a fool for having been tricked. But what can be said for a man like Bismarck? He unites his people with the blood of his neighbors!"

"Come, come, Poincaré. You are being carried away by your feelings. Be reasonable. You lost the war and now you must pay. We Germans want nothing more but to live in peace with you from now on. Your wounds will soon heal. You will forget this war. Let us shake hands and look forward to the time when our countries will meet as friends."

"Never! Never will my people forget this insult! We will always remember how you forced us to sign the treaty in the Hall of Mirrors of our palace at Versailles. We will remember the faces of your soldiers who occupied our country. We will hear the cries of our brothers and sisters in Alsace and Lorraine who have been stolen from us! They are being forced to live as Germans. We will remember! And one day we will present you with our bill!"

"Be careful, Poincaré. It is dangerous for a Frenchman to speak this way to a German!"

"Schmidt, that is one more thing that I will remember!"

## UNDERSTANDING THE STORY

**A.** *Tell which statements show how the Franco-Prussian War affected France.*

1. France won the Franco-Prussian War.
2. France was forced to sign a peace treaty with Germany.
3. France was made to pay for its loss to Germany.
4. Bismarck moved the capital of Germany from Berlin to Paris.
5. The war brought French lands under German rule.
6. France lost Alsace and Lorraine to Germany.
7. German soldiers occupied France.
8. After the Franco-Prussian War, France became Germany's strongest ally.

**B.** *Decide who made or might have made the remarks that follow. Write S for each statement that Schmidt made or might have made and P for each statement that Poincaré made or might have made.*

1. Germans were unreasonable.
2. Louis Napoleon swore to avenge the honor of France.
3. France was forced to sign the peace treaty.
4. Bismarck tricked France into war.
5. France lost the war and now must pay for it.

6. France will never forget this insult.
7. Germany and France must look forward to meeting as friends.
8. Germany stole Alsace and Lorraine from France.

C. Imagine that you are the United States ambassador to France. Schmidt and Poincaré have presented their cases to you. Each tried to convince you that the other started the Franco-Prussian War. Write a report to the president of the United States. Outline the French and German viewpoints. Then add your own conclusions.

## ACTIVITIES AND INQUIRIES

1. Use each of the following key terms in a sentence.
   Alsace-Lorraine                     diplomat
   military occupation                 treaty
2. Imagine that you are a reporter. Your assignment is to interview Schmidt. Write the questions you would ask him about the treaty ending the Franco-Prussian War. Now write the answers you would expect him to give.
3. Imagine that you are the same reporter. Your assignment is to interview Poincaré. Write the questions you would like to ask him about the Franco-Prussian War and the treaty that ended the war. Then write the answers he would give you.
4. Go to the library. Prepare a report on either Germany or France in 1871. In your report, include the country's industries and its agricultural and military strength.
5. The caption of a cartoon is: "You stole Alsace-Lorraine from us!" Draw the cartoon. Who would agree with the cartoon, Schmidt or Poincaré? Do you agree with the cartoon?

# 2. A Secret Treaty

*The French and the Germans* remained bitter enemies. Bismarck, the German prime minister, felt that France would go to war with his country only if other nations helped her. Bismarck worked hard to stop this from happening. He formed alliances with Austria-Hungary, Italy, and Russia. In this story, Bismarck and the Russian foreign minister are about to sign a secret treaty.

See if you can discover the weaknesses in Bismarck's plan to *isolate* France (keep her from having allies). Is it true that "the enemy of my enemy is my friend"?

## Berlin, 1887

"Congratulations, Izvolsky (ish-VOL-skee). Your people will be proud of you. The treaty we are about to sign will once again guarantee Germany's friendship with Russia."

"Herr Bismarck, this treaty does not please me nearly as much as it seems to please you."

"How can you still have doubts, Izvolsky? It is impossible —after all we have said to each other!"

"Why shouldn't I have doubts?" answered Izvolsky. "We Russians are not stupid. We know that you have signed a treaty with Austria-Hungary. Do I have to remind you, Herr Bismarck, that we Russians do not see eye to eye with your Austrian friends?"

"Calm down, Izvolsky. I am not trying to make a fool of you. We need each other. You need the money my country is prepared to lend you. We need your guarantee that Russia will never join France in a war against Germany. We Germans have no interest in your quarrel with Austria. We only want to keep the peace in Europe!"

"Herr Bismarck, you are a brilliant man. I admire you. You have

united your country. But more than that you have forced all of
Europe to fear and respect the power of Germany. Your sole
enemy, France, stands alone. Italy, Austria-Hungary, and now
Russia all join with Germany. But suppose that one day Russia and
Austria-Hungary find themselves at war with each other. How will
Germany choose then?"

"Trust me, Izvolsky. That day will never come."

## UNDERSTANDING THE STORY

**A.** *Write* T *for each statement that is true,* F *for each statement that is
false, and* N *for each statement that is not mentioned in the story.*

1. Germany made alliances with Austria-Hungary, Italy, and
   the United States.
2. Bismarck was the greatest German prime minister of all
   time.
3. Germany tried to isolate France.
4. Russia and Germany signed a treaty in 1887.
5. The Russo-German treaty was planned to prevent all future
   wars.
6. Izvolsky said that he has no doubts about the treaty.
7. The Russians and Austrians were good friends.
8. Russia promised never to join France in a war against Germany.

**B.** *Complete each of the sentences.*

1. The enemy of my enemy is my ———.
2. ———, the prime minister of Germany, formed alliances
   with Austria-Hungary, ———, and ———.
3. The treaty in the story was to guarantee Germany's friendship with ———.
4. Russians did not see eye to eye with the ———.
5. Germany needed Russia's guarantee never to join ——— in
   a war.
6. Germany did not care about Russia's quarrel with ———.
7. All of Europe respected the power of ———.
8. Germany's enemy, ———, stands alone.

## ACTIVITIES AND INQUIRIES

1.  Imagine that you are a United States senator. The president of the United States has made a treaty with a nation that has been hostile in the recent past. The country now says that it wishes to be friendly with the United States. Your job now is either to approve or reject the treaty. How would you vote? Explain the reasons for your action.

2.  Imagine that you are Bismarck's assistant. You have the map of Europe and the world in front of you. Why do you want to have an alliance with Russia? Why do you want to have an alliance with Austria-Hungary?

3.  Pretend that you are Izvolsky. Write a letter to the czar of Russia. Explain about the alliance with Germany. Tell the czar what you think Russia should do about the alliance.

4.  Now pretend that you are the czar. Answer Izvolsky's letter.

5.  Use each of the following key terms in a sentence.

    isolate              secret              guarantee
    isolation            treaty

# 3. The Power Balance

*In spite of Bismarck's efforts* to keep Russia on Germany's side, the two countries went their separate ways. In 1890 Bismarck retired. Kaiser William II (the German emperor) refused to renew the treaty with Russia. Soon France and Russia signed a treaty of their own. Bismarck's nightmare of a Germany surrounded by two enemies was beginning to come true. Europe was dividing into two armed camps, and Britain decided that it was time for her to join one of them.

*Europe in 1914*

In this story, two members of the British Parliament are privately debating England's future. See if you can predict which alliance the English will join. Why did the British have to make a choice of alliances? How had Britain kept a balance of power in Europe?

# London, 1907

"Why should we join with any of them?" asked White. "I say let these foreigners bang their heads together. Let's mind our own business!"

"White, as usual, you make no sense at all," said Brisbane. "Save your speeches for the gallery. Let us try to speak sensibly to each other."

"And what is the sensible thing for Britain to do, Brisbane?"

Brisbane thought for a moment. "There is no question. We must join one of the alliances."

"Why?" asked White. "Why can't we go on just as we have for the past hundred years? Why can't we wait for a war to begin before we decide which side to join? Why should we risk a war now? We have so little to gain by joining either side."

"Stop speaking like a fool!" answered Brisbane. "These alliances have made war more likely than ever. France, Germany, Russia, and Austria-Hungary are preparing for war. If a war starts, its flames will spread across the sea to us. We cannot avoid the war once it begins. But perhaps we can prevent a war by becoming a part of one of the alliances."

"And which side should we join?" asked White.

"That, sir, is a most difficult question," answered Brisbane. "We have been rivals of the French for a long time—especially in Africa and Asia. We are also rivals of the Russians in Asia. At the same time, the Germans talk about moving in on our African territories. They are building a navy that will soon be as powerful as ours. Truthfully, I don't like either side very much. But I do know that Britain must soon make her choice."

"And how can England choose between her enemies?" asked White.

"I suppose," answered Brisbane, "the way that Britain has always chosen."

"And what is that?"

"We have always joined with others against the most powerful country in Europe. We have kept the balance of power on the continent."

"And which country is the most powerful in Europe today?" asked White.

"The country whose navy threatens our sea-lanes is the most powerful, White. She is the nation we must join against. Do I have to draw pictures for you? Or have I answered your question?"

"No, Brisbane. In answering my question you have just answered your own!"

## UNDERSTANDING THE STORY

**A.** *Match each item in Column A with its answer in Column B.*

| COLUMN A | COLUMN B |
|---|---|
| 1. Refused to renew the treaty with Russia | (a) join an alliance |
| 2. Had nightmares of Germany surrounded by two enemies on the continent of Europe | (b) Germany |
| | (c) France and Russia |
| | (d) Kaiser William II |
| | (e) balance of power |
| | (f) Bismarck |
| 3. Continent where the English and the Russians were rivals | (g) Asia |
| | (h) Africa |
| 4. Continent where the English were the rivals of the Germans | |
| 5. Country that England feared was building a large navy | |
| 6. Name given to England's policy of joining against the most powerful country in Europe | |
| 7. Brisbane's idea of what England could do to prevent a war | |
| 8. European countries that had signed a treaty | |

**B.** *Read the following passage about the Triple Entente. Then tell whether the statements that follow are true or false.*

> Czar Nicholas II of Russia was not anxious to ally Russia with democratic France. But in 1891 the French and Russian governments took the first steps toward friendship. By 1894 there was a military alliance between France and Russia. This alliance provided that France would help Russia if Germany attacked her. Russia would help France if she was attacked by Germany. The alliance between Russia and France would last as long as the Triple Alliance of Germany, Austria-Hungary, and Italy lasted.
>
> England was still not a member of any alliance. But the competition between England and Germany for world markets increased. The German navy also challenged the British around the world. England saw that she could no longer stand alone. She sided with France and Russia. The Triple Entente (on-TOHNT) was born.

1. At first, the czar of Russia was not anxious to make an alliance with France.
2. Germany was a member of the Triple Alliance.
3. An alliance between Russia and France protected both from an attack by the United States.
4. England entered an alliance with Russia.
5. France would help Russia if England attacked her.
6. Germany was happy to allow England to have as large a navy as she wished.
7. The alliance between Russia and France would last as long as the Triple Alliance.
8. England realized that she had to join an alliance.

**C.** Assume that most of the world is divided into two alliances. Also assume that the United States is not a member of either alliance. You are the top adviser of the president of the United States. What questions would you like answered before you talk to the president about the alliances? Would you advise the president to join an alliance? Explain. If your answer is yes, on what basis should the United States join? If your answer is no, what should the United States do in the event of war?

## ACTIVITIES AND INQUIRIES

1.  Look at the outline map of Europe in 1914 on page 288. Copy the map. Label the nations of the Triple Alliance. Then label the nations of the Triple Entente.

    a.  What do you notice about the location of the countries in the Triple Alliance?
    b.  What do you notice about the location of the countries in the Triple Entente?
    c.  What are the advantages and disadvantages of these arrangements of countries to the nations of the other alliance?

2.  Use each of the following key terms in a sentence.

    entente              rival                balance of power
    alliance             armed camp

3.  Go to the library. Prepare a report on a war in which Great Britain fought as a member of an alliance. Why did Great Britain join that alliance?

4.  Prepare a poster on England and the Triple Entente. Should it read

    *England Must Join the Alliance!*
        or
    *England Must Stay Out of the Alliance!*

    Upon what did you base your decision?

# 4. An Assassin's Story

*In 1907 France, Russia, and England* joined together and formed the Triple Entente. For the next seven years, the members of both the Triple Alliance and the Triple Entente would risk war. Twice Germany and France almost went to war because of arguments over Morocco. Once Russia and Austria-Hungary threatened to go to war when Austria-Hungary took over Bosnia and Herzegovina. All of these incidents were serious and dangerous. But somehow war was avoided. One incident, however, finally brought the nations of Europe to war. It involved a secret society and the actions of one of its members in the city of Sarajevo (sah-rah-YEH-voh). The Austrian archduke was *assassinated* (murdered). World War I had begun.

See if you can learn why this one incident was explosive enough to lead to war. Why did Princip feel that it was his duty to kill the archduke?

## Sarajevo, July 1914

My name is Gavrilo Princip (PREEN-ceep). I am a Bosnian who dreams. I dream that some day all Slavic people will be united under the flag of one country: Serbia.

I hate the rulers of Austria-Hungary. They do not like the Slavic people. They do not give us the same rights as the other peoples who live in their empire. It is my duty to wake up the Slavic people. They must revolt and join their brothers and sisters in building a greater Serbia!

For months I trained with members of a secret society called the Black Hand. We believed that only violence and terror would make our dream come true. My friends taught me how to use a pistol. I hoped to use this skill very soon.

My friends and I were now ready for our most important mission. We knew that the Austrian archduke, Francis Ferdinand, and his wife were visiting Bosnia on June 28. They were not to leave the country alive! Our leaders told us that the archduke planned to make life easier for the Slavic people when he became emperor. We could not have this! If his reforms helped the Slavic people, they would never revolt. The archduke had to be stopped before he ruined our dreams of a greater Serbia!

The archduke and his wife were riding in an open car. One of our leaders had prepared a bomb. The car stopped at a bridge and the bomb was thrown. The crowd screamed as the bomb exploded. When the smoke cleared, I saw wounded people lying in the street. But the archduke and his wife were not hurt. I shivered to think that we had failed in our mission.

The driver turned the car past the corner where I was standing. It seemed too late for me to do anything. But wait! The car was slowly backing up. I could see the archduke and his wife very clearly. They were sitting just a few yards in front of me. The car was moving very, very slowly. I reached for my gun, moved forward, and pointed it at my enemy. I shot once and hit the archduke in the neck. Then his wife covered him with her body. I shot her too! Long live the Slavic people! Long live Serbia!

## UNDERSTANDING THE STORY

**A.** *Write* T *for each statement that is true and* O *for each statement that is an opinion.*

1. If the archduke had not been shot, World War I would never have started.
2. France, England, and Russia were members of the Triple Entente.
3. Russia and Austria-Hungary almost went to war because of Bosnia and Herzegovina.
4. Nothing could have stopped World War I.
5. Gavrilo Princip was a member of the Black Hand.
6. Princip wanted all Slavic people united under the flag of Serbia.
7. Princip should not have shot the archduke.
8. The archduke was assassinated at Sarajevo.

**B.** *Tell which item makes each statement correct.*

1. Germany and France almost went to war over (*a*) Morocco (*b*) Spain (*c*) England.
2. Princip hated those who ruled (*a*) Russia (*b*) France (*c*) Austria-Hungary.
3. The Black Hand believed in (*a*) the balance of power (*b*) violence and terror (*c*) passive resistance.
4. The Austrian archduke and his wife were visiting (*a*) Paris (*b*) Vienna (*c*) Sarajevo.
5. Princip shot the (*a*) French president (*b*) German kaiser (*c*) Austrian archduke.
6. A country that was not a member of the Triple Entente was (*a*) Italy (*b*) France (*c*) Russia.
7. Princip was (*a*) a member of the Russian underground (*b*) a member of the Black Hand (*c*) a special agent of British Intelligence.

**C.** Imagine that the Black Hand never existed and Princip therefore had not killed the Austrian archduke. Would there still have been a world war? Explain. If you think there would have been a world war, how do you think the war would have started?

## ACTIVITIES AND INQUIRIES

1. Use each of the following key terms in a sentence.
   assassination        Black Hand         Slavic
   archduke             mission
2. Imagine that you are a reporter at the trial of Gavrilo Princip. You are to visit him in his cell and interview him. Prepare the questions you want to ask. Answer the questions as you believe Princip would answer them.
3. Assume that your assignment is to defend Princip. Prepare his defense.
4. Assume that your job is to prosecute Princip. Prepare the case against him.
5. Go to the library. Prepare a report on Princip, the Black Hand, or Archduke Ferdinand.

# 5.  In the Trenches

*Archduke Francis Ferdinand was* assassinated on June 28, 1914. One month later, Austria-Hungary declared war on Serbia. Russia, Serbia's protector, alerted her troops and sent them to the borders of Germany and Austria-Hungary. Germany declared war on Russia.

Believing that the French would soon attack, Germany declared war on France. The British warned that they would enter the war if neutral Belgium was invaded by any of the nations at war. On August 4, 1914, Germany invaded Belgium. England then declared war on Germany. The two armed camps, the Triple Alliance and the Triple Entente, now tried to settle their differences on the battlefield.

When news of the war came, men rushed to join the armed forces. Men in uniform marched through the streets of their cities. Civilians cheered and threw flowers. Soldiers, young and old alike, marched off to the battlefields with a song on their lips. All were convinced that they would soon return victorious and covered with glory.

Let us see for ourselves what the soldiers of World War I experienced when they finally reached the battlefields. What does this story, set in Verdun (ver-DUN), France, tell you about the war? Why does Eric insist that he is not afraid?

## Verdun, 1916

Thousands of German soldiers were standing in their trenches waiting for the signal to attack. For several hours German artillery fire had been hitting the French positions. Now the shelling had stopped. Every German soldier knew that he would soon be given the order to leave his trench and try to capture the French strongholds.

Two soldiers with worried faces were talking. They nervously waited for the attack to begin.

"Hans, are you afraid?" asked Eric.

"Of course, I'm afraid. I'm not a fool or a madman," answered Hans.

"Well, I'm not afraid," said Eric. "Anything, even death, is better than living like this!"

"Eric, don't talk like a fool!"

"Why shouldn't I? Aren't we all fools? Who but a fool would volunteer to spend two years of his life living in mud and fighting with rats for scraps of bread?"

"Enough!" interrupted Hans. "Remember, you are a German soldier. You have taken an oath to protect the Fatherland. It is our duty to suffer if suffering will bring peace to our country. Let us not complain like weak old men. A good soldier must learn to hide his feelings."

"If only I could still believe these things," Eric answered sadly.

Suddenly the command "Charge!" was given. Hans and Eric picked up their weapons and pulled themselves over the trench wall. Now they somehow had to find their way across "no man's land," the area between the German and French trenches. Shells were exploding all around them. Suddenly there was the smell of gas in the air. The soldiers stopped and quickly put on their gasmasks. But some waited too long. Their lungs filled with the poison gas. They choked to death.

Hans and Eric approached the enemy trenches. There was barbed wire everywhere. The two men began to cut their way through. There was a burst of machine gun fire; rows of men fell in their tracks. Through all the noise and confusion, Hans heard one scream. It was Eric. The scream was the last sound he would ever make. Eric's arms and legs had been shot away. The rest of his body was caught on the barbed wire.

Hans stumbled forward and jumped into the enemy trench. He fired blindly, shooting at everything that moved. He saw a Frenchman who was seriously wounded. The man looked at Hans, a plea for mercy in his eyes. Hans hesitated. There was a lump in his throat. He began to back away. Suddenly the madness of the moment gripped him once again. He ran his bayonet through the fallen Frenchman.

Later, when the battle was over, the German general congratulated his soldiers. "Men," he said, "I am proud of you. You have done your duty as soldiers of the Fatherland. Thanks to you, Germany is one step closer to peace!"

At these words, Hans began to cry.


## UNDERSTANDING THE STORY

**A.** *Write T for each statement that is true and F for each statement that is false.*

1. The French were hitting the German positions with artillery fire.
2. Eric said that he would rather die than go on with the war.
3. Hans agreed with everything Eric said.
4. The area between the German and the French trenches was called "no man's land."
5. Poison gas was used as a weapon in World War I.
6. In the story Hans died and Eric lived.
7. Hans decided not to kill the wounded French soldier.
8. Hans cried when he was told that he had brought Germany closer to peace.

**B.** *Study the table below showing the military costs of World War I and complete the statements on page 299.*

### Military Costs of World War I

| Country | Total Armed Forces | Killed or Died | Wounded | Taken Prisoner |
|---|---|---|---|---|
| Austria-Hungary | 7,800,000 | 1,200,000 | 3,620,000 | 2,200,000 |
| British Empire | 8,900,000 | 900,000 | 2,100,000 | 190,000 |
| France | 8,400,000 | 1,357,800 | 4,266,000 | 537,000 |
| Germany | 11,000,000 | 1,773,700 | 4,216,000 | 1,152,800 |
| Japan | 800,000 | 300 | 907 | 3 |
| Russia | 12,000,000 | 1,700,000 | 4,950,000 | 2,500,000 |
| Serbia | 707,000 | 45,000 | 133,000 | 153,000 |
| United States | 4,735,000 | 116,500 | 204,000 | 4,500 |

1. The country that had the largest number of soldiers killed was ————.
2. The country that had the smallest number of soldiers killed was ————.
3. The two countries that had the largest number of prisoners taken were ———— and ————.
4. The country that had the second smallest number of men taken prisoner was ————.
5. The three countries that had more prisoners taken than men killed were ————, ————, and ————.
6. The country that had the largest number of wounded soldiers was ————.
7. The country that had the smallest number of wounded soldiers was ————.

C. Imagine that Hans and Eric fought in the Vietnam War. You are a reporter. Interview both men. Who supported the war? Who opposed it? For what reasons?

## ACTIVITIES AND INQUIRIES

1. Go to the library. Write a report on one of the battles of World War I.
2. Imagine that you are a soldier in a trench during World War I. Write a letter home. Tell what living in a trench is like.
3. Imagine that you are writing a script for a movie about World War I. What would you call your movie? Write an outline for your script.
4. Hans broke down because he no longer believed in the things that he had once preached to Eric. Did you ever stop believing in something? Why? How did you feel?
5. A German soldier and a French soldier would probably have disagreed about many things. On what would they have agreed? Why?

# 6. Make War for Democracy

*When World War I started* in 1914, the United States said that it would not favor one side over the other. The United States was interested only in staying out of the war. In 1916 Woodrow Wilson was reelected president. He told the American people that he had kept the country out of the war—and he meant to keep it out of the war. One year later, however, Wilson asked Congress to declare war against Germany.

In this story, Wilson is meeting with Representative Claude Kitchin of North Carolina. Kitchin is trying to convince Wilson not to send his war message to Congress. Why do you think that Wilson has changed his mind about the war? What are the main arguments that Kitchin uses?

## Washington, March 1917

"And I tell you, Mr. President, that your message to Congress will cost thousands of American lives," argued Kitchin.

The two men had been discussing their differences for over an hour.

"Mr. Kitchin," said President Wilson, his eyes flashing, "may I remind you that I have done everything possible to keep the United States out of this mess? Congress demanded war when the Germans started their submarine attacks on American ships. But I asked for peaceful talks. I got the Germans to stop their attacks on our ships. No one wanted to keep America out of this war more than I. But now Germany has gone too far!"

"Perhaps it is the United States that has gone too far," answered Kitchin. "Why shouldn't Germany try to protect herself from us? Don't our ships deliver goods to Germany's enemies? Isn't it also true that Americans have loaned large amounts of money to England and France? I beg you to think of these things, Mr. President, before you ask Congress to declare war against Germany."

"Mr. Kitchin, Americans have every right to sell their goods to anyone they wish. If private citizens want to lend money to foreign governments, that is not the business of this government. However, there is one thing that is the business of this government. The security of American citizens everywhere must be guaranteed. By God, I'm not going to sit and do nothing while German submarines blow up our ships and kill our citizens!"

"Mr. President, it's still not too late. Stop our ships from carrying goods to England and France. American business can survive without trade with these nations."

"Kitchin," answered the president a bit sadly, "I am no lover of war. In fact, I believe that Americans will pay a monstrous price for getting into this war."

Kitchin interrupted. "Then stop it before it begins. Let Americans continue to live in peace. Mr. President, please don't send that war message to Congress."

"Can't you see, Kitchin," said the president quietly, "a new world is being born? We Americans must help to shape it. Can we really have peace at home when Europe is in this great crisis? America must help to make this world safe for democracy. We can enjoy peace when we join with free people everywhere. We must bring peace and safety to all nations."

Kitchin shook his head sadly. "Mr. President, you are a decent man. I know that you mean everything you say. I'm convinced now that nothing I can say will stop you from sending that war message to Congress. I'm also afraid that, thanks to you, neither of us will ever again see a peaceful world."

*Postscript.* On April 2, 1917, President Wilson went before the Congress and asked for a declaration of war against Germany. On April 4 the Senate agreed with him by a vote of 82 to 6. On April 6 the vote in the House of Representatives was 373 to 50. A state of war existed between the United States and Germany.

# UNDERSTANDING THE STORY

A. *Write K for each statement that Kitchin made or might have made and W for each statement that Wilson made or might have made.*

1. The president's war message will cost thousands of American lives.
2. Germany has been warned to stop submarine attacks against American ships.
3. Germany should protect herself from the United States.
4. Germany has gone too far.
5. American ships should not deliver goods to Germany's enemies.
6. American firms have the right to sell their goods anywhere.
7. The security of American citizens everywhere must be guaranteed.
8. If the war message is sent, we will never again see a peaceful world.

B. *Tell which statements are true.*

1. The United States was eager to get into World War I.
2. Wilson told the American people that he would keep the country out of war.
3. Germany never attacked United States ships.
4. England and France loaned large amounts of money to the United States.
5. German submarines attacked American ships after German leaders had promised not to do so.
6. Wilson believed that the United States would not be hurt by the war.
7. Wilson and Kitchin agreed that America should go to war against Germany.
8. The Senate and the House of Representatives of the United States agreed to declare war against Germany.

C. Imagine that Wilson and Kitchin are candidates for the office of president of the United States today. Which man would get your vote? Why?

## ACTIVITIES AND INQUIRIES

1. Go to the library. Prepare a report on how the entrance of the United States into World War I affected the outcome of the war.
2. Imagine that you are a reporter. Prepare the questions that you would like to ask President Wilson. Then answer the questions as he would have done.
3. Assume that you are the same reporter. Prepare the questions that you would ask Kitchin. Answer the questions as Kitchin would have done.
4. What is wrong with the caption of the cartoon below? Explain. Change the caption so that it is correct.

*"Mr. President, won't you declare war on Germany?"*

5. Study the following selection from the document called the Fourteen Points. This was a plan to end the war and keep the peace. Decide if it is written by Wilson or Kitchin. Explain.

> We entered the war because the rights of our people were ignored.
> We demand that the world be made fit and safe to live in.
> The program of world peace is our program.

# 7. Winners Take All

*In mid-1918 Germany's drive* to Paris was stopped. Russia had been defeated and Austria-Hungary had left the war. The British, French, and American armies were preparing to sweep into German territory. Germany realized that she was on the brink of defeat; she asked for an *armistice* (an end to the fighting). It was now up to the leaders of the winning nations to make a peace plan that would prevent war from breaking out again.

In this story President Wilson is meeting with leaders of the victorious European powers. They are talking about the peace conference that will soon take place.

See if you can guess how the winners treated the losers. Why was Wilson a hero in France? Why were there such great differences of opinion between Wilson and the other leaders?

## Paris, 1919

"Congratulations, Mr. Wilson," said Premier Georges Clemenceau (klem-on-SEW) of France. "How does it feel to be the most popular man in France?"

Wilson blushed. He was the first American president ever to visit Europe. He too was amazed by the way the French people had cheered him.

David Lloyd George, the British prime minister, looked up. "Yes, Wilson, I believe that the European people think of you as a shining knight. You are the one who will give back to them what this war has taken."

"And what do you suppose that is?" asked Wilson.

"I'll answer that," said Clemenceau. "My people want to make sure that Germany will never attack them again. They will be satisfied with nothing less than this security."

"And my people," added Lloyd George, "feel that someone must pay for the war. Germany started the war—why shouldn't she pay for it?"

"Gentlemen," said Wilson a bit sharply, "I didn't come to Europe to sign a peace treaty that will cripple Germany. We must deal justly with the Germans. Otherwise, there will be no lasting peace!"

"Treat them justly!" shouted Clemenceau. "These people have invaded France twice in the last 50 years. They invaded Belgium, attacked passenger ships, and killed innocent civilians. They forced Russia to sign a harsh treaty. They would gladly have picked our bones clean if they had won. You ask for justice for these people?"

"Especially for these people," answered Wilson. "Gentlemen,

*Europe in 1919*

these people believe in me. They asked that the shooting be stopped because they trusted me to see that they would be treated fairly."

"Nonsense, Wilson," boomed Lloyd George. "The Germans asked for a halt because they knew they were beaten. If we follow your advice, Germany will leave this conference the strongest country in Europe. Is that how you plan to build a lasting peace?"

The arguments continued for days. Wilson was no longer so sure of himself. He began to show signs of being tired and nervous. Slowly he gave in on many of his ideas. Clemenceau and Lloyd George were too much for him. At last, the treaty was ready.

"Well, Wilson," said Clemenceau, "you may be proud of yourself. Thanks to you, we have agreed to a League of Nations. Never again will nations have to go to war to settle their differences. History will remember you as a good man who helped to make this war the last war. War is finished!"

Wilson thought for a moment. "I pray, sir, that your prediction will come true—not for my sake, but for the sake of humanity."

*Postscript.* The Treaty of Versailles included a plan for creating a League of Nations. Germany was forced to give up some of her land in Europe and all her colonies overseas. She had to pay a heavy fine to cover the costs of the war. Her army and navy were destroyed. The Germans protested, but they had no choice. They signed the treaty rather than risk starting the war again.

Woodrow Wilson left Paris believing that his League of Nations would right all the wrongs of the treaty. He sent the treaty to the Senate of the United States for approval, but the Senate, which opposed the League, turned him down. Soon afterward, Wilson suffered a stroke from which he never recovered. He died a bitter man. His own people had turned their backs on his dream of world peace.

## UNDERSTANDING THE STORY

**A.** *Tell which statements Wilson would have agreed with.*

1. Germany must be punished so that she will never make war again.
2. Germany should pay the full cost of the war.

3. The winning nations should not take advantage of Germany.
4. The Germans expect to be treated fairly.
5. Germany called for a halt in the war because she knew she was beaten.
6. The League of Nations will prevent future wars.
7. This war must be the war to end all wars.
8. The Treaty of Versailles was very fair to Germany.

**B.** *Write* T *for each statement that is true,* F *for each statement that is false, and* N *for each statement that is not mentioned in the story.*

1. France asked that the fighting be stopped.
2. Wilson, Clemenceau, and Lloyd George agreed on most things.
3. Wilson was very popular with the French people.
4. The German people loved Americans.
5. England wanted Germany to pay the full cost of the war.
6. After Wilson, Clemenceau was Germany's best friend.
7. Wilson was afraid that the war might continue unless Germany was fairly treated.
8. The League of Nations was Wilson's idea.

**C.** Imagine that a war between the United States and another country has just ended. The war has been very ugly. Many people have been killed. The other country has called off the war. Now the United States must make up the peace treaty. How would Wilson make up such a treaty? Would you approve of this treaty? Explain.

## ACTIVITIES AND INQUIRIES

1. Imagine that you are present at the Paris peace conference. You are asked to draw up a treaty that will prevent future wars between the nations at the conference. Draw up your treaty. Explain why it will prevent wars.
2. Assume that you are a newspaper reporter. Which of the men at the Paris conference would you want most to interview? Why? Write the questions that you would like to ask him. Answer these questions as you think he would.
3. Pretend that you are a reporter for a German newspaper. Write an article about what is happening at the peace conference.

Write your opinion of the peace treaty that Germany is being forced to sign. Explain why you feel this way.

4. Go to the library. Prepare a list of Wilson's Fourteen Points. Then make a list of the terms of the actual peace treaty (the Treaty of Versailles). Underline the ideas that you think are good in Wilson's Fourteen Points. Underline the ideas that you think are good in the Treaty of Versailles. Now put together the ideas you like in the Fourteen Points and the Treaty of Versailles. Add ideas of your own. Do you now have a treaty that will prevent future wars? Explain.

5. Assume that the peace conference is over. Germany has just signed the Treaty of Versailles. Draw a cartoon for a French newspaper showing how the French feel about the treaty. Next draw a cartoon for a German newspaper showing how the Germans feel about the treaty. Judging from the feelings in the cartoons, will the Treaty of Versailles end war between the French and German peoples?

6. Look at the maps of Europe in 1914, on page 288, and Europe in 1919, on page 306. Compare them. Notice the changes in the 1919 map of Europe. Tell which item below makes each statement correct.

   *a.* A new country in Central Europe in 1919 was (*a*) Czecho-slovakia (*b*) Germany (*c*) France.

   *b.* A new country in Eastern Europe in 1919 was (*a*) Russia (*b*) Greece (*c*) Yugoslavia.

   *c.* A country that lost territory in World War I was (*a*) Spain (*b*) France (*c*) Germany.

   *d.* A country that gained territory in World War I was (*a*) Germany (*b*) France (*c*) Austria-Hungary.

   *e.* A country divided into many other countries was (*a*) Great Britain (*b*) Austria-Hungary (*c*) Italy.

   *f.* A new country in Northern Europe in 1919 was (*a*) Estonia (*b*) Sweden (*c*) Norway.

   *g.* A country in Central Europe that did not change in size as a result of World War I was (*a*) Austria (*b*) Germany (*c*) Switzerland.

   *h.* A country that lost territory to the new nation of Poland was (*a*) France (*b*) Russia (*c*) Bulgaria.

   *i.* Another Northern European country that did not exist before World War I was (*a*) Denmark (*b*) Lithuania (*c*) the Netherlands.

   *j.* A country north of Italy that was formerly part of an empire was (*a*) France (*b*) Switzerland (*c*) Austria.

# 8. The Monster Rests

*A group of writers and students* are in a smoke-filled cafe on the Left Bank in Paris. Wine flows freely. People are singing and dancing. It appears as if these people do not have a care in the world. Let us see if this is really so. Who do you think the stranger in the story is?

## Paris, 1928

"You there, why aren't you drinking?" asked Pierre, a student in his early twenties. Pierre spoke to a man of about 40 who sat alone watching the crowd.

The man ignored Pierre. He was a stranger; nothing was known about him. Night after night he came to the cafe, but he spoke to no one. People were curious about him. That was why Pierre had tried to strike up a conversation.

"Waiter!" shouted Pierre. "Bring a bottle of wine for my friend!"

The stranger looked up. He seemed to notice Pierre for the first time.

"Do you mind if I join you?" asked Pierre.

The stranger shrugged and turned away.

Pierre sat down and studied the stranger for a few moments. "Where are you from?" he asked.

"Does it matter?" answered the stranger. "It is where I am going that concerns me right now."

"You are a puzzle to those of us who come here often," said Pierre. "No one knows what to make of you."

"Why?" asked the stranger. "Is it because I don't drink and dance and smoke and make jokes like everyone else?"

"Why, yes," answered Pierre. "Everyone thinks that you don't like what goes on in here. Yet you come here every night."

"I come here because I have no other place to go. My world is dead."

"I don't understand," Pierre said. He was beginning to feel uncomfortable.

"The war," muttered the stranger. "My world died in the war."

"But the war ended years ago," protested Pierre. "No one even mentions it now. Why think about old nightmares? Join me in a drink instead."

"There are no answers for me in that wine bottle," answered the stranger.

"But why look for answers?" asked Pierre. "The past is dead. The present is fun, the future is bright. What else is there to know?"

"Then why, if you are so confident of the future, do you live as if there were no tomorrow?" asked the stranger.

"You are beginning to bore me," answered Pierre. He stood up. "Your world created a monster, the Great War. My world destroyed the monster. The war is a thing of the past. We will never see its like again."

"Look again," said the stranger. "The monster is not dead, only resting. It will be back again, and sooner than you think."

"Oh, really?" asked Pierre in a mocking tone. "Well, then, I'd better hurry and finish this drink."

Pierre lifted the bottle to his lips, tilted his head back, and took a long swig. He wiped his mouth with the back of his hand, and slammed the bottle down on the table. "I've left some for you, stranger," he said. "It may help you to close the book on the past."

"Those who ignore the lessons of the past are doomed to repeat its errors," answered the stranger. "The fires of the Great War will rage on for a long time to come. Your generation is only one of many that will be scarred by the flames."

Pierre turned and walked away from the stranger. He rejoined his friends and spoke quietly to them. Some turned to stare at the stranger. A few people laughed.

Suddenly the stranger got up, spilled the remains of the wine on the floor, and walked out.

Pierre and his friends never saw the man again.

# UNDERSTANDING THE STORY

**A.** *Tell which item below makes each statement correct.*

1. The stranger was noticed by others because he (*a*) acted differently (*b*) talked loudly (*c*) drank too much.
2. The stranger lived in (*a*) the future (*b*) the present (*c*) the past.
3. The stranger's world was destroyed by (*a*) fire (*b*) the world war (*c*) imperialism.
4. Pierre said that this was bright: (*a*) the past (*b*) the present (*c*) the future
5. Pierre believed that this was a thing of the past: (*a*) war (*b*) hunger (*c*) poverty
6. The stranger (*a*) agreed with Pierre (*b*) disagreed with Pierre (*c*) joined Pierre in a drink.
7. The stranger believed that this would happen to those who ignore the lessons of the past: (*a*) They would repeat the errors of the past (*b*) They would forget the past (*c*) They would remember only good things.
8. The stranger said that this was not dead: (*a*) a bright future (*b*) a powerful Germany (*c*) the monster of war

**B.** *Complete the following sentences.*

1. Pierre was annoyed because the stranger ——— to no one.
2. The stranger said that his ——— was dead.
3. Pierre said that ——— was a thing of the past.
4. The stranger said that the monster of war was only ———.
5. Pierre wanted the stranger to close the book on the ———.
6. The stranger believed that Pierre's generation would be ——— by the flames of the world war.
7. The stranger was never ——— again by Pierre and his friends.

**C.** Who do you think the stranger was? Give your reasons.

# ACTIVITIES AND INQUIRIES

1. Go to the library. Prepare a report on how World War I continued to cause problems long after the war itself ended.
2. Imagine that you had a chance to speak to the stranger of the story. What questions would you have asked him? How do you think the stranger would have answered these questions?

3. Pretend that you are Pierre's friend. Pierre tells you about his talk with the stranger. What does he say? Do you agree with Pierre? Why?
4. Write a caption for the cartoon below. Which man in the story would agree with this cartoon, Pierre or the stranger? Why? Do you agree with the cartoon?

"Wow!" said Jack. "I can't believe they were that stupid."

Mr. Miller smiled. "I suppose they were stupid at that."

"I mean," Jack rushed on, "it's really dumb to fight a war that no one wants."

"All right, Jack, if you're so smart, how would you have prevented the war?"

"That's not fair. You teachers are always asking us to solve problems that are none of our business."

"Are you sure that World War I is none of your business?"

"How can a war that began and ended years before I was born have anything to do with me?"

"Think, Jack. Is war a thing of the past?"

"I don't suppose so," answered Jack.

"Well, perhaps if we learned why wars took place, we wouldn't have them anymore."

"Okay, Mr. Miller, you're right, as usual."

"Then answer my question, Jack. How would you have prevented World War I?"

Jack thought carefully. "I don't know if I could have done anything to prevent the war. But I would have tried to get the nations to talk things over. I think the war began as soon as they signed secret treaties."

"You know, Jack, every now and then I begin to think there is some hope for you after all."

"Thanks for nothing. But seriously, World War I cost billions of dollars and millions of lives. How did the people who fought this war pay for it?"

"With a lot more than money."

"What do you mean?" asked Jack.

"You'll find out soon enough."

# Twentieth-Century Dictatorships

"Mr. Miller, I still don't know what you mean when you say that people paid for World War I with a lot more than money."

"What do you think I mean?"

"Teachers!" said Jack impatiently. "You're always answering a question with another question!"

Mr. Miller smiled.

Jack continued. "I can only guess that something terrible happened after World War I."

"How did you guess that?"

"Well, if people have to pay for something with more than money, it must be pretty serious."

"True enough."

"But what happened?" asked Jack. "After all, the war was over. Peace treaties were signed. What could have gone wrong?"

"If only it were that simple."

"Okay, Mr. Miller, at least give me a hint."

"I'm sorry, Jack, if I seem to be teasing you," said Mr. Miller. "It's just that our next unit is such an ugly chapter in our history that I'm still upset by it."

"But Mr. Miller, with what, other than money, are people going to pay for World War I?"

Jack had never seen Mr. Miller with such a serious look.

"With their freedom and their lives," replied Mr. Miller.

# 1. Russian Revolution— The Beginning

*World War I brought sweeping* changes to most of the countries of Europe. It had perhaps its greatest impact upon Russia. Russia on the eve of the war was a giant country, with a wide variety of natural resources. In spite of these natural gifts, however, Russia was one of the most backward countries in Europe. For over 300 years, it had been ruled by absolute monarchs—the czars. The great majority of the Russian people were poor and illiterate. They were surrounded by corrupt officials and secret police, and few dared to speak out against the government. Those who did were sent off to the icy wasteland called Siberia. They were usually not heard from again. For these reasons, Russia seemed to stand still as other nations moved forward.

In our story, a crowd has gathered outside the czar's palace. The Russian fleet had just been defeated by the Japanese. Workers are on strike, people are rioting, and revolution threatens. This crowd has come to make serious demands of the czar.

Ask yourself what the crowd wanted from the czar. How would he deal with the crowd?

## St. Petersburg, 1905

"We are just wasting our time," said Sonia, a young Russian. She had joined the mob marching on the winter palace of the czar.

"You'll see," answered her friend Peter. "The czar is a good man. He'll listen to us."

"Do you really believe that your precious Nicholas is so different from those who came before him? His ancestors made slaves of the Russian people, and Nicholas is no different."

"But Sonia," protested Peter, "the czar understands suffering. His own son dies a slow death from an incurable blood disease. Nicholas can only watch helplessly. He would give up his throne if it would save his son. If he has such love for his son, is he not capable of loving and protecting his own people? You'll see, Sonia, he'll help us."

"Peter, how can you be so stupid?" asked Sonia. "If the czar is such a good man, why are so many of us so poor? Whose fault is it that we break our backs at work and go home to miserable shacks? We watch children go hungry while the czar and his friends live in palaces. They feed their dogs better than we feed our families!"

"It's not his fault," said Peter. "Things will be different for us after he hears what we have to say."

"He won't listen," said Sonia, her voice rising angrily. "He thinks of us as lowly dogs who should crawl on our bellies and beg to be petted. He will not listen to those who stand on their feet and make demands of him."

"Sonia, you have been brainwashed by your revolutionary friends," Peter replied. "They say these things about the czar without really knowing anything about him. I can only tell you that you and your friends are in for a surprise today."

"Most of my friends have already been surprised," said Sonia. "They were surprised in the middle of the night by the czar's secret police and taken away. No one knows where they are being held or if they will ever come back. This is the justice that your czar gives to those who stand up to him."

By this time, the crowd had arrived at the gates of the winter palace. Sonia and Peter pushed their way to the front lines. People holding banners and signs were calling out the czar's name. The crowd was respectful rather than angry. Men removed their hats and stood with bowed heads. Women and children stood at attention. Cries of "Little Father" were heard everywhere. It was clear that the crowd expected the czar to make an appearance soon.

Instead, the palace guard appeared. They marched up to the crowd and formed a human barricade. The officer in charge ordered the crowd to leave.

"For the last time," shouted the officer, "go now or else there will be trouble!"

"Not until we've seen the czar," answered many from the crowd.

*Shots rang out. In less than a minute, the streets were red with blood.*

The officer turned and signaled the guard. The soldiers aimed their weapons at the crowd and awaited their next signal.

A man shouted, "Will you fire upon unarmed men, women, and children? We come here in peace. Our only wish is that the czar will hear our pleas."

In answer, the officer signaled his men again. Shots rang out. In less than a minute, the streets were red with blood. Children shrieked as they saw their parents stagger and fall. People ran only to be cut down by swordsmen on horseback. Only a few escaped serious injury or death.

Hours later, people came to claim the dead. Peter, wounded and exhausted, wondered if he would have the strength to bury his friend.

## UNDERSTANDING THE STORY

A. *Decide who made or might have made the remarks that follow. Write S for each statement that Sonia made or might have made and P for each statement that Peter made or might have made.*

1. Trying to see the czar is a waste of time.
2. Nicholas is no different from his ancestors.
3. The czar loves the people.
4. It is the czar's fault that many of our people are poor and illiterate.
5. The czar will help us after he hears what we have to say.
6. The czar uses the secret police to make us afraid of him.
7. The czar would give up his throne if it would save his son.
8. The czar thinks of us as dogs who should crawl and beg to be petted.

B. *Write T for each statement that is true and F for each statement that is false.*

1. World War I hardly affected Russia.
2. The great majority of Russian people were poor and illiterate.
3. The Russian people could speak freely on any subject.
4. Russia was rich in natural resources.
5. The czar's son was dying.

6. The secret police were used to silence those who spoke out against the government.
7. In Russia every person could expect to receive a fair trial.
8. The crowd threatened the czar and threw rocks at the palace.
9. The palace guards killed or wounded many in the crowd.

C. Imagine that the czar's palace guards had not been ordered to shoot the marchers. Instead the czar agreed to meet with some of the people. What would Sonia have said to the czar? What would Peter have said to the czar?

## ACTIVITIES AND INQUIRIES

1. Use each of the following key terms in a sentence.
   backward    corrupt      protest     brainwash
   czar        illiterate   ancestor
2. Peter has just buried his friend Sonia. He writes a letter about Sonia's death. Peter also tells his feelings about the czar. Write Peter's letter. Decide if Peter has changed his mind about the czar.
3. Pretend that the czar is on trial. You are Peter. Write down what you will say when you are called to the witness stand.
4. Imagine that you are a newspaper reporter. Your assignment is to interview the czar. Write the questions you would like to ask him. Answer the questions as you think the czar would.
5. Look at the illustration on page 318. Do you think it would have appeared in a Russian newspaper of the time? Explain.

# 2. Peace, Bread, and Land

*The strikes and riots of 1905–1906* did little to change Russia's government. Nicholas continued to ignore cries for reform. Those who dared to criticize him were either imprisoned or forced to leave the country. Most Russians sighed and shrugged their shoulders. They quietly continued to live out their lives under the direction of the badly run and corrupt Russian government.

World War I, for the moment, helped the Russian people to forget their problems. Eager to protect Russia from her enemies, the people rallied to the support of their government. But defeats at the front and food shortages at home soon caused many Russians to complain bitterly against the czar and his government. Soldiers began to desert the army and crowds began to riot in the cities. An order from Nicholas to fire on the rioters was ignored, and he suddenly found himself helpless and abandoned. On March 15, 1917, Nicholas II gave up his throne.

As our story opens, the new Russian government is facing grave problems. The riots are worse than ever. Small, well-organized groups are trying to take over the government. The world war continues, and Russians suffer even greater losses at the hands of the Germans. The situation is desperate. Russia's very survival seems to be at stake.

Two men, both revolutionaries, are discussing their plans for Russia's future. Both agree that the czar and the nobility must be prevented from returning to power. They disagree on practically everything else. Both men will taste power. One will go on to change the course of Russian history. The other will live out his years in exile, lonely and forgotten.

See if you understand the reasons for the one man's success and the other man's failure.

# Petrograd, 1917

"And you call yourself a revolutionary," muttered Vladimir Ulyanov, better known as Lenin (LEN-in). He was talking to the government leader, Alexander Kerensky (kee-REN-sky).

"Of course, I'm a revolutionary," answered Kerensky. "I am transferring the government from the czar to the people. I am saying good-bye to 300 years of misery and corruption. What else am I if not a revolutionary?"

"A fool," replied Lenin. "You are a fool who has come to believe in his own daydreams."

Kerensky reddened. "Stop talking down to me as if I were one of your schoolboy followers. While you make speeches on street corners, I am putting together a government that will give hope to Russians who love freedom. It will take time. Democracy moves slowly. But one day the people will understand what I have done for them. Then they will return the love I feel for them."

"Love you?" asked Lenin. "They hate you! Fool that you are, you don't even understand why."

"Tell me why," said Kerensky.

"They hate you because you are a good man, and they understand only cruelty."

"I don't understand."

"Of course you don't, Kerensky. You don't understand that the people want to see this war over *now*. They want land and bread *now*. They don't care how they get these things. Our people are filled with hatred. They hate the rich, the educated, and the privileged. They hate all those who make them feel stupid, clumsy, and inferior.They will follow a man shrewd enough to punish those they hate and strong enough to make them fear him."

"No, no!" shouted Kerensky. "The Russian people aren't like that at all! They are brave people who will fight on until this war is over. They will get their land and their bread. But they know that these things take time. They understand that these things must be done properly. They must be done democratically. The people understand, and they will wait."

"Bah!" sneered Lenin. "You lead the Russian people but you don't understand them at all. Your picture of them is a lie!"

*"Russia is about to give birth to a great revolution!"*

"But what of your picture of the Russian people?" interrupted Kerensky. "What an ugly picture you paint of them. I am beginning to think that *you* hate the Russian people!"

"I am above love and hate," sneered Lenin. "Russia is about to give birth to a great revolution. I am the doctor who will deliver this child. I will do anything—use any trick, sacrifice any person—to see the revolution live and grow strong!"

"You're mad!" cried Kerensky.

"Perhaps," answered Lenin. "Perhaps great visions come only to those who are a little mad. Maybe that's why we succeed where others fail!"

"Take care, Lenin," warned Kerensky. "You may become the thing you claim to hate the most!"

"And what is that?"

"The next Russian czar!"

# UNDERSTANDING THE STORY

**A.** *Write* T *for each statement that is true,* F *for each statement that is false, and* N *for each statement that is not mentioned in the story.*

1. The strikes of 1905–1906 did much to change things in Russia.
2. The Russian people wanted a democratic government.
3. Things continued just as before the strikes of 1905–1906.
4. World War I helped to force Nicholas II to give up his throne.
5. Conditions improved after Nicholas II gave up his throne.
6. The Russians continued to fight the war after Nicholas II gave up his throne.
7. Kerensky and Lenin had a great deal in common.
8. Lenin secretly wanted to be the next Russian czar.

**B.** *Tell which statements Lenin would have agreed with.*

1. The Russians should fight on until they win the war.
2. The Russian people must be given land and food immediately.
3. The Russian people can wait for land and bread.
4. The new Russian government must become democratic.
5. The revolution must succeed, no matter what the cost.
6. The Russian people are filled with hatred.
7. The Russian people are sick of the war.

**C.** Imagine that you were living in Russia in 1917. The czar had just given up the throne. Lenin and Kerensky were fighting for power. Which man would you have followed? Why?

# ACTIVITIES AND INQUIRIES

1.  Use each of the following key terms in a sentence.

    reform        desert        exile        vision
    inefficient   abandoned     sacrifice

2.  Prepare a report on the Russian Revolution of 1917.
3.  Pretend that you are producing a television special. Both Lenin and Kerensky want to appear on your show. However, you can choose only one of them. Which one would you choose? Why?
4.  Look at the illustration on page 323. Who is shown—Kerensky or Lenin? Explain. Draw a picture of the other man. Explain how the two pictures show the differences between Lenin and Kerensky.

# 3. Soviet Dictatorship in Action

By August 1917, a small group of revolutionaries led by Lenin was able to seize power over a country of 150 million people. They promised "peace, bread, and land." They called themselves Communists, and they ended the fighting with Germany. They fought a civil war and defeated foreign invaders—all in the space of four years.

Firmly in power, the Communists now faced even more serious problems. How were they to unite the Russian people? Could food production be increased? How could Russia be turned into a modern state? How could the revolution be protected from its enemies?

In 1924 another serious problem was added. Lenin suffered a stroke and died. A brutal fight for power followed. Finally one man, Josef Stalin (STAH-lin), won out over the other leading Communists. He placed himself at the head of the Soviet Union.

Ask yourself what sort of man Stalin was. What plans did he have for the Soviet Union? Could Stalin help to make the Soviet Union into a modern state? What price would the Russians be asked to pay for Stalin's ideas?

## Moscow, 1938

It was 3:00 A.M. Comrade Igor Kirofsky, a high-ranking Soviet official, was sound asleep. Suddenly, there was a loud knocking on the door.

"Who is it?" bellowed Kirofsky, as he tried to rub the sleep from his eyes.

"Open the door, comrade. It is the police."

Kirofsky angrily jumped from his bed and threw open the door. "How dare you come to my house at such an hour? Don't you know who I am? Whoever is responsible for this will pay dearly!"

Two men stepped inside the room. "Please, comrade," said one, "we have our orders. You are to get dressed and come with us immediately. All will be explained to you shortly."

Still muttering angry threats, Kirofsky dressed and left with the men. They soon arrived at a police station that was quite familiar to Kirofsky. He knew that spies and dangerous criminals were usually brought here for questioning. For the first time, he began to feel a little less sure of himself.

Kirofsky was ushered into a well-lighted waiting room. He was told that someone would soon speak with him. He was left by himself. An hour later, a man entered and approached Kirofsky.

"Please come with me," said the man.

"What is this all about?" asked Kirofsky. He seemed far less angry than he had been earlier.

"Please come with me," repeated the man.

Kirofsky followed the man out of the waiting room and down a stairway leading to the basement. He was escorted to another room and asked to surrender his valuables. The door was locked behind him.

Deep in thought, Kirofsky did not notice that the room was a very unusual one. Later, after he had spent some time there, he discovered that the room had no windows. It had a single, glaring light, and it was soundproof. Each day a tray of food was pushed through a tiny compartment that could be opened only from the outside.

Minutes, hours, days, weeks, perhaps even months went by. Kirofsky lost all sense of time. Denied sound, books, and human contact, he retreated more and more into himself. Over and over, he silently asked himself the same question, "Why am I here?"

Slowly, Kirofsky became convinced that he was guilty of some monstrous crime. Why else would he be given this treatment?

He thought many times about Comrade Stalin. Kirofsky was confused. "Did I only think of him as a butcher, or did I call him that to his face?" he asked himself. "Did I tell Stalin I hated him for giving the order to execute rich farmers and scatter their families?

*Over and over again, he asked himself the same question, "Why am I here?"*

Did I accuse Stalin of murdering his closest friends and driving his wife to suicide? Did I criticize him for enslaving the Russian people and forcing them to work in state factories and farms in exchange for scraps of bread? Did I plot to remove Stalin along with the others who have long since been arrested and executed? Did I think these things, or did I do them? I can't remember which. Does it really matter? Doesn't thinking these things or dreaming them make me as guilty as if I had done them anyway?"

Kirofsky had been secretly observed from the beginning. Sensing that at last the time was ripe, the official in charge of getting signed confessions ordered Kirofsky brought to his office.

Kirofsky was taken from the cell into the lighted corridor. His eyes hurt and his legs were weak. He needed help to walk to the official's office.

The official jumped up to greet Kirofsky. "Welcome, comrade," he said, and immediately offered him a cigarette. The official asked

Kirofsky how he could make him more comfortable and help him in any other way.

"What a wonderful man!" Kirofsky thought. "I have plotted against the government, and am therefore guilty of treason of the highest order. Yet this man shows such concern for me. I must listen to him carefully and do what he says because he is a much better man than I."

"Comrade," the official said to Kirofsky, "you have been alone with your thoughts for a long time. I know that you are bursting to speak of them. Why don't you tell me what you have discovered about yourself. I am sure that you will soon feel better."

Kirofsky began to speak. At a signal from the official, a secretary began to write. The minutes ticked by and soon Kirofsky had confessed all his innermost thoughts.

"Comrade," the official said softly, "will you sign what you have just dictated and stand by these statements at your trial?"

"Of course I will!" answered Kirofsky. "A traitor like myself should be tried before the people. I have betrayed my country and I hate myself for it! I no longer care what happens to me. If I could ask for anything, it would be for an end to this life of mine!"

"Comrade," said the official, "the man you called a butcher is not without mercy. He will grant your last wish."

## UNDERSTANDING THE STORY

A. *Complete the sentences below.*

1. Lenin promised ———, ———, and ———.
2. The Communists worried about how to ——— the country after the civil war was ended.
3. After Lenin's death the brutal fight for power was won by ———.
4. Kirofsky was brought to a police station where ——— and dangerous ——— were usually taken.
5. Kirofsky was imprisoned in a room without ———.
6. Kirofsky became convinced that he was ——— of some monstrous crime.
7. Kirofsky thought that he had plotted to remove ——— from power.
8. Kirofsky ——— to many crimes against the state.

**B.** *Match each item in Column A with its answer in Column B.*

COLUMN A

1. Lenin died from this
2. First thing Kirofsky felt
3. What Kirofsky was told at the police station
4. Question that Kirofsky asked himself
5. Man Kirofsky hated
6. What Kirofsky signed
7. What Kirofsky called himself
8. What will happen to Kirofsky

COLUMN B

(a) "Why am I here?"
(b) a traitor
(c) a stroke
(d) a confession
(e) anger
(f) he will be executed
(g) nothing
(h) Stalin

**C.** Although he was not beaten or physically harmed, Kirofsky signed a confession of guilt. Should your police force use methods like those in the story to get confessions? Explain.

## ACTIVITIES AND INQUIRIES

1. Use each of the following key terms in a sentence.

   Communist    unite      retreat    official      confess
   invade       comrade    plot       treason

2. Imagine that Kirofsky is on trial. You are to be his prosecutor. Prepare the case against him.
3. Pretend that you are to be Kirofsky's lawyer. Prepare the case in his defense.
4. Suppose that you are an American reporter at Kirofsky's trial. Write an article describing the trial. Tell if Kirofsky will be found innocent or guilty. Write your opinion of the verdict.
5. Look at the illustration on page 327. Describe the scene. Write your own title for the picture.

# 4. The Prize

*Stalin remained in power* for more than 25 years. During this time, the Russian people saw the government add to its powers at their expense. The government now controlled all factories and farms. It set prices and wages and decided what was to be produced and how it was to be made. Strikes were outlawed. People lived in fear because of the secret police, censorship, and the use of terror tactics.

In 1941 Germany attacked the Soviet Union. Four years of hard fighting followed, much of it on Russian soil. Once again, the Russian people suffered unbelievable hardships.

At the end of the war Stalin was even more firmly in power. No relief was in sight for the Russian people. The war had brought other European countries under Russian control. They too began to feel the sting of the dictator's whip. As time went on, Stalin's appetite for power grew even greater. All Russia trembled before his cruelties. Finally, the year 1953 arrived and brought with it a ray of hope for the Russian people: Stalin died.

Which way would the Soviet Union turn now? Would its new leaders relax some of the controls over the Russian people? These were the questions that were being asked by the Russians as well as outsiders. To this day, Soviet officials deny that the Russian people are not permitted to express themselves freely. Let this story help you to decide if they are telling the truth.

In our story, Boris Pasternak (paz-ter-NACK), a Russian writer, has been notified that he has been awarded a Nobel Prize for his book *Dr. Zhivago* (zhih-VAH-goe). Pasternak has agreed to accept the award. A friend and fellow writer, Ilya Ehrenburg (AIR-on-borg), has come to talk with Pasternak.

# Moscow, 1958

"Well, Ilya," said Boris Pasternak, "are you happy for me?"

"Boris," answered Ehrenburg, "you have written an interesting book, but I am afraid that it is also a dangerous one."

"Dangerous?" asked Pasternak. "Why dangerous?"

"Let us say that there are important people who do not like your book."

"But—"

"Boris, let me finish!" interrupted Ehrenburg sharply. "I have it from the highest authority that you would be wise to refuse the Nobel Prize."

"But Ilya," pleaded Pasternak, "I have already notified the Nobel committee that I am going to Sweden to accept the prize."

"Then you must write them immediately and tell them that it is all a mistake," advised Ehrenburg.

"Ilya, my book has been translated into many languages and is being read all over the world."

"And why have our enemies turned it into a best seller?" Ehrenburg cut in. "Because you have given them more reason to criticize us."

"But I am not a politician," pleaded Pasternak. "I am a writer. I have written the truth as I understand it."

"Boris, the Communist party decides what the truth is. Take my advice. Don't accept that prize."

"The ghost of Stalin continues to haunt this country after all," replied Pasternak.

"Stalin—did you say Stalin?" asked Ehrenburg. "Stalin is dead and everything he stands for is dead as well. Do not speak of Stalin to me."

"Then, why," flashed Pasternak angrily, "am I being asked to turn down the Nobel Prize? Is it because I wrote a book that describes the human soul as free and able to rise above all things?"

"Boris," said Ehrenburg, "stop asking these foolish questions. Tell me that you agree not to accept the prize."

"And if I choose to accept?"

"Then, my friend," said Ehrenburg, "you will be free to leave the country to collect your prize. But you will not be allowed to return. Now what is your answer? I must have it within the hour."

There was silence for several minutes.

"I am an old man," sighed Pasternak. "All that I am—my life and my thoughts—has been shaped by my country. I cannot have a life anywhere else. I will turn down the prize."

"Spoken like a wise man," said Ehrenburg.

"No, I am an old man who wants to be buried in Russian soil," answered Pasternak. "But I have learned a valuable lesson tonight. For the first time, I understand why the government hates my book!"

"And why is that?" asked Ehrenburg.

"It is not Pasternak the writer that the government is concerned with," said Pasternak. "It is Zhivago, the hero of the book. His soul belongs only to himself, and he frightens the government."

"Zhivago is only a figment of your imagination," protested Ehrenburg, half amused.

"No, my friend," answered Pasternak, "he is real enough, and one day the government will have to deal with him."

*Postscript.* Throughout the 1960s and 1970s, Russian artists, writers, and scientists spoke out against the government. Many were jailed, placed in insane asylums, or denied the right to work. Nevertheless, the criticism continued, and it still continues. Alexander Solzhenitsyn was warned many times to stop his criticism of the government. But he dared any punishment, even death, and continued to criticize. Boasting that all Russians may speak out freely, the Soviet government forced Solzhenitsyn to leave Russia in 1974.

To this day, the Soviet government gives no sign that it is willing to allow true freedom of expression. Most people are afraid to speak out because they know it will cost them dearly. However, the Russian "Zhivagos" continue to fight to keep their souls free, and they will meet that price.

## UNDERSTANDING THE STORY

**A.** *Write T for each statement that is true and O for each statement that is an opinion or point of view.*

1. Stalin was the most effective leader the Russians ever had.
2. Under Stalin, the government set prices and wages.
3. Stalin's secret police caused people to live in fear.
4. Since Stalin's death, the Russian people have enjoyed a better life.
5. The Soviet government thought that Pasternak had written a dangerous book.
6. Pasternak won the Nobel Prize for his book.
7. Pasternak's book was translated into many languages because it criticized the Soviet Union.
8. Pasternak turned down the Nobel Prize.

**B.** *Read the selection and answer the questions that follow.*

> The Soviet Union is not a democracy. Millions of people rot in concentration camps and prisons. There is no freedom in the Soviet Union. The Soviet leader has so much power that he can take away any right that he gives. Each year, the terror grows worse. The Soviet Union rests upon a sea of blood, an ocean of tears, and a world of suffering. How can fear, force, lies, and misery make a better person?

1. The person who wrote this selection (*a*) likes the Soviet system (*b*) dislikes the Soviet system (*c*) has no opinion.
2. The author says the Soviet Union is *not* a (*a*) dictatorship (*b*) democracy (*c*) police state.
3. According to the author, millions of Russians are (*a*) loyal to the government (*b*) getting ready to revolt (*c*) rotting in concentration camps and prisons.
4. The author writes that, to this day, the Soviet people still do not enjoy (*a*) freedom (*b*) bread, land, and peace (*c*) decent housing.
5. The few rights that the people enjoy may be taken away at any time by the Soviet (*a*) police (*b*) leader (*c*) army.

6. The author believes that, since the revolution, the terror has (*a*) grown worse (*b*) practically disappeared (*c*) remained the same.
7. The Soviet system rests upon (*a*) justice and equality (*b*) private ownership of property (*c*) fear, force, and lies.

C. Imagine that Boris Pasternak chose to accept the Nobel Prize. The Soviet government ordered him to leave the country and never return. Would Pasternak have chosen to live in the United States? Explain your answer.

## ACTIVITIES AND INQUIRIES

1. Imagine that you are a reporter. You wish to interview Boris Pasternak. Prepare the questions you would like to ask him. Now answer the questions as if you were Pasternak.
2. Now imagine that you are the same reporter. You wish to interview Ilya Ehrenburg. Prepare the questions you would like to ask him. Answer those questions as if you were Ehrenburg.
3. Look through a local newspaper. Imagine that it is a Soviet newspaper, and all the events that happened in the United States really happened in the Soviet Union. Write down three statements in the paper that would not be printed in a Soviet paper.
4. Assume that you are about to move to the Soviet Union. How will your life there be different from your life in the United States?
5. Pretend that you are a Soviet citizen. You are angry because Pasternak has been forced to turn down the Nobel Prize. Draw a poster that shows how you feel. Would you walk around with this poster? Explain.
6. Use each of the following key terms in a sentence.

| | | |
|---|---|---|
| authority | hardship | politician |
| censorship | translate | |

# 5. The Balance Sheet

*Many people continue to speak out* against the Soviet Union. They say that its leaders are guilty of committing many crimes against the Russian people. Yet others speak in favor of the Russian experiment. Some say that while Russia is old, the Soviet Union is still very young. In time, they claim, the Soviet Union will become all that the Russian people hope for.

Others remember what Russia was like before the Communist revolution. For them, the Soviet Union is a great improvement over the Russia ruled by the czars.

In our story an old man and his grandson are discussing the Soviet Union. Both are Russian born, yet each has his own picture of the Soviet Union.

## Leningrad, 1975

"No, Grandpa, I don't agree. I don't agree that the Russia of today is a hundred times better than the Russia of yesterday. How can a nightmare be an improvement over anything?"

"Ah, Leo, you are 30 years old and still a child," said Grandpa. "How can you speak of nightmares when you have never really lived through one?"

"Grandpa, millions have been killed and tortured in this country. And why? Just because they did not agree with the government. The government decides what I read, what I wear, where I travel—indeed, whether I travel at all. Even my education was decided for me by the government. If this life is not a nightmare, at least agree it is a very bad dream."

"I have lived through a different bad dream," answered Grandpa. "I remember a different Russia. In that Russia, people fought over scraps of bread. We worked long hours for wages that

335

barely kept us alive. People in that day would have kissed the hands and feet of the same government leaders you speak against."

Leo looked at his grandfather carefully. "You curse the czars even though they are no longer in power. Yet you would kiss the hands and feet of leaders who are just like them. I don't understand you, Grandpa."

"Leo, the czars were driving Russia to its grave. The Communists have brought life back to our people. Today we have jobs; our children go to school. We are well fed and our government takes good care of us. People once laughed at Russians. Today we are one of the world's most powerful people. I am not ashamed to say that the Communists have done a great deal for Russia."

"But what of the price that we have been forced to pay?" protested Leo. "The killings and the Siberian death camps and the loss of liberty."

"Bah!" said Grandpa impatiently. "Our country was diseased. The Communists cut out the infection. Can you eat freedom? Can you wear liberty? If we have been asked to pay a price for the good things we have today, I say that we have received good value."

Leo muttered, "Humanity does not live by bread alone!"

His grandfather laughed.


## UNDERSTANDING THE STORY

A. *Tell which of the statements are true.*
   1. Every Russian speaks out freely against the government of the Soviet Union.
   2. Some people believe that the Soviet Union today is a great improvement over the Russia ruled by the czars.
   3. Millions of people in the Soviet Union have been killed and tortured.
   4. The Soviet government keeps its people under tight control.
   5. The Russian people are better fed today than they were in czarist Russia.
   6. The Soviet Union gives liberty to all of its people.
   7. Leo spoke highly of the Soviet Union.
   8. Grandpa prefers life in the Soviet Union to life in czarist Russia.

**B.** *Decide who made or might have made the remarks that follow. Write L for each statement that Leo made or might have made and G for each statement that Grandpa made or might have made.*

1. Life in the Soviet Union is a nightmare.
2. The Soviet government decides when and where people may travel.
3. In old Russia, people fought over scraps of bread.
4. Thanks to the Communists, the Soviet Union today is one of the world's most powerful nations.
5. The Soviet government takes good care of the people.
6. Millions of people have been killed and tortured because they disagreed with the government.
7. You cannot eat freedom or wear liberty.
8. Humanity does not live by bread alone.

**C.** Imagine that Grandpa has been given permission to visit the United States. You have been asked to be his guide. What would you take him to see? How would he feel about the United States? Would the Soviet government want people like Leo, who opposes their government, to visit the United States? Explain.

## ACTIVITIES AND INQUIRIES

1. Assume that you are an American reporter. You are visiting the Soviet Union. You have just interviewed Leo. Write an article describing what life in the Soviet Union is like.
2. You are the same reporter. This time, interview Grandpa. Will you change anything in the article you just wrote? If so, what? If not, why not?
3. Write to the Soviet embassy. Ask for materials on the Soviet Union. What would Grandpa think of these materials? What would Leo think? Explain.
4. Go to the library. Prepare a report on the role of women in the Soviet Union today. Do Soviet women need a liberation movement? Explain.
5. The caption of a cartoon is: "The finest freedom is the freedom from hunger." How would Leo reply to this statement? How would Grandpa reply to this statement? With which person would you agree? Explain. Draw the cartoon that fits the title.

# 6. Workers Become Bosses

*Italy had been on the winning* side at the end of World War I. Italy entered the war on the side of Germany but soon switched over to the side of England and France. She made the right choice. But the Italian people had little to be happy about. The Treaty of Versailles had not given them all the land they wanted, and the war had been very costly. Exactly how costly, the Italians were about to find out.

As our story opens, a group of factory workers are arguing. Ask youself why these workers are so unhappy. What are they prepared to do? Would you have gone along with these workers?

## Milan, 1920

"Fools! Fools! You're all a bunch of blind, pig-headed fools!" shouted Vito at his fellow workers. "This stupid plan will never work!"

"What should we do, then—let them starve us to death?" asked Gabriele, the leader of the group.

At this, the other men began to mumble among themselves and to glare angrily at Vito.

"Say what you will," Vito replied. "We are fools to think we can take over this factory and run it by ourselves. What do we know about managing a factory?"

"Can we do any worse than the fat capitalists who own the plant?" asked Tony. "Thanks to them, prices are rising, wages are low, jobs are scarce, and goods are of the worst quality—if you can find them!"

"Still trotting out the Communist line, eh, Tony?" mocked Vito.

"And why not?" Tony replied hotly. "The Communists are the only people who make sense in all of Italy."

"Vito," interrupted Gabriele, "it's about time you woke up to what's happening in this country. All of us here risked our lives in an idiot war, and what's the payoff? We came back to find that the men who stayed home got the jobs or made fortunes from the war. We who faced death now have to stand on breadlines or beg for work!"

"But things will get better," replied Vito. "The government won't let these things go on for much longer."

"Bah!" blurted Gabriele in disgust. "The government is useless! It's run by fools who can't agree over anything! No, it is the people who must solve their own problems. There is no government to help us."

"And so, by taking over this factory, you begin to solve Italy's problems!" sneered Vito.

"It's a beginning," answered Gabriele, and the others nodded in agreement.

"The beginning of the end!" muttered Vito under his breath.

## UNDERSTANDING THE STORY

A. *Tell which item makes each statement correct.*

1. The Italians were unhappy with the Treaty of Versailles because they believed that Italy did not get enough (*a*) land (*b*) money (*c*) medals.
2. The men in the story were thinking about (*a*) getting married (*b*) taking over a factory (*c*) joining the army.
3. This was true of wages and prices in Italy in 1920: (*a*) wages were up and prices were down (*b*) wages were down and prices were up (*c*) wages and prices were up.
4. Vito called Tony a (*a*) socialist (*b*) capitalist (*c*) Communist.
5. Gabriele was angry because the people with jobs were (*a*) former soldiers (*b*) men who never went to war (*c*) Communists.
6. Vito said that things would get better because of help from (*a*) the government (*b*) the army (*c*) the Communists.
7. Which man disagreed with the other two? (*a*) Vito (*b*) Gabriele (*c*) Tony.

**B.** *Which statements show how Italy was affected by World War I?*
1. Italy got all the land she wanted.
2. Returning soldiers could not get jobs.
3. There was a shortage of goods.
4. Wages were higher than ever.
5. Prices were higher than ever.
6. All Italians were sure that the government would solve their problems.
7. Communists wanted the workers to take over factories.

**C.** Imagine that Vito and Gabriele are visiting the United States. How would Vito advise us to solve our problems? How would Gabriele advise us? Which man's advice do you think Americans should follow? Explain.

## ACTIVITIES AND INQUIRIES

1. Go to the library. Prepare a report on conditions in Italy after World War I.
2. Imagine that you are a member of the Italian government. You are meeting with Gabriele. You want him to agree that he will not ask the workers to take over the factory. Write the arguments that you will use to convince Gabriele.
3. Imagine that you are Gabriele. What promises do you want the government to make?
4. Assume that the workers tried to take over the factory. Gabriele was arrested and placed on trial. Prepare the case against him.
5. Now assume that your job is to defend Gabriele. Prepare his defense.

# 7. Benito Mussolini

*The workers' takeover of factories* led to confusion and even lower production. Most workers admitted their mistakes and agreed to give the factories back to their owners. But the property owners had been frightened by this. From now on, they would throw their support and their money to those who promised to help them keep their property.

Out of the ashes of confusion would arise a man whose drive to power could not be stopped. His name was Benito Mussolini (mus-soh-LEE-nee).

Ask yourself how Mussolini will come to power. Should the factory owners have supported him? Does he have the answers to Italy's problems?

## Rome, 1923

You are Benito Mussolini, and you are about to become the most powerful man in Italy. You have worked hard to become somebody. You have been a teacher, a newspaperman, a soldier, and a political leader. Life for you has been hard but interesting.

You are no stranger to violence. You have seen men killed in battle, and you yourself were wounded in the Great War. As a young man, you got involved in several fights and once threatened a man with a knife. You are also outspoken, and you have spent time in jail because of this.

People are not sure what you stand for. You spoke out against the Great War when it first began. Later you were thrown out of the Socialist party for speaking in favor of the war. You claim to be in favor of improving working conditions. Yet you have hired yourself out many times as a strikebreaker.

While others may be confused by your actions, you know

341

exactly what you want: power! You will take any avenue that leads you through the corridors of power, up to the very top.

You are clever enough to know that frightened and confused Italians respect strength and force. This is why you have organized a group that you call the Fascist party. You dress these men up in black shirts and use them to beat up your enemies. Sometimes your men get carried away and force castor oil down the throats of those who speak out against you. This always makes you laugh.

The Communist party has been very useful to you. Every time there is a strike or riot, you blame the Communists, and your men take to the streets and break workers' heads. The factory owners and landowners are grateful to you, and they see that a lot of money comes into your hands.

You have tried to take control of the government by legal means. The Italian people, for the most part, have not given you their support at the polls. You must find another way!

Now you have decided that the time is ripe to make your move. You will simply take over the government by force. The government is weak and the king will do anything to keep his throne. He has already promised you his complete cooperation. Many in the government hate you, and they can stop you only if they stand together. You know that this will not happen!

You have sent 40,000 men to march on Rome to force the government to give in to you. You take no chances—you wait safely in Milan. Should there be trouble, you are ready to make your escape to another country. You have nothing to worry about. The march will go smoothly and will accomplish its purpose. The people will be impressed and the government will be frightened. You will be invited to go to Rome and take control of the government.

You can't possibly know it, but your worst days are in front of you. But you are now about to become the most powerful man in Italy, and today belongs to you!

## UNDERSTANDING THE STORY

**A.** *Match each item in Column A with its answer in Column B.*

| COLUMN A | COLUMN B |
|---|---|
| 1. One result of the takeover of factories by the workers | (a) strikebreaking |
| 2. The workers decided to do this after awhile | (b) Communist party |
| 3. These people supported Mussolini | (c) lowered production |
| 4. Mussolini once belonged to this political party | (d) power |
| 5. Mussolini earned money by doing this | (e) Fascist party |
| 6. This is what most attracted Mussolini | (f) give the factories back to the owners |
| 7. Mussolini organized this political party | (g) Socialist party |
| 8. This political party was blamed for strikes and riots | (h) property owners |

**B.** *Number the events below in the order in which they took place according to the story.*

Mussolini was thrown out of the Socialist party.
World War I broke out.
Mussolini spoke out against World War I.
Mussolini's army marched on Rome.
Mussolini spoke out in favor of World War I.
Mussolini organized the Fascist party.
Factories were given back to the owners.
Property owners supported Mussolini.

**C.** Imagine that Mussolini is in the United States. He wants to become the leader of the American people. Write a step-by-step plan telling how Mussolini would probably try to take power. Would this plan succeed? Explain.

## ACTIVITIES AND INQUIRIES

1.  Use each of the following key terms in a sentence.
    violence              strikebreaker          polls
    Socialist             Fascist
2.  Go to the library. Prepare a report on how Mussolini came to power.
3.  Assume that Mussolini has just come to power. You are going to interview him. Write the questions that you would like to ask him. Now answer the questions as you think Mussolini would.
4.  Imagine that you are an Italian newspaper reporter. Mussolini just became the most powerful person in Italy. Write an article about whether or not you think Mussolini will help the Italian people.
5.  Imagine that you are working for Mussolini. He asks you to draw a poster. The poster is to tell people that Mussolini is going to solve Italy's problems. Draw the poster.

# 8. The Two Faces of Italy

*Riots, strikes, unemployment,* high prices, and murder in the streets were all part of the Italy that Mussolini inherited. Italians wondered if things would get better now that Mussolini was in power.

Did things get better? Gina, a school teacher, has an opinion. Her father has a different opinion. Perhaps you will form an opinion of your own.

## Naples, 1935

"That madman!" shouted Gina. She slammed down her newspaper. "Now he makes war on Ethiopia (e-the-O-pi-a)."

"Quiet!" begged Mr. Mora, her father. "Do you want us to be jailed?"

"And where do you think we are right now?" answered Gina. "Thirty-six million Italians are in prison, and Mussolini is our jailer!"

"Gina, please. Your temper will get us all into trouble. Besides, I don't agree with you."

"Here we go again. My father, the Mussolini lover, is about to make his favorite speech!"

"Yes, young lady, and while I'm at it, I'd like to remind you that I'm your father. I'm entitled to some respect."

"Yes, Father, if you think so."

"Very well, make fun of me. But at least have the decency to admit that Mussolini has done wonderful things for the Italian people."

"For the Italian puppets, you mean."

"Gina, you make me want to cry. You forget that Mussolini has brought us peace and quiet. Most children are being taught to read and write. Our factories are running day and night. Our cities are cleaner. Our farmers are beginning to use electricity. Even our trains are running on time!"

"Yes, of course, we have peace and quiet," said Gina. "How could it be otherwise? The secret police are everywhere. People who speak out against the government are thrown into jail. Strikes are forbidden by law. The newspapers, the radio—even the letters we write—are carefully watched by the government."

"Yes, yes," said her father. "But these people are trouble-makers. They deserve what they get. And who needs strikes? And so what if the government watches over the newspapers and the radio? I trust Mussolini, and I know that he is right!"

"How can you be so blind? Your wonderful Mussolini cares nothing for us. It is for himself that he does these things. He wants to go down in history as the greatest caesar of them all. And my students believe he is that right now!"

"And how can your students think so well of Mussolini?"

"Why not?" answered Gina. "They are surrounded by posters of him. They learn about him in every school subject. Textbooks give him credit for things he never did. We teachers are under orders to drill students to say again and again, 'Mussolini is always right.'

"Then our students go home and listen to radio programs that repeat his name. Newspapers are filled with news of his latest deeds. Their parents sound just like you! Is it any wonder that they think Mussolini is the greatest person in the world?"

"But why do you carry on so?" asked her father. "After all, haven't we come a long way from the days before Mussolini?"

"A long way indeed," answered Gina. "And I fear that the way back will be very hard to find."

## UNDERSTANDING THE STORY

A. Write T *for each statement that is true and* F *for each statement that is false.*

1. Conditions in Italy were good when Mussolini took power.
2. Mussolini declared war against Ethiopia.
3. Gina was a supporter of Mussolini.
4. All Italian people hated Mussolini.
5. Mussolini saw to it that the secret police were everywhere.
6. Strikes were not allowed in Italy.

7. Mussolini's name was never spoken in classrooms.
8. Mussolini's face and deeds were known all over Italy.

B. List four arguments that Gina's father used to convince her that Mussolini had done wonderful things. List four arguments that Gina used to convince her father that Mussolini had done terrible things.

C. Some people say that the United States could use a person like Mussolini to solve its problems. List five problems that Americans face today. How would Mussolini try to solve these problems? Would he succeed? Do you think that Mussolini would be good for the American people? Explain your answer.

## ACTIVITIES AND INQUIRIES

1. Go to the library. Prepare a report on the living conditions of the Italian people while Mussolini was in power. Find a picture of Mussolini. What does the picture tell you about the man?
2. Imagine that you are visiting Italy. Mussolini is in power. Write a letter home telling what is happening in Italy.
3. Pretend that you are working for Mussolini. Your job is to make sure that nothing bad is written or printed about Mussolini or Italy. Look at the letter you just wrote. Underline all statements that Mussolini would not want people to write.
4. Read the following story and answer the questions that follow.

> A wolf was very hungry and cold. He tried to steal a chicken. The wolf was stopped by a farm dog. The wolf begged the dog to let him steal the chicken. The dog told the wolf that if he worked for the farmer, he would never be hungry or cold again. The hungry wolf followed the dog to the farmhouse. Just before the wolf entered the house, he noticed a leash mark on the dog's neck. The wolf ran back into the forest.

Why did the wolf run away? Who is Gina in the story? Who is Gina's father in the story? Who is Mussolini in the story? Explain your answers. What would have happened to the wolf if he had not run away?

5. Imagine that Mussolini read the story of the wolf and the dog. Would he want to change the story? Why?

# 9. Poison in the Streets

*Let us see what was happening* in Germany now that World War I was over. Germany, a defeated country, faced many problems. She owed money to the countries that had defeated her. Her people suffered from food shortages. Many factories were closing, and millions of people were out of work. Prices climbed higher from day to day.

All over Germany, people asked why this was happening. The speaker in our story believed that he had found the answer to this question, and, with it, the solution to Germany's problems. Let us now find out what this man has in mind.

Ask yourself why these things are happening in Germany. How does the street-corner speaker in the city of Munich (MYOO-nik) propose to solve these problems? Does he really have the answers?

## Munich, 1920

"The Jews—they are the ones who are to blame!" cried the street corner speaker. The crowd of onlookers began to grumble among themselves. Some nodded their heads, while others murmured angrily and walked away.

"We did not lose this war!" screamed the speaker. "We were stabbed in the back by Jewish traitors who made money while we shed German blood!"

"How much money is this arm worth?" yelled a one-armed man from the crowd. The crowd stood back as the man pushed his way toward the speaker.

"You have both your arms," angrily said the man facing the speaker. "I have donated one of my Jewish arms to the service of my country! You, sir, are a liar!"

*"How much money is this arm worth?"*

At this moment, four men rushed the one-armed man and quickly moved him away from the crowd. Quietly and viciously they beat and kicked him.

The speaker addressed the crowd once again. "You see how dangerous these Jews are? If you speak against them, they will do anything to stop you. I have seen this man before. He lost his arm in an accident. Now he wants you to believe that he lost it in the war. Don't feel pity for him. He is your enemy, and he is getting what he deserves. Today we punish him. One day soon we will deal with all of his race!"

"But," interrupted someone from the crowd, "even if we deal with the Jews, how will this help solve Germany's problems?"

"The Jews are not the only ones to be dealt with," answered the speaker, his eyes glistening. "We Germans are the master race. We were born to rule, not to serve! All inferiors—Jews, Gypsies, old people, cripples, the mentally retarded, and others of this kind —must be separated from us so that we can fulfill our destiny!"

"And what is our destiny?" cried a young man.

The speaker smiled. "Our destiny is to unite all German people everywhere in the world. Once we have done this, we must provide living space for our people. We must move to the east, take Russian lands, and make the Russians our slaves!"

"But this means another war!" yelled someone in the crowd.

"No," answered the speaker. "The West is afraid to fight. They know that they did not defeat us the first time. They will not want to meet us on the field of battle again. Besides, do they care what happens to a pack of Communist dogs?"

"Young man," cried an elderly Catholic priest, "I have listened to everything that you have said. I am shocked that only one person has spoken out against you!" The priest turned to the crowd and said, "How can you as Christians listen to these ugly things and remain silent? Have you no shame?"

At these words, many in the crowd turned red with embarrassment and lowered their heads. Some began to walk away.

The speaker's face now became red with anger. "You old fool! Don't you know that Jesus Christ was born and died a Jew? When Jesus said turn the other cheek, he meant for us to turn so that the Jews could slap us again. The Jews invented Christianity and gave it to us so that they could continue to control us through Christian teachings. For centuries, Christianity has been used by the weak to control the strong!"

The priest was silent for a moment. He said, "You are a bitter man—your mind is twisted and sick! As angry as the German people are today, they will never listen to you! You will soon crawl back into the sewer you came from, never to be heard from again!"

Having said this, the priest turned and walked away. Others looked around once or twice and slowly began to drift away. Soon there were only a few people left.

One man, middle-aged, his suit a bit shiny and his collar frayed, walked up to the speaker. He said, "Never mind that old fool. You speak of things the way they really are. You have opened my eyes and I am grateful. I would like to know your name."

"My name," said the speaker, brushing his hair away from his eyes, "is Adolf Hitler."


## UNDERSTANDING THE STORY

**A.** *Tell which statements are true.*

1. Germany suffered from food shortages after World War I.
2. Employment was up and prices were down in Germany after the war.
3. Some Germans believed that Germany did not really lose the war.
4. Adolph Hitler believed that Germans were just like any other people.
5. Hitler believed that Germany must one day move against Russia.
6. Hitler felt that the western European countries would not fight to protect Russia from Germany.
7. Hitler blamed many of Germany's troubles on the Jews.
8. Hitler was a very religious man who believed in Christianity.


**B.** *Read the selection and answer the question that follows.*

> The German does not speak much. The people of other races talk a lot. They do not have anything important to say. The German chews his food with his mouth closed. Other races chew with a smacking

noise like animals. Only the German race walks and
stands fully upright. The German has a great mind.
He has great courage. Other races walk like cows and
ducks. They talk with their hands. The German is
very clean. Other races live in dirt. The Germans
have nothing in common with other races. The German has created all things fine and good. Germans
are clearly better than all other races.

Do you agree with the information in this reading selection?
Why do you think the selection was written?

C.  Imagine that you hear a person making a speech in a local park.
He is saying terrible things. He blames one particular group for
all the troubles of our country. He asks that the crowd join with
him in throwing those people out of the country. Would you
stop to listen to this speaker? Explain. Should the speaker be
permitted to make remarks of this type? Explain.

## ACTIVITIES AND INQUIRIES

1.  Use each of the following key terms in a sentence.
    solution           inferior            twisted
    master race        destiny
2.  Study the graph showing the value of the German mark from
    1921 to 1923 on page 353. The graph shows how many German
    marks were worth one dollar during the years 1921 to 1923. Tell
    which item below makes each statement correct.
    a.  Between 1921 and 1923, the German mark (1) became more
        valuable (2) became almost worthless (3) kept the same
        value.
    b.  In 1922, the value of the mark was how many times the value
        of the mark at the end of 1923? (1) 100,000 times (2) a million
        times (3) 10 million times.
    c.  According to the graph, in 1923 the German people could buy
        (1) more (2) less (3) the same with their money than in 1922.
    d.  Compared with 1922, the German people in 1921 were (1)
        better off (2) worse off (3) about the same.
    e.  How would Hitler have explained why the German mark
        became worthless during the years 1921 to 1923?
3.  Look at the illustration on page 349. Describe what is happen-
    ing. Write your own title for this picture.

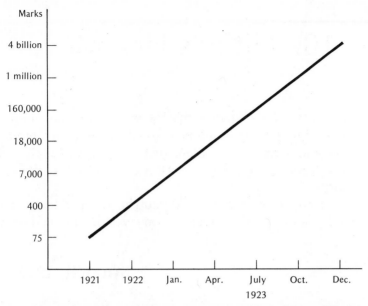

*The value of the German mark per dollar, 1921–1923*

4. Read the following selection. Then explain who was to blame for the German mark becoming worthless during the period 1921 to 1923.

> The government let the mark fall in value in order to free Germany of her war debts. German factory owners rid themselves of their war debts. The army was in favor of the fall in the value of the mark. This would wipe out Germany's war debts and leave her free to prepare for a new war. Most people did not know that the army, the state, and the factory owners were being helped by the fall in the value of German money. All they knew was that a large bank account could not buy even a bunch of carrots and a pound of potatoes, sugar, or flour. People were hungry and they were angry.

5. Study the graph (activity 2) and the reading selection (activity 4) once again. Do you think that the fall in the value of the German mark helped make Adolf Hitler more popular or less popular with the German people? Explain your answer.

# 10. Hitler's First Move

*By 1923 Adolf Hitler felt* that the time had come for him to make his first important move to take over all of Germany. He and his followers planned to march on Munich, the capital of the German state of Bavaria, and to take it over by force.

How could such a small group have hoped to succeed? Why did Hitler think that the time was ripe for a takeover?

## Munich, 1923

Three thousand men raised their beer glasses and cheered as the state commissioner of Bavaria, Gustav Kahr, began to speak. Sitting with Kahr were General Lossow, the commander of the army in Bavaria, and Colonel Seisser, the head of the state police. These three officials were the most important men in Bavaria. They were in the beer hall to conduct a political rally.

While Kahr spoke, a man entered the hall followed by others carrying rifles and pistols. The crowd was so interested in Kahr's speech that only a few took notice of the stranger and his group. Suddenly the man pulled out a pistol, jumped up on a table, and fired a shot into the ceiling.

People quickly turned away from Kahr and stared at the man standing on the table. In no time, his name was whispered throughout the hall. Adolf Hitler was no stranger in Munich.

Pistol in hand, Hitler jumped from the table, ran to the stage, pushed Kahr aside, and shouted, "The revolution has begun!"

All was confusion. While the crowd tried to make sense of what was happening, Hitler and his aides forced the three government leaders into a room next to the stage.

"You must join with me now!" cried Hitler. The three men said nothing. Hitler continued, "The French occupy our country. Factories are closing all over Germany. Millions are out of work. Every day, people are losing their life's savings. Our money has lost most of its value. All Germany is ready to follow the man who will put an end to this, and I am that man! Will you three join with me?"

The men exchanged glances. They shook their heads—no.

Hitler angrily rushed from the room and stood before the confused mob. "I am happy to announce," he said, "that Kahr, Lossow, and Seisser have just agreed to join the revolution!"

Some in the crowd began to cheer.

"They will each hold important positions in the new German government. I will lead the government, and General Ludendorf, our great war hero, will lead the new German army! We will take over Bavaria now. From here, we will march on Berlin. Soon all Germany will be ours, and a new day will begin for all of us!"

At last the crowd understood, and people cheered themselves hoarse.

At this moment, General Ludendorf arrived. Told what had happened, he grew angry that he had not been asked to help plan the revolution. But Hitler assured Ludendorf of how important he was to the success of the movement, and Ludendorf was soon won over.

A cheering crowd behind him, Hitler, with Ludendorf at his side, rushed back to the three Bavarian leaders. He waved his pistol at them and shouted, "Will you join me now?"

The three men exchanged glances. They nodded—yes.

Happier than he had ever been, Hitler danced around the room. For the first time, he really believed that his dream of becoming Germany's leader was about to come true. Hitler, Ludendorf, and the three officials now walked back into the hall together. Instantly the crowd burst into applause, and many rushed over to congratulate the men. Surrounded by admirers, Hitler and Ludendorf did not notice that the three Bavarians had quietly slipped out of the beer hall.

Safely away from Hitler and his lieutenants, Kahr, Lossow, and Seisser quickly agreed that they could not support Hitler's revolution. They made arrangements to gather troops and police to stop Hitler's group.

By morning, Hitler was aware of what had happened. "General," he said to Ludendorf, "we cannot fight the police and the army. We need them on our side. This is not the right time for us to make our move."

"Nonsense!" boomed Ludendorf. "We will march on Munich and take the city before this day is over. As for the army and the police, they will never open fire as long as I lead the march! Germany loves her war heroes too much to risk killing them."

Not convinced, but afraid to back down, Hitler gave the signal for the march to begin. He and Ludendorf led a small group of followers to the center of the city. They were met by a large police force armed with rifles. The two groups nervously faced each other. Shots rang out. Sixteen of Hitler's men and three policemen fell dead. The rest of Hitler's group fell to the pavement to avoid being shot.

One man continued the march. He brushed past the police to the next square. Just as he had said, not a single shot was fired in his direction. Upon reaching the square, Ludendorf turned to see if Hitler was still with him. Hitler was stretched out on the pavement along with the others.

Men cried out to Hitler for help, but he rose, rushed by them, and leaped into a waiting car to make his getaway. Days later, Hitler was found hiding in a friend's house. Hitler was arrested and brought to trial for treason. Newspapers all over Germany printed the story. For a short time, Hitler's name, once known only in Munich, was spoken everywhere.

At the trial, Hitler acted as his own lawyer. He argued before the jury that he was only trying to help Germany. But the jury found Hitler guilty of treason and sentenced him to five years in prison.

"Well," said many Germans after the trial, "I guess that's the last we'll ever hear of Adolf Hitler."

## UNDERSTANDING THE STORY

A. *Write T for each statement that is true and O for each statement that is an opinion.*

1. Hitler planned to take Munich by force.
2. Political meetings in Munich were always held in beer halls.

3. Hitler wanted Kahr, Lossow, and Seisser to join with him in making a revolution.
4. French occupation was the cause of millions of Germans being out of work.
5. Many Germans were losing their life's savings.
6. General Ludendorf agreed to join Hitler.
7. Kahr, Lossow, and Seisser agreed that they could not support Hitler's revolution.
8. Germans would never shoot at a war hero.

**B.** *Complete each of the following sentences.*
1. Munich is the capital of the German state of ———.
2. Kahr, Lossow, and Seisser were the most ——— men in Bavaria.
3. Adolph Hitler jumped up on a ———, pulled out a ———, and fired a shot into the ———.
4. Ludendorf was a great ——— hero.
5. The march on Munich was met by a large ——— force armed with ———.
6. ——— of Hitler's men died in the shooting.
7. Hitler was tried for ———.
8. Hitler was sentenced to ——— years in prison.

**C.** While in jail, Hitler asked himself what had gone wrong in Munich. List the mistakes you think Hitler made. On the basis of this story, do you believe that the German people had heard the last of Hitler? Explain.

## ACTIVITIES AND INQUIRIES

1. Go to the library. Prepare a report on Hitler's march on Munich.
2. Imagine that Hitler is on trial. He is charged with treason. Prepare the case against him.
3. Assume that you have been assigned to defend Hitler at his trial. Prepare the case in his defense.
4. Pretend that you are a member of the jury at Hitler's trial. Would you vote "guilty" or "not guilty"? Explain your vote.
5. Hitler's trial is over. Assume that you are a reporter assigned to interview Hitler in prison. Write the questions you would like to ask him. Now answer the questions.

# 11. An Unholy "Bible"

*By 1928 good times had returned* to Germany, and the breadlines had all but disappeared. The German people seemed pleased with their democratic-republican style of government. Few stopped to listen when the Communists and the Nazis held street corner rallies. The future for Germany and for world peace seemed very bright.

In our story, an American attending school in Germany talks to his German roommate about a book he has just finished reading.

Ask yourself why the American and the German were discussing *Mein Kampf.*

## Berlin, 1928

"Have you read this, Karl?" Bruce held up a book titled *Mein Kampf* (my struggle).

Karl hesitated. He replied, "I suppose many Germans have read it."

"Slept through it, you mean," said Bruce. "It's so boring. Besides, it's filled with half-baked ideas and half-truths."

"You Americans are all alike," answered Karl. "Whatever you don't understand, you call stupid and boring."

"Oh, come on now," protested Bruce. "The clown who wrote this never finished grade school. He has been a failure at everything, even at making a revolution. Why should he be any more successful at writing a book?"

"Say what you will. There are Germans who still think that Adolf Hitler's only crime was that he told the truth," replied Karl.

"What truth, Karl? That Germans are the master race? There is no 'master race.' Nations aren't races. Must France be destroyed, Eastern Europe conquered, and Russia invaded? Should Germany

358

rip up the peace treaty and start to build up her army and navy?"

"What's wrong with those ideas?" asked Karl. "Hitler is only saying what most Germans are thinking."

"Then God help Germany if Hitler should ever come to power," answered Bruce. "And by the way," he continued, "any people who can believe a man who says that all pure Germans are tall and blond, while he himself is short, dark, and an Austrian, need all the help that God can give them!"

"Bruce, I admit that some of what Hitler says is hard to understand. But you have to remember that in the past ten years we Germans have lost a war. We have been occupied by France. Our money became worthless. The Communists have grown stronger. Through all this, our government has sat back and done nothing. I think the German people have had enough of a government that lets Communists speak but tries to shut up Adolf Hitler. Watch what happens in the next election!"

"And what do you think will happen?" asked Bruce.

"I think that Hitler's Nazi party will win a majority in the next election."

"If that happens," said Bruce, "you realize that Hitler will become the leader of the German government."

"Yes, of course," answered Karl.

"And will you vote for the Nazis?" asked Bruce.

"That, my friend, is my business!"

*Postscript.* On May 20, 1928, the German people went to the polls to vote. Out of 31 million votes cast, only 810,000 went to the Nazi party. The Nazis won 12 of the 491 seats in the government.

## UNDERSTANDING THE STORY

A. *Tell which item below makes each statement correct.*

1. By 1928 (*a*) many people were listening to the Communists and Nazis (*b*) few people were listening to the Communists and Nazis (*c*) the Communists and Nazis were in control of the German government.

2. Bruce found the book *Mein Kampf* (*a*) boring and stupid (*b*) exciting (*c*) full of great wisdom.

3. Karl (a) agreed with Bruce (b) disagreed with Bruce (c) had not read the book.
4. *Mein Kampf* showed that Hitler (a) was well educated (b) was an expert on many subjects (c) had little education.
5. Karl believed each of the following except (a) Germans were the master race (b) Germany must stay out of all future wars (c) France must be destroyed.
6. Hitler said that all pure Germans were (a) tall and blond (b) short and dark (c) tall and dark.
7. Karl was angry with the German government because it (a) let Hitler speak (b) let the Communists speak (c) prepared Germans for war.
8. In the election of 1928, the Nazi party won (a) 300 of 491 seats in the government (b) 100 of 491 seats in the government (c) 12 of 491 seats in the government.

B. Imagine that Hitler is visiting the United States. He has written a letter home telling what he thinks of the United States. Write Hitler's letter.

## ACTIVITIES AND INQUIRIES

1. Use each of the following key terms in a sentence.
   breadlines                                half-truth
   street corner rally                       master race
   democratic-republican government
2. Imagine that you are visiting Germany in 1928. You have witnessed a Nazi street corner rally. Write a letter home describing what the Nazi speaker said.
3. During your visit to Germany, you found that many Germans were not interested in Hitler's ideas. Write a letter home explaining why you think the German people at that time were not interested in Hitler's ideas.

# 12. The Fires of Evil

*Prosperous times in Germany* came to an end in 1929. Germany was just one of the many countries to stagger under the jolt of a worldwide depression. Once again, people stopped and listened when Nazis and Communists held their street-corner meetings.

In spite of bad times, however, neither the Nazis nor the Communists could convince the German people to give them control over the government. In fact, no German political party had a majority of the votes in the *Reichstag* (rikes-TAHK), the German lawmaking body.

Field Marshal Paul von Hindenburg, the president of the German Republic, faced the problem of how to create a majority in the Reichstag. Without a majority, laws could not be passed. He had to choose to join with either the Nazis or the Communists to get his majority. Hindenburg chose the Nazis. He decided that it would be easier to control the Nazis than the Communists. He appointed Adolf Hitler the chancellor (prime minister) of Germany.

Hitler became the chancellor of Germany in 1933. But he was still far from his goal of controlling the government. The Nazi party was still a minority, and Hitler could be dismissed any time the majority voted against him.

Had Hitler come this far only to be turned back before he could take control? Since President Hindenburg, the army generals, and the majority of elected representatives were against him, how could Hitler hope to achieve his ambitions?

# Berlin, 1933-1934

"Fire! Fire!"

A crowd of frightened people watched in horror as the fire in the Reichstag building (the government meeting hall) burned out of control. It was February, 1933.

Angry shouts were heard everywhere. "It's the Communists!" "It's a Nazi trick!" "God help us all!"

The next day, a Dutch Communist was arrested and charged with the crime. He confessed on the spot. He did not mention that he had been hired by the Nazis to set the fire.

On the same day Hitler met with Hindenburg and waved a piece of paper at him. "You must sign this, Herr President," pleaded Hitler. "The German people need to be protected from the Communist terror. Granting me police powers will help to do the trick."

Hindenburg, old, tired, and forgetful, pretended to read the document. He nodded his head once or twice and signed.

Later Hitler met with his aides. "The old fool went for it," he said. "Now that the German people have lost their rights of freedom of speech and press, the Nazi party will win the next election. I'll see to it that the Communists are not allowed to hold rallies. In the meantime, we Nazis will say whatever we please about our enemies. We will convince people that there is a plot to destroy the government. The German people will be so frightened that they will trust only the Nazi party. You'll see—this time the German people will give me the majority!"

In March 1933, a general election was held. Over 90 percent of the German voters cast ballots. The Nazis won more votes than ever before, but they still fell short of winning a majority.

Although Hitler was still disappointed by the results, he continued to make himself more powerful. By threatening, bullying, flattering, and promising, Hitler convinced a majority of government representatives to vote to change the constitution. All law-making powers were turned over to the chancellor—Hitler. Next Hitler moved to break up all political parties except the Nazi party. Any who dared to start a new political party would face a stiff jail sentence.

Only two things now stood in the way of Hitler's becoming the dictator of Germany: President Hindenburg and the generals of the German army.

In 1934 the army chiefs met with Hitler and warned him about his storm troopers, who were his own private army. "You must put an end to this business," they demanded. "Your bullies beat up people; they steal and they arrest innocent people. Germany must have law and order. If you can't control these hoods, we will—even if we have to take the government away from you to do it!"

Hitler thought, "I need these men. One day they will help me to conquer Europe!" He decided to go along with them.

"Gentlemen," he said, "I promise that I will take care of the problem. There will be only one army in Germany, and that will be the regular German army!"

As good as his word, Hitler moved against the storm troopers. He ordered the leaders of the storm troopers arrested or shot. Hitler's old political enemies were also rounded up and killed. In one June weekend, on Hitler's orders, over a thousand people were slaughtered.

For these acts, Hitler was congratulated by army leaders and members of the government. He was cheered in the government hall when he announced, "I have saved Germany from those who destroy her by revolution!" No one asked him to prove this charge.

In August 1934 President Hindenburg died. Hitler forced his cabinet to declare that the offices of president and chancellor were now combined into one. He would be called the *führer* (leader). He became the sole ruler of the German people as well as commander in chief of the armed forces.

One of his aides said to him, "Führer (FURE-err), you must be very happy. You are now one of the greats of history!"

Hitler stiffened. "Not yet," he replied. "After all, I have only conquered Germany." He paused. "So far, that is."

# UNDERSTANDING THE STORY

**A.** *Write* T *for each statement that is true,* F *for each statement that is false, and* N *for each statement that is not mentioned in the story.*

1. The Nazi party won a majority in a free election.
2. A Nazi set fire to the Reichstag.
3. President Hindenburg became very fond of Hitler.
4. The Communists were blamed for the Reichstag fire.
5. Under Hitler, all political parties except the Nazis were forced to break up.
6. Hitler wanted the German people to keep their freedom.
7. The army chiefs warned Hitler to do something about his storm troopers.
8. Hitler had many of his storm troopers killed because he was afraid they would plot against him.

**B.** *Match each item in Column A with its answer in Column B.*

| Column A | Column B |
|---|---|
| 1. A Dutch Communist was hired to do this | (*a*) stop the storm troopers |
| 2. Hindenburg gave Hitler powers that had this result | (*b*) arrested or shot |
| | (*c*) set fire to the Reichstag building |
| 3. Hitler was given this under the new constitution | (*d*) bullies and hoods |
| 4. What the army chiefs wanted Hitler to do | (*e*) Germany was saved from a revolution |
| 5. What many Germans called the storm troopers | (*f*) all lawmaking powers |
| | (*g*) the regular German army would be the only army in Germany |
| 6. Promise Hitler made to the army chiefs | (*h*) the German people lost their freedom of speech and the press |
| 7. What Hitler ordered done to the leaders of the storm troopers | |
| 8. How Hitler explained his actions against the storm troopers | |

C. Imagine that the president of the United States wishes to become a dictator. What steps would he have to take? Could he succeed? Explain.

## ACTIVITIES AND INQUIRIES

1.  Below are a number of key terms. Try to fit each one into a sentence to show that you understand what it means.

    minority party      constitution      cabinet
    Reichstag              storm trooper      führer

2.  Go to the library. Prepare a report on what life was like for the German people after Hitler became dictator.
3.  Imagine that you are now living in a dictatorship. Look through your newspaper. Underline everything that a dictatorship would not allow to be published.
4.  Imagine that you are a reporter. You have just interviewed a leader of the storm troopers. He was a close friend of Hitler's. He has told you much about Hitler. Write what this man told you about Hitler.
5.  The Nazis believed that a woman's place was in the home. Married women should not work. Women should keep themselves beautiful for their husbands, stay home, and raise children. Women should stay out of politics. Women should not hold important jobs. Only men were fit to hold important jobs. Write a report on the role of women in Nazi Germany. Did women stay home and raise children while men did all the important work? Did German women agree with the Nazis?

# 13. Knockout

*To his dying day, Adolf Hitler* insisted that the German people were members of the "master race." The laws of nature, he said, had chosen the Germans to rule over all other people.

Many Germans believed Hitler. They laughed when he told them how stupid and clumsy other races were when compared to Germans.

In June 1936 in the United States, Max Schmeling, a German boxer, fought Joe Louis, an American. Schmeling gave Louis a terrible beating, and knocked him out in the eighth round. Afterward, Schmeling told reporters that he had known he, a "superior" German, could easily beat an "inferior" black person.

Louis went on to win the heavyweight championship of the world. Schmeling returned to the United States to try to take the championship away from Louis. He went with Hitler's blessings. Hitler believed a victory by Schmeling would prove that the Germans were indeed superior to all other people.

As our story begins, the fight is about to get underway. Two reporters, one a German, the other an American, are sitting at ringside. They are having their own fight.

## New York City, June 1938

"Your American champion is a coward. He will faint at the sight of his own blood," said Hans, the German reporter.

"Then, why," asked Jimmy, the American reporter, "did Schmeling wait so long to fight him again?"

"Bah! You forget that Schmeling beat Louis to a pulp the first time. Tonight he will do it again!"

"It will be different tonight."

"I agree. This time Schmeling will knock Louis out in the first round!"

"You're sure?" asked Jimmy.

"As sure as I am that the German champion, Schmeling, is a member of the master race. Your American champion, Louis, is a member of an inferior race. Tonight we Germans will win our battle in the boxing ring. Tomorrow will bring even more interesting surprises!'

"Don't count Louis out yet," said Jimmy.

"I will count him out along with the referee," snorted Hans. "Afterward I will watch them carry Louis from the ring, and I will laugh in your face!"

The crowd of 70,000 quieted down. It was time for the fight to begin.

The bell rang. The two men circled each other. Schmeling missed with a right hand. Louis moved forward and hit Schmeling with a left, a right, another right, a left, and a right. Schmeling fell to the canvas. He got up slowly. Louis again hit him with a left and a right. Schmeling fell to the canvas a second time. His face was bloody. He seemed in great pain. Once more, he slowly picked himself up.

Louis met him and threw punches so quickly that they could barely be counted. This time Schmeling fell to the floor and stayed there. The fight was over. Schmeling had to be helped from the ring. The announcer cried out, "The winner and still heavyweight champion of the world, Joe Louis!"

Jimmy turned to look at Hans, but it was too late. The German was no longer there.

## UNDERSTANDING THE STORY

**A.** *Write T for each statement that is true and O for each statement that is an opinion.*

1. The German people were members of the master race.
2. Other races were stupid and clumsy when compared to the Germans.
3. Max Schmeling defeated Joe Louis the first time they fought.

4. Louis was the heavyweight champion of the world when he fought Schmeling for the second time.
5. Louis defeated Schmeling in their second fight.
6. Louis' victory proved that boxing skill had nothing to do with race.

B. *Tell which item makes each statement correct.*

1. Adolf Hitler insisted that the German people were (*a*) like everyone else (*b*) the master race (*c*) inferior to others.
2. Max Schmeling first fought Joe Louis in (*a*) June 1936 (*b*) June 1937 (*c*) June 1938.
3. The second fight between Schmeling and Louis was held in (*a*) Germany (*b*) the United States (*c*) Zaire.
4. Hitler (*a*) was interested in the Louis-Schmeling fight (*b*) was not interested in the Louis-Schmeling fight (*c*) did not even know about the Louis-Schmeling fight.
5. Hans, the German reporter, told Jimmy, the American reporter, that Louis was (*a*) a great champion (*b*) as good a man as Schmeling (*c*) a coward.
6. Hans thought that Louis would (*a*) win by a knockout (*b*) win by a decision (*c*) be counted out in the ring.
7. Louis knocked Schmeling down (*a*) once (*b*) twice (*c*) three times.

C. Imagine that you are Jimmy, the American reporter. You are sitting at ringside next to the German reporter. How would you answer the reporter's claims?

## ACTIVITIES AND INQUIRIES

1. Imagine that you are the American reporter in our story. You are interviewing Joe Louis just before the fight. Write the questions you would like to ask him. Answer those questions as you think Louis would.
2. Assume that you are the same American reporter. Now you are interviewing Max Schmeling after the fight. Write the questions you would like to ask him. Answer the questions as you think Schmeling would answer them.
3. You are still the American reporter. Write an article about the fight for your newspaper.
4. Pretend that you are the German reporter. Write an article about the fight for your newspaper. How will you explain Schmeling's defeat?

"Why so quiet, Jack?" asked Mr. Miller.

" I have a lot to think about," answered Jack.

"Oh? What, for instance?"

Jack spoke slowly. "It's hard for me to believe that this nightmare took place such a short time ago. I thought that monsters like Hitler, Mussolini, and Stalin died hundreds of years ago."

Jack paused and added, "There are millions of people alive today who remember those madmen!"

"I'm one of them," Mr. Miller said.

"That's right, I guess you are," said Jack, looking carefully at Mr. Miller. "Were they really that bad?"

"Worse," answered Mr. Miller, a tense look on his face.

"How do you know?" asked Jack.

"I lost a lot of my family in Europe, thanks to that bunch. Those who managed to keep themselves alive have never recovered their health. And they have a daily reminder of what they went through."

"What do you mean?"

"I mean that they were branded like cattle. Numbers were burned into their flesh. They will take their numbers to their graves!"

"But only Hitler did that."

"Hitler, Mussolini, Stalin—all burned the flesh and scarred the souls of people."

"Mr. Miller, these guys really got to you."

"Yes, Jack, they really got to me."

"Well, maybe it will never happen again. After all, I'm beginning to find out that the whole point of learning about history is so we won't have to repeat it!"

"Jack, humanity has repeated this bit of history for centuries. Entire populations have been run through by the swords of dictators. The Irish, Scots, Armenians, and American Indians have all gone the way of the Jews, Poles, Russian Gypsies, and Czechs. It sometimes seems as if we just don't take the trouble to really learn from our mistakes!"

"But I don't understand. People lived through the horrors of a world war. They suffered at the hands of dictators. Didn't people decide that they had enough of such things?"

"I wish I could say 'yes,' Jack," answered Mr. Miller. "I'd love to be able to tell you that the Great War of 1914 to 1918 was the war to end all wars."

"But you're not going to tell me that," Jack said.

"Come," said Mr. Miller, "it's time to get back to our studies."

# World War II

"But why did the biggest nations in the world fight a second world war?" Jack asked.

"Perhaps they forgot the lessons of the first," suggested Mr. Miller.

"How could they? World War I was only over for 20 years! The world was led by people who had fought the first war! How could they let a second war take place?"

"Calm down, Jack," said Mr. Miller. "I've never seen you so upset. Can it be that history is beginning to get to you?"

"You're darn right it is. When world leaders won't learn from the mistakes of the past, what hope is there for the rest of us?"

"Very well put, Jack. And yet we can't give up hope that people will one day learn not to repeat the mistakes of the past."

"I hope they will. And while we're on the subject, are there any new lessons to be learned from World War II?"

"Yes, of course there are, Jack. For example, one reason why World War I took place is that nations were impatient with one another. Perhaps World War II took place because some nations were too patient with others."

"Mr. Miller, would you be very disappointed if I told you I don't know what you're talking about?"

"Patience, Jack. You will. Trust me, you will."

# 1. The Monster Stirs

*World War I had been* a nightmare. People all over the world prayed that war would never take place again. The leaders of the world tried hard to achieve this. Conferences were called and peace treaties were signed. By 1928 it looked as if the chances for a lasting world peace were very good indeed. Armed with the League of Nations, world trade agreements, and the Kellogg-Briand Pact—signed by League members—outlawing war, the peacemakers looked forward to a rosy future.

By 1930, however, the picture had changed completely. A worldwide economic depression made desperate people look for any solution to their problems. Many democratic governments fell, and dictatorships took their place. The dictators made promises to their frightened and hungry people. They promised jobs and prosperity. They promised to win back the lands lost in the Great War. These promises would be kept in blood. When the time came for the dictatorships to make their move, would the democracies stand up to them? What would happen if the democracies failed to stand up to them?

As the newspaper headlines below tell us, a military dictatorship is about to put the democratic nations to the test.

**September 18, 1931:** Bomb explodes in Mukden (MOOK-den), China, damaging Japanese railway. Japanese blame Chinese. Japanese troops invade Manchuria.

**September 19:** Chinese say Japanese lie, accuse them of blowing up own railway. Claim Japanese are looking for an excuse to take over Manchuria.

**September 21:** Reporter says that Japanese refuse to talk about Mukden bombing. Damage so slight that trains continued to run on schedule after blast.

**September 25:** League of Nations upset by Japanese invasion. Action promised soon. League commission will make full investigation.

**October 5:** United States says Japanese may have broken peace treaties. Statement of United States policy expected.

**November 3:** Chinese refuse to buy Japanese goods. Will not trade with Japanese as long as they occupy Manchuria.

**January 7, 1932:** United States sides with China. Says Japan should pull troops out of Manchuria. Secretary of State Stimson says that the United States will not recognize Japanese gains in Manchuria.

**January 9:** League members applaud United States policy statement. Many hope that League actions will force Japanese to leave Manchuria.

**January 28:** Japanese invade Shanghai, China. Promise to leave Shanghai as soon as Chinese agree to buy their goods again. League outraged.

**February 18:** Japanese rename Manchuria "Manchukuo" (manchoo-KWOH). Say that people in the area demand rule by Japanese. China complains to League.

**May 12:** Japanese Premier Inukai calls for peaceful settlement of China-Japan problems. Japanese military angry at speech.

**May 15:** Inukai assassinated! Observers suspect plot by Japanese military.

**October 2:** Lytton Commission reports to League. Japan accused of aggression in Manchuria. League will seek Japanese agreement to peaceful solution.

**February 24, 1933:** League approves Lytton Report and refuses recognition of Japanese gains in Manchuria. Japan warned about military activity. Stronger actions may follow.

**May 27:** Japan resigns from League! Warns League not to interfere. League expected to vote trade blockade of Japan.

**July 8:** China charges League's failure to act on trade blockade has placed Manchuria in Japanese hands.

*Postscript.* Two delegates to the League of Nations, who had watched the Japanese-Chinese incident from the beginning, shared some thoughts over lunch.

"Well," said the first, "the League has really made a mess of things by it's 'no-action' policy on the Japanese problem. Imagine the message we have given to those people in the world who love peace!"

"Worse yet," said the second. "Imagine the message we have given to those in this world who love war!"

## UNDERSTANDING THE STORY

**A.** *Write T for each statement that is true and F for each statement that is false.*

1. In 1928 chances for lasting peace were good.
2. Dictatorships replaced a number of democratic governments in the 1930s.
3. Manchurian troops invaded Japan in 1931.
4. The Chinese said the Japanese were looking for an excuse to invade Manchuria.
5. Dictators made promises to hungry people.
6. United States Secretary of State Stimson approved of Japan's invasion of Manchuria.
7. Japan changed the name of Manchuria to "Mongolia."
8. The League of Nations refused to approve Japan's gains in Manchuria.

**B.** *Number the events below in the order in which they took place.*

Japan invaded Shanghai, China.
Japanese Premier Inukai assassinated.
Kellogg-Briand Pact signed by League members.
League of Nations approved Lytton Report about Japanese actions in Manchuria.
Japanese railroad in Mukden, China, damaged by bomb.
Japan resigned from League of Nations.
League of Nations formed a commission to investigate Japanese actions in Manchuria.
Manchuria renamed "Manchukuo" by Japan.
Stimson declared that the United States would not recognize Japanese gains in Manchuria.

C. Imagine that you are a member of the Lytton Commission. You have been appointed by the League of Nations to look into Japan's invasion of Manchuria. What would you write in your report about Japan's actions? What actions do you think the League of Nations should take?

## ACTIVITIES AND INQUIRIES

1. Use each of the following key terms in a sentence.

outlaw            invade            crisis
dictatorship      Manchuria         Kellogg-Briand Pact

2. Study the map below of the Far East from 1930 to 1939. Tell which item makes each statement correct.

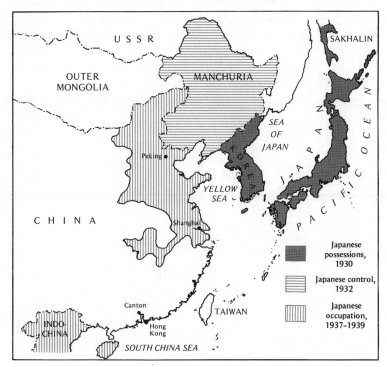

*Japanese expansion in the Far East, 1930–1939*

a. An area in Japan's possession in 1930 was (1) Korea (2) Formosa (3) Outer Mongolia.
b. A country in Asia that does not touch Manchuria is (1) Japan (2) Korea (3) the Union of Soviet Socialist Republics.

    *c.* A Chinese coastal city is (1) Shanghai (2) Canton (3) Hong
       Kong.
    *d.* North of Manchuria is (1) Outer Mongolia (2) the Union of
       Soviet Socialist Republics (3) Korea.
    *e.* South of Peking is (1) Manchuria (2) Outer Mongolia (3) Hong
       Kong.
    *f.* A city in China that was controlled by Japan was (1) Shanghai
       (2) Hong Kong (3) Canton.

3. Imagine that you are a reporter at the League of Nations. You
   are assigned to interview the Japanese representative. Write
   the questions you would like to ask him. Then write the answers you think he would give.

4. You are the same reporter. Now interview the Chinese representative. Write the questions you would like to ask him.
   Answer the questions as you think he would.

5. The caption of a cartoon about Japan and the invasion of
   Manchuria is: "How dare you keep us out of your territory!"
   Who do you think said this? Explain. Were they right to say
   this? Explain. Draw the cartoon.

# 2. Meeting in Munich

*The failure of the League of Nations* to act against the Japanese gave other dictatorships the signal they were waiting for. In 1935 Italy attacked Ethiopia and took it over. Ethiopia protested to the League, but once again the League failed to do its job. Cheered by the League's failure to act, Adolf Hitler began to bring to life the ideas in *Mein Kampf.* In 1935 he began openly to rearm Germany, even though rearmament was forbidden by the Treaty of Versailles. Nothing was done to stop him. In 1936 Hitler moved troops into the German area between Germany and France (the Rhineland). Germany had signed a treaty never to do this. Again nothing was done by the democracies of the West.

When civil war broke out in Spain in 1936, the Germans, Italians, and Russians interfered in spite of the League's warnings. Once again, countries were able to laugh at the League and get away with it.

Hitler realized that he could win territories by bluffing the frightened League members. He was almost sure that war would not be declared against him until it was too late.

He claimed that Austria and Germany should be united because many Germans lived in Austria. This too was forbidden by the Treaty of Versailles, but the bluff was successful. Austria and Germany were united, even though this was against the wishes of most Austrians.

Hitler next cast his eyes upon the country that was to be his key to the gates of Eastern Europe. This country, Czechoslovakia (check-o-slo-VA-ki-a), was well armed, and it was protected by both France and England. Hitler insisted that the Germans living in the western part of Czechoslovakia—the Sudetenland (sue-DATE-in-land)— should be part of Germany. England, France, and Czechoslovakia prepared to go to war rather than let this happen.

As our story opens, a four-power conference—of Germany, England, France, and Italy—has been called in a last effort to prevent all-out war. Ask yourself what Hitler will demand at the conference. What will the others want in return? Who will get the better deal?

# Munich, September 1938

"No! No!" cried Neville Chamberlain, the prime minister of England. "We have gone over this before, Herr Hitler, and you know our position. We will not let you occupy the Sudetenland starting on October 1."

Having said this, Chamberlain turned to Premier Edward Daladier (da-la-DYAY) of France and shook his head slowly. Daladier nodded in return. Daladier knew that Chamberlain was doing his best to prevent a war from breaking out but that Hitler's demands were impossible to meet.

Hitler now prepared to answer Chamberlain. He was furious that Chamberlain refused to give in to him, and once more tried to explain his position.

"Gentlemen," he said, speaking to both Chamberlain and Daladier, "you understand that most of the people who live in the Sudetenland are Germans. You also understand that these Germans have never cut their ties to the Fatherland. Finally you understand that my people, the Germans of the Sudetenland, are surrounded by unfriendly races. They are in great personal danger—"

"Hear! Hear!" interrupted Chamberlain.

"Let me finish!" Hitler thundered. "You must understand why it is so important for me to send troops to protect my people."

"Herr Hitler," said Chamberlain, in what he hoped was a steady voice, "Czechoslovakia is an independent country."

"Nonsense!" Hitler said. "She is a creation of that idiotic Treaty of Versailles!"

"As I was saying," continued Chamberlain, "an independent country does not welcome foreign troops on its soil. As for England and France," said Chamberlain, nodding to Daladier, "we are agreed that we will do what we must to stop the occupation of

Czechoslovakia by Germany, or any other power for that matter."

Mussolini, who had been quiet, now chose this moment to speak. "Gentlemen," he said to the three men, "we are here to keep the peace, not to make a war. Let us be reasonable. Let each side give a little bit."

"What do you suggest?" asked Daladier.

"Suppose we do this," answered Mussolini. "Let Germany transfer to itself any Czech territory in which 50 percent or more of the people are German. And, to satisfy the Czechs, you, Chamberlain, and you, Daladier, will personally guarantee the safety of the remaining Czech territories."

At this, Daladier whispered to Chamberlain, "Czechoslovakia will never accept this."

Chamberlain whispered back, "She won't like this, but what choice does she have? Without our protection she cannot exist for a moment, and she knows it! She will do anything we suggest."

"I tell you what," Hitler said. He had carefully watched the exchange between Chamberlain and Daladier, and cleverly guessed that they were close to giving in to him. "I won't move into the Sudetenland until October 1. I'll take over one district at a time over a ten-day period. And, if you like, you can have an international commission stand watch over Czechoslovakia's new borders. Now is that reasonable enough for you?"

"That sounds reasonable," said Chamberlain. "But how do we know that you will not move against the rest of Czechoslovakia?"

"Mr. Chamberlain," answered Hitler, "it is no secret that I am a racist. We Germans want no Czechs. Besides, I am ready to give my word that Germany wants no more territory in Europe. My word must count for something!"

"To an Englishman," said Chamberlain, "a gentleman's word counts for everything!"

*Postscript.* Neville Chamberlain flew back to England. He was cheered by crowds at the airport when he said that he had returned from Germany "bringing peace with honor." He finished: "I believe it is peace for our time."

On October 1, 1938, however, the German army crossed the Czech frontier and occupied the Sudetenland. By March 1939, Hitler had decided to move on. No longer would he cry that for their protection Germans living in foreign countries had to be reunited with the "Fatherland." The new cry would be the need for "living space" for the German people.

On March 14, 1939, Hitler met with President Hacha of Czechoslovakia and gave him one hour to sign his country over to Germany. Threatened and bullied, Hacha gave in. The next morning, German troops seized what was left of Czechoslovakia.

## UNDERSTANDING THE STORY

**A.** *Write T for each statement that is true and O for each statement that is an opinion.*

1. The League of Nations should have stopped the dictators.
2. In 1935 Hitler began openly to rearm Germany.
3. Germany, Italy, and Russia interfered in the Spanish Civil War.
4. Hitler was the most powerful dictator of the 20th century.
5. Hitler united Austria and Germany.
6. Part of Czechoslovakia was called the Sudetenland.
7. Chamberlain should never have given in to Hitler.
8. You can trust the prime minister of a democracy, but you cannot trust a dictator.

**B.** *Tell which statements Chamberlain would have agreed with.*

1. Czechoslovakia must remain an independent country.
2. A free country does not want foreign soldiers on her soil.
3. Czechoslovakia is the creation of the Treaty of Versailles.
4. Do anything you want, but don't invade England.
5. Without our protection, Czechoslovakia cannot exist.
6. We will defend Czechoslovakia to the last soldier.
7. Hitler is a liar! This means war!
8. I have brought peace for our time.

**C.** The word "appease" means to calm or soothe, to satisfy someone's wants or needs. Have you ever tried to appease someone? Describe the situation. What was the result? Was Chamberlain right when he tried to appease Hitler? Explain. What else might Chamberlain have tried to do?

## ACTIVITIES AND INQUIRIES

1.  Study the map below of Axis military aggressions before World
    War II. Then complete the sentences.

*Axis aggressions in the 1930s*

  *a.* A member of the Axis powers was (1) France (2) Italy (3)
      Belgium.
  *b.* A country controlled by the Axis was (1) Czechoslovakia (2)
      the Netherlands (3) Yugoslavia.
  *c.* A country north of Germany is (1) Denmark (2) Austria (3)
      Spain.
  *d.* The Sudetenland was part of (1) Yugoslavia (2) Albania (3)
      Czechoslovakia.
  *e.* Munich is a city in (1) France (2) Germany (3) Italy.
  *f.* The Rhineland is located between (1) Poland, Germany, and
      Czechoslovakia (2) Germany, Switzerland, and Austria (3)
      Germany, France, and Belgium.
  *g.* Poland is located between (1) Germany and the USSR (2)
      France and Germany (3) Germany and Czechoslovakia.

2. Use each of the following key terms in a sentence.

   racist              aggression          independent
   honor               Axis                international

3. Go to the library. Prepare a report on Hitler, Mussolini, Daladier, or Chamberlain.

4. Imagine that you are a reporter assigned to interview either Hitler or Mussolini. Write the questions that you would like to ask him. Now answer your questions as he would.

5. You are the same reporter. Your assignment is to interview Daladier or Chamberlain. Write the questions you would ask. Then answer the questions.

# 3. A Fateful Decision

*Shocked by the German takeover* of Czechoslovakia, England and France were jolted again when Italy moved into Albania in April 1939. England and France had learned a lesson. Now they knew that they could not bargain with the dictators. Both countries began to arm themselves. Both agreed that the next move by the dictators against an independent country would have to be met with force.

On August 23, 1939, Germany and Russia signed a treaty that cleared the way for Germany's next move. It was not long in coming. On September 1, Germany invaded Poland. Fifty hours later, on September 3, England declared war on Germany. Europe was plunged into the second world war in less than 25 years.

To the horror of the free world, the dictatorships —Germany, Italy, and Japan—made fantastic gains. Poland, Estonia, Latvia, Lithuania, Denmark, Norway, Holland, Belgium, Luxembourg, France, Bulgaria, Yugoslavia and—in the Far East—Hong Kong, Thailand, Indonesia, and parts of China all fell to the dictatorships.

Europeans now took the Japanese seriously. They did their best to stop Japan from taking over other territories in Asia. With the outbreak of World War II, the Europeans prepared to fight with one another. They could no longer keep a watchful eye over their colonies in the Far East. This was the chance that the Japanese had been waiting for. They began to move their troops into East Asia.

One nation, not yet involved in the world war, seemed to stand in the way of Japanese ambitions. This nation was the United States. As our story unfolds, the Japanese Imperial High Command reaches a fateful decision.

Ask yourself why the Japanese were interested in the West's colonies in Asia. Why did the United States seem to stand in Japan's way?

# Tokyo, November 1941

The setting is the headquarters of the Japanese Imperial High Command in Tokyo (TOE-ki-oh).

"Gentlemen, let us come to order," said Prime Minister Tojo. "Stimson says the United States will not recognize our territorial gains in China. We must now decide how to deal with the United States."

There was a sharp outcry from the admirals and generals. All agreed that something had to be done.

The prime minister continued. "We all know that Japan is the most advanced nation in Asia. Therefore, the people of Asia look to us for leadership and protection. Now that the Western imperialists are fighting a war to the death among themselves, we have our chance to rid all Asia of those vultures! I say let us strike fear in the American heart and send her back to the other side of the sea where she belongs!"

At this, the military officers in the room leaped to their feet and shouted their approval. Only one man remained seated— Admiral Yamamoto. It was obvious that he did not entirely share Tojo's opinions.

Admiral Yamamoto spoke. "Gentlemen, we enjoy a profitable friendship with the United States. Americans supply us with oil, scrap iron, and many other valuable materials. We need these things, and the United States needs our business. We all know that they still suffer from an economic depression. I do not think that they can afford to stop trading with us. Americans are reasonable people. I do not think that they are looking for trouble. Let our ambassadors, and not our guns, convince the Americans to mind their own business. Remember, gentlemen, war is costly. The United States may not be as weak and foolish as she appears."

The men spoke excitedly to one another. While they did not cheer the admiral, they were impressed by what he had said. Suddenly an official rushed into the room and gave a message to the prime minister. The room was hushed as Tojo read the message.

Tojo looked up with flashing eyes. He said, "My brothers, the United States has just turned down every one of our demands. The message says that, if we wish to continue to trade, we must give up the parts of Asia that we now protect. Those dogs keep our sons and daughters who live in their country out of their schools. Our Japanese brothers and sisters are not good enough for them! They order us about as if we were mindless children! We have taught the Chinese and the Russians to respect us. Now I say that it is time to let the Americans feel our sting! We will invade their bases in the Philippines."

The officers stood once more and flooded the room with cries of agreement. Not a single officer remained seated.

## UNDERSTANDING THE STORY

**A.** *Write T for each statement that is true and O for each statement that is an opinion or that is not found in the story.*

1. European nations were afraid to stop Japan from moving into East Asia.
2. The Japanese believed that the United States stood in their way.
3. The people of Asia looked to Japan for leadership and protection.
4. Japan would easily frighten the United States.
5. Japan was the most advanced country in Asia.
6. The United States supplied Japan with valuable materials.
7. The United States could not afford to stop trading with Japan.
8. The United States could be convinced to mind its own business.
9. Japan and the United States disagreed about many things.

**B.** *Complete each of the sentences below.*

1. Japan was able to defeat both —— and ——.
2. At the outbreak of World War II, Japan moved troops into ——.
3. One country, ——, seemed to stand in Japan's way.
4. Prime Minister Tojo wanted to use —— against the United States.
5. Admiral Yamamoto thought that the United States could not afford to stop —— with Japan.

  6. The United States was suffering from an economic ———.

  7. The United States would continue to trade with Japan only if Japan gave up ——— she had taken in ———.

  8. The United States kept some Japanese-American children out of American ———.

**C.** The year is 1941. Imagine that you are an adviser to the president of the United States. He asks you how to deal with the Japanese. What advice would you give him?

## ACTIVITIES AND INQUIRIES

1. Imagine that you are a reporter interviewing Prime Minister Tojo of Japan. Write the questions that you would ask Tojo. Answer the questions as he might have done.

2. Now imagine that you are a reporter interviewing Admiral Yamamoto. Write the questions that you would ask him. Answer the questions as he might have done.

3. Go to the library. Prepare a report on the Japanese attack on Pearl Harbor. Was the United States government really surprised that the attack took place?

4. Imagine that you are a Japanese person living in the United States before World War II. Write a letter to relatives in Japan. Tell them what life is like for you in the United States.

5. Draw a cartoon that shows at least one reason why Japan decided to go to war with the United States. Do you think that the Japanese military had good reasons for attacking the United States? Explain.

# 4. The Finest Hour

*The future looked very gloomy* for the democracies. The dictatorships—Germany, Italy, and Japan—were on the move. They won battle after battle. It looked as if nothing could stop the dictatorships from gaining control over the entire world.

What, then, turned the tide in favor of the unconquered countries? Perhaps, more than anything else, the human spirit, which refused to surrender in the face of almost impossible odds.

## London, 1950

You are Winston Churchill, and you have been loved and hated since you were a small boy.

You have been a soldier, journalist, historian, politician, public speaker, and statesman. Yours has been a most exciting life.

You were put in charge of the British navy at the beginning of World War I. You spoke bluntly, stepped on many toes, and made many enemies. You had many original ideas for fighting this war. But they were too far ahead of their time, and most were ignored. Stubborn as always, you fought for your ideas, and finally got to put a few into action. These failed miserably and, ten months after the outbreak of World War I, you were fired from your job as head of the navy.

You told your friends that you were finished. You were convinced that you would never again play an important role in the shaping of your country's history. You retired for awhile to your country home, but it was not long before you returned to public life. You were elected to Parliament.

You watched carefully as Adolf Hitler built up Germany's armed forces. Yours was one of the few voices raised in protest against Hitler's actions. From the first, you called for England to stop Germany before it was too late. As usual, you were ignored.

You begged your fellow Britons to arm themselves after Germany moved into the Rhineland. For your troubles, you were labeled a warmonger.

A year after Chamberlain handed Czechoslovakia over to Hitler, Germany invaded Poland. World War II had begun! Now people had to admit that perhaps you had been right all along. You were asked to head the navy again, and you were happy for the chance. Unknown to you, you would soon be asked to fill a much more important job.

A few months after the outbreak of the war, Chamberlain stepped down, and you were asked to lead the government. You did so gladly. You told the British people that you had nothing to offer them but "blood, toil, tears and sweat." They understood, and they loved you for telling them the truth.

After the fall of France, England was forced to fight alone. You faced your people and gave them the shot in the arm that they so desperately needed. When it seemed that Germany was about to invade your country, you told your people: "We shall defend our island, whatever the cost may be, we shall fight on the beaches, we shall fight on the landing grounds, we shall fight on the fields and in the streets, we shall fight in the hills; we shall never surrender."

Your people believed you.

Your country was bombed and battered. After each bombing your people dug themselves out and were even more determined to fight back. You went into the streets, picked up a shovel, and dug out with the rest. Your people knew that you were willing to put up with anything to bring your country through. They caught fire from your spirit!

Your country's magnificent stand held off the Germans. It gave Russia and the United States time to prepare themselves to fight on your side. No one hated the Russian government more than you, but you were willing to pay any price to defeat Hitler and his crew.

By 1943 the tide had turned in your favor. The Germans, Italians, and Japanese were being beaten back. It was now just a matter of time. The war lasted until September 2, 1945. You lived to see Germany, Italy, and Japan go down to total defeat. You took no small satisfaction at the deaths of your enemies Mussolini and

Hitler. But you were saddened at the death of one of your closest wartime friends, United States President Franklin Delano Roosevelt.

Two months after this great victory, your people turned you out of office. You were shocked. Perhaps you never understood that people wanted to forget the wartime nightmare, and you were a constant reminder of it. Perhaps, too, this was the people's way of saying that a democracy does not reward a great hero with a lifetime key to the powers of government.

You soon got over your disappointment. It wasn't long before you were your old self, making speeches and writing books. You would be brought back to power one more time, but your greatest years were behind you.

You once told your people that, if the British Empire lasted for a thousand years, people would look back at England's stand in 1940 and say, "This was their finest hour."

You are Winston Churchill, and you have been loved and hated since you've been a small boy. But when others stood ready to snuff out your island, you rose to defend it magnificently.

This was *your* finest hour.

## UNDERSTANDING THE STORY

**A.** *Write T for each statement that is true, F for each statement that is false, and O for each statement that is an opinion.*

1. England refused to arm itself until the war began.
2. A democracy is always stronger than a dictatorship.
3. In the first years of World War II, the democracies were very successful.
4. Winston Churchill was the greatest politician the world has ever known.
5. Churchill had been a soldier and historian.
6. Churchill replaced Chamberlain as prime minister of England.
7. The bombing of England stopped as soon as Churchill became prime minister.

**B.** *Tell which statements Churchill made or might have made.*

1. Hitler must be stopped before it is too late.
2. Germany will win World War II; England must surrender.
3. I offer blood, toil, tears, and sweat.
4. We shall defend our island whatever the cost.
5. If we stop bombing Germany, Hitler will leave us alone.
6. We shall never surrender.
7. Mussolini and Hitler will be our friends after the war.

**C.** Suppose that the British had not chosen Winston Churchill to lead them during World War II. Instead Neville Chamberlain remained the prime minister. Do you think that the outcome of the war might have been different? Explain.

## ACTIVITIES AND INQUIRIES

1. Go to the library. Prepare a report on life in Great Britain during World War II.
2. Imagine that you are a reporter. Your assignment is to interview Hitler. You ask Hitler what he thinks of Winston Churchill. Write what you think Hitler would say about Churchill.
3. You are the same reporter. You have been interviewing Mussolini. You asked him what he thought about Churchill. Write down what Mussolini would say about Churchill.
4. Go to the library. Prepare a report on the activities of women during World War II.
5. Use each of the following key terms in a sentence.
   journalist              politician                statesman

# 5. No Escape

*In 1940 Mussolini pushed his* country into World War II. He did this believing that Germany would win the war, and that Italy would then share in the fruits of victory. For Mussolini, this was the beginning of the end. His armies were badly beaten, and his friends turned against him.

Bu July 1943 Mussolini had been pushed out of power, and he was held prisoner for awhile until he was rescued by the Germans. Tired and sick, Mussolini watched with horror as the Germans were slowly driven out of Italy. He knew that if the Italian people captured him, they would deal harshly with him.

In our story, Mussolini and his mistress, Clara Petacci, are trying to escape from Italy. Ask yourself why Mussolini was afraid of his own people. How had Mussolini changed since the days of his rise to power? What lesson had the Italian people learned from Mussolini's rule?

## Milan, 1945

"Clara, tell me once again that things are going to be all right."

"Courage, Benito. In a few hours we will be safe in Switzerland, and then our troubles will be over."

"I wish I could be so sure, Clara. I keep looking to the stars for some message, but they tell me nothing."

"Benito, haven't you faced danger before? You are the smartest, strongest, bravest man I know. When trouble comes, you'll know how to handle it."

"Clara, my Clara, what would I do without you? If it had not been for you, I might have taken my life long ago!"

"You just say these things because you're tired. You'll see, as soon as we're safely out of this country, you'll be your old self."

"Are you sure that nobody can recognize me?" asked Mussolini anxiously.

"Don't worry. In that German outfit no one would mistake you for the great man that you are."

Feeling better, Mussolini moved closer to Clara. He began to relax as the car moved ever closer to the Swiss border.

"Stop! Stop or we'll shoot!"

Mussolini brought his head up sharply and looked through the car window. Just as he had feared, it was a band of Italians who had joined the fight against the Fascists and the Nazis. Mussolini's heart sank.

"You, there," cried the leader, "get out of the car—and you, too!"

Mussolini and Clara Petacci slowly got out of their car.

"Please, sir," stammered Mussolini, "I am only a German officer trying to find my way back to my lines."

"We shall soon see," snapped the leader. "Let's see your papers."

The leader examined the papers and then carefully looked at Mussolini. Mussolini tried to look away from him.

"Wait a minute," said the leader. "Don't I know you? Of course. Men, look who I found!"

Trapped, Mussolini tried to make a run for it, but he was caught quickly.

"What will happen to me?" cried Mussolini.

"What should have happened to you the moment you were born!" answered the leader.

Sometime later, the men held a meeting and made a decision. Their leader, Colonel Valerio, approached Mussolini and Clara. He addressed Mussolini mockingly, "We have decided that you have suffered enough. After tomorrow, you will never suffer again! You are to be shot at dawn!"

Mussolini's mouth opened, and his jaw hung loosely. But he said nothing.

Clara cried out, "Please, leave him alone. Can't you see that he is old and tired? Is this how you pay back the man who has meant so much to Italy?"

At these words, Valerio slammed his rifle butt on the floor. "So much for what Mussolini has meant to Italy! Be quiet, woman, or you will get what's coming to him!"

"Please," Clara cried, "if he must die, let me die with him!"

Valerio bowed. "Far be it from me to say 'no' to a lady. You will get your wish!"

The next morning, Mussolini and Clara Petacci were brought before a firing squad and tied to posts.

"Don't kill us," cried Mussolini. "I'll see to it that you all become rich men! You'll become famous. I'll give you anything that you want . . . only don't do this to me!"

"Mussolini," Valerio cried, "you once called yourself a soldier. Now, prepare to die like one!" He gave the order to fire.

Later the bodies were hung by the heels in the town square. A crowd gathered to look. Newsmen took pictures of the scene. Valerio, watching, turned to his aides and said, "A fitting end for such a man!"

## UNDERSTANDING THE STORY

**A.** *Match each item in Column A with its answer in Column B.*

COLUMN A
1. Country that Italy joined in World War II
2. What happened to Mussolini's armies
3. What Mussolini became as he watched his dreams of glory fade
4. This was the disguise Mussolini used to escape from Italy
5. Country that Mussolini was trying to reach
6. Person who tried to give Mussolini courage
7. Mussolini's final reward

COLUMN B
(a) Switzerland
(b) German officer's uniform
(c) Germany
(d) death by firing squad
(e) tired and sick
(f) they were defeated
(g) Clara Petacci

**B.** *Write* T *for each statement that is true,* F *for each statement that is false, and* N *for each statement that is not mentioned in the story.*

1. Mussolini hated violence and war.
2. The Italian people begged Mussolini not to send them to war.
3. By July 1943, Mussolini had been pushed out of power.
4. Mussolini became afraid of his own people.
5. The Germans tried to protect Mussolini from the Italians.
6. In the story, Mussolini's car was stopped by a band of Italian Communists.
7. The Italians shot Mussolini but let Clara go free.
8. Everyone was impressed because Mussolini died bravely.

**C.** Imagine that Mussolini was not executed but brought to trial. What crimes should he have been charged with? If you had been the judge at the trial, how would you have sentenced Mussolini if he had been found guilty? Explain.

## ACTIVITIES AND INQUIRIES

1. Assume that Mussolini is on trial. Prepare the case against him.
2. Now assume that your assignment is to defend Mussolini. Prepare the case in his defense.
3. Imagine that you are a reporter for a foreign newspaper. You interview Mussolini in his prison cell. Write the questions you would like to ask him. Answer the questions as you believe he would.
4. Pretend that you are a member of the jury at Mussolini's trial. You have heard both sides present their arguments. What is your verdict? Why?
5. Once again, you are a reporter. You are with the Italians who capture Mussolini. Write an article about the way Mussolini behaved from the time he was captured until he was shot.

# 6. Victims

*Many Germans waited to see how* Hitler would behave. He was now the most powerful person in Germany. They said, "Forget what he has written and promised. He said those things only to call attention to himself. Now that he is Germany's leader, he will work only to make our lives better. Our nightmare is over!"

But Hitler soon plunged his country into a world war. And while that war was raging on the battlefields, another one was being fought behind the lines. The victims of this war were innocent men, women, and children.

Ask youself whether the German people really understood Adolf Hitler. Why did Hitler make victims of innocent people?

## Munich, 1944

They say that my mind is gone. Yet I have never seen things so clearly. For the first time I am beginning to understand everything. That is what makes them afraid of me.

They don't know me anymore, my friends in the Commandos. They want to remember only the man who cheered when Hitler spoke of the need to rid Germany of her Jews and other undesirables.

At first we believed that all Hitler wanted us to do was to break a few shop windows and beat up some people. It seemed like a good idea at the time. We didn't like these people. Hitler told us that they were the cause of all of Germany's problems. We believed everything Hitler said.

We frightened many into leaving Germany. Many Germans

agreed with us. Most of those who did not agree were too afraid to speak out. We were teaching the German people how to obey their masters.

But our taste for violence grew. We were no longer satisfied with just clubbing people in the streets. We began to round them up. We made them dig their own graves. We forced them to undress and then we shot them down.

I was a Commando doing my job. Jews, Gypsies, Christians —they were all the same to me. They were the enemies and had to be dealt with harshly. In the concentration camps, gas chambers and giant furnaces were built so that thousands could be killed each day. Our doctors experimented with these people. Bodies were turned into soap and lamp shades. Babies were drowned in vats of cold water. Young girls were used as prostitutes for German soldiers. Many others were worked, starved, and beaten to death. Hitler was not a cruel man. These people deserved what they were getting.

But then Sister Catherine changed everything for me.

I first saw her on the camp grounds two months ago. "What are you, a nun, doing in this camp?" I asked. She stared at me and said nothing.

"Don't you remember me? I'm Albert Bauer. I was a student of yours many years ago." Again she stared and seemed to recognize me. But she quickly turned her face away.

I tried to find out from the others why she had been sent here. No one could tell me anything. I had to know. Perhaps it was all a mistake. I looked up her records. It was no mistake. Sister Catherine had been caught hiding Jewish families. For this she would have to die.

I sent for her. I asked, "Why, Sister Catherine? Why did you hide these people? You are not Jewish."

She said nothing.

Again I asked, "Why did you do it?"

She looked at me and asked quietly, "Why do you murder people?"

I answered, "I do Hitler's work. I follow orders. These people must be destroyed."

"I do the Lord's work," answered Sister Catherine. "All human life is sacred."

I ordered that she be taken back to her quarters.

Weeks passed. I did not see Sister Catherine. But I thought about her all the time. I had to admire her. She was a brave woman. She had risked her life to protect the lives of others. But why did she try to help Jews? And where did she get her strength?

Yesterday I saw her again. She was being marched along with the others to the gas chamber. I walked alongside of her. "Please," I asked, "why did you let this happen to you?"

Silence.

The march ended and people were lined up for entry into the chamber. I began to feel uneasy. My stomach was churning. A lump came to my throat. Now her turn came. She crossed herself and said a silent prayer. Then she took the hand of a child and walked toward the chamber. Just before she entered, she turned and looked at me.

"You see, Albert, Hitler makes victims of us all."

I stood there with my mouth open and watched her disappear into the chamber. I knew what would happen next. The doors would be locked and the gas would be turned on. All inside would die. I had watched this scene many times. It had meant nothing to me. I had always believed that dangerous animals were being put to sleep. But there was at least one human being in that chamber now. And perhaps—perhaps—there were more.

Suddenly my head cleared. I now saw things as they really were. I fell to my knees and begged forgiveness for my sins. My companions looked at me with horror. They grabbed me and took me to my room.

Today I am being taken to a hospital for the mentally ill. The doctors say that I have suffered a nervous breakdown. What they don't understand is that the German people have all suffered a nervous breakdown. All Germany is an asylum.

Sister Catherine was right. We are all Hitler's victims.

# UNDERSTANDING THE STORY

**A.** *Write T for each statement that is true and F for each statement that is false.*

1. Albert Bauer was a soldier on the Russian front.
2. Adolf Hitler plunged Germany into World War II.
3. Sister Catherine at first refused to talk to Albert Bauer.
4. The victims of Hitler's war behind the lines were often innocent people.
5. Albert Bauer could not understand why Sister Catherine was in a concentration camp.
6. The last time Albert Bauer saw Sister Catherine she was being released from the concentration camp.
7. Adolf Hitler said that the Austrians and the French were the cause of Germany's troubles.
8. Sister Catherine helped Albert Bauer understand what had happened to the German people.

**B.** *Complete the sentences.*

1. Albert Bauer was being taken to a hospital for the ——— ill.
2. The Nazis forced people to dig their own ———.
3. Hitler ordered ——— and ——— built so that thousands of people could be killed each day.
4. Doctors were ordered to perform ——— on human beings.
5. Albert Bauer had been a ——— of Sister Catherine's.
6. Albert Bauer could not understand why Sister Catherine had sheltered ———.

**C.** When World War II ended, the Allies brought Nazi leaders to trial in Nuremburg, Germany. They were accused and found guilty of wartime atrocities and crimes against humanity. Imagine that you are one of the judges at these trials. What sentence would you pass on the war criminals?

# ACTIVITIES AND INQUIRIES

1. Go to the library. Prepare a report on life in the German concentration camps.
2. Imagine that you were the last person to speak to Sister

    Catherine. She told you how she felt and why she was going to the death chamber. Write the things she told you.

3. The commandant of a concentration camp is on trial. Prepare the case against him.

4. Assume that the camp commandant is defending himself. Write the things he will say in his own defense.

5. Imagine that you are interviewing a person who was imprisoned in a concentration camp and is still alive. Write the questions you would like to ask this person. Answer the questions as you think this person would.

# 7. The End of the "Master Race"

*Ask yourself why the German* people supported Hitler.
What went wrong with Hitler's dream of power?

## Berlin, April 1945

You are Adolf Hitler, and for 12 years you have been one of the most talked-about men in the world.

You have hurt a lot of people on your climb to the top: Jews, Poles, Russians, French, English, and, most of all, Germans. You have no regrets.

You have lied, cheated, bluffed, bullied, and done anything that it took to get you to the top and keep you there. You have ordered the deaths of millions in prison camps and the deaths of millions more on fields of battle. People call you a madman when you say that you did these things to help the German people become the masters of the world.

You have paid a high price for these 12 years. There have been attempts upon your life. One arm is paralyzed. Your health is poor, and lately you have begun to look much older than you are.

Your dream of making Germany the greatest nation in the history of the world has all but ended. Your armies have been chased out of Africa, Western Europe, and Russia. Your enemies are closing in on you.

All is lost in Italy. The Japanese also are losing battles. You tell people around you that you are hoping for a miracle. Secretly, you believe that all is lost.

You have just learned that your good friend Mussolini was captured and shot. You will never let that happen to you. You have given orders that, immediately after your death, your body is to be soaked in gasoline and burned to ashes. Rather than surrender, you have decided to take your own life.

The latest news is that the Russians are closing in on Berlin. They may enter the city in a matter of hours. You would like to run, but all doors are closed to you.

You are Adolf Hitler, and for 12 years you have been the most talked-about man in the world. But your time has run out.

*Postscript.* On April 30, 1945, Adolf Hitler pointed a pistol at himself and pulled the trigger.

## UNDERSTANDING THE STORY

**A.** *Tell which statements are true.*

1. Hitler did great harm to the European people.
2. Millions of people were killed in concentration camps.
3. Germany was trying to become the master of the world.
4. Germany was winning the war at the time of Hitler's death.
5. Hitler's body was to be burned immediately after his death.
6. At the end of the war, Hitler's health was good.
7. At the end of the war, the Russians were closing in on Berlin.

**B.** *Study the map on page 402 and answer the following questions.*

1. At the end of World War II, which of the following was a country that did not occupy Germany? (*a*) Poland (*b*) Soviet Union (*c*) France
2. The French zone of occupation in Germany was (*a*) in East Germany (*b*) along the border between France and Germany (*c*) in Poland.
3. The city of Berlin was in the (*a*) British zone (*b*) American zone (*c*) Soviet zone.
4. The Soviet zone of occupation was in (*a*) East Germany (*b*) West Germany (*c*) France.
5. The city of Bonn is in (*a*) East Germany (*b*) West Germany (*c*) Austria.
6. France is on the border of (*a*) East Germany (*b*) West Germany (*c*) Poland.

*Allied occupation of Germany after World War II*

## ACTIVITIES AND INQUIRIES

1. Go to the library. Prepare a report on the last days in the life of Adolf Hitler.
2. Pretend that you are making a motion picture. It will be about the life of Adolf Hitler. Write the title of the movie. Write an outline of the scenes in the movie.
3. Hitler has just killed himself. Write his *obituary* (death notice, or biography) for a newspaper.
4. Imagine that Hitler is captured alive. He will go on trial. Prepare the case against him. How will Hitler defend himself? If Hitler is found guilty, how will you punish him?

# 8. A Survivor's Story

*The Japanese shocked the United States* with a surprise attack on Pearl Harbor. The United States immediately declared war against Japan. A long, ugly series of battles followed. The Japanese suffered terrible defeats. By 1945 they were preparing to defend their homeland against a United States invasion.

Ask yourself why the Japanese found it impossible to conquer the United States. Why did the United States use the atomic bomb?

## Tokyo, 1950

I am a Japanese woman. I have been in a hospital for five years, since I was 16. I am here because something terrible happened to me and my people.

Five years ago I was a schoolgirl. I lived with my parents in the city of Hiroshima (he-ro-SHE-ma). Japan was at war with the United States. We were told we were fighting for our national honor. My teacher would point to a map of the world and show us how small our country was compared to the United States. This made me feel proud. We Japanese would not let anyone back us down.

All the boys in my class were afraid that the war would end before they had a chance to fight. They were such fools! I hated the war! It had taken the lives of my two brothers. My father told me to be proud of my brothers. He said that both had died fighting bravely for our divine emperor. They had been rewarded with eternal life in heaven. My father told me not to cry for them. But I heard him cry late at night when he thought I was asleep.

We knew that the Americans were near Hiroshima because their planes flew over and dropped leaflets. These leaflets warned us to leave the city. They said that a terrible weapon would soon be used against us. This frightened many people. But our leaders said it was just another American trick. We were reminded to have faith in the emperor. We had to work hard so that we could win the war. I wanted to believe this with all my heart and soul. But I could not help feeling afraid.

Then it happened. I was miles away from Hiroshima visiting with relatives. I heard a terrible noise. Then I saw fire and smoke. My heart sank. I could see that Hiroshima was in flames. My family was trapped. I tried to run back to my city, but my aunt held me. She begged me to wait. We both held on to each other and cried.

Later, when the fires had died down, I rushed back to Hiroshima to find my family. As I got closer to the city, I began to smell burning flesh. People with parts of their faces ripped away rushed past me. Others had burns all over their faces and bodies. My city had become a furnace.

I ran to where we had lived. But there was nothing where my home had been. I sank to my knees and cried. I would never see my family again.

I wandered around for days. Finally I was picked up by a medical team and brought to this hospital. The doctors told me that I had suffered from exposure to radiation. I was given many treatments. I lost a great deal of weight and was in intense pain. And I was not alone. Hundreds were in this hospital suffering from the same sickness. Many have already passed into the next world.

The doctors still try to cheer me up. They tell me that I will soon be well again. I know better. I am growing weaker. I am being fed through my veins. But my nightmare is almost over. Soon I will be with my family.

An atomic bomb was dropped on Hiroshima on August 6, 1945. Three days later, an atomic bomb was dropped on Nagasaki (na-ga-SA-ki). The Japanese surrendered. Together, the two bombs killed over 120,000 people. About the same number of people were seriously injured.

Japan today is at peace with the world and has a democratic government. It is also one of the wealthiest nations in the world.

The Japanese have kept part of the city of Hiroshima as it was after the atomic attack. To this day, Japan will not stockpile nuclear weapons of any kind.

# Independence, Mo., 1965

United States President Harry Truman was interviewed many times about his decision to drop the atomic bomb. Here are the highlights from one of these interviews.

"Mr. President," said the writer, "didn't you give it a lot of thought?"

"There wasn't much to think about," said President Truman. "We were about to invade Japan. Perhaps a million American soldiers would be killed or wounded. The Japanese would suffer as much or more. The nightmare had to be ended. The bomb took care of all that."

The writer said to Truman, "Dr. Oppenheimer, who worked on the atomic bomb, feels that we made a great mistake. He says that this terrible weapon should never have been used to destroy human beings."

President Truman looked grim. "Oppenheimer is a cry baby. I had to make a decision. I had to think about all the lives that would be lost if the bomb wasn't used. I'm not ashamed of the decision I made."

"Mr. President, you say you wanted to save lives by using the atom bomb. Yet a lot of people lost their lives because of the bomb. If you could make that decision again, would you make it the same way?"

President Truman thought for a moment. "Yes. Perhaps because of what has happened in Japan, no one will ever again use this bomb against human beings."

## UNDERSTANDING THE STORY

A. *Tell which statements show how the atomic bomb affected Japan.*

1. The atomic bomb caused the war between Japan and the United States.
2. The bomb caused the death of the girl's two brothers.
3. The bomb helped bring the war to an end.
4. The bomb caused great suffering for the Japanese people.

5. The bomb practically destroyed two cities, Hiroshima and Nagasaki.
6. The bombings made the Japanese even more determined to win the war.
7. As a result of the dropping of the atomic bomb, the war continued for two more years.
8. The bombing of the two cities has never been forgotten by the Japanese people.

**B.** *Match each item in Column A with its answer in Column B.*

COLUMN A
1. The Japanese attack on this place made the United States declare war.
2. Person the Japanese believed was divine
3. What the Japanese thought would happen to military heroes
4. What the leaflets urged the people of Hiroshima to do
5. President Truman thought that using the bomb would do this
6. Atomic bombs were dropped on these cities
7. Part of this Japanese city has not been rebuilt since the war
8. The type of government Japan has today

COLUMN B
(a) leave Hiroshima immediately
(b) democracy
(c) save many lives in the long run
(d) Pearl Harbor
(e) Hiroshima
(f) emperor of Japan
(g) they would live forever in heaven
(h) Hiroshima and Nagasaki

**C.** Imagine that President Truman has not yet decided whether to use the atom bomb against the Japanese. He asks your advice. Give your advice and explain your reasons.

## ACTIVITIES AND INQUIRIES

1.  Study the table below and answer the questions that follow.

    **Destruction Caused by United States
    Bombing of Tokyo, March 9, 1945**

    | Homes destroyed | 250,000 |
    | Persons made homeless | 1 million |
    | Persons killed | 85,000 |

    This bombing raid on Tokyo did more damage than the first
    atomic bomb dropped on Hiroshima five months later. Why
    then did the Japanese surrender after the United States had
    dropped just two atomic bombs? How would President Tru-
    man use this table to back up his decision to use the atomic
    bomb?

2.  Imagine that President Truman is on trial for using the atomic
    bomb against the Japanese people. Prepare the case against
    President Truman. Go to the library. Prepare a report on the
    bombing of Hiroshima or Nagasaki. Use this report as part of
    your evidence against President Truman.

3.  Prepare the case in favor of President Truman. Go to the
    library. Prepare a report on the American invasions of Japan's
    islands in the Pacific Ocean. Use the *casualty figures* (numbers of
    dead and wounded) as evidence to support President Tru-
    man's decision to use the bomb.

4.  You are a member of the jury hearing the case against Truman.
    Vote "guilty" or "not guilty." Explain the reasons for your
    vote.

5.  Pretend that you are a Japanese reporter covering the trial for
    your country. What questions would you like to ask President
    Truman? How will he answer these questions? Are you satis-
    fied with his answers? Explain.

# 9.  Enrico Fermi

*The attack on Pearl Harbor* had caused the United States to declare war on Japan. Days later Germany declared war on the United States. For the second time in the 20th century the United States was involved in a world war.

The United States spent billions of dollars to produce guns, tanks, planes, and other equipment. Millions of men were drafted. The survival of the free world was at stake. Every weapon would have to be used to make sure that Germany and Japan were defeated.

One of the greatest weapons used to win the war was the human mind. The scientists from all over the world who came to the United States in the 1930s helped to develop new weapons of war. Many of these scientists came from Hitler's Germany, Mussolini's Italy, and from areas of Europe that were occupied by dictators. The scientists had sworn to help defeat the dictatorships. This is the story of one of these scientists.

## Washington, 1952

My name is Enrico Fermi (FAIR-me). From the time I was a little boy, I have been interested in how things work. I would take things apart and put them together again. This helped me understand them. Later I turned to math and physics. I studied in Italy, Germany, and Holland. I was graduated with honors, and I was told that I had a brilliant future. On graduation from the university, I was immediately hired to teach math and physics at the University of Rome. I was 22 years old.

Teaching left me time to experiment. I became interested in the behavior of atoms. My goal was to bombard atoms with atomic bullets. I formed a team with some friends. We decided to use radium. The experiments began. There were disappointments. Nothing happened when we bombarded the first few atoms. Then we began to get results. We got our best results using uranium. We had made something new. But what was it? It took us five years to find out.

In the meantime, I faced other problems. Mussolini came to power and turned Italy into a dictatorship. I did not want my children to become followers of Mussolini. Besides, my wife was Jewish, and Italy began to pass laws that took rights from Jews. It was only a matter of time before my wife and children would suffer. I wasted little time. In 1939 we gathered our belongings and left for the United States.

It was here in America that I learned what had happened in my experiment. I found that I had not created something new. I had instead done something that no powerful atom-smashing machine had been able to do. I had split the atom. Now my work was clear. I would have to learn how to control the atom's great power and put it to work.

I joined a team of scientists. We believed that splitting the atom would create a chain reaction, and a tremendous amount of energy would be given off. The team would now try to prove this theory in the laboratory.

It was important that my team succeed. World War II had just begun. Hitler was terrorizing all of Europe. We were afraid he would soon terrorize the rest of the world. And Hitler's scientists were also experimenting with splitting the uranium atom. If Hitler learned the secrets of the atom, the world would be doomed. My friends and I told the president of the United States about the power of the atom.

President Roosevelt met with us and listened. He agreed that atomic research should begin immediately. But we were not given enough money for our experiments, and we complained. On December 7, 1941, Japan bombed Pearl Harbor. Days later, Germany declared war on the United States. Now we were given all the money we needed.

The experiments went well. This time we discovered something new—plutonium. We found that plutonium was more powerful than any other known explosive. We thought that we could use plutonium to split the uranium atom. Now we had to find out if we could build an atomic bomb.

On December 2, 1942, we were ready for our final test. Our experiment had cost $353 million. How we hoped that this last test would be a success! It was! That afternoon we proved we could create a chain reaction that would go on by itself. Furthermore, we were able to control the chain reaction. The atomic bomb was born before our eyes.

From that day on we worked around the clock. We worked to build three atomic bombs. We had to agree on the right amount of materials for the bomb. A bomb dropped from a plane could not be controlled. If we made a mistake there would either be no explosion or an explosion that would destroy us. Finally, we were ready. On July 16, 1945, at Los Alamos, New Mexico, we exploded our first atomic bomb. The results were better than we dared hope.

Now we had two bombs left. They were used against the Japanese. One was dropped on Hiroshima, the other on Nagasaki. These bombs put an end to the war and ushered in a new age—the atomic age.

Some scientists are very critical of me. They say that I have created a monster. They predict that the bomb will one day be used to destroy the world. But I disagree. I believe that knowledge is always better than ignorance. I also believe that atomic power will someday be used to improve rather than destroy life.

## UNDERSTANDING THE STORY

**A.** *Tell which statements are true.*

1. Many scientists left countries ruled by dictators and came to the United States.
2. Fermi's goal was to find a new poison gas.
3. Fermi's Italian team got its best results by using uranium.
4. Fermi left the United States for Italy.
5. Fermi discovered that he had split the atom.
6. President Roosevelt was not interested in atomic research.
7. Hitler's scientists knew nothing about splitting uranium atoms.
8. The discovery of plutonium was important in the building of the atomic bomb.

**B.** *Complete each of the sentences below.*

1. One of the greatest weapons used to win the war was the
——— ———.
2. Many scientists came to the United States to escape from
———.
3. Fermi escaped from Italy, which was controlled by ———.
4. Tremendous amounts of energy are given off by splitting the
———.
5. The dictator of ——— was interested in learning the secrets
of the atom.
6. The United States became interested in atomic research after
an attack by ———.
7. The atomic bomb used ——— and ——— to produce its
tremendous power.
8. Atomic bombs were dropped on the Japanese cities of ———
and ———.

**C.** Imagine that you are the president of the United States. Government scientists are working on a weapon even more terrible than the atomic bomb. Would you let their experiments continue? Explain.

## ACTIVITIES AND INQUIRIES

1. Imagine that you are a famous scientist. Write a letter to the president of the United States. Try to convince him to support atomic research.
2. Imagine that you are another famous scientist. Write a letter to the president of the United States. Try to convince him *not* to support atomic research.
3. Go to the library. Prepare a report on another scientist whose work helped to develop the atomic bomb. Among those you may write about are Einstein, Szilard, Teller, and Oppenheimer.
4. The dropping of two atomic bombs ended World War II. Many people argued that we should not have used atomic bombs. Imagine that Fermi is being placed on trial. What are the charges against him? Prepare his defense. Next prepare the case against him. If you were a member of the jury, would you find him guilty or not guilty? Explain.

# 10. Meeting at Yalta

*When World War I ended,* the winners met and signed the Treaty of Versailles. This treaty shaped world history for the next 20 years. As World War II drew to a close, the probable winners decided to meet to discuss treatment of the losers. They also wanted to prevent future wars. Once again, an agreement would shape world history for years to come.

The three most important men in the world—Franklin Roosevelt of the United States, Winston Churchill of Great Britain, and Josef Stalin of the Soviet Union—met to talk over some very important problems. All three had at least one thing in common: They wished to see the downfall of Hitler. Beyond that, however, there were problems that seriously divided the three men.

Could England and the United States trust Russia? Could Russia trust England and the United States? Would Russia agree to join the fight against Japan once Germany was defeated? And, perhaps most important of all, would the Soviet Union permit free elections in the East European countries she had recaptured from the Germans and now occupied (for example, Poland)?

Ask yourself why Roosevelt, Churchill, and Stalin had trouble coming to an agreement. How did they try to prevent future wars? Did the Yalta conference bring lasting peace?

## Yalta, February 1945

As the conference opened, Churchill said to Roosevelt, "We could not have found a worse place than Yalta for a meeting if we had spent ten years looking!"

"You know that Stalin refused to meet anywhere but in Russia," Roosevelt replied. "Besides, now that we have given in to him on this point, perhaps he will give in to us on others."

Churchill shook his head from side to side.

Stalin now cleared his throat and nodded to President Roosevelt. The conference began. "Mr. President," Stalin said through his interpreter, "would you like to make some remarks to open the conference?"

Roosevelt, a charming man and a great speaker, thanked Stalin. "My friends," said Roosevelt, "let us work together in a spirit of friendship and cooperation so that all people will know that the powerful nations are of one mind."

At this, Churchill, Stalin, and the staff members of the three men burst into applause.

Now Stalin spoke. "Gentlemen, as long as we three live, none of us will allow our countries to make war on other nations. But, after all, none of us may be alive in a few years. A new generation may come that will not know the lessons that we have learned. We must try to build a lasting peace. We must remember that the greatest danger for the future is the chance that our countries will one day turn on one another."

"Hear, hear!" said Churchill, speaking directly to Stalin. "It is good that you speak this way. Now perhaps we can settle this Polish business."

Stalin frowned. Churchill had touched upon the most difficult question of the conference: how to deal with Poland.

The three men knew Poland's history only too well. Made independent after World War I, Poland was attacked first by Germany and then by Russia at the start of World War II. The Poles fought hard, but when it became clear that they were doomed to defeat, Polish officials escaped to England. There they formed a government in exile. This government was immediately recognized by England and the United States.

In the meantime, in 1941, Germany attacked Russia, and Russian troops were driven out of Poland. The Russians left behind a group of Polish Communist leaders who formed an underground movement. They continued to fight on against the Germans.

Now that the war was coming to an end, an important question was to be answered: Which group should govern Poland? Should it be the one in London, recognized by the British and the Americans? Or should it be the one in Poland, recognized by the Russians?

Churchill now continued, determined to make his point. "Gentlemen, Britain can be happy only with a plan that will leave Poland a free and independent state. Poland must be mistress of her own house. I say that we should agree on a temporary government now and call for free elections in the near future. Let the Polish people decide which government will represent them. Let us all agree to recognize that government. If we can agree on this, we will leave this table knowing that we have brought the world one step closer to lasting peace!"

"Not so fast!" said Stalin. "I hope you gentlemen haven't forgotten that twice in the past 30 years Russia has been invaded through Poland. We Russians must look very carefully before we decide to recognize any Polish government! Besides, there already is a government of Poland. The Polish people support the Lublin government. They need no other government."

Roosevelt looked tired and upset. He had come to the conference to make sure that the Russians would continue to cooperate to bring the war to an end. The Polish question could wreck everything.

"Aren't you forgetting the Polish government in London?" asked Roosevelt. "England and the United States believe that the London government represents the Polish people."

Stalin replied quickly. "Nonsense! The Lublin government remained in Poland. It did not abandon the Polish people in their hour of need. *Your* Polish government is in London, thousands of miles away from the Polish people. What do the Poles in London know of the needs and dreams of the people in Poland? Why aren't they in Poland now?"

Roosevelt seemed worn out by the argument. He said, "We will accept the Lublin government. But it should be reorganized to include Polish leaders from Poland and London."

"I agree," said Churchill. "However, I must insist that elections be held in Poland as quickly as possible. And these elections must be absolutely free. There must be no interference with the voting of the Polish people."

"I accept," said Stalin. "The Lublin government will be enlarged. I have nothing to fear from free elections. I agree to hold them within a month or two. The Polish people will choose the government that has fought not from London, but from within Poland itself."

Both Roosevelt and Churchill brightened at these words. Perhaps the conference was going to be successful after all.

"One more thing, Premier Stalin," said Roosevelt, "you have read my Declaration on Liberated Europe. You know that it calls for the right of all peoples to choose through free elections the form of government under which they will live. Will you put your signature to my declaration?"

Stalin hesitated for a moment. "Mr. President, I approve of your declaration, and I will sign it!"

This, for Roosevelt, may have been his greatest personal triumph.

Later Roosevelt met privately with Churchill. "Didn't I tell you that we could get Stalin to give in to us?" asked Roosevelt.

"Mr. President," said Churchill, "it seems to me that you have worked a miracle! Stalin has signed your declaration. He has promised free elections in Poland and other countries in Eastern Europe. He has also agreed to enter the war against Japan, as well as to support Chiang Kai-shek. One thing bothers me, though."

"What is that?" asked Roosevelt, a bit annoyed that Churchill was not as elated as he.

"I keep remembering an old Russian saying: 'You have to buy the horse twice when dealing with a Russian!'"

*Postscript.* Franklin Roosevelt was convinced that he could talk Stalin into continuing to cooperate with the West. But Roosevelt died later in 1945.

In spite of the agreement at Yalta, free elections to reorganize the government of Poland were not held. An election in 1947 was strictly controlled by Soviet authorities. Only candidates of Soviet choosing were permitted to seek office. Poland became a Communist state.

Winston Churchill remarked afterward that an "iron curtain" was falling across Europe. The Russians were ignoring Roosevelt's declaration. They were turning the nations of Eastern Europe into Communist dictatorships.

# UNDERSTANDING THE STORY

**A.** *Tell who made or might have made the statements that follow. Write C for each statement that Churchill made or might have made, R for each statement that Roosevelt made or might have made, and S for each statement that Stalin made or might have made.*

1. Great Britain wants a free, independent Poland.
2. Twice in the last 30 years we have been invaded through Poland.
3. Let the Polish people decide who will represent them.
4. I have nothing to fear from free elections in Poland.
5. Will you sign my Declaration on Liberated Europe?
6. Russia will enter the war against Japan.
7. We could not have found a worse place than Yalta for our meeting.
8. You have to buy a horse twice when dealing with a Russian.
9. We want nothing more than peace and freedom.

**B.** *Tell which item makes each statement correct.*

1. The meeting of world leaders in the story was held at (*a*) Washington (*b*) Geneva (*c*) Yalta.
2. Which of these men was *not* present at the conference? (*a*) de Gaulle (*b*) Roosevelt (*c*) Churchill
3. Stalin preferred to attend conferences in (*a*) the U.S.S.R. (*b*) the United States (*c*) France.
4. The leader who was afraid that these three nations might turn on each other was (*a*) Roosevelt (*b*) Stalin (*c*) Churchill.
5. The most difficult problem at the conference had to do with (*a*) Poland (*b*) Czechoslovakia (*c*) England.
6. Russia had been invaded twice in 30 years through (*a*) Turkey (*b*) Poland (*c*) Germany.
7. The Declaration on Liberated Europe was written by (*a*) Roosevelt (*b*) Churchill (*c*) Stalin.

**C.** The leaders of major nations meet with other heads of state from time to time. These meetings are usually called "summit conferences." Assume that you are an adviser to the president of the United States today. Which heads of state would you recommend that he meet in a summit conference? Why? What topics should the president and the other leaders discuss?

## ACTIVITIES AND INQUIRIES

1. Use each of the following key terms in a sentence.

   declaration          downfall          free election
   liberated            generation
   iron curtain         interpreter

2. Imagine that you are a reporter at the Yalta Conference. You ask Churchill how the conference is going. Write down what you think he would say to you.

3. You then ask Roosevelt how things are going at the conference. Write down his answer.

4. Finally you speak to Stalin and ask him about the conference. What would he tell you?

5. The caption of a cartoon is: "You have to buy the horse twice when you buy from a Russian!" Why did Churchill say this? How would Stalin complete this sentence: "When you deal with an Englishman, you have to ————"? How would Roosevelt answer Churchill? How would Roosevelt answer Stalin?

# 11. The Costs of War

World War I took, all told, 10 million lives. The war's dollar cost was put at $400 billion (in 1920 dollars).

In 1920 a well-off American family had a home worth $2,500 and furniture worth about $1,000. The home was on five acres of land worth $100 an acre. In 1920 the money that had been spent on World War I could have bought land and built and furnished a home for every family in the United States and ten other countries that fought in the war.

In addition, a $5 million library and a $10 million university could have been built in every large city in these 11 countries. And, from what was left, enough money could have been set aside to pay yearly salaries of $1,000 to 125,000 teachers and 125,000 nurses.

But, you ask, how does this apply today? How do you build and furnish a house so cheaply? How can you build so many libraries and schools and pay such low salaries?

You are right, of course. But if you multiply all of the 1920 dollar figures by ten, the costs of salaries, homes, libraries, and schools are a little more realistic.

Now multiply the dollar costs of World War I—$400 billion—by ten. Change the number killed to 40 million persons. Now you have the human and dollar costs of World War II.

Can we afford a third world war?

## UNDERSTANDING THE STORY

A. *Complete each of the sentences below.*

1. World War I took ——— lives; it cost ———.
2. World War II took ——— lives.
3. The money spent on the war could have paid for a ——— and ——— in every ——— in ——— countries.
4. Each city could have a $5 million ———.

5. Each city could have a $10 million ———.
6. There would have been enough money left over to pay the salaries of 125,000 ——— and 125,000 ———.

**B.** *Study the table of lives lost in World War II. Tell which item makes each statement correct.*

**Lives Lost in World War II—Military and Civilian Casualties**

| Country | Military Casualties | Civilian Casualties |
|---|---|---|
| China | 1.3 million | 22 million |
| Germany | 3.5 million | 780,000 |
| Japan | 1.3 million | 672,000 |
| Poland | 5.8 million* | |
| U.S.S.R. | 11 million | 7 million |
| United Kingdom (Great Britain and Ireland) | 264,000 | 92,000 |
| United States | 292,000 | 6,000 |
| Yugoslavia | 305,000 | 1.2 million |

*Separate figures for civilians and military are not available.

1. The country that suffered the largest number of civilians killed was (*a*) China (*b*) Yugoslavia (*c*) the U.S.S.R.
2. The country that suffered the largest number of combatants killed was (*a*) the United States (*b*) the U.S.S.R. (*c*) Germany.
3. The total number of U.S.S.R. civilians killed was (*a*) more than three times that of China (*b*) greater than that of all nations combined, with the exception of China (*c*) greater than the number of U.S.S.R. combatants killed.
4. The country that suffered the smallest number of civilians killed was (*a*) Great Britain (*b*) Japan (*c*) the United States.
5. The country that suffered the smallest number of combatants killed was (*a*) Great Britain (*b*) the United States (*c*) Japan.

6. A country that lost more civilians than combatants was (a) the U.S.S.R. (b) Germany (c) China.
7. Two countries whose combat losses were about the same were (a) Japan and Yugoslavia (b) China and Japan (c) Germany and China.
8. Another country that lost more civilians than combatants was (a) Yugoslavia (b) the United States (c) Great Britain.
9. The three countries that lost the largest total number of civilians plus combatants were (a) the U.S.S.R., China, the United States (b) Germany, China, Great Britain (c) the U.S.S.R., China, Germany.
10. The three countries that lost the smallest total number of civilians plus combatants were (a) the United States, Great Britain, the U.S.S.R. (b) Yugoslavia, the United States, Great Britain (c) Germany, Japan, Great Britain.

C. Assume that you are one of a group of experts. You are discussing the question "Can our world afford another world war?" What position would you take? Explain. What one fact would you use from the reading to prove that the world cannot afford a third world war?

## ACTIVITIES AND INQUIRIES

1. Go to the library. Use an almanac or another source of general information. Look up the following about the war in Vietnam: the countries that were involved and the number of wounded and killed on each side.
2. Imagine that you are an infantry soldier in battle during World War II. In a diary describe your experiences in one day of the war.
3. Pretend that you are a reporter during World War II. Your assignment is to interview Allied soldiers returning from battle. Write the questions you would like to ask the soldiers. Then answer the questions as you think they would.
4. As a reporter during World War II, you also have the chance to speak to Axis soldiers returning from battle. Write the questions you would like to ask these soldiers. What answers would they give to your questions. How different would the answers of the Allied soldiers and the Axis soldiers be? Explain.

5.  Look at the illustration below. Can one side really say it won a war? What would be another good title for the illustration?

*Who won?*

"Well, anyway, it wasn't like World War I," said Jack.

"How was it different?" asked Mr. Miller.

"No one seemed to want World War I. But there sure were a couple of people who pushed for World War II."

"Good thinking, Jack. Do you see any other differences?"

"First," Jack answered, "I think that World War I began because some countries took too many chances. It looks like World War II began because some countries didn't take enough chances."

"What do you mean?" Mr. Miller asked.

"Well," Jack replied, "if the democracies had taken chances and had stood up to Hitler and his gang right away, the dictators might have backed down."

"That's good. Anything else?"

"It looks like the good guys won and the bad guys lost. I wasn't sorry to see how Hitler and Mussolini ended. But I saw something in World War II that reminded me of World War I."

"What was that?"

"I think that both wars ended in the same way."

"How do you mean, Jack?"

"It seems to me that neither war was really ever settled. The winners of World War I didn't really agree with one another. The same was true of the winners of World War II. You'd think that after two all-out wars this world would have learned its lesson."

"It had better learn this time," Mr. Miller said.

"I agree," said Jack. "This world can't afford a third world war. Mr. Miller, World War I led to all sorts of problems. And I understand that these problems are still with us today. Maybe I'd better not ask what followed World War II."

"I don't think you have a choice," said Mr. Miller.

"I don't follow you."

"It's very simple. History has finally caught up to you. From here on, you are no longer going to just read about history. You now have a front row seat. You see, the past and the present are now one!"

"I still don't understand."

"You will."

# The Present Day

"You know, Mr. Miller," said Jack, "I'm almost sorry that we are about to study the present."

"Why?"

"I haven't finished thinking about the lessons of the past."

"Neither have I," replied Mr. Miller. "And, to tell the truth, I don't ever expect to stop studying the past."

"You said that to me once before."

"Yes, Jack. And I remember that you wanted to study only the present. You wanted nothing to do with the past."

"That was a long time ago," said Jack. "I was worried about inflation and crime and things like that. Is that what we are going to study now?"

"That and more. Much more."

"Such as?"

"Just little things, such as whether or not humanity has a future on this planet."

"Mr. Miller, don't play around like that. I may take you seriously."

"I think you should," said Mr. Miller with a straight face.

"Do you really think that we don't have a future on this planet?" asked Jack, a worried look on his face.

Mr. Miller looked hard at Jack. "I think that your own answer to that question will be more important than my answer."

"And how will I be able to answer that question?"

"Well," replied Mr. Miller, "let's begin by taking a good look at the present."

# 1. The Missiles

*The years following the end* of World War II have been difficult ones. Riots, revolutions, civil wars, and wars between nations have occurred all over the world. The world's two superpowers, the United States and the Soviet Union, have made angry faces at each other. They have supported different sides in battle—sometimes just with arms, sometimes with men and arms. But they have been careful not to confront each other in all-out war.

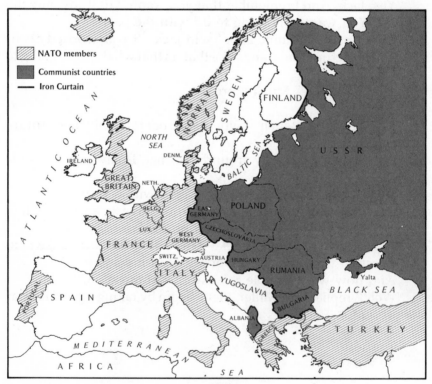

*Present-day Europe*

The United States stood by while the Soviet Union took over Czechoslovakia in 1948, put down a riot in Poland and a revolution in Hungary in 1956, and built a wall between East Berlin and West Berlin in 1961. The United States even sided with the Soviet Union in 1956 in the Middle East. At that time, Israel, England, and France invaded Egypt. The Soviets threatened war if those countries did not pull back at once.

The Soviet Union watched as the United States sent guns to Greece in 1947 to help put down a Communist threat. She stood by as the United States rearmed Western Europe in 1949 by forming the North Atlantic Treaty Organization (NATO). The Soviet Union did not send troops to Korea in 1950 or to Vietnam in 1962, even though the United States was sending both arms and men to those places.

Both nations fought with speeches, threats, help to other nations, and in the United Nations. But neither used direct force against the other.

Why have the superpowers, the United States and the Soviet Union, stopped short of going to war with each other? Is it that both have weapons that can destroy the entire world many times over? Is it that both have learned to live with each other? Is it that they have learned the lessons of the past?

Perhaps some of these answers will be revealed as we examine the incident that nearly brought the two giants to all-out war.

## Moscow, April 1962

"Impossible! The United States will never stand for it!" cried Alexei Adjhubai (ahd-juh-BUY). He was speaking to his father-in-law, Nikita Khrushchev (KROOSH-chof), premier of the Soviet Union.

"Don't be a fool!" replied Khrushchev. "They will never know the truth until it is too late. We will fool them into thinking that we are building bases in Cuba for short-range ground-to-air missiles. Instead, we will build bases for missiles that can hit the United

States. These bases will be so well disguised that United States planes won't be able to spot them. Besides, this is their election time. Kennedy will be too busy making speeches to give this his full attention."

"But," protested Adjhubai, "what is the point of doing this if the United States is never to know that we have placed ground-to-ground missiles in Cuba?"

Khrushchev smiled. "When the time is ripe, I will tell young Mr. Kennedy everything. He will complain and call me names—but that's all he'll do. Who knows, he might even propose a deal. Perhaps he'll trade some of his foreign bases. It is something to think about."

Khrushchev did more than just think about it. Beginning in late June, several ships per week left the Soviet Union carrying missile parts, fuel, and technicians to Cuba.

## Washington, September 1962

The American government was beginning to show concern over the number of Soviet ships that arrived daily in Cuba. Attorney General Robert Kennedy had invited Soviet Ambassador Dobrynin (doe-BREE-nin) to meet and discuss this with him.

"Mr. Ambassador," said Kennedy, "I must warn you that President Kennedy will take the strongest possible steps if he finds that your country is building missile bases in Cuba."

"Mr. Kennedy," said Dobrynin with a wide grin, "Premier Khrushchev is very fond of your brother and would do nothing to embarrass him. We Russians have no need to build missile bases in any other country but our own. Believe me, all we want is to live in peace with your country—not push you to the edge of war."

## Moscow, September 1962

"The Americans are becoming suspicious," said Adjhubai. "What do we do now?"

Khrushchev thought for a moment. "The Americans place great store in a man's word. I will put them off the track by giving them mine."

# Washington, September 1962

"Mr. President," said an executive assistant, "we are getting a cable from Moscow."

The president rushed over and studied the cable as it was transmitted over the machine. "It's from Khrushchev," he exclaimed. "He says that nothing will ever cause him to build ground-to-ground missile bases in Cuba."

"Do you believe him?" asked one of the president's advisers.

"I'd like to," answered the president.

# Washington, October 1962

"Mr. President," said MacGeorge Bundy, the special assistant on national security, "the Cuban photos prove it! The Russians *are* building ground-to-ground missile bases!"

"Are we certain?" asked the president.

"Absolutely!"

"That idiot Khrushchev!" The president bit his lip in anger. "Only yesterday he said that we should all join hands and keep the peace. And all this time he has been playing nuclear war games!"

"Well, then, God help him!" interrupted Bundy.

"God help us all!" said the president.

## UNDERSTANDING THE STORY

**A.** *Write T for each statement that is true and O for each statement that is an opinion.*

1. The United States should have helped the Hungarian people in 1956.
2. The United States and the Soviet Union did not want to go to war with each other.
3. The United States and the Soviet Union backed opposing sides in various wars around the world.
4. The United States should not be on the same side as the Soviet Union.
5. The Soviet Union set up missile bases in Cuba.

6. The Russians told the Americans that they wanted peace.
7. The Russians should not have sent missiles to Cuba.
8. The Russians said that they would never send ground-to-ground missiles to Cuba.

B. *Tell which statements President Kennedy made in the story.*
   1. I will never say another word to Khrushchev.
   2. I'd like to believe Khrushchev.
   3. We are certain that the Russians are building missile bases.
   4. You can't believe the Russians.
   5. Let's send a few missiles to Moscow.
   6. Khrushchev is playing nuclear war games.
   7. Castro would never make a deal with the Russians.
   8. God help us all.

C. Imagine that you are Khrushchev's adviser. He asks you whether the Soviet Union should build missile bases in Cuba. Khrushchev also asks what the United States might do if the bases were built. What advice would you give Khrushchev? Explain.

## ACTIVITIES AND INQUIRIES

1. Go to the library. Prepare a report on the life of John F. Kennedy, Nikita Khrushchev, or Fidel Castro.
2. Imagine that you are a reporter. You are assigned to interview President Kennedy in Washington, D.C. Write the questions that you would like to ask him about the Cuban missile crisis. Then write the answers you think he would give you.
3. Imagine that you are a reporter. Your assignment is to interview Nikita Khrushchev in Moscow. Write the questions you would ask him. Answer the questions as you think he would.
4. Study the map of the Caribbean on page 429 and answer the following questions.
   *a.* Using the scale of miles on the map, we estimate that the distance from Havana to Key West is (1) 125 miles (2) 250 miles (3) 375 miles.
   *b.* The distance from Havana to the Panama Canal is (1) 200 kilometers (2) 1,600 kilometers (3) 600 kilometers.
   *c.* Cuba is west of (1) Mexico (2) Haiti (3) the Panama Canal.

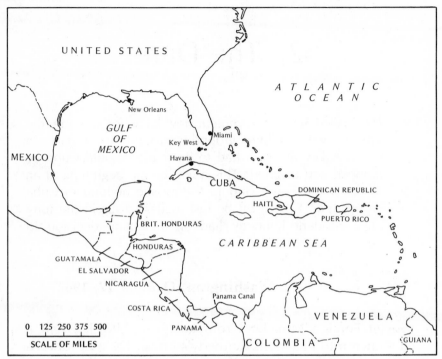

*The Caribbean*

*d.* An island to the south of Cuba is (1) Puerto Rico (2) the Dominican Republic (3) Jamaica.

Study the map once again. Why was the United States concerned that Soviet missiles were placed in Cuba?

5. Use each of the following key terms in a sentence.

| cold war | superpower | war games |
|----------|------------|-----------|
| missile  | NATO       |           |

# 2. The Dare

*The United States government* now knew for sure that the Russians were building ground-to-ground missile bases in Cuba. A key decision had to be made. Should Cuba be bombed and invaded? This might be the beginning of an all-out nuclear war. Should the missile buildup in Cuba be ignored? This might be just as dangerous in the long run. President Kennedy had an agonizing decision to make.

## Washington, October 17, 1962

Soviet Foreign Minister Gromyko (grow-MEE-ko) had just been shown into President Kennedy's office. He was concerned by rumors that Kennedy knew something about the Russian missile buildup in Cuba. He was there to find out as much as he could.

"Mr. President," said Gromyko, "let me come directly to the point. My government would be most happy if you Americans would make peace with Cuba instead of always threatening her."

"Your government," said Kennedy, "asks that we make peace with Cuba while at the same time it prepares Cuba for war!"

"Not so!" replied Gromyko. "We are shipping only farm tools and some small defensive weapons to the Cubans. Speaking for Mr. Khrushchev, I pledge that the Soviet Union will never ship ground-to-ground missiles or any other offensive weapons to Cuba."

President Kennedy gripped the edge of his desk. He looked at Gromyko and said firmly, "I must warn you that the United States will never allow offensive weapons in Cuba. We will take any step—I repeat, any step—necessary to rid Cuba of them!"

"Don't worry, Mr. President. Your country will never have to take those steps."

Gromyko smiled to himself. His report to Khrushchev would be a good one. While Kennedy was suspicious, he did not know about the missiles that were being put together in Cuba.

## Washington, October 18

"What do you think, Bobby?" asked President Kennedy of his brother, the attorney general.

"Well, Mr. President," said Robert Kennedy, in a somewhat formal tone, "it doesn't look good. The military chiefs want to invade Cuba immediately. Who can blame them? After all, the Soviet missiles in Cuba can kill 80,000 Americans. Do you see any other way?"

"Bobby," said President Kennedy, "I keep thinking how Europeans jumped into World War I after the assassination of the Austrian archduke. That was an ugly chapter of history. I for one don't want that history repeated!"

## Washington, October 19

"Well, Bob," said President Kennedy to his secretary of defense, Robert McNamara, "give me the bad news."

"Mr. President," replied McNamara, "an invasion of Cuba will need 250,000 men and 2,000 air strikes. At least 25,000 of our men will die in battle."

"Why can't we just hit the bases with a surprise air attack?" asked Kennedy.

"An air attack may not destroy all of the missile sites and missiles in Cuba," McNamara replied.

"Then unless the Russians bend, we have no choice," said Kennedy.

"We have no choice, Mr. President."

## Washington, October 22

"In here, sir," said the presidential assistant to Soviet ambassador Dobrynin, as he ushered him into the president's office.

"Mr. President," said Dobrynin with a wide smile, "what a great pleasure to see you again. How may I serve you?"

"Mr. Dobrynin," Kennedy said crisply, "please read this."

"May I ask what I am reading?" asked Dobrynin, still smiling.

"It is a speech I am going to make to the American people in exactly one hour."

Dobrynin began to read. Slowly the smile faded from his face. He opened his mouth to speak but Kennedy continued.

"Mr. Dobrynin, we are done with lies in this office. Tell Premier Khrushchev that the American people will never allow missile bases and missiles in Cuba. Now they are ready to make good their warning!"

Unsmiling, Dobrynin replied, "I will deliver your message to Premier Khrushchev."

## UNDERSTANDING THE STORY

**A.** *Tell which statements are true.*

1. The United States decided to ignore the Soviet missiles in Cuba.
2. The Russians wanted to build a missile base in the United States.
3. Gromyko said the Russians were shipping farm tools to Cuba.
4. President Kennedy said the United States would never allow ground-to-ground missiles in Cuba.
5. The Russians wanted to use Cuba as a base for invading England.
6. American military chiefs suggested an invasion of Cuba.
7. President Kennedy was afraid of starting a world war.
8. The Russians wanted their Cuban bases to be as well built as their bases in Puerto Rico.

**B.** *Who made the remarks that follow? Write K for each statement that Kennedy made. Write D or G for each statement that Dobrynin or Gromyko made.*

1. You are preparing Cuba for war.
2. Why can't we hit them with a surprise air attack?
3. Your country has nothing to fear from us.
4. We will not allow missiles in Cuba.

5. We are shipping small defensive weapons to Cuba.
6. I keep thinking how Europeans jumped into war after the assassination of the Austrian archduke.
7. I am going to make this speech to the American people in one hour.
8. I will deliver this message to Khrushchev.

C. Pretend that you are the adviser of the president of the United States. He has just learned about the Soviet missile bases in Cuba. What advice would you give him? Why?

## ACTIVITIES AND INQUIRIES

1. The caption of a cartoon based on our story is: "We want to live in peace with you." Who do you think is saying this? Why is he saying this? Does he mean it? Explain your answer. Draw the cartoon.
2. You are a reporter. Your assignment is to interview Robert Kennedy about the Cuban missile crisis. Write the questions you would like to ask him. Then write the answers you would expect to receive from Robert Kennedy.
3. Assume that you are the same reporter. You have also been assigned to interview Robert McNamara. What questions would you ask him? How would McNamara answer your questions?
4. Go to the library. Prepare a report on the North Atlantic Treaty Organization (NATO). (See the introduction to Unit XI, Chapter 1.) Was NATO the cause of Khrushchev's putting missiles into Cuba? Explain.
5. Study the map of Communist and non-Communist Europe after World War II on page 424. Then check the item that makes each statement correct.
   a. A nation that is not a member of NATO is (1) Spain (2) Great Britain (3) France.
   b. The NATO nation that touches the U.S.S.R. is (1) Turkey (2) West Germany (3) Yugoslavia.
   c. The NATO nation on this map that is farthest from the U.S.S.R. is (1) Great Britain (2) Iceland (3) Portugal.
   d. A Communist country bordering on the U.S.S.R. is (1) Finland (2) Poland (3) Switzerland.

    *e.* The northern European country that belongs to NATO is (1) Finland (2) Rumania (3) Norway.

    *f.* Two Communist countries that border on West Germany are (1) Denmark and East Germany (2) Czechoslovakia and East Germany (3) Austria and Hungary.

    *g.* A country that borders on the U.S.S.R., but is *not* one of her allies is (1) Greece (2) Bulgaria (3) Finland.

6. Use each of the following key terms in a sentence.

| | |
|---|---|
| offensive weapons | attorney general |
| defensive weapons | secretary of defense |
| expert | premier |
| ambassador | |

# 3. Face to Face

*Tension mounted in Washington* and Moscow as the two governments prepared for a showdown. President Kennedy had announced that the United States navy would stop and search all Russian ships within 500 miles of Cuba. We would turn back any Russian ships carrying missile parts. Would Khrushchev stand for this? Would he stand by and permit the United States to stop and search his ships? Would he stand by if the United States chose to bomb and invade Cuba—especially if Russian lives were lost as a result?

## United Nations, New York, October 23, 1962

A meeting of the United Nations Security Council was in progress. Two men, Adlai Stevenson of the United States and V. A. Zorin of the Soviet Union, were arguing furiously with each other.

"Gentlemen," said Zorin, addressing the Security Council members, "once again I ask that you vote to condemn the United States for its war-mongering, imperialistic stand against the freedom-loving Cuban people! Let us unmask the United States government once and for all. Let the world see her for what she is. She is a troublemaker who would bring us to a third world war in order to have her own way!"

"Mr. Zorin," said Stevenson, his eyes flashing, "if a third world war is at hand, it is because your government—not mine —has willed it!"

Zorin began to answer but was interrupted by Stevenson.

"Mr. Zorin, do you still say that there are no Soviet offensive weapons in Cuba? Just answer yes or no!"

"Who are you to ask me a question in such a manner? I am not in an American courtroom, sir! In due time, you will have your answer!"

"You are in a courtroom, sir—a courtroom of world opinion! Answer my question, please."

"You will have your answer when I am ready to give it to you!" answered Zorin.

"All right, then," said Stevenson, "perhaps this will help to speed your answer along."

Stevenson handed a batch of photographs to the council members. These photographs left no doubt that missile bases were being built in Cuba.

Zorin gathered up his papers and without so much as a nod quickly left the room.

## Caribbean Sea, aboard a U.S. destroyer, October 24

"Sir, they keep coming!" said naval Lieutenant Hodges to Captain Ford. Hodges' voice was strained.

"Do you see anything else on the radarscope?" asked Ford.

"Only what I saw before, sir. Two Russian ships are moving rapidly toward our position, and 30 more are following behind them!"

"How much longer will it be before they get here?"

"The two ships should be here in about 25 minutes, sir."

The two men exchanged glances. Despite the air-cooled room, drops of perspiration formed on the lieutenant's brow.

"Sir," said Hodges, his voice rising, "something is happening! A Soviet submarine is moving into position between the two ships!"

"Quick," said Captain Ford to his communications officer, "wire the White House. Tell them that we are standing by for instructions!"

Moments later, a message was received from the White House.

"What are our instructions, sir?" asked Hodges.

Captain Ford, in a serious tone, said, "Our instructions are to do whatever is necessary to stop those ships!"

The minutes ticked by. The Russian ships drew closer. The entire crew waited, each man a heartbeat away from disaster.

"Captain!" shouted Lieutenant Hodges, "the Russian ships

have stopped! They have stopped dead in the water! Some are even beginning to turn around and head back!"

The captain bowed his head and whispered, "Thank God!"

## Moscow, December 5

"Well," said Adjhubai to Khrushchev, "you have given your enemies the weapons with which to pick you apart!"

"Times have been better for me," agreed Khrushchev with some reluctance.

"Your enemies call you a coward. They say that you gave in on everything. You let the Americans stop and search our ships. You let them bluff you into tearing down the missile bases and removing the missiles from Cuba!"

"My enemies are fools!" said Khrushchev. "Would they rather I had gone to war because that hothead young American president kept pushing me? They should build a statue in my honor. If it were not for me, those idiots would not be able to draw the breath with which they say those ugly things!"

"They are right about one thing," said Adjhubai.

"What's that?"

"The United States won a big victory over the Soviet Union!"

"Wrong, Alexei," replied Khrushchev quietly. "We are all on the winning side. Humanity is the winner!"

## UNDERSTANDING THE STORY

**A.** *Write* T *for each statement that is true,* F *for each statement that is false, and* N *for each statement that is not mentioned in the story.*

1. The United States stopped the Russian ships.
2. The United States should not have been afraid of Cuban missile bases.
3. The debate between the United States and the Soviet Union took place in the League of Nations Security Council.
4. The United States said that the Soviet Union was an imperialist troublemaker.

5. Stevenson said that a third world war would be blamed on the Soviet Union.
6. The United States and the Soviet Union wasted too much time talking.
7. Khrushchev thought his enemies were fools.
8. Khrushchev said the United States won a victory over the Soviet Union.

B. *Tell which item below makes each statement correct.*

1. An argument took place in the United Nations between the representative of the United States and the representative of (*a*) Cuba (*b*) the Soviet Union (*c*) Saudi Arabia.
2. The United States was accused of wanting to start a (*a*) missile base in Panama (*b*) missile base in Cuba (*c*) third world war.
3. The Soviet Union denied that there were (*a*) offensive Soviet missiles in Cuba (*b*) Soviet spies in the United States (*c*) farm tools being sent to Cuba.
4. The American representative at the United Nations was (*a*) Robert Kennedy (*b*) Adlai Stevenson (*c*) Robert McNamara.
5. The Soviet delegate was told that he was in a courtroom of (*a*) the United States Supreme Court (*b*) the World Court (*c*) world opinion.
6. The captain's instructions were to (*a*) stop the Russian ships (*b*) leave Russian and Chinese ships alone (*c*) ask the United Nations for help.
7. The Russian ships (*a*) turned back (*b*) rammed the American ships (*c*) changed course and headed for Florida.
8. Khrushchev said that humanity (*a*) lost (*b*) won (*c*) should get ready for World War III.

C. Pretend that you are on the United States destroyer with Captain Ford and Lieutenant Hodges. You see the Russian ships coming. What are you thinking about? What should Captain Ford do?

## ACTIVITIES AND INQUIRIES

1. To whom does the caption of the cartoon on page 439 refer? Explain. Suppose they had not blinked. What other outcomes were possible? How would the Russians explain their actions?

*They blinked!*

2. Assume that you have been given the job of writing a television special. The program will tell the story of the Cuban missile crisis. What people would you have in your story? What scenes would you include? What other endings would you suggest? Is another ending more exciting than the real one? Explain.
3. Suppose that your class is going to stage a debate between Soviet and American delegates to the United Nations. The topic is the Cuban missile crisis. Prepare the case for the American side.
4. Now prepare the case for the Soviet side of the Cuban missile crisis.

# 4. The Lesson

*Our story begins in 1944*. The tide of war is turning against the Japanese. But in French Indochina, in the area that we now call Vietnam (ve-et-NAHM), Japan is still in control.

The first half of this story takes place in a small jungle camp near the Vietnam-China border. An American special forces team has joined a band of Vietnamese guerrillas. The American soldiers are teaching the Vietnamese how a small group can fight a large army. The Vietnamese are using this training to drive the Japanese from their country.

In our story, American Colonel David Johnson is talking to Ho Chi Minh (hoe chee min). Ho is the leader of the Vietnamese Communists. Each man likes and respects the other. The second half of the story tells what happened to Vietnam 20 years after the meeting of Ho and Johnson.

### Vietnam, 1944

"You Americans are different, you know," said Ho Chi Minh.

"How do you mean that?" David Johnson asked.

"I mean that you are not like the French."

"And what makes Americans different from French people?"

"Your history is like ours," Ho replied. "You fought the English for your independence. We will soon fight the French for our independence. Our peoples have much in common. You are teaching us how to destroy our enemies and we are grateful."

Johnson was pleased. "Ho, you and your men are good students. You learn quickly. The Japanese have better weapons and more men. Yet each time you fight them, you hurt them more than they hurt you. Your enemies will have to think twice before they make war against you!"

"David, I hope that when this war is over you will bring back a message to your people," Ho said. "Tell them that we Vietnamese want only to get back our own country. Tell them that we will fight anyone—the Japanese, the French—who stands in our way! And tell them this, please. I hope that the United States and Vietnam can be good friends."

"You know a great deal about the history of my country," David said to Ho. "But I know nothing of your country's history. What can you tell me?"

Ho answered, "My history is a very proud one. My people have suffered at the hands of foreigners through the ages. The Chinese ruled us for over 1,000 years. My people fought more than ten wars with them. At last the Chinese were chased from my country. Today the Japanese and the French are the enemies of my people. Tomorrow others may try to rule us. No matter. We are a stubborn people. We have learned how to suffer and wait. We are in no hurry. The longer we wait, the greater will be our enemies' defeat!"

## Vietnam, 1945–1976

At the end of World War II in 1945, Ho asked the United States government to help him stop the French from regaining control of Vietnam. The United States government did not trust Ho. He was a Communist. Instead the United States decided to help the French regain control over Vietnam.

The French were armed with heavy weapons. They had well-trained army and air force troops. The United States sent more guns and money. Ho's army was a small band armed with light weapons. Ho would not admit defeat. His army lived and worked alongside the people of Vietnam. The soldiers used hit-and-run tactics. They ran from the French in the morning and attacked them the same afternoon. The French suffered defeat after defeat. At last, in 1954, the French gave up. They gave up Vietnam. Vietnam was divided into two parts: the North had a Communist government in Hanoi, and the South had a non-Communist government in Saigon.

Slowly the United States began to take the place of the French in Vietnam. At first, Americans helped only to train and supply the South Vietnamese army. Then American soldiers were sent to advise the South Vietnamese. By 1964 United States planes were dropping bombs on North Vietnam. Less than a year later American troops were in battle. Both sides suffered heavy losses. The

North Vietnamese fought to control the entire country. The Americans fought to keep the Communists from gaining control over more people. The United States also fought to help the South Vietnamese choose their own way of life.

The war became uglier. Communist troops tortured and killed both soldiers and civilians. Vietnamese peasants were afraid not to help the Communists. People who didn't help the Communists had their throats slit as examples to others. Life became very cheap in Vietnam.

The ugliness of the war also touched the American soldier. Reports from the battlefield told of American soldiers who shot up entire villages. Men, women, and children were killed. Americans believed that the enemy was everywhere. People in the United States were told of atrocities in Vietnam. Who was to blame? There was a public outcry against the war. Demands for peace were everywhere.

In 1973 the United States signed a peace treaty with North Vietnam. The North agreed to end the fighting if American troops would go home. The United States had trained the army of the South very carefully. It had supplied the South with many weapons and was ready to keep on doing so. The American government felt that South Vietnam could now take care of itself.

The ceasefire did not end the war in Vietnam. Fighting went on between the armies of the North and the South. The United States watched from the sidelines. The soldiers of North Vietnam won province after province, city after city. On April 28, 1975, South Vietnam surrendered to North Vietnam. Saigon, the capital city of the South, was renamed "Ho Chi Minh City." Another long war had come to an end.

*Postscript.* In 1976 North and South Vietnam were unified into one nation under the control of North Vietnam.

## UNDERSTANDING THE STORY

**A.** *Number the events below in the order in which they took place.*

Ho Chi Minh asked the United States to help him.
American advisers helped the South Vietnamese army.
Japan controlled Vietnam.

United States planes bombed North Vietnam.
Ho's army used hit-and-run tactics against the French.
World War II ended.
North Vietnamese troops defeated South Vietnam and occu-
    pied Saigon.
The United States signed a peace treaty with North Vietnam.
The United States decided to help the French in Vietnam.
The French surrendered in Vietnam.

**B.** *Tell which statements show how the United States was involved in Vietnam.*

1. The United States army never tried to train the South Vietnamese army.
2. The United States helped the French in their fight against Ho
   Chi Minh.
3. Later the United States turned against the French and
   helped Ho Chi Minh.
4. The United States took the place of the French in Vietnam.
5. The United States fought to keep the Communists from
   gaining control in Vietnam.
6. The United States was involved in an ugly, brutal war in
   Vietnam.
7. The American government supplied the South Vietnamese
   army with many weapons.
8. After the United States forces left, the North and South
   Vietnamese became great friends.

**C.** Assume that you are an adviser to the president of the United
States. The year is 1950. The president tells you that the United
States has several choices in Vietnam. We can help the French
or we can help Ho Chi Minh. Or we can remain neutral and
stay out of Vietnam. What advice would you give the president? Explain.

## ACTIVITIES AND INQUIRIES

1.  Use each of the following key terms in a sentence.
    special forces        combat        hit-and-run tactics
    ambush                ceasefire
2.  Go to the library. Prepare a report on the activities of the French
    in Vietnam or the United States in Vietnam.

3.  Imagine that you are Colonel David Johnson. You are speaking to Ho Chi Minh. Ho tells you that the United States and Vietnam can be friends. But he adds that his people will fight anyone who stands in the way of independence for Vietnam. What would you tell Ho Chi Minh? How do you think Ho would answer your remarks?
4.  The caption of a cartoon is: "We are a stubborn people. We have learned to suffer and wait." Who is the speaker? What does he mean by "suffer and wait"? Is it possible to win freedom by "suffering and waiting"? Draw the cartoon.
5.  Study the map of Southeast Asia below. Tell which item makes each statement correct.

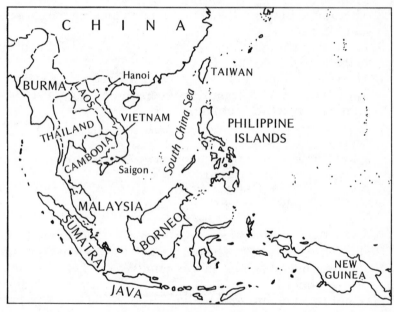

*Southeast Asia in 1976*

*a.* The capital of North Vietnam is (1) Hanoi (2) Saigon (3) Bangkok.
*b.* The country north of North Vietnam is (1) Malaysia (2) Indonesia (3) China.
*c.* The country situated between Thailand and North Vietnam is (1) South Vietnam (2) Laos (3) Cambodia.
*d.* The country situated between South Vietnam and Thailand is (1) North Vietnam (2) Laos (3) Cambodia.

# 5. The United Nations Hosts the Revolution

*In the spring of 1945,* delegates of 50 nations drew up the United Nations Charter. The purpose of of the United Nations was to keep peace among nations. The nations hoped that peace could be achieved through the cooperation and goodwill of the member nations.

The United Nations has been tested many times. In 1950 it sent troops to Korea to help end the war. It also sent forces to parts of Africa, Asia, and the Middle East to end local wars. The United Nations has, however, often failed to stop wars. It has also failed to settle many of the problems that keep nations hostile toward one another.

In our story, one such problem is being brought before the United Nations. Yasir Arafat (ara-FAHT), the leader of the Palestine Liberation Organization, speaks before the United Nations General Assembly.

Arafat speaks for a people who have been homeless for many years. Many of them once lived on lands that now belong to the state of Israel. The people lost their lands when they ran away during the first Arab-Israeli War in 1948. These people want to go back to their lands. Israel says "no!"

Israel says that these people left their lands because they did not wish to become citizens of Israel. The Palestinians, they say, will never agree to become citizens of Israel. Many Palestinians are terrorists who attack and kill innocent civilians. They will not rest until the state of Israel is no more. Israel adds that the Palestinians should become citizens of other Arab countries. Israel also says that the Arab countries would rather keep the problem alive than finally bring peace to the Middle East.

Has the United Nations changed much since it was first organized? Do its members still believe in working together to solve the problems of the world? Our story should help answer these questions.

# United Nations, New York, November 1974

"Here he comes!" whispered many of the delegates seated in the General Assembly of the United Nations.

A short man, dressed in a windbreaker and brown trousers, walked to the microphone. He wore a *kaffiyeh* (kee-FEE-ya, a head covering). A pistol holster could be seen when he opened his jacket. All the delegates except the Israelis were present. The delegates had come to hear Yasir Arafat speak.

Arafat clasped his hands over his head as boxers do after they have won a fight. Delegates from Asian, African, Middle Eastern, and Latin American countries stood up and cheered. Many of these delegates too had fought for the cause of nationalism. Arafat was one of their own.

The European delegates sat politely. Many remembered the early years of the United Nations. Then the United States and Western Europe controlled the General Assembly. Now they were outvoted by Asian, African, Middle Eastern, and Latin American countries all joining together. Times had changed!

Arafat cleared his throat. He began to speak. "I have come bearing an olive branch and a freedom fighter's gun. Do not let the olive branch fall from my hand!"

"What do you think he means by that?" asked an assistant to the delegate from the United States.

The delegate shrugged. "Who knows? To his friends, his speech will be a promise of peace. To his enemies, it will be a threat of war. Only one thing is certain. Nothing will be solved here today."

Outside the United Nations, small riots were taking place. Arabs carrying signs cried their support for Yasir Arafat. They were faced by Jews who raised clenched fists at them. Riot police managed to keep the two groups apart.

Inside the United Nations, Arafat was finishing his speech. He had spoken for almost 100 minutes. He had promised that Jews would be able to live in peace in the Middle East—once the state of Israel no longer existed. Arafat's remarks had been greeted with wild applause. The state of Israel must fall. It was a tool of Western imperialists.

Arafat stopped. He had finished his speech. Again delegates from the Asian, African, Middle Eastern, and Latin American countries stood and cheered.

Arafat smiled, walked away from the microphone, and sat down.

Now the Israeli ambassador returned to the auditorium. He stepped to the microphone. He was angry. He said, "The United Nations has disgraced itself by inviting the murderer of innocent men, women, and children to speak before it!"

The Western delegates applauded. There was no answer from the Asian, African, Middle Eastern, and Latin American countries. They had left the assembly as soon as the Israeli rose to speak.

The British delegate turned to the United States delegate. He asked, "We have come a long way here at the United Nations. Where do you think we are now?"

"We are in the hands of the revolution!" answered the United States delegate.

## UNDERSTANDING THE STORY

A. *Write T for each statement that is true, F for each statement that is false, and O for each statement that is an opinion.*

1. The United Nations sent troops to Korea.
2. The United Nations had often failed to stop wars.
3. The United Nations should be moved from the United States to Switzerland.
4. Arafat spoke for all Arab nations.
5. Arafat was an Iraqi Arab.
6. All Palestinians should go back to live in Israel.
7. The United States and Western Europe no longer controlled the General Assembly.
8. Terrorists have no right to hurt people.

**B.** *Tell which statements Arafat made.*

1. Israel should be allowed to exist in peace.
2. I come bearing an olive branch.
3. The state of Israel must fall.
4. The United Nations has disgraced itself.
5. Jews will be able to live in peace once the state of Israel no longer exists.
6. Do not let this gun fall from my hand.
7. Israel is a tool of Western imperialists.
8. Someday I will be president of Egypt and Syria.

**C.** Imagine that you are the secretary general of the United Nations. You have been asked for your advice. Should Arafat be permitted to speak at the General Assembly, even though his people are not members of the United Nations? What advice would you give? Explain.

## ACTIVITIES AND INQUIRIES

1.  Use each of the following key terms in a sentence.

    charter            freedom fighter      terrorist
    cooperation        Palestine            kaffiyeh
    General Assembly

2.  Go to the library. Prepare a report on the successes of the United Nations through the years.
3.  Assume you are a reporter. Your assignment is to interview Israel's United Nations representative. Ask him what he thinks of Arafat's speech. Answer the question as you think the Israeli representative would and then explain the answer.
4.  You are the same reporter. You are now interviewing Arafat. Fill him in on what the Israeli ambassador told the General Assembly. Also tell Arafat what the Israeli said to you. Write down what you think Arafat's answer would be.

5. The olive branch represents peace. What is wrong with the cartoon below? What does Arafat really mean? Can his methods bring peace to the Middle East? Explain.

*"Do not let the olive branch fall from my hand!"*

# 6. Five Minutes to Midnight

*We turn the pages of history* and finally come upon our own times. We would like to be able to say that wars are a thing of the past. But our world remains dotted with trouble spots. Nations still use war as a means of settling their differences.

Nowhere in the world is the threat of war stronger than in the Middle East. Since the birth of the state of Israel, the Middle East has been the scene of several wars.

Ask yourself why this area is such a trouble spot. Why does trouble there threaten the rest of the world? Perhaps our two college students—one an Israeli, the other a Syrian—can help us answer these questions.

## New York City, 1976

Avram had ten minutes to eat his lunch and get to his science class. He looked around the crowded college cafeteria and saw one empty seat. A young woman sat at the table. He knew that her name was Leila.

"May I sit here?" asked Avram.

Leila nodded her head. Avram put his tray on the table and placed his books next to his chair.

Both Avram and Leila were foreign exchange students. Avram was an Israeli, Leila a Syrian. They attended a science class together but had never spoken. After a minute of silence, Avram spoke.

"Thank you for letting me sit here," said Avram. "We Israelis don't often get such invitations from Arabs."

Leila looked up sharply. "Perhaps it's because your people behave as rudely as you are behaving now."

"I apologize for my rudeness," said Avram. "Israelis have been pushed so many times that I suppose we're always ready for a fight."

*The Middle East in 1976*

"Please don't make such innocents of the people of Israel. After all, it was you who pushed your way into the Arab world. And you have taken lands that belonged to the Arab people. You Israelis deserve to be pushed. And we Arabs won't stop pushing until we have pushed you into the sea."

"Dear lady," said Avram, "every time you push us you leave behind more of your lands. Perhaps it is time for the Arabs to stop this foolishness. We don't want your land. We want to break bread with you at the peace table."

"Wonderful words," answered Leila, "and Israel repeats these same words before the United Nations and the world. Yet while Israel speaks of peace, she builds on the Arab lands which she has stolen. And generations of homeless Arabs waste away in the desert."

"We have stolen nothing. It is you who try to steal our land by making wars. This land has belonged to us for centuries. Even your holy book, the Koran (KOH-ran), proves it. And you know that many Arabs live in Israel. They are granted citizenship and even hold seats in our government. Most of them live better in Israel than anywhere else in the Middle East."

Leila interrupted. "What about the Arabs you have made homeless?"

"If the Arab countries are truly concerned about the homeless

Arabs, why don't they invite them into their own countries? After all, we Israelis invite Jews from all over the world to live in our country."

Leila said, "We don't take these Arabs into our countries because we never want to forget that Israel has stolen their homeland! You invite Jews to settle in your country because you need soldiers to fight your wars."

Avram answered, "You don't take the homeless Arabs into your countries because you want to use them as terrorists against Israel. And while it is true that the Arabs greatly outnumber us, we invite Jews to Israel for reasons other than building up our armies."

"I know. You're going to tell me all about the concentration camps."

"Yes, my people crawled out of the world's ghettos to go to Israel. They went from countries that had tortured and chased them. They have risen from the ashes of the concentration camps. After two thousand years of persecution, they have the right to live as free people in a land of their own!"

Leila spoke through clenched teeth. "My homeland is not a homeland for Jews!"

"You may be a brilliant student, but you don't know your history," said Avram. "You refuse to understand that all Jews have lived in Israel for thousands of years. Some have actually lived and worked there. The others have lived and worked in Israel in their hearts and minds. In recent times we bought diseased swampland from Arab landlords. We paid dearly for this land—not only with money but with sweat and blood. We worked hard and made this once-barren land a showplace for the world. The Bible, the Koran, our history, and now the United Nations all give us the right to claim this land. And we will not be moved. Never!"

"But we are becoming more powerful," said Leila. "Our Arab countries are rich in oil, and we can buy anything we want. The Russians supply us with tanks, guns, and planes. Our armies are getting stronger. Can you really stop us from pushing you into the sea one day?"

Avram answered. "We are not without resources. So long as the Russians supply you, the Americans will continue to supply us. Besides, your hundreds of millions of people hardly frighten our 3 million people so long as we have atomic weapons. It has taken too many centuries to reclaim our homeland for us to give it up without a fight."

"And so Arab and Israeli will go on locked together in a death struggle," said Leila.

"Unless we learn to speak with one another."

"What do we have in common to speak about?" asked Leila.

"A great deal," answered Avram. "We are both concerned with homeless people. You are concerned with homeless Arabs and I am concerned with homeless Jews. Perhaps if we help one another, we can make a good home for both."

Avram and Leila looked quietly at each other. The class bell rang. They gathered their books and coats and walked off silently to class together.

## UNDERSTANDING THE STORY

**A.** *Write T for each statement that is true and F for each statement that is false.*
1. War is a thing of the past.
2. The threat of war is great in the Middle East.
3. The two people in the story are an Israeli and a Syrian.
4. Avram and Leila shared a table in a college cafeteria.
5. Leila believed that Israel had stolen lands from the Arabs.
6. Avram and Leila had never spoken to each other.
7. Avram and Leila disagreed about the Middle East.
8. Avram believed that Israel should be a homeland for the Jewish people.

**B.** *Write A for each statement that Avram might have made and L for each statement that Leila might have made.*
1. We want to break bread with you at the peace table.
2. Generations of homeless Arabs waste away in the desert.
3. My people have risen from the ashes of the concentration camps.
4. My homeland is not a homeland for Jews.
5. Can you stop us from pushing you into the sea?
6. Our people have the right to live as a free people in a land of their own.

7. Arabs and Israelis are in a death struggle.

8. You are concerned with homeless Arabs. I am concerned with homeless Jews.

C. Suppose that Avram and Leila came to you for advice. They would like to know how their countries can live in peace. What advice would you give them?

## ACTIVITIES AND INQUIRIES

1. Use each of the following key terms in a sentence.

   Israeli                                      Arab
   terrorist                                    homeland

2. The caption of a cartoon is: "Our people have risen from the ashes of the concentration camps!" Who do you think said this? Explain. What does Israel mean to the survivors of the concentration camps? Draw the cartoon.

3. Study the map of the Middle East on page 451. Tell which item makes each statement correct.

   a. The Suez Canal connects (1) Israel and Egypt (2) the Mediterranean and the Nile River (3) the Mediterranean and the Gulf of Suez.

   b. An Arab country to the southwest of Israel is (1) Egypt (2) Jordan (3) Syria.

   c. An Arab country east of Israel is (1) Egypt (2) Jordan (3) Lebanon.

   d. Which of these Arab countries does not actually touch Israeli land? (1) Jordan (2) Saudi Arabia (3) Lebanon

4. Go to the library. Prepare a report on Arab-Israeli wars from 1948 through 1973.

5. Suppose that Leila and Avram have a history exam. They are asked to give a possible solution to the Middle East problem. What would Leila write? What would Avram write?

# 7. Last Chance?

*Many people have begun to take* a long, hard look at Planet Earth. They do not like what they see. They talk about the coming shortages of important natural resources, such as oil and coal. People are also talking about the shortage of our most vital natural resource: food.

In our story, Dr. Paul Ehrlich (AIR-lick), a biologist, is holding a press conference. He wants to make people realize that there is a food crisis. How serious is this crisis? Will we face starvation in our lifetime? Let us see how Dr. Ehrlich answers these questions.

## Washington, 1970

"Dr. Ehrlich," called out a reporter from *The New York Times*. "Would you please repeat those figures?"

"Gladly," said Dr. Ehrlich. "It comes down to this. Soon we are not going to be able to grow enough food to feed all the people who live on this planet. There are over 4 billion people living on the earth right now. A hundred years ago there were only a billion people on the planet. The world's population used to double every 1,500 years. Today it doubles every 80 years! We cannot continue to feed so many people!"

"What do you suggest?" asked the reporter from the Chicago *Tribune*.

Dr. Ehrlich answered immediately. "We must limit every family in the world to no more than two children."

"But," sputtered the editor of the *National Review*, "that's unthinkable! People have the right to bear as many children as they wish."

The other reporters listened with interest. Most agreed with the editor of the *National Review*. They found it hard to take Dr. Ehrlich's statements seriously.

"Ladies and gentlemen," said Dr. Ehrlich, "I see that most of you do not believe what I am saying."

"Oh, we believe you," said the reporter from the New York *Daily News*. "It's just that we don't think the world has anything to worry about for a few hundred years. By that time, scientists like yourself will have invented new ways of feeding the world."

"Ladies and gentlemen," said Dr. Ehrlich, "we don't have a few hundred years left! The crisis is now. Oil, lead, zinc, tin, and water are already in short supply. As for food, right this minute, people are starving to death! All over the world, millions of people are starving. By the year 2000, the world's population will have grown from 4 billion to 7 billion. How many people will starve then?"

"But, Dr. Ehrlich," protested the reporter from the Washington *Post*, "don't we have enough food to feed the world's people right now? Isn't it just that some countries have too much food and others have too little?"

Dr. Ehrlich shook his head. "If all the world's food supply were evenly divided, there would still not be enough to go around. And, of course, air pollution and water pollution make our problems even more serious. Plants depend upon oxygen and water to live and grow. If plants do not grow or are killed by polluted air and water, the animals that eat these plants will have no food. Soon, animal life will die off. If plants and animals die off, what will remain for human beings to eat? With an exploding world population, and with increasing pollution of air and water, the world's food supply is threatened."

At last the reporters began to understand what Dr. Ehrlich was trying to tell them.

"Is there anything we can do?" asked the reporter from the *Village Voice*.

"That's why I called this news conference," said Dr. Ehrlich. "Families will have to have fewer children. We must stop waste and pollution, and governments must pass tough laws to make sure we stop. Then *perhaps* there may still be time."

"And if this isn't done?" shouted several reporters.

"Then," said Dr. Ehrlich, "we have nothing to look forward to but pollution, starvation, and war. Human life will disappear and will be replaced by a creature who will inherit the earth."

"What creature?" cried the reporter from the New York *Post*.
"The one creature that life on earth will be fit for," replied Dr. Ehrlich. "The cockroach!"

## UNDERSTANDING THE STORY

**A.** *Complete each of the sentences below.*
1. People talk of shortages of natural resources such as ——— and ———.
2. There will also be a shortage of our most important natural resource— ———.
3. We are not going to be able to grow enough food to feed all the ——— who live on this ———.
4. The population of the world doubles every ———.
5. The crisis is ———.
6. All over the world, millions of people are ——— to death.
7. Even if all the world's food were evenly divided, there would still not be ———.
8. We must stop ——— and ———.

**B.** *Match each item in Column A with its answer in Column B.*

| Column A | Column B |
|---|---|
| 1. What we face in our lifetime | (a) now |
| 2. The number of people now living on earth | (b) stop waste and pollution |
| 3. What happens to the number of people on earth | (c) starvation |
| 4. What Dr. Ehrlich thinks each family must do | (d) have as many children as they wish |
| 5. What most people think families have a right to do | (e) 4 billion |
| 6. When Dr. Ehrlich thinks the crisis is | (f) doubles every 80 years |
| 7. What Dr. Ehrlich says human beings must do | (g) the cockroach |
| 8. Creature that will inherit the earth from human beings | (h) have no more than two children per family |

**C.** Assume that you are a member of the President's Commission on Natural Resources. You have been asked to make a report on the resources of the United States today and in the future. What would you tell the president about our country's resources? How will the careless use of American resources affect the rest of the world?

## ACTIVITIES AND INQUIRIES

1. Use each of the following key terms in a sentence.

   planet                      population           environment
   natural resources           pollution

*Last chance!*

2. Go to the library. Prepare a report on an important natural resource.
3. Look at the illustration on page 458. What is the message of the picture? Write your own title for the illustration.
4. Draw a poster that will encourage people to stop waste.
5. Write an outline telling what the students in your class can do to prevent the waste of resources.

"Congratulations, Jack," said Mr. Miller. "You got one of the highest grades in the class."

"Thanks, Mr. Miller. Please don't think that I'm just being polite when I tell you that I really enjoyed your subject."

"My subject? History belongs to all of us."

"There you go again, Mr. Miller. And now I suppose you'll start to talk about the past and the future, just as you did at the start of the term."

"Was I wrong?"

"Do you want the truth?"

"Of course."

Jack hesitated. "The truth is, I'm not sure that I've really learned anything about the future or even learned to understand the present. But I have learned something for myself."

"What's that?"

"Well, I learned that I'm a lot tougher than I thought."

"How did the course teach you that?" asked Mr. Miller.

"It didn't happen right away," answered Jack. "It took a long time. But after studying about the rise and fall of empires, wars, revolutions, and the many problems that threatened people's lives, I finally got the message."

"What was it?"

"It got through to me that, in spite of all the problems, people survived. Time after time, people built on top of the ruins to make a new life."

"And what does that have to do with you?" asked Mr. Miller.

"I finally began to think that if I had lived during any of those times of crisis, I too would have made it. After all, if the human race has survived—why wouldn't I have made it too?"

Mr. Miller smiled. "Do you remember how worried you once were about the problems that face us today? Do you still feel the same way?"

Jack laughed. "I think I'll survive. I think we all will."

# Glossary

**absolute monarchy**   form of government in which a king or queen has complete control of the nation's affairs

**A.D.** (anno Domini)   all years since the birth of Christ

**Age of Reason**   period in Europe (17th and 18th centuries) during which people began to search for truth through observation of nature and scientific experimentation

**balance of power**   means of preventing any one nation from becoming strong enough to overpower others; a coalition of one group against another

**barbarian**   outsider, foreigner; one not as civilized as others

**B.C.** (before Christ)   all years before the birth of Christ

**capitalism**   economic system that encourages private ownership of property and personal profit through the use of capital (money)

**Church (Roman Catholic Church)**   dominant religious organization in Western Europe from the fall of Rome (476) to the early 16th century

**civilization**   way of life of a nation or a part of the world; refinement of ideas, manners, and tastes

**Congress of Vienna**   council of European leaders that drew up the peace treaty following the Napoleonic Wars (1815)

**colonialism**   (*see* imperialism)

**commonwealth**   a group of people organized under a system of laws; also, English government during the reign of Oliver Cromwell (1649–1660)

**communism**   economic system in which all means of production are the property of the state or government

**Crusades**   Christian military expeditions to regain the Holy Land (Palestine) from the Moslems during the Middle Ages

**Declaration of the Rights of Man**   description of the rights of French people, written during the French Revolution

**democracy**   form of government that provides for the expression and realization of the wishes of the majority of the people

**dictatorship**   government ruled by one person or a group of people; the wishes of the majority are not considered or recognized

**divine right**   belief that a monarch rules because of God's wishes or plans

**domestic system**   economic system under which goods were made by hand in the home

**empire**   extensive lands or territories controlled by one nation; originally, lands ruled by an emperor

**Estates General**   legislative assembly of France before the Revolution, made up of three estates

**factory system**   making of goods by machine in a special building set aside for that purpose (a factory)

**fascism**   form of 20th-century government in which a dictator rigidly controls political life; its economic system is a form of capitalism

**feudalism**   economic and social system during the Middle Ages; the nobility owned the land; the serfs lived on and worked the land and fought wars to defend it

**First Estate**   high clergy in the Estates General

**Glorious Revolution of 1689**   replacement of Stuart kings of England by William and Mary of Orange (Netherlands); supremacy of Parliament over king established

**guild system**   association or group of men during the Middle Ages who controlled the manufacturing and sale of a product in a town or city

**humanism**   revival of Greek and Latin classics during the Renaissance; emphasis upon secular (worldly) matters and activities

**imperialism**   process in which a powerful nation takes control of a weaker one; empire building

**indulgences**   pardons for sins

**Industrial Revolution**   shift in technology from handcrafts made at home to machine-made goods produced in factories

**Inquisition**   Roman Catholic Church court that sought out and punished those who disagreed with Church doctrines

**League of Nations**   organization formed after World War I to keep the world at peace

**"Liberty, Equality, Fraternity"**   slogan of the French Revolution

**Magna Carta**   charter signed by King John of England in 1215 which granted certain rights to English barons

**manor system**   medieval system of farming

**nationalism**   feeling held by a group of people that they belong together as a separate nation

**Middle Ages**   period between the fall of Rome and the Renaissance (476–1400)

**New World**   continents of the Western Hemisphere (North America and South America), discovered by Columbus

**Old Regime**   system of privileges and absolutism in France before the Revolution

**Orient, the**   lands of Asia, such as China and Japan

**parliament**   lawmaking body whose members discuss national problems and pass laws

**Petition of Right**   statement of rights written by the English Parliament and signed by King Charles I in 1628

**philosophes**   writers and thinkers in 18th-century France

**Reformation, Protestant**   upheaval in the Church during the 16th century that resulted in the formation of many separate Christian churches

**Reign of Terror**   period during the French Revolution marked by violence and death

**Renaissance**   revival or rebirth of learning and interest in earthly life during the 15th century

**revolution**   a great change; the overthrow of a government; a change in manner of thinking or production

**Second Estate**   nobles in the Estates General

**serfdom**   system whereby people were bound to the soil as farmers and were controlled by the nobility

**social contract**   theory of government in which the people have agreed to be governed by certain persons

**Third Estate**   middle-class persons, lower clergy, farmers, and workers in the Estates General; represented 98 percent of the French people

**Triple Alliance**   agreement of mutual protection by Germany, Austria-Hungary, and Italy; the Central Powers during World War I

**Triple Entente**   agreement of mutual protection by England, France, and Russia; the Allied Powers during World War I

**United Nations**   world organization formed after World War II to prevent war and promote freedom

**West, the**   Western Europe and North America

# Index